Library of Congress Catalog No: 99-65735
ISBN: 1-55671-086-0

Printed in the United States of America

08 07 06 05 04 03 02 01   10 9 8 7 6 5 4 3 2 1

Copies of this and other publications of SIL International may be obtained from

International Academic Bookstore
SIL International
7500 W. Camp Wisdom Road
Dallas TX 75236-5699

Voice: 972-708-7404
Fax: 972-708-7433
Email: academic_books@sil.org
Internet: http://www.sil.org

Globe-Trotting in Sandals:

A Field Guide to Cultural Research

Carol V. McKinney

A Publication of
SIL International
Dallas, Texas

SIL International

Volume Editor

Rhonda L. Hartel

Production Staff

Bonnie Brown, Managing Editor
Laurie Nelson, Production Manager
Margaret González, Compositor
Hazel Shorey, Graphic Artist

Globe-Trotting in Sandals:

A Field Guide to Cultural Research

Contents

Contents

Preface

"Where do I start when I go to the field to do my research?" asked Nancy, a gradu-
ate student who had just completed a social science research methods class.

Nancy's question, one that she felt had been inadequately answered by her previous research field methods class, points to the need for a practical book on the nitty-gritty of
fieldwork. My goals in writing this book were to provide field methods options and to give
direction to those doing cultural research, whether for a degree program or for some other
purpose. In focus are those who conduct linguistic field research and also desire to gather
cultural data as a component of their fieldwork. For example, texts are rich sources of information about culture; they are also essential for linguistic analysis. Further, several text
genre, such as some described in the chapter on oral traditions, are useful for purposes of
both linguistic and cultural analyses.

What is distinctive about this field guide is that it focuses on data-gathering field methods from an insider's or emic perspective. In order to gather data from this perspective,
field methods presented provide practical guidance for you, the fieldworker, as you engage
in your adventures in cultural research. For example, engaging in participant observation is
designed to help you gain the perspective of an insider of that culture. Each chapter is designed to give you an introduction to a particular research method. I have also included an
extensive bibliography for you to consult for further information on any particular research
method.

This field guide revolves around specific research methods. Other than in a few areas,
such as oral traditions, music, and values, it tends not to focus on specific content areas of
culture. For example, there are no chapters on religion, political organization, economics,
or social organization, though some cultural information is included where it is relevant to
these areas.

Numerous examples from my own research as well as from that of other researchers are
included in order to provide the human side of this adventure, and sometimes misadven-
ture, and to illustrate types of situations you may encounter. The personal data come from
my husband and my fieldwork with the Bajju people of Nigeria, West Africa.

This book speaks of cultural research rather than other possible descriptions of this activity. For example, one could also have characterized this type of social science research as
anthropological, ethnographic, sociological, sociolinguistic, linguistic, or historical. My reason for using the broad, general phrase "cultural research" is that each of these fields,
while having its own emphases in fieldwork, tends to make use of similar field methods,

especially when working with predominantly oral societies. I wanted to write a general field guide useful to researchers in several related social science disciplines.

I am deeply grateful for the comments and suggestions of those who have read earlier drafts and portions of this manuscript. I wish to thank Katy Barnwell, Stephen Beckermann, Alex Bolyanatz, Hank Bradley, Mary Clarkson, Gillian Hansford, Tom Headland, Kath Higgens, Kalon Kelly, Marlin Leaders, Marv Mayers, Barbara Moore, Beth Pinney, and Bob Priest. I am grateful for the input of Tom Avery and Ken Hollingsworth, both ethnomusicologists, who reviewed the chapter on music and made a number of beneficial suggestions for improving it. I thank Ken McElhanon for his comments on the chapter on worldview. My thanks to Mary Huttar and Carol Orwig for their insights on the chapter on language learning. Pat Townsend and Wayne Dye carefully read through this manuscript and made many helpful suggestions. It is a better book for their input. Thank you. I wish to thank Frank Robbins, Tom Crowell, David Ross, and Andy Gallman, who have encouraged and supported me in this project. I am grateful to my students who have patiently read parts of this manuscript, listened to me expound on many of the subjects included, and provided useful comments on it. My thanks to the SIL library staff who patiently checked out books and articles for me, and even at times renewed them without my asking when I had not returned them on time. My thanks especially go to Claudia Griffith, Ron Pappenhagen, and the late Dottie White who took an interest in this project and encouraged me in it. Paul Griffith, Bob Reed, and Norris McKinney provided computer support for this manuscript, and I am grateful for their help.

I would like to express my gratitude to my Bajju friends, who will probably recognize my foibles and who could no doubt add more. They shared themselves, their culture, and their language with us. Many of them call our family *bashong Bajju*, the 'red Bajju'. The Bajju have four color terms, and the skin color of "white" people falls into their red color category. Thanks particularly go to Musa Asake who read an earlier draft of this manuscript. He encouraged me by his comment that if all fieldworkers followed the principles set forth in this manuscript, people would not object to fieldworkers studying them. Thanks also go to Samuel Waje Kunhiyop who collaborated with me in fieldwork and has encouraged me in writing this manuscript. I am also grateful to Haruna Karick who worked together with me in fieldwork.

Finally, my very deepest gratitude goes to my husband, Norris McKinney who, as my encourager, has helped immeasurably in editing this manuscript, and who has been my companion in fieldwork. I would also like to thank our children Mark, Eric, Susan, and Christy who shared fieldwork with us. In fact, Christy joined our family at Evangel Hospital, Jos, Nigeria, when we were in the midst of fieldwork. Our Bajju friends claim her as one of theirs and insisted that her ethnic identity was Bajju when answering questions of census takers in the now discarded 1973 census.

Christy suggested the title for this book. Since most fieldwork centers around everyday activities, I am assuming that most fieldworkers choose everyday footwear such as sandals. Therefore, I wish you *bon* fieldwork as you trot around the globe in sandals, engaging in the adventure of cultural research!

1

Introduction to Cultural Research Methods

As Haruna and I chugged along a dirt road on his motorcycle towards a rural village to administer an interview schedule,[1] he exclaimed, "I can't believe I'm actually doing fieldwork! I studied about this in university, but never dreamed that I'd ever have the opportunity to do any, and among my own people, too!"

Haruna's obvious joy and excitement parallels the emotions of many who engage in fieldwork, a rite of passage for cross-cultural workers. Participants usually look forward to rites of passage with anticipation, excitement, and anxiety; when conducting fieldwork, these emotions may also be accompanied by feelings of culture shock and stress. After successfully completing fieldwork, you have a sense of accomplishment, an expanded perspective, and an understanding of basic principles taught in the social sciences that comes through experiential learning.

This book presents some of the most common practical field methods for collecting cultural data from an insider's perspective. Since fieldworkers continue to be creative in the methods they use and since there are numerous means of data collection, this book makes no claim to include all possible ethnographic field methods.

While concentrating on practical field methods for collecting data from an insider's perspective, this book also suggests some analytical tools to apply to the data you collect. Since ethnographic research involves description, analysis, and explanation of cultural data, both methods and analyses are important in the cultural research process. While methodology and analysis may theoretically be separated, in practice the fieldworker combines these two activities in the fieldwork process. When engaging in data collection, some analysis is essential for various reasons. For example, preliminary analysis may indicate omissions or areas where you need to collect more data. It can indicate areas where that which is intuitively obvious needs support to substantiate it. In general, as you go along, some analysis keeps data collection on track and points to areas for further research.

This book assumes that you have studied cultural anthropology or a similar area within the social sciences, and it reviews only a few of the concepts that are covered in such a course. Thus, important topics such as the nature of culture, holism, cultural relativity, and other basic social science concepts are assumed to be part of your knowledge. Anthropology as a social science draws from the biological sciences (e.g., physical anthropology, also termed biological anthropology, and archeology) and from the humanities (e.g., ethnology

---

[1] A technical term for a research instrument, discussed in chapter 9.

and linguistics). It involves objective quantifiable facts as well as "soft data" (e.g., study of worldview, oral traditions, and religion) that do not lend themselves easily to quantification. The field methods presented in this book seek to address both areas. They deal with both etic and emic field data.

This book addresses the topic of cultural RESEARCH. Research refers to systematically collecting data and analyzing it. It is the systematic aspect of research that sets it apart from other forms of problem solving.

Why cultural research?

Why conduct cultural research? That question has various answers depending upon your goals. Some conduct cultural research in order to be able to interpret one culture to persons in another culture. Other researchers engage in cultural research purely for scientific interest. For example, a fieldworker may desire to understand what gender role differences observed in one culture occur universally. Others do cultural research to address particular issues (e.g., what is the incidence of AIDS in this population?). Another important reason to do cultural research is because a group of people has requested it to help them address a specific felt need.

Cultural research addresses questions such as: Why do people behave as they do? What functions, if any, do specific behaviors have within the culture? Do these behaviors occur cross-culturally or are they culture specific? Answers to these and other questions come from the collection of basic descriptive data and, if necessary, quantitative data in order to make inferences about specific hypotheses proposed.

Cross-cultural comparisons

Researchers may focus on collecting descriptive data for cross-cultural research comparisons which serve to advance our knowledge of cultural generalizations and universals of human behavior. For example, Murdock and others who have set up and used the Human Relations Area Files have substantially advanced our knowledge through their careful cross-cultural research (Murdock and White 1969).

Within cross-cultural research people choose different foci, such as conversion, gender studies, religion, political economy, economics, social organization, art, the local medical system, material culture, and different forms of decision making.

Pragmatic reasons

Some engage in cultural research for pragmatic reasons. Many development agents seek to understand the basic problems people face so that they may alleviate some of them. Cultural research may inform policy decisions and their application. Practical implications and applications of cultural research are myriad.

Research for development should begin with the expressed needs of the local people, particularly people who are affected directly by any development project. The local people must be in focus in the planning, research, implementation, and evaluation of the development project. By involving the local people in the initial planning and development of a project, their underlying assumptions and worldview can be understood, which can either assure the success of the proposed project or lead to its failure. Any development project must address the question of what importance the local people give to the project: Would they prefer that project or some other project?

If you plan to be involved in culture change, for example, by introducing literacy to illiterate or semi-literate people, you need to understand the culture within which that change is to take place. Just as you would not think of adding a new component to a computer without understanding the existing components, so, too, you need to understand the culture within which you plan to introduce a literacy program. Understanding the culture allows you to avoid unintended consequences.

Translation into another language

If you are engaged in a language project where material is translated from one language into a second language, you need to understand the semantic domains of the terms used in the translation process. Cultural research provides that understanding, especially of the basic categories, the cultural meanings, the ethno-information in that second language. Failure to do cultural research may result in your skewing the translated material, resulting in mistranslation that communicates a different message from the one intended, or worse, communicates nonsense.

Writing an ethnography

In the early days of cultural anthropology, the goal of field research centered on writing an ETHNOGRAPHY. An ethnography is a general description of the culture, including its social organization, political structure, economy, religion, and material culture.

Some traditional, theoretical, anthropological ethnographies seemed almost to be out of touch with the people they described. More recently, some authors are writing narrative ethnographies. A NARRATIVE ETHNOGRAPHY reestablishes that touch by keeping the people in a prominent position. The reader feels like he or she is there interacting with the people written about in the ethnography. See Abu-Lughod (1993) for an example of a narrative ethnography. Narrative ethnography consists of narratives and conversations that do not present the culture systematically. It does not directly address theoretical issues, except perhaps in an introduction or conclusion. Yet it does give the reader an insider's or emic perspective of a culture that comes from what is written about specific individuals.

Problem-orientated field research

Field research which focuses on specific problems or topics predominates in the social sciences. With the realization that there is so much involved in understanding another culture, researchers will often specialize in some facet of the culture, then develop hypotheses, collect data to confirm or fail to confirm them, and write up the results. Some examples are irrigation systems, agricultural practices, and practices of traditional healers. Research into the latter may have the goal of implementing a culturally sensitive mass media campaign for combating dehydration through oral rehydration therapy. For example, problem-oriented field research was done by Green, who studied practices of traditional healers in Swaziland with the goal of integrating them into the modern health delivery system (Green 1986:118).

Methods described in this book apply to field research on limited problems and work within the increasing subspecialties of the social sciences. Some subspecialties within anthropology include ethnology and ethnography, cultural materialism and Marxist anthropology, medical anthropology, development anthropology, agroanthropology—which focuses on the interaction between agriculture and people—nutritional anthropology, psychological anthropology, urban anthropology, and cultural ecology.

Research for theory construction

Researchers who collect data for the purpose of theory construction do so by the inductive approach. It involves the development of theories based on direct observations. Conversely, a cultural researcher can begin with or develop a specific theory, then collect data to prove or disprove it. The DEDUCTIVE APPROACH moves from theory construction to direct observation to confirm, modify, or disprove the theory. Both approaches have contributed significantly to our understanding of human behavior, and both have their place within cultural research.

Having noted that theory construction can use both inductive and deductive approaches, this field guide concentrates on the inductive approach. The goal is to understand what people actually do, say, and think; to understand the culture from the perspective of an insider of the culture.

Cultural research from etic and emic perspectives

A primary goal of cultural research is to discover the insider's perspective, that which is EMIC (see Headland, Pike, and Harris 1990). As a researcher you start with the ETIC, the physical data of what is going on; you record data that are both significant and insignificant from an insider's perspective. You do so because initially you do not know what is significant from the perspective of an insider in the culture. As research continues, you sort your data into cultural domains that are meaningful to members of the research culture. This emphasis on the insider's perspective emerged early in the discipline of anthropology. For example, Malinowski's purpose in fieldwork was "to grasp the native's point of view, his relation to life, to realize his vision of the world" (1967:25).

In order to discover the emic perspective, ask questions such as: what is going on, who are the actors, why are they behaving as they are, and what is the significance of their behavior? These questions need to be asked in a culturally appropriate way. (See the side box for an example.)

Clues to the insider's perspective come from FOLK TERMS, terms that identify specific cultural domains. For example, terms such as *rappelling* and *belaying* occur within a mountain climbing context. When

---

Why no "why" word?

For months, in the research Norris and I did among the Bajju of southern Kaduna State in Nigeria, West Africa,[2] we failed to find any Jju word for "why." It is not a question word that Bajju use frequently, unlike many Americans. They were already socialized into their culture; hence, use of a why question was unnecessary. Our discovery of the phrase "because of what" or in free translation "why" occurred when we heard it used in context. Since initially we were unable to ask "why," we learned how to interact without using that phrase. Coming with our American perspective we would have vastly overused it if we had learned it early on. While we were in the village, however, Americans sent the first men to the moon. Then our Bajju friends asked us, "Why?!"

---

[2]The Bajju people speak the Jju language. Non-Bajju refer to them as the *Kaje*, a term other researchers have most often used in the literature. The term *Kaje* probably derives from *Kajju*, the Bajju term their geographic area. The word *Kaje* also translates from Hausa as 'You go'.

researching a mountain climbing social situation, a fieldworker would seek to discover the meaning of these emic folk terms.

Gender-related issues need to be kept in mind from the beginning of research in order to do adequate emic research. What is the perspective of men and of women about the questions you are researching? Often those two perspectives differ. Part of the reason for keeping gender issues in focus comes from the division of labor that occurs in cultures. Men do some things while women do other things. Both perspectives need to be studied to avoid the imbalances of past researchers.

By doing etic research you look at objective observations; this approach must complement the emic perspective. The etic approach utilizes social science categories that allow for cross-cultural comparisons. Some combination of etic and emic approaches in data collection is essential for an adequate understanding of what is going on and its significance. Some etic data collection and analysis also allows for quantitative research with the possibility of using statistical tests that can be applied to the data.

It can be argued that expatriate field researchers can never gain a complete insider's perspective. The very presence of an outside researcher changes the context so that people do things differently when you are there than when you are not present. Even so, cultural researchers seek to understand the insider's perspective to the extent possible.

Models for collecting ethnographic data

Whatever your goal for conducting fieldwork, use of a model for cultural research can be helpful. Realize, though, that there are no perfect research models that can be followed in a cookbook fashion that can assure success in field research.

Some find it helpful to select a specific ethnography or other research write-up to serve as a model for them to follow and build upon in their research. Selection may be based on some cultural similarity (e.g., a similar religion or subsistence base), a similar theoretical perspective, the same or a similar culture area, or similar research methods used. Use of an ethnographic model can lead you to investigate areas of the culture that you may not have thought about before, thus helping to provide direction to your research. (See the side box for an example.)

Writing

Writing should begin early in your fieldwork. This is true even if you find that you must rewrite the material later. Writing early helps you find the holes in your data that need to be researched. Write with a specific audience in mind. Usually, writing for an individual enables you to reach a wider audience, while writing for a wider audience may reach no one.

Bwiti, an ethnographic model

When doing research on Bajju religious change, I selected *Bwiti*, an ethnography by Fernandez (1982) about the Fang in Gabon, as a model. The Fang have similarities to the Bajju that include a migration history, Christian influence, wide use of proverbs in daily life, a horticultural subsistence base, and the presence of independent churches. In comparing the Jju data I was collecting with that of the Fang, I began to look for more information on topics similar to those Fernandez reported on, e.g., I looked for more information on Bajju genealogies, and I sought ways to integrate Jju proverbs with specific ethnographic data. In both these instances, I was less than successful, yet I did gain through searching for similarities. I discovered that the Bajju do not keep long genealogies as the Fang do.

Goals of writing

Both in collecting data and in writing, you should limit your goals to manageable sections or modules. For example, you might write a module on marital patterns or on residence. Gradually, individual modules combine to build your research write-up. If your goal is to write a complete ethnography of the culture, you may find yourself discouraged because the task seems too daunting. By writing in modules, however, you gradually develop an ethnography. Cultural researchers increasingly view writing complete ethnographies as lifetime projects that are rarely done following a person's initial fieldwork.

Recently, some have been writing ethnographies in such a way that they include themselves in their writing, thereby recognizing that they are contributing to and changing the field situation by their very presence (see Stoller and Olkes 1987). Anthropologists have been taking the issue of the self and its portrayal of the other seriously. Questions emerge such as, Who are we writing for? What if members of the research community read what we write? Would they say, "Yes, this accurately reflects our culture and what occurred when the ethnographer was here," or might they say to another person, "You aren't fooled by this description of my people, are you?"

Quotations and vivid descriptions

In your research write-up include specific quotations of what people actually said and vivid descriptions of what occurred. Including word-for-word quotations and descriptions enables your readers to feel as though they are experiencing the culture, and they can then visualize what you are writing about. Knowing this prior to beginning your field research will help you to collect more useful data. Be sure to credit those whom you quote.

Professional strangers

Fieldwork takes time, often a lengthy period, interacting with others within a cross-cultural or subcultural context. During this time, you become a "marginal native" (Freilich 1970), a "professional stranger" (Agar 1980), a guest, a foreigner, perhaps a loner, marginal both to your own culture and to that of the research community. Jennings feels that fieldworkers fall into the category of being "not-quite-indigenous but not-quite-outsider position during their fieldwork" (1995:14). Increasingly, scholars are focusing on the intense experiences of the culture of fieldworkers (Van Maanen 1988).

Being a guest or stranger implies that people will often stop what they are doing to entertain you when you show up at their houses. This may frustrate your efforts to engage in unobtrusive observation of their local patterns of behavior. It also entails an obligation on their part to take care of you.

Overview

Cultural data collection needs to conform to sound ethical principles, the topic of chapter 2. Rynkiewich (1976:59) notes that "Some anthropologists would still argue that ethics and the methods and theories of anthropology should be kept separate. I would argue that they never were nor could be separate."

Chapter 3 addresses the important topic of preparing for fieldwork, including selection of a research topic, research design, literature review and proposal development, research hypotheses, research affiliation, the length of research, and making health preparations. This preparation precedes initial fieldwork, the topic of chapter 4, which addresses issues such as site selection, rationale to present to the community for living at that site, and building trust and respect relationships. Chapter 5 presents participant observation, process observation, circular stages in ethnographic research, goals, and everyday pragmatics (e.g., managing cultural shock, confusion, and stress). Participant observation is a fieldwork technique that is foundational to all good cultural research.

Chapter 6 focuses on language learning, presenting specific suggestions to help in learning another language. It also addresses the question of which language to learn and the possible use of interpreters in field research.

Chapter 7 discusses keeping an ethnographic record, which includes your field data notebooks, a topical database, photographs, artifacts, tape recordings, and anything else that documents the culture in focus. In general, all data gathered using various field methods are part of the ethnographic record.

Informal interviews, the topic of chapter 8, is an extremely important means of investigating the emic perspective of members of the research community.

Chapter 9 is on constructing and implementing an interview schedule or questionnaire, and it includes a minimum census database to collect. It covers sample selection, age estimation, and possible bias in data collection. Chapter 10 gives some introductory suggestions for statistical analysis of the data collected with a research instrument.

Chapter 11 deals with collection and analysis of demographic data, including significant aspects of the composition and dynamics of specific populations studied. Demography can serve to identify segments of a population that are illiterate or literate, monolingual or multilingual, and so forth.

Chapter 12 looks at mapping the research site. This research technique is one that you can do early in fieldwork when you are still in the early language learning stage. It helps to identify significant places within your research area. Chapter 13 is on material culture, also a topic that you can begin studying early in your research.

Chapter 14 focuses on collection of kinship data; and kinship rests on marriage and descent, the topics of chapter 15. Collection of kinship data provides a good way to meet and understand people who live together in social groups. It has long been a mainstay of ethnographic research.

Chapter 16 discusses collection of life histories, while chapter 17 explores gathering data on social networks.

A cognitive approach to worldview, the topic of chapter 18, is particularly important for those doing linguistic research and translation into the language of the ethnic group in focus. It addresses the topics of systems of knowledge and thought, cosmology, worldview, folk terms, and categorizations in culture. Besides providing suggestions for collecting such data, this chapter presents some analysis suggestions.

Chapter 19 is on values, which are accepted ideals of behavior. Values are universal in culture, and they indicate how people should and should not behave. They grow out of people's worldview and provide the ideals towards which people strive.

Chapter 20 describes oral traditions, including folktales, proverbs, riddles, performances, origin narratives, epics, and other verbal traditions and gives suggestions for collecting them. Oral traditions articulate cultural values, teach worldview, contribute to social control, as well as entertain people. Chapter 21 looks at the analyses of oral traditions. Chapter 22 considers music, a specific type of oral art.

Chapter 23 presents data collection through rapid assessments (RA), a methodology frequently used by those interested in introducing culture change in a culturally relevant and appropriate manner. Chapter 24 is on social impact analyses (SIA). Chapter 25 briefly explores a few other field methods, including time allocation studies and event analysis. Finally, chapter 26 deals with completion of fieldwork and the write-up of your research results.

While each of these field methods is important for specific purposes, when doing fieldwork you should select the specific field methods that will be of most use for collecting the data needed for your purposes. Be aware that no single field method can be applied equally well in all cultures. You need to be sensitive about when it is appropriate to use the various field methods described in this guide book.

2

Ethics in Cultural Research

Doing ethical fieldwork—and indeed living ethically in general—is not about follow-ing prescribed formulae, but precisely about thinking *over the processes and situations that you are involved in.* (Wilson 1993:198)

Fieldwork involves an ethical responsibility to those people studied. All ethnographic re-search involves dealing respectfully and responsibly with people, as Pratt and Loizos state, "...responsible and sensitive research is always conducted consultatively, together with the people affected, rather than inflicted upon them from above, or outside" (1992:1). Conse-quently, the American Anthropological Association (AAA) has set forth ethical principles to provide guidance in fieldwork (1990). Further, the AAA maintains an Ethics Committee and regularly addresses ethical issues in the *Anthropology Newsletter* (see also Cassell and Jacobs 1987).

In the United States when researchers conduct research on humans, the research subjects involved must sign *informed consent forms* which list the procedures to be performed and the possible risks involved. An informed consent form specifies that the subject may dis-continue participation in the research at any time without prejudice to that person. These forms are most widely used in the medical field, a practice that grew out of the medical ex-periments on human subjects against their wills by the Nazis in Germany during World War II. For projects in courses in cultural anthropology field methods, it is important for students to receive permission from those whom they study. (See Cassell and Jacobs 1987:81–92 for informed consent forms that can be used for projects in cultural anthropol-ogy field methods classes.)

When you work cross-culturally, the local people frequently perceive that you will collect information from them, then publish those data and become rich while the local people re-main as poor as before. Similarly, people may perceive that your taking photographs is de-signed to exploit them, to present them as primitive, and then to sell their pictures for profit. You need to address the concerns of people whom you study, such as their concerns about your motivations, reasons for being there, goals, and the possible impact of your research.

The principles discussed here are from the principles of ethics the AAA set forth. They are based on respect for those studied. Stoller and Olkes state,

> As anthropologists we must respect the people among whom we work. We have
> long been concerned that our studies not produce difficulties for the people we

9

have studied. For me, respect means accepting fully beliefs and phenomena which our system of knowledge often holds preposterous. (1987:229)

In a working relationship with the people studied, it is essential that you come to understand the people's *worldview*, defined as their set of basic assumptions about reality (see chapter 18). They work within those assumptions; our interaction with them must be in terms of those assumptions. To do otherwise is to be irrelevant to the local social situation. The question may be raised as to the extent to which you need to accept their worldview as your own while working cross-culturally such as Stoller and Olkes suggest that they do in the above quotation. I would suggest that understanding and working within that framework are sufficient; the extent to which it is adopted as part of your core worldview is up to you to determine.

Social responsibility

One issue of ethics that fieldworkers have concerning the data they collect is a social responsibility towards the people. For example, should knowledge you collect be used for the purpose of meeting the needs of human beings, and thereby contributing to a just and safer world? Fieldworkers who view collection of cultural data with a social responsibility in mind look at the complexity of the problems people face, problems such as poverty, ignorance, illiteracy, inadequate and differential provision of health care, and injustice. Cultural research examines indigenous perceptions of oppression and categorization from an emic perspective, and thus may document problems.

An example comes from De Waal's research (1989) on the meaning of "famine" for the people of Darfur, Sudan, during the period 1984–1985. He found that for them the word "hunger" includes "famine" within its semantic domain. This word also implies poverty, powerlessness, shortages, and suffering. The people did not focus on starvation per se. Their concern was to maintain their subsistence base and way of life over the long term rather than to keep all possible people from starving. De Waal found people to be very reluctant to sell all their assets, such as land and animals, in order to satisfy their hunger. From the perspective of their worldview De Waal examined the relevance of the local survival strategy as it related to those who contributed international food aid.

Sometimes field researchers find themselves in difficult situations where the involvement of multinational corporations, logging companies, mining operations, and the like may be proposed to the local people and receive their initial approval for a project in their area. You as an outsider may be aware of consequences that have not been adequately explained to the people, such as the environmental degradation of clear-cutting of the rain forest by a logging company. It is at this point that you may choose to be involved by raising awareness of the local people so that they can be better equipped with the knowledge necessary to decide on and argue their own case.

Some researchers would argue that research for the sake of knowledge is sufficient reason for collecting cultural data, without the necessity of pragmatic purposes or social responsibility. Clearly, there is a place for both approaches to cultural research.

Principles for ethics

In this section some of the principles for ethical field research set forth by the American Anthropological Association are presented. The AAA first proposed these principles, then the membership voted to adopt them. While these principles have been set forth by anthropologists, they are applicable more generally to anyone who works cross-culturally because they are based on respect for those with whom we study and work. They apply whether you are a cultural anthropologist, linguist, translator, literacy worker, sociologist, other social scientist, development agent, businessman or woman, missionary, or any other category of cross-cultural worker. In reading through these principles of ethics it may help you to substitute your own category of cross-cultural worker for the word "anthropologist" in order to raise your awareness of the applicability of these principles to your fieldwork.

Principle I. *Anthropologists' first responsibility is to those whose lives and cultures they study. Should conflicts of interest arise, the interests of these people take precedence over other considerations. Anthropologists must do everything in their power to protect the dignity and privacy of the people with whom they work, conduct research or perform other professional activities. Their physical, social, and emotional safety and welfare are the professional concerns of the anthropologists who have worked among them.*

Principle I.A. *The rights, interests, safety, and sensitivities of those who entrust information to anthropologists must be safeguarded.*

If you engage in anthropological fieldwork, missionary service, linguistic fieldwork, translation and literacy work, development projects, or other cross-cultural activities, you may find yourself answering to various interest groups. These groups may include sending and funding organizations, national governments of your own and your hosts' countries, special interest groups, and the local people. Each group may have a different agenda, and you may feel caught in the middle. According to the principle stated above, your paramount responsibility is to safeguard the people you study. According to this principle their rights, interests, safety, and sensitivities come first.

Principle I.A.1. *The right of those providing information to anthropologists either to remain anonymous or to receive recognition is to be respected and defended. It is the responsibility of anthropologists to make every effort to determine the preferences of those providing information and to comply with their wishes.*

Principle I.A.1.a. *It should be made clear to anyone providing information that despite the anthropologist's best intentions and efforts anonymity may be compromised or recognition fail to materialize.*

Principle I.A.2. *Anthropologists should not reveal the identity of groups or persons whose anonymity is protected through the use of pseudonyms.*

Anonymity has long been an important principle in cultural research. If you desire to reveal the identity of the individual who supplied some data, then that individual should give his or her approval for your doing so. If that individual refuses to do so, then you need to respect his or her wishes.

Sometimes you gain information that is important for accomplishing your research goals, but if you revealed your sources, those sources could face difficult consequences. This type of problem occurs particularly when you document oppression, a phenomenon that is all too common for minority ethnic groups. The protection of anonymity in this situation is vital.

The issue of anonymity continues to receive attention. Historians who are beginning to collect oral histories are careful to document accurately and carefully each source of information. You may find yourself perplexed over this issue, as Henige explains.

> The problem [of confidentiality], and the consequent soul-searching, become the greater when dealing with the recent past, when the reputation, integrity, and even safety of living people—perhaps important people—may be brought into question. It is not hard to imagine any number of situations where this could happen: collaboration with an enemy or colonial power; rigging elections; financial wrongdoing; crimes against humanity. Possessing this kind of information, and it matters little whether it is true or not, the historian [or other social scientist] holds, however unwillingly, the well-being of some of his informants in his hands. In some cases he can do nothing with information of this nature, not even try to cite it anonymously if there is the possibility that it can be traced to a particular person or even used as a means of random reprisal....If he has *any* doubts about the wisdom of using them he must begin by relying on any cultural familiarity and specific knowledge he has gained in the field and, where possible, supplement these by communicating with his informants, asking advice from members of the society...or seeking the aid of other scholars....If his doubts persist he can refrain from using his information, or perhaps manage to couch it in terms that suggest he has based his conclusions on a variety of details from scattered sources, but this must be done with care. (1982:114–115)

Participant observation, an important and powerful cultural research method, may reveal information that can be used either to affirm other people's rights and interests or to invade or violate their way of life. It is also an intensely personal experience for you. Cultural research assistants become your friends and colleagues. For example, one student after engaging in participant observation with a student from Taiwan, honored that Chinese student as best man in his wedding. Fieldworkers who do not become friends and colleagues with their local research assistants and the people studied are more apt to use derogatory pejorative terms to refer to them, terms such as "natives, primitive people, savages, pagans, or uncivilized people." Such individuals do a disservice to the local people as well as to others who conscientiously seek to develop good relationships.

This principle of anonymity and respect for the people has led researchers to submit manuscripts of articles and books to knowledgeable members of the ethnic groups studied for their comments, corrections, deletions, and additions. This procedure may result in additional time before articles or books can be published, but review by the people studied is well worth any delay in publication. Their reviews aid in maintaining good public relations as well as assuring better quality data. In my experience, review by local individuals has resulted in more accurate manuscripts. Local reviewers have corrected my mistakes, and frequently they have volunteered important information that has substantially improved the quality of my manuscripts.

There are educated individuals in most ethnic groups worldwide. Some, when reading what past researchers have written about them, realize that false or distorted information has been published. They are sensitive to this issue and, therefore, they appreciate the opportunity to comment on current manuscripts.

Spradley provides us with an example of such respect in research. After recording a long life history of James Sewid, a Kwakiutl native American in British Columbia, Spradley realized that he had a book length manuscript. Spradley and Sewid signed the contract with Yale University Press as co-authors (Spradley 1980:21). In this way the rights, interests, and sensitivities of Sewid were protected. As a co-author, he had the responsibility of assuring the accuracy of the manuscript, and he also had the right to delete whatever he desired.

Another issue related to showing respect for the people is to be aware that people often prefer not to share with the general public all aspects of their culture. For example, Jennings states that the Nubians "...feel that the honor of their village, and of all Nubians everywhere, lies in covering up the negative aspects of their lives and in setting forth only the positive" (1995:15). He further notes "...that our informants will hold us accountable for what we publish about them" (p. 14).

When working with local scholars who provide data, give them recognition. This is usually done by co-authorship. Not to do so can be viewed as a form of academic imperialism and arrogance. Simply to put the source of the data in a footnote is unacceptable when a local scholar has done the work of collecting the data and perhaps has done some of the analysis.

Principle I.A.3. *The aims of their professional activities should be clearly communicated by anthropologists to those among whom they work.*

Those studied have the right to know the aims of the research. You can state those aims simply such as, "I want to learn about your way of life." Gradually, as language ability and trust increase, explain in more detail the aims of your specific research.

Be prepared to answer questions from people within the research community, questions such as, Why are you here? Who sent you? Will others come to work with you? What organization(s) do you work for? Who is funding you? Why do you want to learn about us? What benefit, if any, will we receive from your research? How long will you be here? How do we know that your government has not sent you as a spy? Will you give us a copy of your results? In response to such questions be honest and answer consistently. When it is appropriate, be brief in answering such questions. When first entering another culture when you might be struggling to communicate in another language, providing adequate answers may be difficult, but giving honest answers in a culturally appropriate manner is essential. Further, it helps to answer consistently, so that you give the same answer to each person who asks you.

People may make multiple requests of you. It is important not to make promises that you do not keep. The local people will remember what you promised and their expectations and opinion of you will be shaped by your words and actions.

Consult with local scholars and community members on topic selection and appropriate field methods. Local input into the direction of the research has often guided researchers to profitable areas to explore, areas which address the *felt needs* or the *expressed desires* of the community. It is helpful to the research community if you focus on their needs. For example, if they are faced with declining crop yields due to the spread of a specific type of insect or weed, they will appreciate assistance in knowing how to deal with their current problem. This is also true for development agencies. For example, in Nigeria, Faith and Farm wanted to begin aiding farmers with improved crop yields. When they asked the local people what their needs were, however, the response was,

> "Our need," they explained, "is to control termites. They damage our houses and churches, they make us re-thatch almost every year, and they destroy the contents of our grain stores; and they kill young trees and some other plants." (Batchelor 1993:13)

Therefore, Faith and Farm focused on termite eradication first, then worked on crop improvement. The termite eradication generated goodwill towards further cooperation. This development agency tapped into what problems and motivations the local people had.

Personally, Norris and I sought advice from Bajju elders when questions arose concerning the direction of our research. We also consulted expatriate colleagues. If there was a significant difference between their responses, we followed the advice of the Bajju elders, which we found to be relevant, effective, and insightful, because they understood the local culture.

Government officials, national scholars, and local leaders all want input into what research they will allow to be conducted within their jurisdiction. This issue is discussed further in the section "Selection of a research project" in the next chapter.

One frequent problem with western researchers' aims in the study of minority cultures is their tendency to concentrate research on the traditional to the exclusion of anything modern. To insiders in that cultural situation that research perspective usually fails to be relevant to their current interests. It results in making their culture look backwards and perhaps quaint to outsiders.

Focus on the traditional has led some to write in the ETHNOGRAPHIC PRESENT, an abstract concept that refers to a point in time when that which is described existed. Sometimes the ethnographic present is defined as the time period when all the traditional aspects of the culture functioned to the exclusion of anything modern. Use of the ethnographic present has enabled some to ignore history and culture change by presenting only synchronic data. If you choose to write using the ethnographic present, do so with much caution. Studying aspects of a culture should include the total historical context, both traditional and modern, as well as culture change.

If you choose to use the ethnographic present, specify the approximate date(s) to which your writing applies. For example, Nutini and Bell (1980:9) placed the *compadrazgo* 'godparent' system in Mexico within its historical context; for the purpose of writing carefully about the research they undertook, they stated that the ethnographic present extended from the time of writing to approximately a century earlier. In order to cover this time period they used data from regular depositories (civil and church archives) and from the literature, as well as data they collected over a period of approximately twenty years. This placed their study firmly within its larger historical, religious, economic, social, and political contexts.

Communicating the aims of research, then cooperating with the host society can lead to what some adult educators who work within a political economy theoretical model term PARTICIPATORY RESEARCH. It is a method that breaks down the distinction between researchers and the researched. The people themselves are involved in the production, participate in collection and development of knowledge, and use of that knowledge as the basis of mobilization for action. The researcher works in partnership with the community in all phases of the research. Orefice quotes Le Boterf who sets forth one of the main characteristics of participatory research as follows:

> The choice of problems to be studied is not made on the basis of a group of hypotheses previously established by the researchers, it arises from the concrete social situations that the people investigated, who participate in the research process, want to study and solve. The activity of researchers and practitioners is to help the groups concerned to formulate and analyze the problems that they themselves decide to study. (Orefice 1988:43)

Cooperation with individuals in the host society frequently involves working with researchers and research assistants in that country. This may involve MENTORING local social science students. (See the side box for an example.)

Principle I.A.4. *Anthropologists must not exploit individuals or groups for personal gain. They should give fair return for the help and services they receive. They must recognize their debt to the societies in which they work and their obligation to reciprocate in appropriate ways.*

In order to fulfill this principle, inquire into the current local salary scale for people who are similarly qualified (e.g., hold similar degrees) and are doing similar work in order to set the amount of REMUNERATION. For example, if your assistant spends four hours per day with you, the hourly wage paid should be in line with the locally set salary scale. Sometimes it is appropriate to write up the CONDITIONS OF SERVICE for your assistant(s).

There are instances where hospitality, gift giving, and/or reciprocal service may be more appropriate than monetary remuneration. Discuss the nuances of how to fulfill this principle with insiders of the research community, particularly with elders and the educated, and with other researchers who have worked there or who are currently working there. Their insight can aid you in making wise decisions about what is appropriate remuneration for those who work with you.

The question of remuneration also comes in if you hire household help. If you choose to employ a cook, a gardener, a person for general household help as with the laundry, house cleaning, washing dishes, carrying water, etc., discuss the issue of remuneration ahead of time with others who have employed household help, preferably in a similar location in order to ascertain the going salary scale. As Cassell states,

> Refraining from hiring desperately poor people who need the money is hardly an answer [to the problem of whether or not to hire local household help]. But having some sense of the local rules for interaction between employers and employees, and knowing ahead of time what sort of problems you are going to face and how you intend to deal with them, would be helpful. (Cassell 1987:7)

If you do hire local help and if they are injured when in your employment, you are responsible for their medical care. (See side box on next page for an example.)

Principle I.A.5. *Anthropologists have an ongoing obligation to assess both the positive and negative consequences of their activities and the publications resulting from those activities. They should inform individuals and groups likely to be affected of any consequences relevant to them that they anticipate. In any case, however, their work must not violate these principles of professional responsibility. If they anticipate the possibility that such violations might occur they should take steps, including, if necessary, discontinuance of work, to avoid such outcomes.*

Mentoring

When I was conducting research on Bajju religious change, the principal of a post-secondary school requested that I work together with a thesis student who was writing on a similar topic. That informal cooperative arrangement proved to be extremely beneficial to both of us. He knew the appropriate people I could benefit from interviewing, and I provided some direction to our research. Further, he had a motorcycle that we used to go on narrow trails back into the hinterland to interview people.

Principle I.A.6. *Whether they are engaged in academic or nonacademic research, anthropologists must be candid about their professional identities. If the results of their activities are not to be made public, this should be made clear to all concerned from the outset.*

This principle looks at positive and negative consequences of the activities of cultural researchers. Often those of us who engage in cultural research find out information that is sensitive for personal, cultural, or legal reasons. When this occurs, it presents special problems for us. There are no standard procedures or formulae for dealing with this type of situation. Often it helps to discuss with others who have encountered similar situations to see how they handled it. Further, when probing into areas that are potentially sensitive, obtaining accurate information may be difficult.

Types of research where you might likely encounter this type of problem include: study of illegal activities such as the drug culture, black market activities, illegal immigration, and smuggling; closely guarded secrets with respect to cultural or religious practices (e.g., initiation rites); sexual practices; personal characteristics with respect to shame and dishonor; lending (a sensitive topic in Asia due to the usurious practices of moneylenders) and borrowing (sometimes considered a sensitive topic in Africa); economic status (especially problematic for the very rich and very poor) and expenditures. The sensitivity of the information may be based on the kind of information sought, the potential uses of that information, the trust relationship that has been established between you as the fieldworker and the respondent, the language used in the interview, and even the setting of the interview (e.g., when an interview on a sensitive topic is conducted in a public place, you are less likely to get the types of data you want than when conducted in private). Further, your opinion of what is sensitive information may differ from the local perception of what is sensitive.

> ### Ishaku
>
> Ishaku came to work for us when fifteen years old. He was a delight to have around. Not only did he do what he was asked to do, he assisted my understanding of the local culture. For example, he shared with me about the "empirical," the supernatural realm of witchcraft.
>
> One day while helping Norris with something on the roof, I watched in dismay as Ishaku fell off the roof past the kitchen window. We took him for medical attention for his broken leg. While he was recovering he frequently came to our house to play with our new puppy. When Norris went to the doctor one day, the doctor told Norris to tell Ishaku to "stop dancing on his leg" so that it would heal more quickly!
>
> It was definitely our responsibility to continue paying Ishaku's salary and medical bills while he was recovering, because we were his employers.

Christensen writes, "Nevertheless, where personal information is clearly sensitive it is essential to preserve both the privacy of the exchange and the anonymity of the information" (1993:125). Having said that, if the information is needed to fulfill research goals, sometimes a frank direct approach is called for, and this type of approach may result in greater respect between you the fieldworker and the interviewee. Be aware that in some cultures certain information may not be readily shared with a fieldworker, dependent on that fieldworker's age, sex, and marital status. For example, Christensen found that respondents refused to share information on either livestock or credit with a female researcher but were quite ready to provide that information to a male fieldworker (p. 127). From their perspective they did not discuss this type of information with females. Similarly, you may find that information on local use of birth control methods is data you could expect to obtain from women but not men. In an African context important or sensitive information is less apt to be shared with an unmarried fieldworker than with a married fieldworker with children, who is considered an adult. For example, Christensen found that "...older, married enumerators (of either sex) were most readily accepted by the villagers [in Burkina Faso], and that maturity and ability to get along with people were more important enumerator attributes than IQ or level of education" (p. 130). Having said this, note that expatriate fieldworkers often fall into the "other" or "visitor/stranger" category. As such, do not let your marital status deter you from conducting a research project, but be aware of potential problems in this area.

Unfortunately, anthropologists, linguists, missionaries, and other cultural researchers occasionally find themselves accused of engaging in clandestine research, such as being employed by the CIA or other intelligence gathering agencies. Such accusations can be devastating. It is well worth the efforts necessary to avoid such false accusations, if possible, by not being associated with organizations that are engaged in secret activities. Further, do whatever local research obligations require, including obtaining the necessary permission for the study and providing reports, articles, and books written to appropriate individuals, institutions, and local organizations.

Principle II.B. *Anthropologists bear a positive responsibility to speak out publicly, both individually and collectively, on issues about which they possess professional expertise. That is, they have a professional responsibility to contribute to the formation of informational grounds upon which public policy may be founded. Anthropologists should make clear the bases upon which their positions stand.*

This issue is mentioned in the section "Social Responsibility" earlier in this chapter. In many instances cultural researchers have an obligation to share understanding with government officials, mission executives, and others engaged in development of the local area whose proposed policies and projects may affect the local people. The knowledge you gain in your fieldwork may be such that you can make a significant contribution to what happens to them, so use that knowledge for their benefit.

Principle II.C. *When engaging in public discourse anthropologists should be candid about their qualifications, and they should recognize and make clear the limits of anthropological expertise.*

When working cross-culturally, you may find yourself characterized as "Doctor..." when you know very well that you do not have a doctor's degree. Be honest about what qualifications you have with those who need to know. Also recognize and communicate that there are limits to what you and your field of study are qualified to do. Many field researchers have limited funding, so they are unable to fund large development projects. Many do not have the knowledge, skills, and aptitude to do any number of things that they are asked about. Be candid and honest concerning what you and your field of study can and cannot contribute.

Relevance of research to a community

It is important to explore ways in which your study can be helpful to the local people. (See side box on next page for an example.) Southwell addresses this issue as follows:

> Pacific Island nations have had much experience with western researchers over the past years. Researchers have come to them, staying for months or a year. They say they want to be friends, but soon leave to go and write up (sometimes even make up?) the results to gain personal academic and financial benefit.

This has come to be resented in some Pacific Island nations as a form of exploitation of their resources. The question they now ask over and over is, "How will your research project directly benefit our community or nation?" (1989:6)

You can make your research relevant to the community that is being researched in various ways. One way is by publishing on the group involved, especially publishing within the country where the ethnic group lives, and by providing some leaders of that ethnic group copies of everything you write about them. Some obligations of a research affiliation with a local university include publication in local journals as well as provision of the final results to the university and the community researched.

Another way to make the research relevant to members of the community being researched is by publishing books (or booklets) in their language on topics of interest to them, such as health, ways of improving local crops, local oral traditions (e.g., histories, folktales, proverbs, etc.), animals, and geography. In traditionally oral societies where more and more children go to school, elders find that there is less time to transmit to the next generation their stories, proverbs, and oral history, but they do not want to loose this information. They often appreciate help from outside researchers in preserving this material for posterity.

> **Topics requested by Bajju elders**
>
> When we discussed with Bajju elders what topics they would like us to include in books, they most often stated that they wanted us to include their oral literature. They feared it would be lost to the next generation if something were not done soon. In order for some of those stories to be written down, we conducted a couple of writers' workshops where Bajju writers wrote down some of their oral stories.

As mentioned before, one way to assist the indigenous people is to help them meet their specific expressed needs. For example, in many areas of the world, minority groups find themselves pushed onto undesirable and unproductive land (Tracy 1988). An important aid is to help them obtain official title to their ancestral lands. Whatever help you might render to indigenous ethnic groups, calls for much wisdom to decide what is appropriate, what is best in each local situation, and how much time and other resources to devote to those activities.

It is naive of fieldworkers to think that they can concentrate on research without doing things that benefit local communities studied. Frequently, members of the local community will ask you to provide ambulance service to the hospital or to provide for their medical needs. (See side box for example.)

Making your research relevant to the people in your daily life during your period of research is important. For example, Wilson states,

> **Practical help**
>
> In the village where we lived, people asked us to provide aid and/or advice in a multitude of areas, from adjusting glasses, to house construction, ambulance service, electrification projects, transportation, aid with literacy, to use of our rope and bucket to get a goat out of a well. Most requests fell into the category of practical aid with everyday problems.

A first priority must be to make the daily experience of the research as enjoyable as possible for all concerned. Be interested in "them" as people as well as data, share genuinely of yourself, be prepared to grow together with people, and develop your sense of humour. Locals remember researchers and "learn" from them through their personal relationships—not their monographs.

Fieldwork as a cross-cultural endeavour is an opportunity for those studied as well as for the researcher. (1993:188–89)

By contrast, some have failed to make their research relevant and their results available to the local community and thus, have failed to show them respect. (See box for example.)

Respect shown by fulfilling promises

While in Nigeria in 1984, I collected wordlists from several languages closely related to Jju, the language of the Bajju (Kaje) people which we were studying. At one village I collected a wordlist from a pastor who told of a researcher who had lived with them for fifteen months. He related a perceived lack of respect for the research community: the previous researcher had promised to mail them a copy of the final write-up of her linguistic analysis of their language. The pastor complained that it was two years since she left, and they had heard nothing from her nor had they seen any of her results. While that length of time is not unusual for the write-up of data collected for that extended period of fieldwork, from the perspective of the local community it was. They felt that they had invested heavily in teaching her their language with no apparent results to themselves. Their previous experience with that researcher made them less willing to cooperate with the next one, namely me. I later learned that she, in fact, had completed her write-up and degree, but she failed to provide the local community with a copy.

Ethics as a byproduct of cultural research

While this chapter has focused on researchers' ethical responsibilities in conducting cultural research, cross-cultural research, itself, can contribute to raising the social consciousness of people through its results. For example, by studying the results of raising the drinking age in a population by one or two years, research has pointed to the resulting reduction of the number of highway accidents caused by drinking alcoholic beverages. Social science indicates possible consequences of proposed programs or legislation by looking at all people who might be affected by those programs, including possible biases due to factors such as racism, gender and age discrimination, and economic considerations.

Summary

In summary, the principles of ethics discussed in this chapter are listed.

1. A researcher's primary responsibility is to the people being studied.
2. A researcher should safeguard those who trustingly provide information.
3. A researcher should communicate the aims of the research.
4. A researcher should cooperate with the host society in his or her research.
5. Those who supply information have the right to remain anonymous.
6. There should be no exploitation of informants for personal gain.
7. There should be no clandestine research.
8. A researcher should reflect on the foreseeable repercussions of his or her research and publication.
9. The anticipated consequences of the research should be communicated to those affected.

Mann reminds us that,

> Each field situation is unique and presents a multitude of problems for the re-
> searcher: theoretical, methodological, and ethical. One thing common to all
> anthropological inquiry, however, is the necessity for personal involvement of
> some sort with one's informants. The anthropologist deals with people and, be-
> cause of this, fieldwork is subject to all the complexities, ambiguities, and
> unpredictability inherent in any form of social interaction. Thus, it is seldom
> possible to anticipate, or to completely control, the types of problems that arise
> in a given research situation. (1976:107)

To the extent possible you do need to anticipate ethical dilemmas and be prepared to
deal with them. Also be prepared to make decisions on-the-spot in accordance with the
general principles of ethics and integrity when dealing with people in the research
community.

Proceed with preparation for cultural research with these ethical principles in mind and
the relevance of the proposed study to the community to be researched. That preparation is
the topic of the following chapter.

3

Preparation for Field Research

We could start with a systematic collection of relevant literature under the rubric nomadic hunting-gathering societies. (Pelto and Pelto 1978:4)

Whether studying a hunter-gatherer society or some other type of society, there is initial preparation for fieldwork that includes (1) carefully thinking through the research project, (2) developing a focused research design, (3) researching the literature on the ethnic group and/or topic selected, (4) formulating your ideas into research hypotheses, (5) establishing an appropriate research affiliation in the country where you plan to do the research, (6) deciding on the length of field research, (7) making health preparations, including obtaining necessary immunizations and prophylaxes, (8) acquiring funding for the research, and (9) collecting and purchasing the necessary equipment. The first seven of these topics are discussed in this chapter.

Selecting a research project

Your first decision prior to field research is selecting a specific topic to study. Questions to answer are, what topic and focus should you select, what data should you collect, what field methods are appropriate to use in order to collect the data you desire, what should you do with those data, and what theoretical perspective best suits your purposes?

Selecting a good research project depends on a host of pragmatic factors. Are you planning on doing STRATEGIC RESEARCH, research into specific problems faced by the community in focus? For example, the existence of AIDS in a community points to the need for research on local sexual practices, the subcultures of prostitutes and intravenous drug users, attitudes and practices in the care of terminally ill patients, racism, ethnicity, gender issues, and the economics and availability of medical care. Other strategic research projects might deal with the effects of drought, depletion of fuel resources, migration, the plight of refugees, the possibility of ETHNOCIDE[3] of a group, and urban overcrowding as evidenced by the existence of shanty towns with inadequate provision of facilities and services to the population (e.g., water, sanitation facilities, electricity, and medical delivery systems).

In response to problems people face within specific cultures, some researchers have focused on APPROPRIATE TECHNOLOGY (AT) to solve those problems. They seek to address

---

[3]Ethnographic research and subsequent awareness of the results of that research by the wider community can help reverse the denigration and resultant ethnocide of those groups. For more on causes of ethnocide see the UN Development Forum, as quoted in *World Christian* 1989:31–32.

topics such as what technology is appropriate within the specific cultural context, what decision-making procedures should be followed in order to introduce AT projects, who will evaluate those projects, who might contribute what to AT projects, what are long term sustainable uses of AT, what modifications should be done with existing AT projects, and what are reasons for success or failure of specific projects?

Most development agencies have research goals of providing practical projects to benefit the people. For example, World Bank is concerned with causes of poverty, particularly within rural areas. Poverty is reflected in poor nutrition, low rural health standards, unemployment and underemployment, and inadequate shelter. Once specific causes are identified through research, it seeks to use that knowledge to develop strategies for rural development that benefit small-scale farmers and others affected. Projects likely to result from such research include nutrition programs, preventive health services, and educational information, seeds, fertilizer, equipment, facilities, and ready access to markets.

Many countries establish their own priorities concerning the types of research they will allow to be done and the terms on which the research is to be conducted (Henige 1982:25–26). Consequently, you need to propose your project in light of those priorities.

Some select a research project because of their theoretical interests and perspectives. For example, if you are guided by a political economy model, you might focus on topics such as modes of production, class structures, oppression, or aftereffects of colonialism.

If you are searching for cultural universals, cross-cultural research projects would be appropriate. You might choose to work with databases such as the *Human Relations Area Files Quality Control Sample* (QCS) or the *Standard Cross-Cultural Sample* (SCCS) (Murdock and White 1969). The Human Relations Area Files contains entries from at least 350 cultures around the world. This database is being entered onto CD-ROM for ready reference. In 1994 there were sixty cultures entered onto the CD-ROM (Bernard 1994:344). It is an important resource that you might want to check with respect to your research project, whether or not your project is cross-cultural. For cultures in the QCS that have not yet been entered onto CD-ROM, you would need to look at research in related cultures that are in the QCS. A library with this material would have it available on microfilm. Murdock and White's SCCS is a database of 186 societies, and is another good resource of ethnographic data on specific cultures that is particularly helpful for cross-cultural comparisons.

In deciding upon a research project, you need to consider which level(s) or scale of analysis to use when conducting your research. This can be at the MICROLEVEL, such as focusing on the craft of calabash carving, or at the MACROLEVEL or global level. Large scale analyses take into account economic, political, and cultural contexts. At this level you might research the international marketing processes for specific commodities such as cocoa, coffee, tea, tin, etc. Whichever level you select as the major focus of your research, small scale research on a local system or large scale analysis, the two must be linked.

In a microlevel example of calabash carving, the specific patterns carved may characterize a particular area of the country and may be used by specific subcultures. For example, an expatriate drew a picture of a Bororo Fulani woman with a carved calabash on her head. The artist indicated the fact that she was a nomadic Bororo Fulani by gold wrapped around her braids. However, when knowledgeable Fulani saw that drawing, they pointed out that pastoral Bororo Fulani do not use calabashes with that particular carved design. That pattern is used by the semi-settled Fulani in the area. In this example, the microlevel research on calabash carved patterns needed to tie specific calabash carving designs in with the larger regional level focus of a distinction between different Fulani subgroups.

Similarly, in the example of studying the international cocoa marketing process, researchers would need to include the effects of cocoa pricing at the international level on the household budget of individual cocoa farmers. The focus of any research needs to acknowledge that the topic is embedded within a total cultural context that goes from the macrolevel or global perspective to the microlevel: from the international, to the national, to the regional, and finally, to the local level. Cultural researchers speak of understanding globalization and localization as opposite ends of a continuum for perspectives on cultural research.

Since one important goal of ethnographic data collection is theory building based on cross-cultural and comparative research, you need to remain aware of the larger picture in your data collection. For example, when Nutini and Bell (1980) studied the *compadrazgo* system in Santa Maria Belen in Tlaxcala and Puebla, Mexico, they kept the larger questions in focus, questions such as, How does RITUAL KINSHIP function in general (e.g., within ethnic groups embedded in modern, urban settings)? What is its geographic distribution? What forms does it take, and does it function differently in social interaction within differing levels of sociopolitical complexity (e.g., within peasant societies and in modern cities)? The specific qualitative and quantitative data collected enabled them to work towards a much broader understanding of ritual kinship.

In Central America the focus of research has often been on the community. Reasons for this focus include the fact that communities in Central America are typically endogamous. Further, each community or cluster of a few communities tends to speak one dialect. Geographic factors, such as mountains and valleys where people live, contribute to linguistic diversity and marriage patterns. By contrast, in Africa many cultural researchers have looked at larger populations, even at entire ethnic groups. Part of the reason for this is that African groups practice clan exogamy, so intermarriage between persons in different villages is common. Communities in Africa maintain ties with their members who live in urban areas, as well as with those in other villages. Thus, there are more villages and people included within the same basic culture and language area.

From the perspective of some, ethnographers have a reputation for looking at the quaint and exotic, at areas of culture that are dying out and, thus, tend to be irrelevant to the current problems of the people. While some ethnographers continue to do so, perhaps the majority no longer do that type of research except to the extent that past practices shed light on current issues. The cutting edge of ethnography is making your research relevant to current issues in today's world. This is not to say that SALVAGE ANTHROPOLOGY has no place within ethnographic research. Salvage anthropology is a means of documenting past or nearly past cultural practices, especially when the ethnic group in question is near extinction or is experiencing very rapid cultural change and losing its cultural distinctives.

Contrastively, some cultural researchers do focus on the traditional and by so doing affirm those customs, traditions, and practices as valuable and valid ways of living. Some may mourn the passing of a colorful heritage of their community. By documenting those practices, crafts, beliefs, and cultural traditions, you may contribute to a greater value being placed on them and perhaps contribute to their revival or reassertion, though perhaps only in limited spheres. By so doing some researchers are making ideological statements. Others who study the traditional may seek to understand the present in light of the past history of the ethnic group. This type of research is termed RESCUE ANTHROPOLOGY. Common reasons for endangered cultures, where the traditional is dying out, include factors such as destruction of ecosystems within which ethnic groups live (e.g., destruction of rain forests, presence of mining companies, the construction of a dam and consequent flooding of people's fields), drug and alcohol abuse, activities involved in producing illegal drugs and trafficking, economic and political exploitation, population decline, and the death of the remaining elders who knew their former way of life.

One aspect of selection of a research project that a fieldworker may not be aware of is its possible or potential political significance. This grows out of a number of factors including rivalry between different ethnic groups, situations of political repression and domination, problems with previous fieldworkers who did not contribute to the community which provided the data, and so on. Any fieldwork topic can have potential political significance.

Research proposal

Prior to embarking on systematic cultural research establish a research design. Many researchers write research proposals, an essential step if seeking financing from various funding agencies. The process of writing a research proposal will help you clarify your thinking about what you will actually be doing in a field situation.

A research proposal typically includes a statement of the problem, literature review, hypothesis or hypotheses to be tested, field methods to be used, statement of the relevance of the proposed research, proposed budget including any equipment needed, a time table, references cited, and relevant appendices to the proposed project, as well as your curriculum vita (CV) that includes references who can be called upon to evaluate you and your chances of succeeding in any research project. You might also want to consult various authors who have written on research design and proposal construction (see Brim and Spain 1974). It will help you in writing your research proposal to consult with people who have worked in the area where you plan to work.

Literature review

Careful research involves a literature review, that helps you know what others have done on the same or a similar topic and/or ethnic group. Read on that topic and/or culture as well as on closely related groups living within the same culture area where there are clusters of similar cultures. A CULTURE AREA, as defined by Nanda, is "a broad geographical area in which a number of different societies make similar adaptations to a particular ecological zone and through diffusion come to develop similar cultural patterns" (1980:341). Wissler (1917) developed the concept of a culture area to help bring some systematization to the vast array of cultural observations. Cultures within the same culture area may share the same mode of production for their food acquisition and may have a similar culture and history. While useful, be aware that radically different cultures can exist within the same ecological zone. So, reading about related cultures within the same culture area is helpful and especially important if the specific ethnic group in focus has had little or nothing written about it.

While it is important to search out results of other fieldworkers, maintain a healthy skepticism about what you read. This skepticism is for a variety of reasons: (1) other researchers may have spent insufficient time in the research communities to have delved very deeply into the culture, (2) the culture may have changed resulting in out-of-date information, (3) the description may have been written in the ethnographic present that ignored more current aspects of the culture, (4) the researcher may have been mistaken, (5) the researcher's results may have been colored by his or her theoretical position so that what actually occurred in that culture was obscured, or (6) the researcher had an inadequate grasp of the local language or worked only through the trade language. Nevertheless, current research needs to build on what others have written, and it may refute, confirm, expand, or modify earlier results. Previous research has observations made at that time in history that are invaluable. Though the theoretical model that informed the research may have changed and become outdated, the observations and data themselves have value.

Once you arrive in the country where you plan to do research, continue doing your literature research in local university libraries and archives, and seek out local documentation that may not be available outside the country. Examples of useful archives to consult include government reports, national archives, newspaper archives, photo collections, industrial data, medical records, school records, wills, deeds, tax rolls, and land-holding records (Bernard 1988:294). You may also find personal documents such as diaries, letters, biographies, and autobiographies. Be aware, however, that some of these sources may not be publicly accessible in some countries or may be politically sensitive.

You might also consult dispensary records, mission archives, local church records, and mission station books. (E.g., Roman Catholic missionaries keep station books at each mission station that record comings and goings, baptisms, and other special events.) You may want to consult census data at the local or national census office. (See side box for an example.)

> **Check local sources**
>
> In research, I found theses in a university library that had been written in Nigeria and were unavailable outside the country. I also read colonial documents in the National Archives in Kaduna and consulted unpublished local church and missionary records.

You can check British colonial archival material in former British colonies. French archival material is sealed in France for fifty years. In former French colonies, however, the same or similar material is not sealed, so check there.

All records, reports, theses, dissertations, newspaper and magazine articles, and other materials that document the culture are important for ongoing research. They form part of the ethnographic record of that culture.

Computer assisted searches

In order to conduct a systematic and thorough literature search, use a computer-assisted search. Begin by drawing up a list of key subject words that define the ethnic group and the topic for your study; include synonyms, alternate spellings, and generic subject terms. Next check card catalogs, indexes, and utilize computerized literature searches. Some scholars begin with the most recent publications on the subject, then consult those published earlier.

Many library systems have resources available for the researcher to conduct computer assisted searches based on the term(s) he or she specifies. One retrieval system used by libraries is DIALOG with the *Social Science Citation Index* (SSCI) which is issued three times per year. Hard copies of the SSCI are published for periods of five years (1981–85, 1986–90, etc.). It includes three indexes: citation, source, and subject. The citation index contains authors' names, alphabetized by last names, and the year the reference was cited. The source index has primary authors, again alphabetized by last names, together with an identification that specifies whether it was cited in a book, article, review article, etc. All references that are cited in the *Citation Index* are also cited in the source index. The address of the author of a particular reference in the source index is included to help the researcher contact him. The subject index uses pairs of words taken from titles of articles. If an article has a catchy title but it does not contain words that really tell you what is in that article, you may have a hard time finding what you are looking for in this resource. (See side box for an example.)

Other resources for conducting computer assisted searches to consult include the *Science Citation Index* (SCI) and the *Arts and Humanities Citation Index* (A&HCI). The following reference can assist in searching for information:

Brody, Ferm and Maureen Lambert 1984 Alternative databases for anthropological searching. *Database* 7:28–32.

General bibliographic references

The following resources might aid you in locating bibliographic references:

> **Birth weight, Africa search**
>
> In assisting in research on birth weights of Bariba infants born in a clinic in northern Benin (Sargent, McKinney, and Wetherington 1986), I used the key terms *birth weight* and *Africa* in a computer-assisted search. I specified all references published in the preceding five years containing both key terms. Based on the results of the computer search, I then consulted each article listed.

Abstracts in Anthropology (AIA) (1970 ff.). Abstracts found in this reference are typically from 50 to 200 words long. It abstracts articles from seven important journals in anthropology: the *American Anthropologist*, the *American Ethnologist*, *Current Anthropology*, *Ethnology*, *Human Organization*, *Journal of Anthropological Research*, and *Man*. In addition, it covers other journals whose materials might not be readily available for fieldworkers. For example, it references *Oral History*, published in Papua New Guinea, and *Caribbean Studies*, published at the University of Puerto Rico.

Anthropological Index (AI) to periodicals in the *Museum of Mankind* library (incorporating the former *Royal Anthropological Institute* library) and *The Library Catalogue*. This reference covers entries from a variety of sources, including ones from eastern Europe and various third world nations. For example, it has references from the *Journal of the Indian Anthropological Society* and the *Bulletin of the National Museum of Ethnology* in Japan.

International Bibliography of Social and Cultural Anthropology (1953 ff.). This reference is produced under the auspices of the International Committee on Social Science Information and Documentation, a UNESCO-funded group that works out of Paris. This group also produces indexes on economics, political science, and sociology, in addition to anthropology. These references have both an author index and a subject index. If you are studying topics from eastern Europe, various third world countries, or other parts of the world this is a good reference to consult.

International Bibliography of the Social Sciences. This bibliographic series includes volumes for sociology, economics, political science, and social and cultural anthropology.

Congressional Information Service (CIS). The CIS, the *American Statistical Index* (ASI), the *Statistical Reference Index* (SRI) and the *Index to International Statistics* (IIS) provide references to publications put out by government agencies, private foundations, and industries. The CIS consists of two volumes published annually that have an index on topics listed by subject headings and abstracts. *CIS Annual* (1970 ff.) provides a guide to publications of the United States Congress. CIS is available back to 1789 on CD-ROM.

American Statistical Index (ASI) (1973 ff.). This is an index of U.S. federal government publications other than from Congress; it does not include journals from government agencies. Those are covered by the *Index to US Government Periodicals*. In the ASI you can search for statistics on particular cities, countries, topics such as tariffs, farm sector data, ethnic groups (e.g., Alaskan Inuit, native Americans), etc.

Statistical Reference Index (SRI) (1980 ff.). This reference looks at statistical publications from both state government and private sources. The documents cited in this reference are all on microfiche.

Index of International Statistics (IIS) (1983 ff.). This resource presents data from around the world on a multitude of topics that may be of interest.

Current Index to Journals in Education (CIJE) (1969 ff.). This is a monthly index which covers a large number of social science journals. This index contains references that are not in the SSCI.

Geographical Abstracts (GA) (1966 ff.). This resource has volumes on social and historical geography, regional and community planning, and economic geography. GA is particularly good for international issues.

The Catalog of the Peabody Museum Library and Anthropological Literature (AL). In that the library of the Peabody Museum of Archaeology and Ethnology, the Tozzer Library, has the largest collection of anthropological literature in the world, consultation of the *Catalog* is likely to be worth your efforts. Initially, the *Catalog* was published in 1963, followed by four supplements. From 1979 ff. the Tozzer Library has published a quarterly journal, known as *Anthropological Literature*. From 1986 ff. the holdings of this Library have been available through the on-line database called HOLLIS. To access it via computer you can use HOLLIS via Telenet to HOLLIS.HARVARD.EDU. This reference is particularly important for references for North, Middle, and South America.

The Tozzer Library. For information on the Tozzer Library that may have useful anthropological information see: Weeks, John M. 1987. Tozzer Library. A 'national' library for anthropology. *Current Anthropology* 28:133–137. The Tozzer Library (formerly the Library of the Peabody Museum at Harvard) contains what the *Cultural Anthropology Methods Newsletter* (CAM) terms the world's largest anthropology bibliography. It can be accessed through Internet and Telnet. For further information on this useful resource see CAM 1992 Vol. 4(1):1–3.

The World Bibliographical Series. Oxford, England; Santa Barbara, California; and Denver, Colorado: Clio Press. The goal of this series is to have a volume of bibliographic information with annotations for every country in the world. Each book has a general introduction to the country in focus. By 1993 there were volumes for 163 countries.
Further resource books are as follows:

Cooper, Harris M. 1989. *Integrating Research, A Guide for Literature Reviews*. Applied Social Research Methods, Vol. 2. Newbury Park, Calif.: Sage Publications, Inc.

Koenig, Mary M. and John M. Weeks. 1989. *Introduction to Library Research in Anthropology*. Boulder, Colo.: Westview Press.

Weeks, John M. 1991. *Introduction to Library Research in Anthropology*. Boulder, Colo.: Westview Press.

The series *Annual Review of Anthropology* (1959 ff.; from 1959–1969 published as *Biennial Review of Anthropology*) is helpful for finding information on particular topics. Each article provides an update on the topic in focus, summarizes past literature on that topic, and includes extensive bibliographic references. In addition, there are *Annual Reviews* in economics, psychology, and sociology.

Area and topical bibliographic references

There are a number of useful bibliographic references for area and topical studies. The following list is suggestive of where you might begin your search for bibliographic references.

Africa

African Bibliography (year of data), Works on Africa Published during (year). Compiled by Christopher H. Allen. Edinburgh: Edinburgh University Press. (1985 ff.; published annually). This bibliographic resource focuses principally on the social and environmental sciences, the humanities, and the arts. It has both author and subject indexes.

The Making of Modern Africa, A Guide to Archives. 1995. Compiled by Chris Cook. New York: Facts On File, Inc. This book brings together information about archival resources that are largely in Britain, Western Europe, and Africa for the period from the Congress of Berlin in 1878 until the end of colonial rule in Africa. Many of the resources listed are in personal or local collections. Cook includes brief notes as to the accessibility of the various archives or restrictions on their use.

Cumulative Bibliography of African Studies.

International African Bibliography (1971 ff.; published quarterly). While each issue has a helpful index, the annual index is more complete and is arranged by author, subject, country, and ethnic group. Egypt is the only African country not included in this index.

Asia

Bibliography of Asian Studies, that was preceded by the *Far Eastern Bibliography* (1941–1955) and the *Bulletin of Far Eastern Bibliography* (1936–1940).

Cumulative Bibliography of Asian Studies.

Australia

Annual Bibliography, produced by the Australian Institute of Aboriginal Studies, beginning in 1975, as well as a *Newsletter.*

Latin America

Handbook of Latin American Studies, prepared by the Hispanic Division of the Library of Congress and published since 1935.

HAPI: Hispanic American Periodical Index.

Pacific

Pacific history bibliography and commentary (published annually).

Papua New Guinea

New Guinea periodical index: Guide to current periodical literature about New Guinea.

Islam

Index Islamicus, a catalogue of articles on Islamic subjects in periodicals and other collective publications. It covers the period of 1906–1975 in five volumes; then from 1977 there is *The Quarterly Index Islamicus.*

Linguistic Anthropology

Communications Abstracts (1978 ff.).

Language and Language Behavior Abstracts (1967 ff.).

Linguistic Bibliography (1948 ff.).

MLA International Bibliography (1981 ff.). This index covers over 3,000 journals from around the world. It includes references to literature, language, folklore, etc. It is updated quarterly.

Research hypotheses

Prior to beginning fieldwork formulate your ideas into research hypotheses to guide your field research. One or more hypotheses to be tested follows the literature review section in a research proposal. In the field, these hypotheses usually undergo modification in light of the local situation and the interests of the community. Hypotheses enable you to decide what field methods are relevant to use to collect data in order to test them.

Suggestions for developing hypotheses

In order to develop useful hypotheses Otterbein (1990:6) suggests the following procedures as an aid:

1. From published literature select a theory to be tested.
2. Identify the basic concepts of the hypothesis within the explanation. He notes that some hypotheses may serve only one level of sociopolitical complexity (e.g., bands),

while other hypotheses are needed to specify specific variables (e.g., the presence or absence of a specific trait).

3. Create hypotheses using those variables identified in step two.

For further information on the form of hypotheses, see the section on hypotheses in chapter 10.

Hypotheses aid in setting goals

Hypotheses provide direction for setting daily, weekly, monthly, and yearly goals for research. Set goals in segments so that they can be accomplished within the allotted time. In most research settings, personal relationships are far more important than accomplishment of research goals. Southwell captures this well by stating,

> In contrast to…[a Western time orientation] we have many third world societies where time is not a major focus. In Melanesia it is not of great importance just when an event may take place. What is important is that all the personal relationships are in place and in good order. So the event is discussed, maybe repeatedly, until a consensus is reached to the general satisfaction of all involved. The event [e.g., a wedding, or accomplishment of your research goals] can then take place without a negative effect on relationships. No one has been excluded or ignored; harmony is maintained in society. (1989:5–6)

Western scholars are often time-oriented while people in other cultures tend to be event-oriented or personal relationship-oriented. Research goals need to take into account the specific orientation of the culture in focus.

The research proposal, in addition to having a literature review and a statement of hypothesis (or hypotheses), suggests possible research findings, shows how these tie in with the results of other researchers, and relates to the theoretical perspective of the research design. Finally, it includes (perhaps in appendices) a proposed schedule of research activities, a tentative budget, and a list of references cited. This research proposal serves as a basis for requests for funding, a guide to research on the field, and the basis for a request for research affiliation. (See CAM 4(1):6–12 (1992) for information on anthropology grant proposals and funding sources.)

Research affiliation

In order to obtain a visa to many countries you must have a research affiliation with some institution that works in that country. Many universities have a category of research affiliation for projects to be conducted within the country. Obtaining such an affiliation involves submitting the research proposal, which then must go through the necessary channels.

Henige (1982:26) points out that since a research affiliation may be difficult to obtain, have an alternative project or two in mind. In any event, you should recognize that obtaining a research affiliation is often time consuming; however, the persevering researcher may be well rewarded for his or her patience.

Once you arrive within the country where you plan to conduct your research, you should count on spending a significant amount of time getting your papers in order before beginning the research. This may include obtaining a residence permit from the ministry of internal affairs. In some countries the police or the military maintain road blocks where people must produce the necessary papers on demand. Some countries keep track of expatriates at local police stations where you must check in upon arrival in the area and must check out when moving to another location. It is important to find out the local regulations and follow them in order to have the minimum of hassle and be able to spend the maximum amount of time on your research goals.

While a university research affiliation is the road most social scientists follow, others affiliate with other organizations already working in the country. In that case, representatives of the specific organization make the necessary arrangements for you to obtain your visa.

Length of cultural research

One year is a minimum period of time spent in the research area by most who are working on Ph.D. degrees in cultural anthropology; some scholars say it should be fourteen months (Foster et al. 1979:324); and some researchers may choose to stay longer. This period allows you the opportunity to observe the annual agricultural, social, and ritual cycles. Students working on an M.A. degree typically choose more limited projects and spend shorter periods in the field. Length of research is often limited by funds, with inadequate funding necessitating shorter research periods.

Multiple research trips

Some cultural researchers make multiple trips to their research sites and accumulate years of fieldwork experience. Howell (1987, paper presented at the meetings of the American Anthropological Association) has investigated the question of how much time anthropologists spend doing fieldwork. Concerning the number of fieldtrips, she states that in her sample

> The average number of fieldtrips for the 204 fieldworkers is 18.8 trips. The median number of trips is 9, reflecting the degree of skew in the distribution caused by a minority of fieldworkers who have done as many as 100 fieldtrips (12)[*] or even as many as 200 (2)....Men report a somewhat larger number of field trips than women. The anthropologists who work primarily in the more distant areas of the world: Latin America, Africa, Southeast Asia, and Asia-Pacific report fewer fieldtrips (average under 15 trips) than those who work in North America and in Europe (average over 25). (Howell 1987:48–49)

> *The numbers in parentheses refer to the number of anthropologists for whom the number of fieldtrips apply.

Howell also addressed the question of the total number of months spent doing fieldwork. She states,

> The average number of months in the field for all of the fieldworkers is 41.8 months, with a median of 35, in other words, between three and four years of continuous exposure to field hazards. We saw earlier that an average of 22 years has elapsed since the first fieldwork these people did, so they have been averaging, overall, a little less than 2 months per year over the course of their career. (1987:5)

The main reason for repeated visits and long-term field research is the opportunity thus afforded to delve into a society in detail and to study that society as it experiences change over time. Such research enables scholars to develop theories about the processes of culture change that are not possible to construct from data collected in a one-year period. Furthermore, many cyclical events in cultures have cycles longer than one year (e.g., the American presidential electoral system).

Benefits of long-term field research

Benefits of long-term field research to the social sciences in general include the finding by Foster et al. (1979:325) that the increased "awareness that social systems are more complicated, or at least more dynamic and open-ended, than previously realized...". For example, the bias some held in social science theory towards functional and equilibrium explanations has been shattered through results of extended periods of research that have shown people move from very traditional societies to active participation in modern states within very short time periods.

Another benefit of long-term field research is that you can move from the "outsider" category to more nearly that of an "insider." As a result you may be privy to information that the people within the community do not readily share with outsiders. You may be more accepted and respected by the community.

The principal results of long-term field research are greater depth and quality of understanding of the culture and knowledge to build more accurate explanatory theories of human behavior. Indeed the extent to which traditional aspects of society are retained in the face of modernizing influences continues to intrigue some.

Other categories of people who can make use of the field methods in this book spend extended periods in the field. They plan on living cross-culturally for an extended time, without the strictures that some cross-cultural social scientists feel. For example, many people in categories, such as missionaries, translators, famine relief agents, doctors, nurses, development workers, teachers, and literacy workers, plan on living cross-culturally with only relatively short periods spent in their home countries.

Health considerations and hazards

Prior to leaving for the field take all necessary preventive health precautions that are available. Health considerations include finding out about diseases endemic to the area of your proposed research. They also include consulting medical personnel about precautions you should take in order to stay healthy and taking the necessary inoculations prior to leaving for the field. Do not limit your inoculations to those required for entry into the country where you plan to work, but take others, too, as a preventive measure.

Purchase and take with you one or more basic field medical guides such as those by Werner et al., entitled *Where There Is No Doctor* (1992) and the Spanish version *Donde no hay doctor* (1980), by Dickson entitled *Where There Is No Dentist* (1983), and by Vanderkooi entitled *Village Medical Manual* (vol. 1 on Principles and Procedures and vol. 2 on Diagnosis and Treatment, 1986). These resources can help you with your own health and with the health of those who come to you for help.

If you are going to an area where malaria is endemic, begin taking your malarial prophylaxis two weeks prior to leaving for the field in order for the medicine to build up in your system. In many countries prescriptions are not necessary in order to purchase what are prescription drugs in North America or Europe. So, for example, if you find that this is the case in the country where you plan to do research, you need to purchase only enough malarial prophylaxis to get you there and to take until you find where you can purchase more locally.

Once there, be aware that the water supply in many areas is not potable. When that is the case, you need to purify your water by filtering and/or boiling prior to drinking it. One type of water filter that is widely used is a Katadyne silver nitrate filter.

In planning to go abroad recognize that you have the potential of contracting the diseases that are endemic to your research area. For example, many fieldworkers have suffered from various intestinal illnesses that result in diarrhea and malaria. Malaria is the type of illness that is likely to occur when you are sick with something else, when you are tired and run down, and, for women, when you have a baby while on the field.

In order to make your fieldwork easier and more enjoyable, be sure to get adequate rest. If you are in a malarial area, sleep under your mosquito net. Check your shoes each morning before putting them on to be sure that a scorpion has not gotten into them overnight.

Soapy water

When we first went to the village, a friend accompanied us. In the morning he set up his shaving mirror and bar of soap on top of our water barrel. It was only when we began to drink soapy water that we realized that his bar of soap had fallen into the water. We quickly cleaned the barrel out and had it refilled. However, three weeks later when we had a couple of women over for dinner, we served them drinks with ice cubes. Only when we began drinking soapy drinks did we realize that the ice in their drinks was made from that soapy water!

Since illness occurs when you are on the field, you need to maintain flexibility in your schedule of activities during your fieldwork. If possible, factor extra time into your schedule to allow you to be ill without jeopardizing completion of your goals.

Soon after arriving inquire from others about available medical facilities. This involves checking on which hospitals and clinics exist and which are likely to provide good care. You should know that in many countries hospitals do not provide food for patients. Rather, the patient's family or friends will stay with the patient and provide food for him or her.

Check out the local medical scene including the local pharmacist, druggist, or chemist to ascertain the quality and availability of medicines in that country. Since many countries do not require prescriptions in order to obtain medicines, it makes sense to read in your health manual and, when necessary, to do some self-diagnosis prior to going to purchase the necessary medicine. After living cross-culturally in a situation where medicines are available without prescriptions, it can be frustrating to return to your home country where a medical doctor must approve each prescription. That aspect of returning home can contribute to reverse culture stress.

Remember to take prescription medications with you. While some medicines, such as aspirin, malaria prophylaxes, and common antibiotics, are likely to be readily available, other medicines that you need may not be. You can also check with others who are or have been in that country to ask about what is likely to be available locally. It is advisable to bring disposable syringes with you. In countries where AIDS is a major health hazard, avoid blood transfusions.

Staying healthy when working cross-culturally involves being careful about what you eat and drink. It is important, however, that you accept the hospitality of your host or hostess by eating the food prepared for you. Sometimes it is better to deal with any intestinal bugs that you might pick up afterwards. Do avoid fresh salads. In most countries bottled drinks are safe to drink; check with people locally, however, to confirm that this applies in the country where you work. Also hot cooked foods are usually safe.

When you find yourself sick in a cross-cultural situation, this is a good opportunity to find out how illness is viewed by the local population. For example, in Africa one is not sick alone. Among the Bajju, one's bedroom is generally off limits when people come to greet you, but if you are sick or injured, they come greet you in your bedroom.

Be aware of the possible health hazards, difficulties, and dangers you might face in the field (see Howell 1990). Potential health hazards include exposure to the elements (resulting in sunburn, heat stroke, and dehydration), high altitude sickness, lightening, fire, cold, boating and water accidents, malnutrition and dietary deficiencies, weight loss, and food poisoning.

There are hazards associated with animals such as creatures of the water (leeches; jellyfish; water snakes, e.g., anacondas and various sea snakes; stingrays). Which problem you encounter depends on where you conduct your research. Encounters with dangerous sea animals are more likely to occur when doing research in the Pacific area and South Asia, while anacondas are a potential hazard in South America.

Land creatures also present problems such as encounters with venomous snakes; scorpion stings; bee, wasp and insect stings (e.g., African killer bees, mosquitoes, tsetse flies, army ants); mammal bites and attacks (e.g., dog bites, bat bites, rhinoceros and dwarf buffalo charges, crocodiles or alligators, monkey bites, rat bites, lions); horse or mule accidents; and criminal attacks. The list of critters that can cause illness also includes worms and other parasites. Hookworms enter through one's skin, so it is advisable to wear shoes (e.g., tennis shoes). Schistosomes or blood flukes also enter through one's skin by walking in water where they cycle through snails. To prevent coming down with schistosomiasis avoid going into streams and rivers.

Be aware that different hazards are specific to different areas of the world. For example, the hazard of dog bite is greater when working in Europe than anywhere else in the world; however, the potential of rabid dog bites is greater elsewhere.

Accidents that result in injuries can occur. Automobile and truck accidents are only too common. Taxi drivers in some countries drive dangerously. As one friend stated, "It worked best if I kept my eyes closed in that taxi ride from Enugu to Jos! The driver left no margin for error."

Finally, infectious diseases can take their toll on fieldworkers. In some third world countries people die more often from infectious diseases than from old age. Many fieldworkers have come down with hepatitis and diarrheal diseases. Again, by taking the hepatitis immunization before leaving for the field, that hazard should not hinder your research. And by watching what you eat and drink you can lessen the likelihood of coming down with diarrhea. This brief discussion of health hazards and

An unearned greeting

When Norris was riding a motorcycle to return it to a friend, I was following him in the car. He inadvertently rode into some sand, and he, together with the motorcycle, fell. Other than for a few skin abrasions, he was unhurt. The next day a large group of women came to greet him on the occasion of his accident. They felt relieved that he was unhurt, and he felt rather embarrassed for having gotten into the sand, fallen, then received such unearned attention. If he had really been hurt, he would likely have reacted differently.

Road accidents

When we first went to Nigeria, the Biafran war was being fought to keep southeastern Nigeria from seceding. I assessed the situation we faced daily, then wrote my parents that automobile accidents posed a greater immediate hazard to us than the war.

fieldwork dangers points to the need to take necessary precautions and be prepared to deal with health problems when they arise.

Summary

Preparation for field research includes selection of a research project, giving consideration to strategic research and specific projects desired by the research community (participatory research). Suggestions for conducting a literature review include use of computerized searches and specific bibliographic references. Both a literature review and research hypotheses are part of the research proposal. It is usually necessary to arrange for some research affiliation within the country where you plan to conduct your fieldwork. At least a year in the field is desirable for good ethnographic research at the Ph.D. level; less time is often sufficient at the master's level. Taking the necessary health precautions should be part of one's prefield preparation. With these preparations complete, including obtaining funding, you are ready to begin your field research.

4

Beginning Fieldwork

When you leave...you won't be remembered for what you achieved, but for how you fitted in. (Batchelor 1997:20)

Beginning fieldwork involves activities such as selecting a research site, presenting a rationale for living in the research site to members of the target community, establishing trust relationships with individuals in the research community, engaging in participant and process observation, setting goals for ethnographic research, and handling the everyday pragmatics of field research. The first three of these concerns will be looked at in this chapter.

During this time period you may realize that village living is far more time consuming and tiring than expected. Initially, culture shock may be acute. The loss of familiar cues, the lack of language ability, and the newness of surroundings can result in incredible stress. Yet even with all those issues to be dealt with, remember that the people want a relationship with you, one that involves mutual trust and respect. You will be remembered by the local people for how you fitted in, so begin well.

The following account recalls a few of the personal experiences that Norris, our children, and I had during the first month of our fieldwork among the Bajju.

Local village elders and pastors selected the teachers' quarters of the school as the site for our residence. Due to a fire which occurred during its occupancy by previous residents and the generally dilapidated condition of the compound, no one lived there other than Shajo, a village drunk. On our first day in the village some men beat Shajo, hoping that he would leave the compound to us. Their efforts, however, did not produce their desired results. Though we moved into the mud-walled buildings, throughout the time we lived there Shajo continued to live in some of the connecting buildings such as the local kitchen hut. He added a dimension to our village living that was unique, to say the least.

The local people received us warmly. Group after group came to welcome us, to give us gifts, and to meet the *batures* (white people) who had come to live with them. They brought us gifts of grapefruit and eggs, two commodities they were sure *batures* ate. We soon filled our kerosene refrigerator with over 200 eggs and a large number of grapefruit! Only later did we learn that Bajju females traditionally do not eat eggs; to do so means that one would "eat" one's own children. To "eat" in this instance means to perform witchcraft against them. No wonder one man later asked me if we "ate" people!

The villagers had worked hard on the previously unlivable school teachers' quarters in order to make them livable for our family. They had lined the drive with whitewashed rocks; they whitewashed the outside of the buildings; they put in larger windows; and they painted tar on the bottom two feet of the walls of the mudbrick buildings, both the inside and outside, to aid in waterproofing them. The tar on the inside walls never dried. Whenever our clothes or bedding touched it, the tar transferred to them; and I never figured out how to get the tar out of clothing. We eventually had to replaster the inside walls.

Everyday living took much longer than I had expected. All our water had to be carried from the well in the school yard across the road. All cooking started from scratch. And there was the never ending fight to keep dust out of the buildings. That dust included both the dust brought in on people's shoes and the airborne harmattan dust. When we saw the harmattan dust coming, we'd close all the windows, but the louver windows proved to be no match for the fine dust. One hour after dusting our furnishings, the dust was so thick that we could easily see our fingerprints in it.

One of my vivid recollections of that first month in the village was going to bed more tired than I ever remembered being in my entire life. And villagers were there to visit with us first thing in the morning.

Since the people selected the village and specific compound in the village where we were to live, site selection was not an issue for us. For most fieldworkers, however, it is one of the first decisions they need to make in a field location.

Site selection

An important early step in fieldwork is selecting a site at which to reside and carry out research. In some research proposals, researchers identify the specific site. In other proposals, researchers may specify the topic(s) of research and an ethnic group to study, but not the specific site(s) where they will conduct their research.

Criteria for selecting a specific location will differ depending upon your research goals. A specific site may depend on obtaining official permission to conduct research within that location. This permission may need to be obtained at several levels: the national level as, for example, from an office of research within the appropriate government ministry; the regional level, as from a local university or government office; and the local level, as from the chief, leaders, or elders.

> **Use of official rest house?**
>
> When Norris first looked for a research residence site for our fieldwork, the District Head offered the official rest house. While this building would have been quite adequate, it was located out of the Bajju area so we declined because it would have been difficult to accomplish our goals from there.

Many fieldworkers, while conforming to necessary government requirements for research, distance themselves from the government. This is especially true when the government preys upon the local people, and when you would be unable to collect reliable data if sources identified you with the government. This will mean finding accommodations other than government rest houses. Harriss recounts her situation as follows: "I also have tried to avoid the taint of living in government rest houses—though in Sri Lanka, when my choice was between a rest house and a brothel, I capitulated!" (Harriss 1993:142).

Pelto and Pelto recognize similar considerations (emphasis added):

> To accept housing in, for example, the governmental office building, the rectory, or the police station requires careful consideration of the local people's attitudes towards those authorities.

In some relatively tight communities, with well-developed boundary-maintenance mechanisms, fieldworkers may find that they *must* accept the dictates of local authorities with regard to the selection of residence, if they have been successful in obtaining permission for the research activity. (1978:180)

Criteria for selecting a village or town in which to live might be similar to those that I used for selecting a village in which to administer an interview schedule. I set up the following criteria: (1) the village had a population that was not thoroughly intermixed with other ethnic groups; (2) the village needed to be readily accessible by road, though not necessarily a main, paved road; (3) the village needed to be one of the long-established Bajju villages; and (4) the chief needed to approve of the research. I added a fifth criterion specific to my research project, namely, that some members of the village had converted to Christianity, because my research focused on reasons for Christian conversion (McKinney 1985:350–351).

Locations may be selected for being typical of the culture or atypical, their accessibility or remoteness. Sometimes researchers select a specific project and site because it has been studied before and, therefore, data are available for a diachronic study (see Howell 1979), or because others have not studied that situation and, therefore, one can engage in a synchronic study. Whatever criteria you have for the site to be selected, that site should fulfill the specific goals of your selected topic, interests, and theoretical problem to be studied.

It is helpful to have a residence site that puts you where the action is, for example, near the center of the village. If there are social cleavages within the village, the site selected should enable you to avoid appearing to be partisan to one side or the other. In addition to the house being appropriate in terms of where it is situated in the research site, it should also be appropriate in terms of meeting your needs.

Even with the best intentions and carefully thought through research objectives, convincing the local population of your goals may prove problematic. Kurin writes concerning his problems,

I was full of confidence when—equipped with a scholarly proposal, blessings from my advisers, and generous research grants—I set out to study village social structure in the Punjab province of Pakistan. But after looking for an appropriate fieldwork site for several weeks without success, I began to think that my research project would never get off the ground. Daily I would seek out villagers aboard my puttering motor scooter, traversing the dusty dirt roads, footpaths, and irrigation ditches that crisscross the Punjab. But I couldn't seem to find a village amenable to study. The major problem was that the villagers I did approach were baffled by my presence. They could not understand why anyone would travel ten thousand miles from home to a foreign country in order to live in a poor village, interview illiterate peasants, and then write a book about it. Life, they were sure, was to be lived, not written about. Besides, they thought, what of any importance could they possibly tell me? Committed as I was to ethnographic research, I readily understood their viewpoint. I was a *babu log*—literally, a noble; figuratively, a clerk; and simply, a person of the city. I rode a motor scooter, wore tight-fitting clothing, and spoke Urdu, a language associated with the urban literary elite. Obviously, I did not belong, and the villagers simply did not see me fitting into their society. (Spradley and McCurdy 1987:46–47)

A research site should be such that you can observe and participate in the daily round of activities. You need to hear the language spoken and have opportunities to use it in order to gain fluency. Some have been able to fulfill their research goals by living with a family, for example, in one or more buildings, such as the entrance hut within a compound. Sometimes it helps allay any distrust the local people may have about you if you live with a highly respected family within the community. Other researchers have lived in rented quarters, in the residence of a local family, in a tent or trailer, in a house built specifically for them, in an unused building associated with a home of a local family, in a school or other building built for some specific purpose, or in a nearby city from which they commuted to their village location.

Pelto and Pelto report on a survey they conducted concerning research sites:

> In a survey of fifty-one anthropologists (Pelto and Pelto 1973), we found that the most usual habitation during field work was a rented house (or apartment) in the research community. We also found that the fieldworker is typically accompanied by his or her spouse (usually no children), and the cuisine usually consists of locally available foods; the fieldworkers usually cook for themselves instead of taking their meals with the local people. (1978:182)

Freeman provides a specific example in his selection of a village home:

> When I first chose the house I would live in for the two years of my study of Muli's village, I anticipated both the need for privacy for interviews and ready accessibility to the village. Accordingly, I chose a house located in a secluded spot just outside the village limits. (1979:14)

In selecting a site for research the issue of privacy arises. Many researchers value a certain amount of privacy, and thus, they may find living with another family in a cross-cultural situation stressful. This value on privacy may not be shared by people in the cultural situation where you are living. For example, Bernard (1994:161) found when doing his fieldwork in Greece that in Greek the closest word for privacy was "being alone," a word that also translates as loneliness.

A related problem is what the local people define as work. Among the Bajju in a village context, work meant farming or some other form of physical labor. To simply sit and do paper activities at a desk was not defined as work; hence, from their perspective we could be interrupted when we were doing so. Needless to say, at times we felt rather frustrated when trying to do desk work. I always consoled myself by remembering that we were getting good language practice by interacting with people. Sometimes one's spouse can greet visitors and take care of their needs. We found that it worked best to accept interruptions graciously.

Once you select your village site, the next step is IMPRESSION MANAGEMENT (Pelto and Pelto 1978:182). This step involves providing some rationale to the research community for your living there.

Rationale for residing in the research site and role of researcher

Either prior to or soon after settling into your research site but prior to beginning fieldwork, you must communicate to the local leaders and other appropriate people in the population your reasons for residing there. Rationale should be stated in such a way that they are understandable to the local people. Your rationale may be that you have come to study their culture, to write a book about them, to help them with some development project, and to study their language in order to do translation and literacy work. Give them your specific reason for being there, e.g., "I'm here to learn about you so that I can finish my degree."

In addition to providing them with a rationale for your being there, early in your time there you need to establish some SOCIAL ROLE understandable to the local community that is relevant for your research project. The role of "neutral outsider" may be foreign in some cultures, so you may have to define and develop a new role within the community. Some find themselves following in the footsteps of other researchers, with the local community already having expectations that may or may not be realistic. For example, Cheryl Grieves related the following about language learning:

> Local Margi individuals told one researcher who wanted to learn their language that he needed to get some 3" by 5" cards. That was what the Grieves had used effectively previously. (personal communication, Jos, 1976)

A locally acceptable role places you into understandable niches within the social structure. Since the role of neutral observer or benign visitor may not be acceptable, taking a locally defined role may provide in-depth data that would not be available readily otherwise. For example, Hirschkind (1991:245) took the role of immigrant farmer in the southern highlands of Ecuador. In that role she gained firsthand experience interacting with neighbors and discovered aspects of the culture that had gone unreported previously in the ethnographic literature. To assume such a role is to integrate while participating in the community. This approach can highlight three major areas regularly misrepresented in cultural research—the mundane, the inarticulate, and the asocial.

Some fieldworkers have apprenticed themselves to local specialists in order to understand the special knowledge they have, knowledge they treat as proprietary. Apprenticeship may be the most effective route to take if seeking some knowledge, as for example, that of herbalists, diviners, midwives, blacksmiths, and other craft specialists.

In some cases, you may find no locally acceptable role for doing research in the community. In that case, you may need to explain carefully and even negotiate with the people what the role you desire entails. Such negotiation should include what types of data you intend to collect, what will be done with those data, possible uses of the data, what you expect from them for your project (Marshall and Rossman 1989:65), and what they can expect from you.

In spite of good intentions, most researchers remain "visitors" or "strangers" within their research communities throughout the time of fieldwork. Within an African context the local chief, or a local government official, or some other person in authority is responsible for any strangers within the area. For example, Fernandez, who worked among the Fang in Gabon, received a letter from a family that offered him a house which stated, "We consider you to be our stranger and shall look after your well being" (1982:28).

Children in the field

Many field researchers are accompanied by their families when conducting fieldwork. When it is a question of taking one's children with you or not doing fieldwork at all, most opt to take the children. Having your children with you involves an understanding of the beliefs and practices about children in the culture being researched. For example, children are part of people's lives in many countries. They are not shuttled off to some age-grouped meeting or separate activity. Children are valued and welcomed into any and most all situations, with the nearest adult available to hold and indulge them. For example, Cassell found in her fieldwork in Jamaica that,

> People in Mango Ridge emphasized the joy, the comfort, the company offered by children, as opposed to the middle-class American stress on the responsibility, stress, and work children represent. (1987:18)

Children are often part of the adult world of work as well. While some of the excesses of child labor have been curbed, child labor continues in many countries throughout the world.

When taking children to the field, the fieldworker faces a unique situation. Children can unlock opportunities and knowledge that are unavailable as readily to a single person or to a married couple without children. In addition, they can present a host of issues that a single researcher does not face. A few specific issues include the following: What influence will children have on the selection of your field site; what about your children's education; what impact will your fieldwork have upon your children and what contribution will your children make to your fieldwork; what impact will the local beliefs and practices about children and child rearing have upon your children and vice versa; who can discipline children and how will your children react to being disciplined by adults other than their parents; what specific health considerations will having children with you have on your fieldwork; and what will be the long-term consequences of your fieldwork on your children? A few of these issues are considered below.

Prior to going to the field with children, fieldworkers often face questions from their friends and families about the advisability of doing so. At this point you may have to do some convincing of grandparents that you will do the best you can to bring their grandchildren back to them safely. The fear of the unknown can be problematic to them, as it is to most people (see side box for an example). Concerns that friends and family may raise include health hazards (e.g., malaria, diarrhea, etc.), sanitation concerns, civil war, primitive living conditions, road hazards, etc. In seeking to explain taking your children, while not neglecting the issues raised by friends and family, it may help to emphasize the positive benefits fieldwork can bring to your children. For example, they will become bicultural or multicultural, fluent in another language, understanding of geography and cultures vastly different from their home country, comfortable with people and cultures different from their own, and so on.

Some parents feel that having children accompany them leads them to set up an independent household rather than living with a local family as some single fieldworkers have done. Doing so allows more control over cooking, sterilizing water, and sanitation in general. It also gives a private place where the family can have time by itself to maintain some of the regular family customs, such as reading to children at bedtime and praying with them.

Snakes and scorpions

When our African colleagues, Iliya and Asabar, moved into the dorm at a school in Dallas, Texas, they read a brochure about local hazards. Asabat had difficulty sleeping that night for fear of snakes and scorpions!

Eric's concern

When living in Unguwar Rimi, Nigeria, Eric, our younger son, was concerned about the poor health of some of his local playmates, the boys who came each afternoon to play soccer with him and Mark, his brother. The boys came to us because we had the ball. His way of dealing with their ill health was to give them chewable vitamins. He told them that they were candy!

Prior to going to the field, do your best to prepare your children for what they are likely to encounter. Talk with them, give them readings or read to them about the field situation, view videos, talk with others who have been there, answer their questions, and so on. Once in the field children suffer culture shock and stress just as adults do. Knowing what to expect may mitigate some of the culture shock, yet knowing does not eliminate culture shock. During the time when their culture shock is most acute you need to be especially sensitive to them. Spend time with them, and try to explain to them what is going on in the culture around you. Unfortunately, when first in the field, you may be struggling with some of the same issues your children are dealing with. It may help your children to deal with their culture shock by keeping their own fieldnotes or diary. Occasionally, it helps to take a break away from the research site. (See some of the other suggestions for dealing with culture shock in chapter 5.)

In many cultures a person is not considered to have attained full adult status until he or she has a child. Fieldworkers without children are often excluded from certain information specifically because they have not attained an appropriate level of maturity within that culture to have specific information shared with them. For example, Klass found that after his wife had a daughter, his and his wife's status in a village in Trinidad changed. He states,

> The village women's perception of Sheila as a mature adult began with their awareness of her pregnancy. After the actual birth, the changes that occurred in her relationships with the women were therefore subtle rather than dramatic. In Morton's case, however, there were sharp changes in the behavior of certain men, particularly older men, immediately attendant on the birth of the child. One older man, for example, who had always been polite but reserved, greeted Morton a few days after the birth in a startlingly relaxed and familiar way. After a pleasant conversation, Morton expressed his enjoyment of the meeting, indicating his regret that they had never had a long and intimate conversation before. The older man smiled and explained that he viewed Morton as a "family man" now, someone like himself. (Klass and Klass 1987:144)

The Klass's also found that the birth of their daughter led to commiseration because they had a girl rather than a boy, the preferred sex of a child. As Klass states, "Many of our village friends…tried to comfort us for what they perceived as our disappointment" (1987:142).

There are hazards that arise as a result of taking children to the field with you. Both you and your children are subject to the diseases endemic to the area. You as a family are also potential accident victims, as driving may be more hazardous than in your home country. Some fieldworkers have experienced the loss of children when abroad. For example, the Hitchcocks experienced the death of their year-old son from an unexplained cause. The day before he had been playing happily, and bedtime went well after a full day in the village. When they awoke the next day their young son was dead. That experience placed his mother among the ranks of other Magar women in Nepal. Hitchcock writes,

> Grief-stricken, I sat on a mat outside the hut with my little girls, surrounded with all the understanding anyone could hope to have at such a moment. The older village women came to sit with me, expressing their sorrow in the common language of tears. One of them held up three gnarled fingers. She had lost three sons; another at her side had lost five. (1987:180)

There are daily health hazards in many field sites. Sometimes medical care is not readily available. It is important to come equipped with antibiotics, antivenom, a stun gun for use on snake and scorpion bites, bandages, and other medical supplies in order to cope with medical emergencies and illnesses when they arise.

Overall, taking one's children with you often turns out to be advantageous. For example, Cassell found that "the presence of the children was an advantage. They guaranteed not only my intent—someone up to no good would not bring children with her—but also my identity—a six year old and a nine year old will tell anyone who asks anything they want to know" (1987:10). She further states, "Children make us as accessible to the people we study as they are to us" (p. 258).

One aspect of taking children to the field is the long-term consequences of the field experience on them. Those consequences will not be the same for each child even within the same family due to individual temperaments and experiences. Some will be angry with you for taking them abroad. Others adjust well and appreciate having been raised with a broader perspective than most children from their own culture. Some remain marginal to their own culture, feeling that they do not really belong to either culture. Some even choose to live permanently with the group or in the country where their parents studied. They have often learned the language and culture as insiders. That is home to them.

Building trust relationships

An essential component of beginning fieldwork is the establishment of good working and trust relationships of mutual respect with individuals in the research community. Rapport and trust are built over time based on mutual interactions in which you and members of the research community learn to trust each other's integrity, abilities, and reliability. Mayers states, "Verbal and nonverbal cues of behavior alert one to the true nature of the trust relationship, whether it is building or being undermined. These cues are different for each society and need to be learned as part of the language and culture" (1974:40).

For example, Stoller found that although he spoke Songhay, one of the important languages in Niger, he had to establish himself as one to be trusted in the local community. As the people put it, they did not "know" him. The language-speaking ability that he had gained as a member of the Peace Corps was not sufficient to enable him to begin immediately with his research as he attempted to do. He spent only a few days settling into the village of Mehanna before beginning his study of the relationship between language usage and local politics (Stoller and Olkes 1987:8). He began with a language-attitude survey administered to a select sample of 179 people, particularly asking what language(s) each person spoke. When he found that one individual had deliberately lied to him, he checked others' responses. Over the next period he found that everyone had lied to him for a variety of reasons, "What's the difference? We do not know you. We know you, but we do not trust you. Since you are too young, we cannot tell you the truth, but we are too polite to tell you to go away. And so on..." (p. 9).

The breakthrough for Stoller came with the advice of Abdoulaye, an old Islamic cleric, who advised Stoller on how to learn about the Songhay. He told him that going around asking personal questions and writing down answers would continue to elicit lies. In order to avoid this problem, the cleric advised Stoller to sit and listen. Abdoulaye used the proverb, "One kills something thin in appearance only to discover that inside it is fat," to make his point (p. 11).

Progress for Stoller and Olkes seemed slow. Even when sitting and listening, people refused to allow them to tape-record discussions or take notes. As months went by, they felt more and more isolated and felt that accomplishment of their research goals was impossible. A change occurred, however, after Stoller physically disciplined a boy who had thrown a rock at him. A group of men, including some elders, surrounded him. Stoller described his situation as follows:

> As they surrounded me, they seemed to suck up the air from my space. I had trouble catching my breath. One of the football players grabbed my upper arm.
> "We wondered," he said, "how long it would take you to understand."
> "Understand what?"
> "We wondered how long it would take you to understand how Songhay deal with children."
> The football player laughed. So did the others.
> "You mean?"
> "You white people are as slow-witted as donkeys. The children will not bother you again."
> The old cleric who had previously given me such good advice broke through this circle of humanity.
> "Monsieur Paul, you have listened, which is good. But now you have acted and have become a person in this village..." (Stoller and Olkes 1987:17)

Stoller's work took off. After that people readily shared information with him. If they were sharing important concepts and words with him, they would tell him to fetch his notebook as important words needed to be recorded accurately.

Discussion

This chapter discussed the beginning of your fieldwork. It involves obtaining the necessary research permission at various levels to conduct your study. It also includes finding a place to live and providing the people with a rationale for your living there. Their concerns need to be addressed honestly and in a culturally appropriate manner.

The issue of children accompanying you in your fieldwork was also discussed. Children can help you relate as an adult with the people among whom you live. They help in building good interpersonal relationships. The possible long-term consequences of your fieldwork on your children was also discussed.

The most important part of beginning your fieldwork is building trust relationships. As in the example from Stoller and Olkes cited, building trust takes time. It is an activity that cannot be hurried; it is time consuming and can be tedious. It relates to developing and maintaining the goodwill of the local community towards your research project. It is essential to build a trust relationship before you try to collect sensitive information. Developing trust involves abiding by local conventions of showing courtesy and respect. It also involves being genuinely concerned for and willing to be involved with the local people.

When distrust creeps into relationships with members of the research community, communication either becomes distorted or breaks down completely. The result is frustration, inaccurate or no data, and poor interpersonal relations.

One key research method for building trust is participant observation. This will be discussed in the next chapter.

5

Participant Observation

Most of our days were spent by Yolanda among the women and by Robert among the men. She sat with the women in their houses, worked with them in making manioc flour, went with them to the gardens, bathed with them, and helped them take care of the children. When she was not off with them, one or more women were usually in our house. Mundurucú women are eminently gregarious, and she soon became included in most of their activities. She did not have to search for informants or seek ways to intrude herself in their midst. Quite to the contrary, she sometimes wished for more privacy. Even today, she recalls nostalgically the hot afternoons when she would settle in her hammock only to be aroused out of slumber by the women, who would shake her hammock insistently, calling out. "Iolantá, are you awake?"
(Murphy and Murphy 1974:ix–x)

The activity of Yolanda among the Mundurucú in Brazil is termed PARTICIPANT OBSERVA-TION. It is the technical term for listening, observing, and participating in a culture setting, a technique mentioned briefly in chapter 2. This research method involves participating while also observing in another culture as a means for understanding that culture (See Kluckhohn 1940, Vidich 1955, McCall and Simmons 1969, Spradley 1980, and Spradley and McCurdy 1975). Participant observation is "experiential learning" at its best. You do not "fade into the woodwork" when engaging in participant observation, but become a participant engaging actively in the local social scene. By completely immersing yourself in the other culture you observe daily occurrences first hand, and you acquire an understanding of the insider's point of view. Anthropology has contributed this research method to the social sciences.

By engaging in participant observation you learn overt, explicit cultural behavior and the tacit rules and associated behavior. You gradually find that various patterns become internalized, a process that occurs sometimes without your even realizing the meaning of the cultural behavior until reflecting upon it later. For example, Norris observed that in greeting, men in northern Nigeria shake right hands then each man touches his right hand to his chest, so Norris did likewise. Only later did he learn that the gesture of touching his chest means, "You are welcome to me."

Participant observation involves understanding and adopting local gestures and posturing. For example, Hausa men may shake a clinched fist at someone of higher status such as an *emir*, a paramount chief, a gesture accompanied by the phrase that translates as, "May you have long life." In this context a raised fist indicates great honor and respect given to one to whom you attribute power. Since a raised closed fist in a western context indicates hostility, it helps to know that a Hausa person is communicating the opposite of this by the same gesture. This example shows that a researcher cannot simply carry over the connotation of specific behaviors from his own culture to the new cultural context.

Posture often expresses respect. For example, people in Asia bow their heads, and sometimes their upper body, to show respect. They are symbolically giving the other their heads, their most important part. In Africa posture also indicates respect. The person of lower status indicates respect by bowing, bending over, squatting, or even lying prone on the ground to one of higher status. In some traditional contexts no person's head is to be higher than or on the same level as that of a chief. Therefore, if he sits on a chair, everyone else sits on the floor.

Use of specific hands may also indicate respect. In some contexts, use of the right hand or both hands indicates respect, while use of the left hand only shows disrespect. The left hand is reserved for unclean activities. I saw one expatriate violate this when she used her left hand to give a cup of coffee to an important chief, and he visibly flinched at the insult implied by that action. She seemed unaware that she had just gravely insulted him; her actions did not correlate with what was emic in the cultural context that was new to her.

> **Attracting a seller's attention**
>
> Among the Bajju I did not learn how to attract the attention of a seller in the market until I became a seller. This occurred the afternoon Norris and I sold our village household belongings before returning to the United States. By the end of the afternoon my elbows hurt, as people had sought to get my attention by grabbing them. In almost eight years of living in Nigeria I had failed to notice that particular cultural behavior!

When engaging in participant observation, you need to maintain your own integrity. You may feel yourself torn between two cultures, your own and that of the community you are studying. This tension may result in your feeling marginal to both cultures, perhaps without feeling accepted in either. Tonkin discussed the need for feeling acceptance.

> This [acceptability] is a personal as well as a professional need, for without a measure of support from others, as Evans-Pritchard pointed out, "disorientated craziness" results (1973:4). The investigator is not just a social being but one bereft of more familiar props. People impose participation on you in their terms, you cannot help but try to achieve it in yours. (1984b:219)

The question of maintaining your own integrity comes when studying the effects of various stimulants. You may find that acceptance of them when offered is important for the sake of conducting your research. The degree to which you can engage in participant observation with respect to taking various stimulants depends upon you and your values. To refuse to do so in all instances, however, may marginalize you even further than you already are as an expatriate. For example, Kennedy (1987:123), when researching the stimulant *qat* in North Yemen (the Yemen Arab Republic), felt it important to enter into the afternoon *qat* chewing sessions. In Yemeni society a majority of the male population in the nation chews *qat* daily or weekly, and thus its use is extremely important, indeed central for understanding that society.

In some Latin American rain forest ethnic groups the use of *chicha*, a fermented beverage, is widespread. If a guest refuses to drink *chicha* when offered, that individual has rejected the hospitality of the group, and that refusal can quickly lead to expressions of hostility towards him or her. In West Africa the gift of kolanuts, a mild stimulant comparable to drinking coffee, expresses hospitality. Similarly, in southeast Asia use of betel nuts is common.

While engaging in participant observation, throughout the research period you are being observed by members of the community. In this process of mutual observation all those involved learn to what extent they can trust each other and become willing to share knowledge, worldviews, and social relationships. The extent to which you succeed in participant observation may well determine the effectiveness of your fieldwork and the accuracy of the information you gather.

One important question concerning participant observation is whether the specific agenda of the researcher may negate its effectiveness. For example, is a missionary who engages in participant observation unable to do so because of his or her specific agenda or biases? Or does the theoretical perspective of a Marxist anthropologist so color his or her involvement that objective participant observation is impossible? All researchers come to participant observation with their own basic assumptions and agendas, any of which could conceivably distort the information they obtain through participant observation. However, having a specific agenda per se does not mean that those who do are unable to engage in participant observation objectively. This is a research tool that all who do cultural research need to use irrespective of their particular agendas and theoretical orientations.

While other field methods mentioned in this book may be utilized at various times as appropriate to the particular research undertaken, participant observation continues throughout the research period.

Process observation

PROCESS OBSERVATION supplements participant observation by focusing on group dynamics which people use to accomplish tasks. You observe the roles assumed by different members within a group, the interaction between participants in the process, and the means of decision making utilized.

In group interactions there are task and maintenance functions. When doing process observation note the following: Who initiates an action and how? Who keeps the group's dynamics moving along smoothly? Do people listen perceptively, or do some people move ahead with their own agenda without really listening? One clue as to whether or not listening with understanding is occurring is whether or not there is REFLECTIVE LISTENING. This is also termed ACTIVE LISTENING or RESPONSIVE LISTENING. Those engaged in reflective listening repeat the essential points that the other person states in order to confirm their understanding. Ways of reflective listening may differ from culture to culture, though in most cultures it involves some interaction, whether verbal assent and/or nonverbal assent (e.g., nodding). For example, Bajju men express assent by producing nasally released clicks, a vocal but non-verbal sound. One word of caution concerning this type of listening is that it can become stilted unless the listener does indeed listen and interact actively with what the speaker is communicating.

Group dynamics and decision making

Group dynamics and decision-making processes differ from culture to culture. Individual decision making, so common in many industrial societies, is uncommon in many other cultures. If you move from one model of decision making to another, it is important for you to understand and fit into the local decision-making structure. A few types of decision making are discussed below.

Consensual decisions

CONSENSUAL DECISION MAKING has been used to refer to a variety of different decision-making processes. For example, decision making in many African groups involves a consensual decision-making process. Each individual has the opportunity to express his or her opinion in the group discussion about an issue. Gradually, a group consensus emerges; when this happens, the individual with the most status, whether from education, wealth, age, or other culture-specific status criteria, expresses that consensus decision. After that individual presents the group consensus, no one else speaks to that issue in that meeting. Individuals who participate in arriving at a decision will likely feel responsible for carrying it out. If people are not involved in the process, they may not feel such an obligation. Once a decision is reached, those who hold a minority position may campaign to have their position adopted through consulting with others between meetings with the goal of having the issue reconsidered at the next meeting. African decisions tend not to be final; they are always open to change, reconsideration, and refinement.

Another type of consensual decision making occurs among the Pocomchi in Guatemala who arrive at decisions by consensus, though with little discussion (Ted Engel, lecture, Dallas, 1986). Their decision-making process involves shared underlying understandings of what is culturally appropriate. While consensus exists, it does not involve much discussion.

Decisions by a council of elders

A council of elders may make decisions through consensus, and their decisions then apply to all those under the council. The reasoning is that these people know the local situation, they represent their constituency, and elders have the wisdom and maturity necessary to make wise decisions. This is the traditional pattern in many societies.

Individual decisions

With individual decision making each person has the right and responsibility to make decisions that apply to him or her. Usually, that right comes when the individual reaches adulthood. The areas in which individuals may make their own decisions is culture dependent. In general, demographers consider an individual an adult when he or she reaches fifteen years of age. In some societies an individual reaches adulthood after being initiated. In others, individuals have full adult responsibilities at eighteen or twenty-one years of age.

Within any society some individual decisions are made. However, the domain of group decisions versus what is left up to the individual differs from society to society. One tendency for fieldworkers who come from cultures with individual decision making is to force that process on people who are used to making group or multi-individual decisions.

Autocratic decisions

An autocratic decision-making process is a widely used model. This involves a top down approach in which a leader or a small group of ruling elite makes the decisions. The leaders involved in a particular decision differ from society to society. Sometimes at the national level it is the federal military council or head of state. At the local level it may be the influence of local religious or political leaders. In many cultures those leaders are based on class or caste membership, wealth, education, and/or authority. For example, in many Buddhist societies, the monks and elders strongly influence decisions, especially with respect to religious matters. A council of elders may make decisions for the entire group, and people under them are expected to abide by their decisions.

Included within autocratic decision making are decisions reached by a small select group who reach their decision before the meeting called to discuss the issue. Basically, the second meeting is to inform the larger group of what their decision is. If you want to have an input into basic decisions, then you need to establish good personal relations with the decision makers. Developing good interpersonal relations takes time but in the end you may find that you have an opportunity to have some input into the decisions reached. This is often the pattern found in China.

Most often autocratic decision making is done by one individual who decrees what people are to do. Those under him or her may feel frustrated by having little input in the decision. Some cultures work well with autocratic decision making, especially when the autocrat is benevolent and cares for those under him or her.

Democratic decisions

In a democratic decision-making process all people can have input, usually through voting with some variation of the majority deciding on what is the accepted decision. "Some variation" refers to the fact that sometimes it can be by a simple majority vote, at other times a two-thirds vote is required, and at still other times a three-fourth vote is necessary. What constitutes a "majority" for specific decisions is culturally defined. The constitution or charter specifies the number of votes required for a decision to be arrived at. Votes in a democratic decision-making process can be on who will fill various elective positions, on specific issues, on a constitution or charter, on financial issues, and so on.

A major problem with a democratic decision-making model is that it is hard on the minority who may have voted against an issue or candidate. They may feel left out of the process and thus may press to have the issue reconsidered. They may renominate the defeated candidate at the next election.

Judicial decisions

A common decision-making means is judicial or legal decision making through the use of courts. This is common within western cultures. We also find that some groups have their own court system. For example, the Bintukwa or Ika in Colombia have a court system for reaching judicial decisions. They may spend several days or weeks discussing conflicts within their community (Tracy 1988:113–14). People remain at the meeting house throughout the time the court is in session leaving only to sleep after which they return to the deliberations. Local leaders repeatedly ask the same or similar questions of those accused of transgressions with the goal of checking whether the defendants answer consistently each time. By this means they seek to validate responses by checking whether or not an individual repeats the same story or changes it. If he or she changes it, that person is likely to be found guilty. Issues discussed in court frequently center around land disputes.

Participant observation and process observation are both parts of an ethnographic research cycle.

An ethnographic research cycle

The steps outlined by Spradley (1980:29) for an ETHNOGRAPHIC RESEARCH CYCLE consist of (1) selecting an ethnographic project, (2) asking ethnographic questions, (3) collecting ethnographic data, (4) making an ethnographic record, (5) analyzing the ethnographic data, and (6) writing an ethnography. Steps two through five are recursive, with writing the ethnography taking place throughout the research period. As writing proceeds, new ethnographic questions come to light, and the cycle repeats itself.

This research cycle needs to be augmented by steps (1a) reading in the literature and (1b) formulating and refining hypotheses. The goals of ethnographic research vary; however, the specific goal of the cycle Spradley proposed is to write an ethnography, a description of a culture or of a specific social situation. Today most anthropologists conduct research on specific topics of culture, and develop and test hypotheses. As such they tend to have more limited goals than an ethnography. Research builds on what others have done as reported in the literature; hence, a literature review is essential preparation. Hypotheses provide guidance as to what may be governing behavior. Hypotheses are statements about what is going on and why; research results serve to prove or disprove them. As you collect data, new hypotheses may develop that then need investigation.

For example, Elsass used the following hypothesis in his analysis of the different survival capacities of the Bari in Colombia and Venezuela and Arhuaco (Ika or Bintukwa) in Colombia: "The hypothesis we are using here is that the more invisible or 'powerless' the organization, the greater the problem of surviving Western society without being absorbed through ethnocide" (1987:59–60).

Based on this hypothesis he presented ethnographic data from both ethnic groups to support it. This hypothesis might be compared to a CULTURAL THEME and CULTURAL THESIS (Spradley 1980:140–41). Spradley stated that cultural themes are arrived at inductively. "For purposes of ethnographic research I will define a cultural theme as *any principle recurrent in a number of domains, tacit or explicit, and serving as a relationship among subsystems of cultural meaning* [italics in original]....A thesis is the central message, the point you want to make...the major themes you have discovered in ethnographic research represent possible theses" (Spradley 1980:141, 169).

Whether arrived at inductively or formulated deductively, hypotheses formulation, refinement, and testing are important in ethnographic research. They aid in setting research goals.

Goals in ethnographic research

Set specific goals for your cultural research. These ethnographic research goals can be broken down into daily, weekly, monthly, yearly, and total research period goals. After each goal, write the estimated amount of time you think will be needed to accomplish that goal.

One important time consideration in setting goals is the amount of time required to learn the language. Tonkin addresses this issue,

> Time is your greatest enemy. Six months is the *least* time it takes normally to get a working ability in a completely new language. Within

the last few years, British student research grants have shortened: instead of two years or more, it will get harder to have even a year in the field. It is simply not possible for most people to do linguistically sensitive ethnography or

---

Posted goals

In my research I post my goals over my desk. Under each goal I write an estimated time for completing it, how I intend to fulfill that goal, and I check it off once it is accomplished. Those goals provide both direction and a sense of satisfaction as I accomplish them.

specialized study of language use in this time if they have to start from scratch linguistically too. (Tonkin 1984:185)

Since in many village sites basic living simply takes longer, goals should allow for flexibility and should be viewed as general guides to research but not as rigid task masters; however, they are important to guard against time passing quickly without direction in your research.

Research assistants

Early in fieldwork most researchers team up with one or more research assistants who are insiders to the culture and, therefore, able to provide invaluable help. Such colleagues have been titled variously over the years. Those titles include research assistants, locally-recruited fieldworkers, key informants, informants, and colleagues.

While some cultural researchers hire their own research assistants, others allow community leaders to select them (see side box). Once you have hired one or more, you need to explain clearly the nature of your project. They need to buy into the project and believe in it. Further, treat them fairly. This involves establishing a sound professional relationship with your assistant(s). Pay them an adequate salary, provide a pleasant work environment, make the job rewarding, and when necessary protect them.

Working with research assistants often involves your training them for the work you want them to do. You need to be clear in your instructions. It helps to work together with them for a while so that they can learn by your mentoring them. As Healey states, "…good research assistants are not born, they are trained" (1975:347).

Research assistants can contribute in a number of areas; they can

> ### Research assistants
>
> In Norris' and my field research, Norris spoke with some of the elders of the community who then selected research assistants for us. Our reasoning for doing so was that the elders knew who was trustworthy, who was likely to be helpful, and who had the time to work with us.

1. Write texts about the local culture. These texts can include oral traditions, such as folklore, origins narratives, or proverbs;
2. Translate collected texts into another language;
3. Sketch an insider's map of the area, or sketch cultural artifacts and rituals;
4. Assist with administering an interview schedule or questionnaire;
5. Enter data into a computerized database;
6. Select persons to be interviewed and conduct interviews, especially with local specialists;
7. Provide his/her life history;
8. Gather data for a time allocation study or for a social network study;
9. Critique your write-ups for accuracy in terms of the language and culture;
10. Work on a dictionary of the local language; and
11. Provide direction as to profitable areas for you to explore.

This list can be extended endlessly. Research assistants often take on your research project as their own and can provide invaluable help. Without the help of local research assistants most cross-cultural research projects would fail. Research projects become team efforts, and as such they benefit significantly from the input of each member of that team.

When writing up your results, be sure to give your research assistant(s) credit. If the contribution of your research assistant has been extensive, sometimes co-authorship with you is appropriate. After working with a fieldworker, some research assistants have studied and become independent social scientists themselves. If you find that your research assistant is talented and interested in pursuing a study program in cultural studies, by all means encourage him or her to do so.

Occasionally, you will be able to work together with a trained local social scientist. This type of collaboration can benefit both of you, and when that happens, co-authorship of materials is appropriate.

In order to balance this discussion of working with local research assistants, note that doing so is not without its problems. As Harriss relates her experience with local assistants,

> Common difficulties with assistants—and faults from which I am myself not exempt—include putting answers into respondents' mouths, and asking questions in the form of assertions which require mere agreement by the respondent. Talking to traders requires street wisdom and technical knowledge, neither of which is necessarily possessed by the holders of good degrees and fluent English. (1993:146)

When working with a local research assistant be aware that sometimes a patron-client relationship is the model he or she is working within. You become the patron and he or she is the client, and as the client that person may have expectations of you that you may be unaware of. For example, if that person becomes ill or injured, you may be responsible for medical bills. You may also be responsible for providing transportation, as by providing a motorcycle loan.

Everyday pragmatics

As you begin fieldwork, you quickly discover that you face a host of factors in dealing with the practical aspects of daily research. For example, individuals who relate to you first are often marginal to their own cultures. Sometimes you find yourself relating to the outcasts, the drunks, the people who just do not fit in to their own culture. You may also encounter local con men, who contact outsiders for their own purposes.

You may face the dilemma of retaining your own cultural identity while also being involved in the local society. You affect the lives of those you study, and you in turn are personally affected by your fieldwork experiences. You bring with you your own presuppositions or worldview. The question may be raised as to whether or not it is possible to be an objective observer. Recognizing one's own presuppositions and cultural background help in relating effectively cross-culturally and in being objective to the extent possible.

Another pragmatic factor is deciding where to "hang out" during the quiet periods of field research. What you do with your spare time is often carefully observed and can affect the types of data members of the research community are willing to provide. What hanging out does is to help build trust relationships, and those trust relationships enable people to engage in ordinary conversations with you, conversations which can teach you a lot.

Lesson on local brews

In Norris' early language learning, one of the village drunks showed up with samples of different types of grains. He came to coach Norris on what type of brew each made, and he described how each was made.

Members of the target population also get to know you as an individual and, thus, are more willing to share with you.

One temptation that should be avoided is to ask too many questions too quickly after arriving in the field. There are things people do not want to tell an outside researcher until they get to really know that individual. For example, information about wealth and economic status are often not readily shared.

Major factors which the vast majority of fieldworkers who work cross-culturally must deal with are culture shock, confusion, and stress. Even with the best preparation, extensive reading in the literature, and an awareness of culture shock, it still occurs and must be dealt with.

Culture shock, confusion, and stress

CULTURE SHOCK is the psychological anxiety and its consequences that people experience when entering and working within another culture. Oberg states that culture shock is,

> precipitated by the anxiety that results from losing all our familiar signs and symbols of social intercourse....These cues which may be words, gestures, facial expressions, customs or norms are acquired by all of us in the course of growing up and are as much a part of our culture as the language we speak or the beliefs we accept. (1960:177)

Culture shock is not necessarily a problem to be solved but rather an experience to help you understand yourself better. For example, Adler states,

> Culture shock is thought of as a profound learning experience that leads to a high degree of self-awareness and personal growth. Rather than being only a disease for which adaptation is the cure, culture shock is likewise at the very heart of the cross-culturally [sic] learning experience. It is an experience in self-understanding and change. (1987:29)

Culture shock results from a number of factors including the following:

1. An inability to understand and predict the behavior of others or to act appropriately within the new cultural situation;
2. The loss of control over events and one's ability to initiate events;
3. Intrapersonal factors such as a person's age, extent of previous travel, language skills, independence, expectations, assertiveness, courage, resourcefulness, ability to tolerate ambiguity, and similar characteristics;
4. One's physical condition, including special dietary and medical needs, and the ability to tolerate stress;
5. Interpersonal factors including your support group both at home and abroad. This support group includes resource persons whom you can call on when in need of medical, financial, mechanical, social, legal, and practical help;
6. Geopolitical factors including local, regional, national, or international tensions. These may critically affect you, as you may be perceived locally as a representative of your country of origin;
7. Spatial and temporal factors such as the place and length of the trip, the climate and problems associated with it, your need for and sense of privacy, travel conditions, sense of time and space, the degree of isolation, housing and its location. There may

be a contrast between your time orientation, and the event or personal-relationship orientation of the people you work with;

8. Conceptual and ideological factors such as a fatalism that pervades some religious systems, and different etiologies for everyday events and illnesses;

9. Language factors such that you cannot communicate about even the most basic needs you have;

10. Employment factors such that your range of employment opportunities may be severely circumscribed;

11. Status factors such as being treated as a child because you are not married or do you have children;

12. Value differences, and behavior that derives from those values, between your home culture and the target culture. These value differences are in any number of areas including attitudes towards authority, toward those of different social and ethnic groups, towards moral issues, respect and politeness, food preferences, privacy, sanitation, health, and so on;

13. Daily inconveniences such as the breakdown of the infrastructure in the country. This may include mail being unreliable or opened and censored, the electricity and water being erratic, the sewer system being either nonexistent or problematic, traffic problems (e.g., it is no longer the car on the right that goes first, but the car whose driver has the higher status, or, in Mexico, when approaching a one-lane bridge, it is the driver that flashes his headlights first that crosses the bridge first), washboard surfaces and numerous potholes in the road, and so on;

14. Differences in economics. These may involve rampant inflation, devaluation of the currency, high prices for basic subsistence needs including housing that you know costs much less in your home country, shortages or lack of availability of things you need or want; and

15. Feelings of alienation from people in your home culture, from the target culture, and from yourself.

Culture shock most often occurs in areas where the research society's culture differs from yours. The greater the cultural distance of an individual from that of the host culture, the greater will be that individual's social difficulty in the host culture (Furnham and Bochner 1986:215).

How do you know when you are suffering from culture shock? When you find that you have difficulty simply getting up to face the world, a world that is so confusing and different from what you are used to, it is likely that you are suffering from culture shock. If you find that you are continually making up excuses for staying in your own little world, or if you find yourself psychologically escaping through excessive sleeping or wakefulness, or reading, or whatever other method of escape that you choose, then recognize that you have culture shock. You may find that you are increasingly stereotyping your hosts negatively. It is almost as if you feel they have created these difficulties just to irritate you. You may find that you increasingly want to interact only with people from your own country and avoid those of your host culture. Alternately, over identification with the culture may also indicate culture shock. Over identification refers to rejecting your own culture, and accepting everything in the new culture uncritically. You, as it were, "go native." Culture shock may cause depression to set in which consists of feelings of anger, sadness, and a realization that your usual ways of interacting will not lead to the outcome you desire.

Culture shock may be divided into two overlapping periods (Dye 1974:62). The first is CULTURAL CONFUSION—the initial perplexity, bewilderment, disorientation, frustration, and sense of helplessness that results from a loss of cultural cues. The second is CULTURAL STRESS—the continued anxiety that comes from change to a new way of living. While cultural confusion may attenuate within a few weeks or months, cultural stress tends to continue throughout the period of living cross-culturally.

Dealing with cultural confusion is important when beginning fieldwork. The loss of familiar cues and the lack of language ability can bring on intense psychological stress. You have cultural confusion and shock when you have symptoms such as not wanting to interact further with members of the research community; sitting for hours under a mosquito net, feeling depressed; experiencing an inability to cope with the simplest things necessary for survival; or having trouble sleeping for fear of thieves, snakes, or scorpions, or alternatively, over identifying with the culture; having trouble dealing with anger appropriately.

Value differences can affect how you deal with culture shock; these relate to different worldviews of cultures. For example, Americans tend to value individualism and self-reliance, truthfulness, cleanliness, privacy, punctuality, empiricism, competition, fair play, personal achievement, equality, science, and technology. For some people religion is compartmentalized and may play a significant role only on holy days or at rites of passage such as birth, puberty, marriage, and death, while for others it is not. For members of other cultures, values may differ markedly. For example, Mbiti asserts that, "Africans are notoriously religious, and each people has its own religious system with a set of beliefs and practices. *Religion permeates into all the departments of life so fully that it is not easy or possible always to isolate it*" (1970:1, italics added).

The American value of competition and fair play, whereby all competitors play by the same rules leads to an emphasis on task completion, winning, informality, being direct and even confrontational in relationships. Issues are dealt with directly and intentionally. This way of approaching issues often leaves out politeness and etiquette that are so necessary for building good interpersonal relations. This approach runs contrary to the way so many other cultures function. For example, Hiebert reports that, "Japanese culture places a high premium on manners and on working indirectly to achieve one's purposes. Skill in social maneuvers is esteemed. Bluntness or open confrontation embarrasses friends and is ridiculed by others" (1985:129).

Competition and personal achievement are also problematic when working cross-culturally. Hiebert states,

> This emphasis on competition and personal achievement is foreign to many societies, such as the Hopi Indians of North America, the Kikuyu of Kenya, and the Thai, who are taught at an early age not to compete or take issue with others, especially those of their own age or older. Consequently, in school they help each other complete their homework and do not try to be the first to complete their lessons. Nor do they disagree with their teachers, who are their elders. And in sports they do not like to keep score because they do not want to win over others in their group (p. 129).

The more your values correspond to those of the other culture, the less culture shock you will experience. Further, the more that you and those researched share the same basic assumptions, the greater will be your ability to communicate and understand each other. For example, a Christian may be more likely to understand an African's religious perspective than an atheist would.

Your involvement with another culture is a factor that can increase stress, but when it is combined with communication it acts to decrease stress. Hence, you need to spend time with the people and learn to communicate with them.

Culture shock often has four stages:

1. Honeymoon stage. This stage lasts for a few weeks to a few months and is characterized by feelings of elation and optimism. During this stage you tend to see the new culture through a tourist's perspective which is often at the superficial level that focuses on what is new and different.
2. Critical stage. At this stage you feel hostile toward and critical of your hosts, and even aggressive towards them. You may find that you reject all or part of your host culture. You may feel lonely, disorientated, angry, sad, helpless, and irritated. By contrast, you may find that you idealize your home culture.
3. Initial recovery state. In this stage you are able to laugh at yourself. You learn more about the host culture, have had a start at language learning, and are gradually adjusting. This stage is marked by increased understanding of the culture around you.
4. Adjustment stage. In this stage you have learned the implicit cultural rules for behavior in the host culture, accepted the other culture as a valid way of living, and have adjusted to it.

Cultural shock relates to ETHNOCENTRISM, our human tendency to judge other cultures in terms of our own cultural background. In judging, the other culture is usually seen as inferior to our culture. Hence, Aboagye-Mensah believes, "Ethnocentrism is an intellectual, emotional, and cultural attitude of a particular group of people who regard the identities and values of other groups of people as false, inferior, or immoral as compared to their own" (1993:130).

While ethnocentrism, a characteristic of people in all cultures, contributes to the survival of cultures, it gets in the way when working cross-culturally. It hinders people from understanding and appreciating another culture. It leads to our being judgmental, paternalistic, and critical of others.

Through interaction with the research community, resulting in increased language ability and understanding of the culture, culture shock gradually lessens. Specific short-term activities that might help decrease culture shock are to read a book, take short breaks outside the research area for rest and relaxation; talk about problems with others (e.g., with members of the local community who may explain to you why they do what they do); exercise (e.g., take walks, swim, jog, etc.); listen to music; draw, sew, or engage in other such activities that you find relaxing; write your problems in a journal; or visit with members of your own culture.

In your quest to conquer your own culture shock it also helps to do task-oriented work such as (1) make a map, (2) take a census, (3) inventory household items, (4) collect genealogies, and (5) write field notes about your own responses to the culture, in other words, study yourself (Bernard 1994:160). In the midst of culture shock realize that many of your values are not absolutes, but rather they are dependent upon your own cultural background.

A very important antidote to culture shock is to maintain your sense of humor, including the ability to laugh at yourself. Barley (1983, 1986) wrote two entertaining books on his adventures and misadventures while studying the Dowayo in Cameroon. He maintained his sense of humor in the midst of formidable problems, potential discouragements, and clearly impossible situations. He writes,

It was perhaps appropriate to my present halfway position that I should end up standing in for the local schoolteacher, teaching English while he recovered from one of the vague agues that afflict everyone in the area....

As in various other institutions of learning, many of the pupils had assumed false identities. Rules concerning the number of times a single pupil may take the same examination are sidestepped by borrowing the identity of a younger brother or sister. Some of the putative sixteen-year olds in the class had gray hair. A disconcerting number had the same names. The problem was exacerbated by twins. Having sought the term for 'twins' in a French-English dictionary they had discovered that they were 'binoculars' and referred to themselves by this term. "This is my sister, Naomi, *patron*. We are binoculars."

I taught them rudiments of the English tongue from a book that dwelt lengthily on such phenomena as Ascot racing, Bonfire Night and the ever-incomprehensible Yorkshire pudding. This they internalized as 'chaud-froid pudding'. In a splendidly medieval collapsing of microcosm and macrocosm one of my pupils had declared, "The blood makes twenty-four revolutions of the body per day." Yet another wrote me an essay containing the surprising intelligence that, "People get headaches standing in the sun because they produce too much oxygen" (1986:153).

He continues his adventures as follows,

We walked along, chewing on bananas, pleased to be away from the cold and gloom of the mountain. Suddenly, there was a cracking noise. My front teeth, repaired in England after the car-crash of my previous visit to Dowayoland, snapped neatly in two, leaving me bemused and edentate.

It is one of the marks of people who have lived in the bush that they are seldom in awe of the skills of others. They are quite prepared to build houses, plan whole villages and execute minor surgical operations with a verve and self-confidence egotistical in the extreme. Given that the skills of any available dentist would be extraordinarily basic, self-treatment looked a much more viable option. As so often when in trouble Matthieu and I headed for the mission.

The teeth being made of some sort of plastic, it was deemed sensible to effect a repair with some sort of resin glue. Fortunately, my mission friends, Jon and Jeannie, had a tube in their tool-kit. Unluckily, it took six hours to harden. A hope-inspiring footnote on the label warned that the resin hardened faster if heat was applied. A solution was quickly devised. The teeth were smeared with glue held in place by two clothes-pegs and heated with a hair-drier. On the whole, the practice was only slightly more uncomfortable than normal dental practice though one did tend to get rather thirsty. Two attempts failed owing to the dampness of the surfaces. Again, a solution was devised. We would heat the teeth in the oven to dry them. This was a hazardous proceeding. Jon and Jeannie only possessed an ancient wood-burning stove whose temperature was virtually uncontrollable. I had a ghastly vision of the teeth melting. The cook stroked away manfully, flashing his own excellent dentition. Luck was with us. With a deft flick of the wrist, Jon whipped out the hot teeth, slapped on glue and clipped on the clothes-pegs. A blast of hot air from the hair-drier completed the treatment. The next few minutes were not pleasant. We had forgotten to allow for the fact that the heat in the teeth would percolate through to the roots. But they stayed in place and lasted till the end of the trip. The only problem was that they rapidly turned green as if in emulation of my monkey friend (Barley1986:86–87).

One area that can be stressful in a field situation is what happens when you suffer injury in a cross-cultural context. For example, one American teacher of English in China while riding her bicycle to work was hit by a truck and knocked off her bicycle. The driver stopped his truck, got out, and came over to her to survey the situation. His response was to begin laughing uproariously. By so doing he was communicating that this situation could be taken care of. It was not one that required anger or sympathy. To the American, however, it seemed an inappropriate response and as such contributed significantly to her distress (example provided by Carol Clark, personal communication, March 18, 1991, Houston). If she had been seriously injured, the driver's response would have been quite different.

Similarly, experiencing illness in another country can be very stressful, especially where the health delivery system is inadequate. Health delivery systems even if adequate can still be stressful due to cultural differences. In Africa one is not sick alone. People come to greet and empathize with the patient. For example, one fieldworker contracted hepatitis while living in a village, and most of the people in the village came into her bedroom to greet her because she was ill.

Fieldworkers frequently encounter asocial and antisocial aspects of society that include theft, lies, envy, jealousy, suspicion, meanness, unpaid loans, and on occasion even violence. These aspects of cross-cultural relationships can make fieldwork trying and contribute significantly to cultural stress.

Some have proposed various scales to enable people to measure the amount of stress they experience. When working cross-culturally fieldworkers typically find their scores so high that they are off the scale of acceptable amounts of stress, amounts that can lead to some physical and/or emotional breakdown. You can do various things to modify the stressful situations you encounter, such as making changes in your own attitudes and developing more realistic expectations of yourself and your situation. To reduce stress, factor in additional time for basic everyday tasks that in many developing countries tend to take longer than you might expect.

Realize that though culture shock is real, it is usually not terminal! Furthermore, most humans need a certain amount of stress in order to work effectively; it is only when stress becomes excessive that people may find themselves overwhelmed.

REVERSE CULTURE SHOCK tends to occur when you return to your home culture. It occurs because of the vast differences between the cultures you are dealing with. Multiple choices may face you over which products to buy, whereas in the field situation no choice was available. For example, a fieldworker who returned to the United States cried over the decision of which brand of shampoo to purchase in a supermarket. She had had no such choice for the preceding years in the field situation. Sometimes the sheer availability of food can result in reverse culture shock. (See side box on next page.)

Even while in cultural shock and stress, you begin your cultural research. Often you begin by observing and beginning to participate in events of the research culture.

Events

Events—occurrences or sequences of behavior—are important in ethnographic research. You, the fieldworker, begin to analyze the components of a culture by studying events, including the interaction of actors, activities, settings, behaviors, communications, and timing of events.

You begin by getting the overall picture of what is going on in the field context. Initial survey observations involve looking at the larger picture, a process termed "grand tour observations" (Spradley 1980:77). Next you narrow your focus to smaller components of culture. The smaller units of experience are your "mini-tour observations." In grand tour observations you identify the major features of the social situation. There are at least eleven components of grand tour observations.

> ### Reverse culture shock
>
> Reverse culture shock occurred to my daughter Susan and me when we went to a supermarket for groceries the evening we returned to the United States. We pushed the shopping cart to the fruit and vegetable section of the store, the first section of the store we entered. There we realized we were both in tears. I looked at Susan and said, "Look, we're both rational human beings. What's wrong with us?" She replied, "Mom, it's because it's so rich!"

One component is understanding how space is used. This includes making a sketch of the setting (see chapter 12 on mapping). You also note what actor(s) or participant(s) is involved, and what activity or activities he is engaged in. Note what physical objects are present (see chapter 13 on material culture). What acts, or single actions, are people engaged in? What events or set of related activities are occurring? Note the timing or sequencing of events, too. What goals, desired results, or purposes do participants have? What feelings or emotions are expressed by both the participants and yourself as the fieldworker? What indirect participants or observers of the events are present? These indirect participants could be promoters, initiators, planners, funders, evaluators, spectators, reporters, etc. And finally, what worldview assumptions and values underlie the event? These components of the situation provide the framework within which events may then be analyzed.

When events occur, go, observe, participate when appropriate, and write them up as fieldnotes. You cannot adequately cover a ritual by simply asking your research assistant to tell you what happens. If you try to do this, you will have a selective understanding of what occurs. You need to go and observe.

Passive adaptational research

Freilich (1970:24) considers the topics covered in this chapter as part of the PASSIVE AD-APTATIONAL STAGE of research. At this stage you are spending time finding housing, learning the language, hiring help, learning how to get around, and developing rapport. You also begin to observe events. The next chapter discusses the important topic of language learning in field research. While language learning forms part of the beginning fieldwork stage, it continues throughout the research period.

6

Language Learning

Properly conducted language learning is one of the few occasions in which an adult can go through a deep experience of poverty, of weakness and of dependence on the good will of another. (Illich, as quoted in Batchelor 1993:19)

If you and the people you plan to study and work with do not speak the same language, you need to begin learning their language. After you have acquired a residence and requisite resident permit, and explained your presence to the people you are living among, turn your attention to the challenging and practical activity of acquiring the language, an activity that is essential for solid field research. As Devereux and Hoddinott state,

> Without some command of the local language, all social and professional interactions will be restricted to those people—often a small minority—who speak your language. This provides a limited insight into the community, as well as exacerbating feelings of loneliness and alienation. (1993:16)

Learning the local language enables you to avoid problems such as Margaret Mead experienced in Samoa where people deliberately falsified information they told her. As Bernard states,

> According to Brislin et al. (1973:70), Samoa is one of those cultures where "it is considered acceptable to deceive and to 'put on' outsiders. Interviewers are likely to hear ridiculous answers, not given in a spirit of hostility but rather sport." Brislin et al. call this the "sucker bias" and warn field workers to watch out for it. Presumably, knowing the local language fluently is one way to become alert to and avoid this problem. (1994:145)

A language mix-up

One day a pastor arrived on his bike to greet Norris and me. We were new in the village and in the early stages of language learning. I became confused as to which of the greetings to use, and ended up using the one that a man would use to welcome another man. Norris, who had just awakened from a nap, knew that he had to use the opposite greeting from the one I had used, so he greeted the pastor with the greeting a woman would use. Realizing what we had just done, I wished the ground would have opened up and swallowed us. However, since that did not happen and since it really was so ridiculous, I found myself laughing at the two of us. Meanwhile, the pastor stood there with his mouth wide open in wonder!

Use of the local language enables you to gather data, first from an etic or outsider's point of view and then more importantly from an emic or insider's perspective. Remember that language and culture learning are an inseparable dyad. Much of culture is communicated through the language. Knowing the language enables you to conduct your field research effectively and to communicate for basic survival in everyday living situations.

If possible, you should study the language before commencing field research; however, many minority languages spoken in areas where cultural researchers conduct their studies are not taught in university or in other schools. Many languages have little or nothing by way of well-established orthographies, written grammars, or language-learning materials available. When this is the case, you must do your language learning in the field context. Language learning in that type of situation involves learning through oral means. You listen, mimic, memorize, practice, and communicate as you learn the language. You need to acquire the new language in such a way that you develop automatic speech habits that you can use to communicate. Those automatic speech habits require lots and lots of practice.

To help you in language learning, prior to your field research you can benefit from studying linguistics so that you have some knowledge of how languages work. For example, in studying linguistics you need a course in articulatory phonetics that will help you learn to recognize and make sounds that are different from those in your own language. In a phonetics course you will also receive practice in writing down sounds in the International Phonetic Alphabet (IPA). The course should include the study of sounds, tone, stress, and intonation (see the side box). You also need a course in phonology in which you learn about sound systems. Study of phonology includes elicitation of minimal or analogous pairs of words to help you find the contrastive sounds in that language (e.g., note the contrast in the vowel sounds in the minimal paired words "hat" and "heat"). And finally, you need a course in grammatical analysis to help you be aware of how words, phrases, clauses, sentences, and discourses function in language. What is the range of possibilities of grammatical constructions you will likely encounter?

Some of the following suggestions are meant to serve as practical aids for language learning. They do not cover all of the areas of language that a linguist would likely explore. Further, they are meant to be suggestive only.

Nasalize that vowel!

The Robarcheks found learning the Waorani language in Equador difficult. Over time, through patient efforts, they began to feel more confident in the language. They did make mistakes, however. For example, they state, "One day, after we had been working intensively on the language for several weeks, Carole, beginning to feel a bit more confident, leaned out the window and shouted to Mïngkaï, as he passed by, "Is your father biting yet?" The young man stopped in mid-stride, open-mouthed and puzzled, and then grinned as he realized what she had intended to ask: "Has your father arrived yet?" The difference was that she had forgotten to nasalize one vowel (Robarchek and Robarchek 1998:33–34).

First, however, some issues related to language learning are considered, including the benefits of acquiring a working knowledge of the local language. Also considered are related issues such as whether to use interpreters, people who help you by translating what others say. Would not use of interpreters be easier than learning the language yourself? Then the important issue of which language to learn is discussed.

Benefits of a working knowledge of the local language

The benefits of language learning in cultural field research far outweigh the effort put into it. For example, Naroll noted that ethnographers who lived in the research community for a year or more tended to report the presence of witchcraft accusations and fears significantly more often than *short stayers* (Naroll 1962, as quoted in Pelto and Pelto 1970:265). Those who lived there longer learned to speak the language, so that they were able to hear about witchcraft accusations and fears.

Most ethnographers collecting data for their doctoral research spend a minimum of one year in their initial in-depth investigation. That length of time is usually sufficient to gain a working grasp of the local language, though certainly not sufficient to gain an extensive knowledge of it.

Use of interpreters

Use of interpreters for conducting cultural research must be viewed as a stop-gap measure only. Field researchers tend to use them initially until their grasp of the language is sufficient to do without them.

Obbo described problems resultant from use of interpreters as follows:

> During the late 1960s and the 1970s...the research assistants were male, with no more than a junior high school education. While investigators trained their assistants in data collection, it was clear that distortions resulted from the double impact of a foreign researcher who did not speak local languages and assistants with limited skills in English.
>
> Unlike other social scientists, anthropologists who could not learn the local languages were troubled by such barriers to their understanding of the actors' cultural points of view. Still more severe distortions of information resulted when research assistants consciously or unconsciously ignored, interpreted, or reformulated the responses of informants who (the assistants felt) had not provided a proper image of their society. (1990:295)

A haranguing interpreter

One day approximately four months into my fieldwork I sent my interpreter away. I was trying to communicate with a woman whose baby had been cut deliberately and who came seeking medical attention for the baby. Instead of carefully translating my questions to the mother, I recognized enough of what my interpreter was saying to her to realize that he was haranguing her for what had happened and thus was being less than helpful. I recognized that my poor Jju was better than his haranguing Jju. Unfortunately, even with both of our poor efforts at communicating, the baby died. Later the mother did not seem to blame me for it but was appreciative of my trying to tell her that her child would die without adequate medical care.

Which language should you learn?

When considering language learning, you must first answer the question of which language to learn, whether the national language, the trade language, a pidgin language, the local language, and/or other related dialect(s). In order to conduct your proposed project effectively sometimes you must learn more than one language, one of which will likely be the national language. Owusu concurs with the need to learn more than one language when he writes concerning field research in Africa,

Command of several local vernaculars is necessary because of the increasing tendency of Africans to shift from language to language within a single interaction context or social field as a result of the mixing of different speech communities. Unfortunately there is a growing tendency among Africanists (and anthropologists working in other geographic areas as well) to assume rather naively, even as they pay lip service to the importance of the use of native languages, that since European languages are now widely used throughout Africa, satisfactory scholarly ethnographies based on fieldwork can be written without mastery of the relevant vernaculars. (1978:313)

The mixing of languages by bilingual and multilingual individuals within a single speech event such as Owusu mentions occurs often. This is termed CODE SWITCHING, and it happens when people find that they can express certain concepts better in one language and other concepts better in another language. People switch between different linguistic codes in order to communicate adequately. This can result in communication problems for those listening who are not fluent in all of the languages involved. In that situation SEMI-COMMUNICATION occurs where people understand only part of what is being said. When all participants in a linguistic interaction do not share an equal knowledge of the language(s) of a conversation, semi-communication results (Scotton 1975:78).

If you find it necessary to learn more than one language, it may encourage you to know that many find it easier to learn another language once they have learned a second language. In other words, each language a person learns seems to come easier than the one before because the person also learns how to learn a language.

A trade language

Cultural researchers often choose to learn only a trade language. Trade languages usually have language learning material available, and they may be taught in universities and other contexts. The trade language will likely help you in your field research since many speakers of various languages are apt to know it to some extent. Learning a trade language will enable you to communicate with people of several ethnic groups, while learning a minority language will enable you to speak only with people of the ethnic group for whom it is their mother tongue. If your research calls for work with several ethnic groups, then the trade language is the appropriate language for you to learn.

Pragmatic reasons for learning the trade language include the following:

1. It is a language of wider communication so that you can do research with several ethnic groups.
2. Literature, language learning materials, dictionaries, and courses are likely to be available to help you in your language learning.
3. Many people, including speakers of minority languages, speak it to some extent, though their knowledge may be only at the market level.
4. Knowledge of the trade language may help you when dealing with local government officials, traders, and others who may not have knowledge of the minority language(s) in the area.
5. The direction of language shift in the area may be towards use of the trade language by more and more people.
6. It is the language of greater prestige than minority languages.

A minority language

Just as there are valid reasons for learning a trade language, so, too, there are pragmatic reasons for learning a minority language. Some of these reasons are as follows:

1. The mother tongue is the language of the home and heart.
2. Knowledge of the minority language will enable you to delve more deeply into the culture of the people you are studying.
3. You will be able to communicate with all speakers of the minority language, including all ages and both genders.
4. You will likely be more accepted by the local people as one of them since you can speak like they do.
5. Your learning their mother tongue contributes to their pride in their language and culture. This is especially true where outsiders may have denigrated their language and culture. It instills in them the knowledge that they can be proud of their own heritage rather than having to cross an ethnic boundary to be accepted.

In northern Nigeria the usual pattern of researchers, missionaries, development workers, and others is to use Hausa, the trade language. Among the Bajju over sixty percent of the people asserted that they spoke Hausa at the market level or less (McKinney 1985:403). Problems with exclusive use of the trade language include skewed data and reliance on interpreters when working with members of minority groups who may have limited knowledge of the trade language. For example, use of Hausa may cut researchers off from some segments of the society, such as women who tend to have less command of the trade language.

If you use a trade language when dealing with people for whom the trade language is a second language, you may find that you are asking yourself, "How much of what I'm asking do they understand? Is semi-communication occurring?"

Bajju have a Hausa political overlay; researchers who use only Hausa end up describing that overlay. For example, concerning the Bajju, Van der Valk stated, "Little is known of their rulers system [sic] before their conquest" (1981:7); however, when using Jju in conducting research for that group, that knowledge of the traditional political system is readily available. Thus, which language you use may determine the data you are able to collect.

Learning an oral language

For purposes of language learning in cultural field research, the focus here is on learning to speak an oral language. As children we learned to speak a language by hearing and practicing speaking it; it is also possible to do so as adults.

As preparation for engaging in language learning, some researchers take tests that identify their particular learning style. While two styles are mentioned here, an oral learner and a visual learner, there are other learning styles as well. It helps to know your learning style(s) so that you can use it to your advantage in learning another language. Some people seem to "absorb" another language by simply listening to it, while others tend to be more analytical. The absorber type of language learner hears the language spoken, then mimics it, and begins to use it. The learning style for this language learner may be that of an oral or auditory learner. Contrastively, an analytical type of person may need to understand the components of the language through writing and analyzing the language before he or she feels free to begin using it. The learning style of this type of language learner may be that of a visual learner.

Given your particular learning style you need to begin using the language to communicate. In learning another language, make allowances for your particular learning style. If you are not a language absorber, do not despair; you can still learn to speak another language.

Some specific suggestions for your acquiring another language include consulting the literature about that language; being immersed in hearing the language spoken day after day in its natural setting; learning some useful words (both content and function words), phrases, and sentences; memorizing; role playing with one or more speakers of the language; developing frame or substitution drills in the language; working at word associations; exploring different semantic domains; mimicking and tracking; and communicating in that language. A language learning kit may help you as you begin to learn another language. Means for compensating for your language learning deficiencies are considered at the end of this section. Your ultimate goal is being able to understand and communicate.

Language literature review

Prior to beginning your language learning, read the literature for information about the language you will be learning. Find out what language family it belongs to and what phonological, grammatical, and semantic features you are likely to encounter. Also read about languages that are within the same language family. You may wish to contact some of the people who have written on the language or on related languages in order to solicit their help.

Having some idea about what you are likely to encounter should help you in language learning. For example, Jju, the language spoken by the Bajju people, has a complete series of fortis-lenis consonant contrasts. When students in a linguistics field methods class used Jju as the language they studied for the semester, all of them missed half of the consonants. They failed to find the fortis-lenis consonant contrast. Once they knew that that contrast was present, they relistened to their data tapes. One student found a fortis-lenis consonant contrast in the first sentence he listened to!

Motivation is key to language learning

Motivation is the key component for effective language learning. By motivation is meant your inner drive, your desire and ability to focus on a task, and your sense of purpose that leads to action. In this case the task or action is to learn another language. When you need to use another language to purchase food needed for survival, it is amazing how motivated you can be to learn that language! Remember that good fieldwork is dependent upon your working in the primary language of the research community.

If you are monolingual, you may feel apprehensive about learning another language. Perhaps your language learning efforts in high school and university have resulted in only a reading knowledge of another

> **Motivation is key**
>
> While stumbling through learning a little Tzeltal in southern Mexico, I had little motivation to learn that language since I knew I would be there for only a few months. When I discovered that the person who was to help us build our shelter (*champa*) was a monolingual Tzeltal speaker, I wished I had worked harder at learning his language earlier. While gestures helped, words, phrases, and sentences in Tzeltal would have been more useful.

language. Whereas, you may be very uneasy about learning another language, you may find that it is much easier to learn than when you studied another language in high school and university.

When people around you speak another language, you feel motivated to learn that language. You hear it from morning to evening; you need to use it to purchase food, to communicate with your neighbor, and to collect data.

If a few people speak English, though poorly, it is still worth your while to learn their language. Otherwise you will be limited in who you may speak with by being unable to communicate in their language.

Brown states that there are at least two basic types of motivation for language learning:

> *Instrumental* motivation refers to motivation to acquire a language as means for attaining instrumental goals: furthering a career, reading technical material, translation, and so forth. An *integrative* motive is employed when learners wish to integrate themselves within the culture of the second language group, to identify themselves with and become part of that society. (Brown 1994:153–154, italics in original)

Total immersion

The best approach to language learning is TOTAL IMMERSION in the language community. Total immersion involves interacting with members of the speech community intensely such that you hear the language spoken daily. As you hear it, patterns of that language gradually begin to make sense and to be embedded in your memory. This requires a full-time effort in language learning on your part for the first few months of your field research. In total immersion you seek to communicate in the local language on a wide variety of topics and in a broad range of contexts. (See the following for information on language learning: Brewster and Brewster 1976, Burling 1987, Healey 1975, Marshall 1989, and Oxford 1990.)

One of the difficulties of total immersion in the early months of language learning is that you are also suffering from culture shock. Learning the language and culture, however, does contribute to decreasing your culture shock.

Since the local people may desire to learn your language, it may take some effort to convince them that their language is the one in which they must communicate with you. In most parts of the world today, you will probably find someone who knows some English and who would like to practice it with you. It is tempting to work solely with those who speak a common language with you. This approach would probably cut you off from the majority of the population.

You may feel embarrassed by your initial halting attempts to learn the other language, especially when you seek to converse with people who know your language better than you know theirs. One way to avoid such possible embarrassment is to practice the target language with those who do not know your language. Monolingual speakers often feel cut off from outsiders to their culture and, therefore, appreciate it when you seek to communicate with them.

You might also want to have someone from the speech community, for example, your research colleague, a friend, or household help, in your home daily. When that person is present, make an effort to speak the language with him or her. Be careful also to go out to speak with and listen to others. A counter example concerning learning Xavante monolingually as reported by McLead is as follows:

> When we first arrived at the Post...we asked for a Xavante woman to help us with the housework as well as doing language work with us. The Post official sent us a different woman each week, some of whom were quite unsuitable as language helpers, and so after a few weeks of frustration we asked if we could have the first girl to help us indefinitely, as she had been quite helpful (when we could persuade her to sit still). We learned later that this was a bad policy, for two reasons. First, the other Xavante women became jealous of her weekly earnings of cloth and thread. Second, by keeping to the first reasonably helpful person, and neglecting to try out other women, for many months we failed to discover those women who were really capable of being good teachers. (Healey 1975:281)

There are a couple of significant factors involved in what was occurring with Xavante language learning. First, these fieldworkers needed to be out in the community learning the language, something which they recognized. Second, the Xavante are an egalitarian group with no person more important in status than any other person. Hence, in order to maintain the egalitarianism of the Xavante culture, the McLeads needed to have a different woman each week.

One pitfall of language learning is that you learn sufficient so that those around you learn your version of their language, but others within the language community cannot understand you. Do not allow yourself to fall into the language learning trap of only being able to communicate with a few who have learned your variety of their language.

Many of us end up spending long hours at our desks writing up our field data. When people come, some fieldworkers feel that they are being "interrupted." It is important, however, to be available and seize the opportunity when people come to talk with you. Communication is key to language learning, so instead of viewing people who come as interruptions, recognize that people who stop by to greet you and talk with you are adding to your knowledge of the language and culture.

Brewster and Brewster (1976:11) proposed a LANGUAGE LEARNING CYCLE, and they stated that COMMUNICATION is the indispensable part of the cycle. Communication or the exchange of information is the name of the game. This means that you do not focus too much on the intricacies of grammar or of the sound system; rather you speak with and listen to people in their language in order to communicate. Burling (1987:5) notes, "The most successful language learners are often those who can get themselves into a situation where they can hear a vast amount of the language without being under pressure to speak." For example, if you rent a room in the home of a local family, you will then hear them communicate with each other daily. Hearing the language spoken in its natural context day after day is an integral part of language learning. This is part of the reason for living near people who are speaking the language.

In some situations the people of the target culture will expect you to speak well in their language as a condition for them to allow you to use their language. These are situations where people learn by observation of others and by listening to others. Groups for which this is true include Native Americans, such as the Navaho, and groups in Latin America. If you plan to do your field research in such a situation, you must spend lots of time listening and quietly learning the target language before using it to any extent. Whether in situations where learning the language quietly is expected, or ones in which you can use the language immediately without offending others, listening is an extremely important part of language learning.

In other situations, where you have no language in common with speakers of the research community, you will need to learn the language monolingually by beginning to speak the target language immediately. You will be amazed at your ability to communicate through use of gestures, a rudimentary knowledge of the grammar, and a poor grasp of its phonology. As you work at communicating and understanding what is being communicated to you, gradually your speaking ability improves. Usually, you will understand far more of the target language than you are able to speak.

When learning another language, focus your attention on what the other person is trying to communicate to you. In focusing on comprehension, meaning is central. To this end you need to concentrate on and learn the words being spoken. To your knowledge of specific words add some rudimentary knowledge of the grammar, knowledge that includes some understanding of morpheme and word order. Some languages, such as English, have a basic subject-verb-object (SVO) word order. Other languages are VSO and others SOV. Less common are languages with word orders OVS and VOS. Comrie states concerning language universals in regards to word order,

> In its original form, this [word order typological] parameter characterizes the relative order of subject, verb, and object, giving rise to six logically possible types, namely SOV, SVO, VSO, VOS, OVS, OSV...the distribution of these types across the languages of the world is heavily skewed in favour of the first three, more especially the first two, but we can now cite solidly attested examples of each of the first five basic word orders, and it is probably only a matter of time before reliable attestations of OSV languages become available.... (1981:81)

It helps tremendously in language and cultural learning if you do not try to keep to a rigid time schedule. This can pose a conflict for many who come from time-oriented cultures.

Find out the common pattern of time use where you are, then conform to it to the extent possible. For example, among the Bajju from five to approximately seven p.m. is greeting time. Having dinner at six p.m. simply is not possible without having multiple interruptions.

Early language learning attempts

Early attempts at language learning can prove disheartening when you find that you can converse only at the level of a four year old or younger. Kurin found that this level of achievement fell far short of the expectations of villagers,

> Their idiom is rich with the terminology of agricultural operations and rural life. It is unpretentious, uninflected, and direct, and villagers hold high opinions of those who are good with words, who can speak to a point and be convincing. Needless to say, my infantile babble realized none of these characteristics and evoked no such respect. (Kurin 1980, as quoted in Spradley and McCurdy 1987:48–49)

As Kurin's language proficiency increased and as he asked questions about kinship relationships, the local populace changed their perception of him. Then they viewed him as being a spy. To counter the misconceptions, Kurin took the time and put forth the effort to build trust relationships that are essential for conducting good cultural research. Gradually, his language ability increased to the point that he was able to build those essential trust relationships.

Useful words and phrases

In your language learning, begin with the greetings and farewells. Learn words that you need for purposes of common courtesy such as "welcome," "hello," "good-bye," "thank you," "you're welcome," and "excuse me." As you begin learning these phrases, learn also the gestures that accompany them. For example, in Kenya when greeting another person, shake that person's hand with your right hand, and with your left hand grasp the elbow of your right arm to indicate respect to the person you are greeting.

Be aware that in greetings there can be differences for males and females. For example, in Jju to welcome a guest, a woman would say *mbaa* to a man or woman, and a man would say *mbaa* to a woman and *maban* or *mahaban* to a man. There is also a different form of the word "yes" used by men from that used by women.

Learn basic useful phrases that you need for your vocabulary, such as ones in the language similar in function to the following English expressions. These are suggestive only and hopefully, they will help you begin to get into the language. Note that in learning the greetings and leave-taking phrases, you need to learn who greets first, and you need to learn both your phrases and the other person's phrases. Many languages have more elaborate greetings and leave-taking phrases than those below.

1. Greetings. "Good morning." "Good afternoon." "Good evening." "Greetings to you in your work." "Are you around?" "Yes, I'm around." "How are you doing?" "How is your work?" "How is your wife?" "How are your children?" "How is your household?"
2. Leave taking phrases. "Until later." "Good-bye." "Until I/you come." "Good night."
3. "What is this?" or "What do you call this?"
4. "What is that?" or "What is that over there?"
5. "Please repeat" or "Please say it again."
6. "Say it slowly." "Say it at normal speed."
7. "What does ____ mean?"
8. "How do you say ____?"
9. "What is your name?" Check on what is the local equivalent. For example, some say "What are you called?" or "What do they call you?" (Note that in some cultures people do not tell others their names. And even in cultures where it is all right to tell names to other people, people may typically be referred to by kin terms. Mothers may be called the mother of their oldest child; e.g., I was often called "Mama Mark.") "What is his/her name?"
10. "My name is _____?" "His/Her name is _____?" "They call me _____."
11. "What type of work do you do?" or "What is your work/occupation?" and "Where do you work?"
12. "Where are you going?" "I am going to ____ (the river, the market, home, ____'s house, etc.)."
13. "What time is it?" (Note that different languages have other ways of reckoning time other than by a watch, e.g., sunup, morning, when the sun is at its zenith, when the sun is low on the horizon, evening, night, or when you can tell the difference between a black and white thread.)
14. "How do you get to ____?"
15. "How many?"
16. "How much does ____ cost?"
17. "Please."
18. "Pardon me."

19. "Thank you."
20. "Come in."
21. "Sit down."
22. "Did I say it right?" or "Is that right?"
23. "Yes", "No", "I'm not sure." (Note that sometimes there is a different affirmative word used by females than by males. Among the Bajju women use *ii* and men tend to use *ee*.)
24. "What is it used for?" or "What is its purpose?"
25. "What does it smell/sound/feel/taste like?"
26. "What color is it? " Learn the colors too. (Note that some languages have words for three or four colors only. Other color words may be borrowed or may be indicated by use of modifiers, e.g., very red.)
27. "I don't know."
28. "I don't understand."
29. "Where is the toilet/water closet (the wc)/loo?" Learn the directions, too, so that you can understand the answer to this question.

Learn such essentials as the names of days of the week, numbers (cardinal and ordinal), directions, honorifics, some function words (e.g., in English these include *a, an, the, for, to,* prepositions, pronouns, etc.), and affixes. In order to speak correctly, you need to understand when to use which function words.

You may encounter grammatical function words that can defy your discovering their meaning for a while. Careful observation of their usage can often bring their function to light.

In your language learning, work on learning the following grammatical categories:

1. Questions. How are questions asked, and what are useful question words or expressions (e.g., who, what, when, where, why, which, how)?
2. Commands. How do you give commands (e.g., sit, stand, go, come, enter, leave, eat, sleep, do, make)?
3. Interjections. What are some commonly used interjections, and when are they likely to be used?
4. Statements. How do you make statements?
5. Verbs. What tenses and aspects are used with verbs? Tense and aspect indicate time and mood or a type of action. Do verbs fall into classes? What affixes occur with verbs? In some languages verbs may be used in serial verb constructions, or verb chains. For example, if translated literally into English a serial verb construction might be as follows: "I went then met John and we talked then danced when the music began." In some languages the subject is not repeated after its first mention in a verb chain.
6. Adverbs. What adverbs are used to modify verbs?
7. Adjectives. For most languages the number of adjectives forms a fairly limited group. Adjectives include colors, qualities (e.g., big, small, long, short, fat, thin, old, new, good, bad, sweet, sour, etc.), feelings (e.g., good, bad). What adjectives occur in the language? Do they precede or follow the nouns they modify?
8. Quantifiers. Quantifiers include concepts such as "lots, many, few, all, none, much," and numbers. What quantifiers are present in the language you are learning?
9. Antonyms. Antonyms involve contrasts between opposites: e.g., tall versus short, big versus little.

10. Comparative and intensifier constructions. Comparative constructions such as "John is taller than Jack" involve two or more persons, objects, or groups that are compared with one another. Intensifier constructions occur with words like "small, smaller, smallest."

11. Pronouns. Languages have pronouns of various types: subject, indirect object, direct object, and possessive. If you are working with a Bantu language, you will find that there are different pronouns for each noun class, including different ones for subject, object, indirect object, and possessive. When you are learning all of these pronouns, it can seem rather daunting. Once you have learned them, however, you no longer have to ask what is the referent for a particular pronoun, such as we often do in English; it is quite clear. Some languages have inclusive and exclusive pronouns for first- and second-person plural.

12. Negatives. How is the negative expressed? How are statements negated?

13. Nouns. Nouns are names of things, including both concrete objects and abstract concepts (e.g., love, hate, blessing, forgiveness, etc.). Nouns name body parts, physical parts of the environment, objects in the house, animals, birds, fish, plants, etc. Nouns are the usual response to your question, "What is this?" When looking at nouns, also look at whether a verb may be nominalized and a noun verbalized, and how this is done. Are nouns divided into noun classes? In a noun class system nouns fit into a class of semantically similar nouns. Any noun borrowed into a language with a noun class system must fit into one of the noun classes. Sometimes all borrowed nouns fit into one class.

14. Relationals. These include conjunctions and prepositions. Relationals bind phrases and clauses together into sentences. They include words like "and, but, however, or." Prepositions include words such as "on, in, upon, by, of, at, into, under, on top of." Sometimes a relational concept is embedded within a noun or verb.

15. Locatives. Locatives refer to place. They include words and phrases such as "here, there, near, far, up, down, on top of, under, underneath, to the side, over here, over there."

16. Temporals. Temporals refer to time. They include "today, yesterday, long ago or the distant past, tomorrow, the distant future, when, while, now, then, morning, noon, evening, day, week, month, year, dry season, rainy season" (and parts of them); and in general the local concepts for time. For example, when does today begin?

While engaged in language learning, you can collect kin terms to use to study the kinship system. See chapter 14 on kinship for help in collecting kinship data.

A ubiquitous nasal

When learning to speak Jju, we encountered a nasal consonant within the verb phrase that clearly was an infix with some grammatical function. Though we asked our language helper about it, he was unable to tell us its function. He seemed to know when it needed to be there, however, and when it should be omitted. For a long time we struggled with understanding what our "ubiquitous nasal" was doing. Only later did Norris discover that it marked the beginning of a relative clause while *ni* marked its end!

Memorization

Learn content words by memorizing them and using them in context. Burling (1987:18) suggests that you work from the target language back to your own language rather than vice versa. This keeps the focus on learning the target language. To work from your own language to the target language ties you to your language.

Memorizing frequently used words, phrases, and idioms helps you in communicating. You may not be able to separate each component of what you are learning, yet you can use them to make yourself understood. Rote memorization and use of phrases in their appropriate context helps (Brown 1994:120). Brown terms this learning PREFABRICATED PATTERNS. He states that this may be the basis of "tourist survival" language learning. Learning formulaic expressions gives the appearance that you know more of the language than, in fact, you know. Such expressions can also have the effect of keeping the conversation going.

Some language learners memorize a story that they go out and tell. That story provides an entrée into a context where you can learn more of the language.

In memorizing review the material frequently. Going over and over it helps you retain it.

Role playing

When engaging in language learning, it often helps to do role playing with one or more persons in order to practice interaction in the language. For example, you can practice the greetings with someone, including the gestures and movements that accompany greetings. Be sure to trade off so that each person has the opportunity to learn both sets of greetings. You can also practice being the seller and buyer in a market with one or more other persons. Role playing can contribute to gaining fluency in the areas practiced.

Frame or substitution drills

It helps to put content words (e.g., nouns and verbs) within a FRAME and to develop SUBSTITUTION DRILLS using frames. A frame or carrier is a phrase or sentence that leaves a place for a word or phrase to be inserted. For example, you can use a frame such as "There is a _____ over there." Then insert a list of nouns in the slot within the frame. Through rote memorization you learn both the content words and the frame. Using a tape recorder practice frame drills. You can also practice the frame or substitution drills with your spouse, co-fieldworker, or language assistant.

The drills need to come from natural language used in situations in which you are likely to find yourself. For example, what words, phrases, clauses, and sentences might you use on a trip to the market? Practice these types of utterances, then use them when you go to the market. If you find new words and phrases that you need there, note them and add them to your drills in order to expand your knowledge of the language.

Mnemonic word associations

Another means of learning content words is to derive some association with either the sounds or the content of the words. For example, in Jju the word for tree is *kakon*. In order to derive some association to help learn this word, it can be associated with a pine "cone" that grows on a pine tree. By extension its meaning can encompass any tree. Use of such mnemonic associations helps in language learning.

Reduplication within words also helps with memorization. Examples from Jju include *əgwagwa* 'duck' and *tolotolo* 'turkey'. The words sound like the sound of these fowl.

Semantic domains

Begin to explore different semantic domains for vocabulary and idioms. Though you may communicate well concerning much of daily life, you may find yourself lost in discussions when a new semantic domain emerges. For example, what words are associated with the semantic domains of farming, herding, fishing, midwifery, the local medical system, and so on? As you explore new semantic domains, you will, in fact, be engaging in language and culture learning. This is content-centered language learning.

Be aware that words have different areas of meaning or semantic space in different languages. For example, the Jju word *kahwa* translates into English as 'abdomen, stomach' and 'womb' or 'uterus'. If a woman is "with *kahwa*," she is pregnant. Hence, one Jju word translates into several different English words. Often there is not a one-word-to-one-word translation into another language, but each language has its unique semantic space for any particular word.

Mimicry and tracking

Mimicking and tracking also aid in language learning. To help you with mimicry, tape record your language material. Record the word, phrase, or sentence in your language first, then record it in the target language, leave a period of silence equal to the length of your mimicking the utterance, then record the utterance a second time, followed by another silent section. In using this tape, you learn the meaning of the utterance, listen to it, mimic it, listen again in order to pick up phonetic features you might have missed, and finally, mimic it again. You can continue this process with other utterances that you want to learn.

Sometimes it is helpful to track a text you have recorded. In tracking, try to mimic the speaker in unison as nearly as possible. Repeat the words, tone, and intonation immediately after hearing them spoken. Tracking helps you to learn language as connected speech. It is best to use a tape recording when you practice tracking a text. To do this with a speaker of the language is a quick way to lose a friend.

Mimicry helps to imprint the patterns of the language in your brain. It also helps you learn to speak with the correct sounds, rhythm, and intonational patterns.

> ### A daughter's example
>
> When I was learning to speak Jju, my one-year-old daughter, Christy, was learning to talk. She started speaking with the word "Hi." That word elicited a response, and her language learning took off. I took some of my clues for learning language from listening and watching her learn her first language. I watched as she repeated words, phrases, and sentences over and over. She provided me with a role model for my language learning.

Be aware that there are times when mimicry is inappropriate. For example, when you study ethnic and occupational subcultures within your own society, people who speak a particular dialect may feel that you are belittling or ridiculing them if you mimic them. If you are studying that subculture, you do need to learn the key words in order to adequately understand people in that context.

Understanding is the primary goal

A language is far too complex to be learned all at once (Burling 1987:13). While eventually you need to learn to speak correctly in terms of the sounds of the language, its grammar, its tone and intonation, and its semantics, you begin gradually with the recognition that learning to speak the language well takes time. Begin by focusing on understanding, particularly content words.

Most non-native speakers of a language speak it with somewhat of an accent. That accent reflects the sounds we carry over from our native language. Burlings advocates a realistic attitude towards our foreign accents when learning another language.

Too much emphasis on pronunciation does little except foster discouragement and takes up time that could be better spent on more important matters. No one really understands why some people acquire relatively "good" accents while others do not, but the fact is that some people do learn to speak understandably, and even fluently, while still retaining powerful foreign accents. The goal of a flawless accent, like the goal of being "adopted into the tribe," has more to do with vanity than with reality (Burling 1987:43).

Filing

If you are working with a language without a dictionary, keep a file of the words you collect. Usually it is helpful to develop a bilingual file, including the vernacular language and your mother tongue. Sometimes a trilingual file is important, one that includes the vernacular, your mother tongue, and the trade language. For further information on filing see chapter 7 on keeping an ethnographic record.

Language-learning kit

Evelyn Pike (1983:6) recommends setting up a language-learning kit. Within your kit include your tape recorder, pictures (e.g., pictures you have taken locally, magazine pictures, etc.), artifacts, and other items that you can use when a guest drops in to visit. Also include a notebook to write down new vocabulary and grammatical constructions. Have this kit handy so that you can practice the language with your guests with some props to stimulate conversation. The props in the kit will keep the conversation relatively circumscribed, and ensure that you get some repetition of lexical items, phonology, and grammatical constructions. As such your language-learning kit needs to have things indigenous to that culture.

Develop a set of questions that cover different semantic domains that you can go out and ask of different people. By asking these questions you continue to expand your knowledge of the language.

Compensating for your language learning deficiencies

As you seek to communicate something in another language, you will quickly find some areas where there are deficiencies in your knowledge. There are a

When is tonight?

Shepherd found temporals confusing when working with the Magar people in Nepal:

"Another thing that caused me much confusion was their reference to 'tonight'. It certainly gave me plenty of trouble when I was trying to unravel the present and past tense in the Magar verb system. I finally got a clue to the problem when someone told me about the dream he had 'tonight'. After endless questioning, it became clear that their 'day' must begin at nightfall, not at midnight or daybreak. Thus, *last night* was literally 'today's night', meaning the night that began today. *Tonight*, however, was literally 'this evening' while *tomorrow night* was just that—'tomorrow night'." (1982:181) couple of approaches that you can take to such deficiencies. First, you can make intelligent guesses by looking for some clues in the situation that may help your understanding. Second, you can use some compensating strategies—switching to a trade language or your mother tongue, seeking help, acting out what you are trying to communicate, selecting another topic to converse on for which you do have more control of the language, making up a new word based on a word that you know in the other language that people may be able to understand, and selecting other words that may help you communicate. By these means or by using some circumlocution or a synonym you may be able to communicate with people, and they in turn will be able to help you say it appropriately.

Total physical response

By TOTAL PHYSICAL RESPONSE (TPR) linguists mean that language learners respond to the language with their bodies as well as verbally. For example, if your language teacher commands "Stand up," you then stand up. There are a number of commands that require physical response from you as the language learner.

Language learning plateaus

As you progress with learning a language, you will likely find that at times you reach a plateau, when it seems like you are not progressing in your language acquisition. It helps to be aware that this happens to many people who are engaged in language learning. Persevere with your efforts. Continue to communicate and to work at understanding the language. At some point you will notice that you are moving on in your language learning and acquiring more of the language. Reaching plateaus in language learning implies that there are levels of language proficiency.

Levels of language proficiency

The United States Foreign Service Institute (FSI) developed a rating scale from zero to five as a self-rating checklist for your language speaking proficiency (as quoted in Brewster and Brewster 1976:370–72).

1. Level zero. Level zero represents no speaking ability in the language. It is the level that the majority of people in the world have for most of the world's languages.
2. Level zero plus. At the level zero plus you can use at least fifty words in their appropriate contexts. This is the beginning stage of language learning.
3. Level one. At level one you have an elementary speaking proficiency. You can communicate sufficiently to travel using the language (e.g., you can get a room, order simple meals, handle your travel requirements, tell time), and you can communicate a minimum of what you need in order to be courteous in the language. However, you still make frequent errors in pronunciation and grammar. You can also recite texts and drills that you have memorized.
4. Level one plus. At this level your language ability is improved, though you usually find yourself limited to fairly familiar material. Your pronunciation is also improved, and you have increased your vocabulary.
5. Level two. At the second level you have a limited working proficiency with the language. At this point you are no longer limited to a range of memorized texts, sentences, and phrases to cope with specific situations. You can give simple instructions,

explanations, and descriptions while still getting lost when it comes to using more complicated material. You may find yourself using various circumlocutions in order to avoid patterns or vocabulary that you have not yet mastered.

6. Level two plus. At this level your rate of speech and your fluency are increasing.

7. Level three. At this level you have a minimal professional proficiency in speaking the language. You are able to handle all social and work requirements including any specialized vocabulary that you need to conduct your research. You can conduct all conversations on general topics with relative ease.

    At this level you will likely still have an accent that comes from your mother tongue. People understand you, however, and you have established some friendships with speakers of the language.

    You need to get to this level in your language learning as a minimum in order to conduct your cultural research with any amount of certainty. Prior to reaching this level you will remain uncertain about the accuracy of the data you collect. The greater your grasp of the research language, the better.

8. Level three plus. Your grasp of the language is increasing as well as your fluency. At this level you are understanding idiomatic speech used by native speakers. You may still be making some grammatical errors as you construct sentences. And your vocabulary is increasing.

9. Level four. The fourth level is that of full professional proficiency in your use of the language. At this level you use the language with proficiency, and you correct yourself when you do make errors in using the language. Your conversation has a high level of fluency, and your knowledge of the vocabulary has improved significantly.

10. Level four plus. At this level you are just short of native speaker proficiency. You have also acquired cultural knowledge such that you understand and can work within the worldview of the people whose language you are learning.

11. Level five. This level is that of complete native-speaker proficiency. At this level you have complete fluency and you use the language idiomatically. Your work is not hindered by your knowledge of the language.

This scale is meant to help you evaluate your language learning. Are you making progress? What can you do to get off the plateau you are on to continue learning more of the language? Some self-evaluation and monitoring helps when learning another language.

> **A son's language proficiency**
>
> My guess is that my son, Mark, is at level four plus or five in his knowledge of French. For example, while in Paris he talked for an hour with a Frenchman. At the end of that hour the man had figured out that Mark might not be French, so he asked my American son, "Are you Swiss?"

Language assistants

Most fieldworkers who learn a language in a field setting work with language assistants or consultants who help them daily with the language. Use of language consultants who know your language to some extent can help you break into the system of the other language. They can help you with pronunciation, grammar, and semantics of the target language. Your progress may encourage them that they are doing a good job of teaching you their language.

Use of language consultants needs to be combined with talking with others within the speech community. In some communities there is a regular visiting time of the day when people go out to visit with their neighbors. Among the Bajju that time of day is from about five to seven p.m. This is a great time to engage in language learning. It is the period when people come to visit with others solely for the purpose of greeting them.

In many societies it is appropriate to visit with another person solely for the purpose of greeting. You might say something like "I just came to greet!"

Among the Bajju, every morning people greet each member of their compound. In our case the elderly head of the household who lived directly behind us came each morning to greet us. He felt it was his duty to do so. If there is such a daily greeting pattern, you need to become part of it in order to practice using the language.

Equipment for language learning

In addition to your data notebook for jotting down words and phrases, you will want to make use of a tape recorder for language learning. There are several possible uses. For example, you can develop frame drills that you record, listen to, and repeat. Record the usual greetings and farewells to help you memorize them. You may wish to record texts for tracking, memorizing, and using their content for your cultural research.

Tape record utterances that are longer than single sentences. Natural speech involves elisions, phonological changes, intonation and tonal patterns, rhythmic patterns, morphophonemic changes, and discourse-dictated patterns. It is this type of language use that distinguishes oral communication from carefully learned speech and written language.

When using a tape recorder, record a text (e.g., a short story or stretch of connected speech), then go over it with your language consultant. Listen to the text for understanding of what is being spoken. In listening to natural speech, make it your goal to understand what is spoken without having to look up the meanings or follow your transcription of the recording.

Some use video cameras for language learning purposes. As you view and hear speakers using the language in its natural setting, you can learn the nonverbal data, the gestures, body language, and other extra-linguistic information that go along with using the language. Further, you can view people's lip and mouth movements in order to help you in mimicking sounds. While tape recordings are helpful, they do not capture all of the types of data that videos do.

In order to build your repertoire of words, begin to enter your data into a filing system on your computer. This is the beginning of a practical functional dictionary that you can consult when you need to.

Learning another language is hard work for the majority of us. It takes time and effort, and can be discouraging. It can also be exciting and exhilarating when you realize that you can understand, think in, and communicate through another language. It opens another worldview to you, another way of viewing life.

Keys to language learning are observing, listening, mimicking, practicing, communicating, and enjoying the language and the people who speak it.

7

The Ethnographic Record

Fieldnotes are an anthropologist's most sacred possession. They are personal property, part of a world of private memories and experiences, failures and successes, insecurities and indecisions. They are usually carefully tucked away in a safe place. To allow a colleague to examine them would be to open a Pandora's box. (Bond, in Sanjek 1990:273)

In fieldwork, begin keeping an ethnographic record early. The ethnographic record consists of anything that documents the culture in focus. This includes fieldnotes, photographs (pictures taken with a camera), pictures (includes photographs, as well as pictures drawn, painted, or sketched), artifacts, tape recordings, video tapes, written documents (books, letters, diaries, census and tax records, church registers, deeds, etc.), any cultural databases available, and anything else on that culture. This chapter will focus on fieldnotes, a cultural database for the management of ethnographic data, personal journals, and logs.

Some organized system for recording, managing, and retrieving the ethnographic data you collect needs to be developed. This will enable you to find information readily when you need it. For example, if you want to write a paper on the local medical system or on the interaction between local and cosmopolitan medical systems, those data should be readily available through the database management system you use. This avoids your having to search through piles of unorganized papers and notebooks to find what you want when you want it.

Types of cultural data files

First, as you collect cultural data, write it in a field data notebook. Next, transfer the relatively unorganized data from your data notebook into a systematic topical database.

Data notebooks

When you first collect data, enter them into bound hardback notebooks, or the locally available equivalent, such as exercise books of the kind used by local school children. Number each page within each notebook, and include a table of contents inside the front cover or an index at the end of the notebook. This can save time when you are looking for specific information by directing you to the place where the appropriate data are located. If you have several data notebooks, number each notebook.

The format for each entry in the data notebook should include the following:

1. Date and time;
2. Source of the information: e.g., name of individual(s) who provided the data, direct observation, an article or book (include relevant reference information), indirect observation as reported by some named individual, overheard text, etc.;
3. Place you collected the data;
4. Other information that might be significant to your specific research project (e.g., weather information, other relevant activities that are occurring at that time, etc.); and
5. Cultural data.

An example of a sample entry in a data notebook might look like example 1.

(1)   1/24/84
                                                                                                               Jos, Nigeria
                                                                                                               Adamu
                                                                                                               Informal interview

The position of District Head at Zangon was held first by a Hausa, then by an Atyap. No Bajju has held that position. Bajju have been struggling to obtain such a position since they understood its significance.

Take your data notebooks with you as you go out to collect data. If it is inappropriate to record the data on site or nearby, or if something significant happens when you have left your notebook home, you can enter your data soon after you get home. Alternatively, enter it directly onto the computer as soon as possible. Short term memories are limited; therefore, it is important that you write up your data on a daily basis so as not to forget important information.

A two-step process in recording field data is first writing CONDENSED NOTES and then EXPANDED NOTES. Spradley asserts that, "All notes taken during actual field observation represent a condensed version of what actually occurred. It is humanly impossible to write down everything that goes on or everything informants say. Condensed accounts often include phrases, single words, and unconnected sentences" (1980:69).

These condensed notes are also called SCRATCH NOTES. Condensed notes are written as soon as possible after collecting the data. From your condensed notes you then write expanded notes which fill in details and information that were not recorded on the spot.

When in a field situation, you should plan on spending time daily writing up your fieldnotes. This time becomes a regular part of your research day. This write-up consists of expanded notes which you transfer from your data notebooks into a topical database. While some researchers write expanded notes, then enter them into a topical database, it will save you time and effort to enter the expansion of your notes, categorized appropriately, directly into your database.

If you tape record data, you should plan to spend six to eight hours transcribing each hour of tape.

The woes of sketchy notes

One anthropologist, who realized that her time in a New Guinean village was very limited, wrote only sketchy notes so that she could write about more things while there. When she got to the capital the sketchy condensed notes were almost useless because her memory of their content had faded and many were indecipherable.

Transcriptions of recorded text can take place over several days since tapes preserve data better than most people's memories. Some fieldworkers not only tape record interviews with individuals when they are collecting data, but they also dictate their fieldnotes into a tape recorder. To do so would be particularly helpful when you come home tired after a full day of work and find that you have neither the time nor energy to enter the data on the computer that day. While tape recordings can be used appropriately, you will also want to have other means for keeping your notes. As much as possible, keep your data notebooks current.

Within fieldnotes specify the language you used, whether the national language, the trade language, the local language, related dialects, the investigator's language, or some form of amalgamated language that includes several of these languages. Further, be aware that when using social science terms in note taking, distinguish between what the respondent uses and social science vocabulary. For example, a man with two wives would likely refer to "my two wives," while within the social sciences the researcher would likely write that the man has a "polygynous marriage with two wives." As you take notes include folk terms that are used by the people themselves, and that may later be useful to you in your understanding of folk categorization of local knowledge. Realize that your early notes are likely made when you do not yet have a full understanding of what some of these terms mean, and you will later regret the loss of information if you record a mistranslation.

Quotations need to be written verbatim. Later you can use word-for-word quotations to add color and anecdotal data to your write-up. Data written verbatim with the speakers identified may prove to be useful in substantiating hypotheses, documenting data, and providing examples when writing up your research results.

You need to identify the speaker(s) in your data notebook and database. You can use initials of speakers to quickly identify them, different colored pens, or some other means for speakers' identification. If using initials, have a code table somewhere in your data that gives full names. Your key to speakers should probably be kept somewhere other than in your data notebook. If your research is on some sensitive topic, such as on the drug culture or corruption in government, use some encryption code to identify speakers. As such it makes the source of those data unavailable if by any chance the data were to fall into the wrong hands. Basically, it would serve to hide data (Bernard 1994:193), and, thus, protects the anonymity of your sources (see AAA Principle 1.A.1 in the statement of ethics).

From the condensed fieldnotes in your data notebook, next enter your expanded notes into a topical database.

Topical database

Most field researchers manage their data with computerized topical database management system (DBMS). A topical database consists of data filed in separate fields (categories) according to topic. You take relevant cultural data from your data notebooks, and file them according to some filing system.

Various DBMSs available may be used for handling ethnographic data. Any DBMS needs to allow for topical categorization of data, ready retrievability, and ease of use. Computer programmers continue to develop good DBMSs that you can examine in order to find a suitable one before commencing your field research.

One DBMS currently available for field linguistic and cultural research is SHOEBOX (see the appendix for information on obtaining SHOEBOX). It deals with six types of databases: anthropology notes, anthropology outline, lexicon, texts, grammar outline, and parse lexicon (Wimbish 1990:51). Besides providing a template for data entry, it helps in data analysis through organizing data, searching for key words, organizing references and specific examples, retrieving the data desired, etc. SHOEBOX can handle seven files at one time.

Computer hardware continues to be developed that has increased speed and memory and decreased power consumption. Computer price reductions occur continually, so delay final selection of both software and hardware until just before you desire to use them, in order to make use of state-of-the-art technology and programs. Learn how to use your computer and accompanying software before leaving for a field location since help may not be available there.

Database for cultural data. The most commonly used filing system for cultural data is the *Outline of Cultural Materials* (OCM) which is used in the Human Relations Area Files (HRAF) (Murdock et al. 1987). It is a pragmatic system of classification with some overlapping of categories. Further, inherently related categories are in the same section. The OCM system consists of a numbering code: it uses two digits for main topics, and three digits for subtopics under each main topic. An example of the OCM filing system of religious beliefs (from Murdock et al. 1987:ix) is shown in (2).

(2)   77 Religious Beliefs
                              771 General character of religion
                              772 Cosmology
                              773 Mythology
                              774 Animism
                              775 Eschatology
                              776 Spirits and gods
                              777 Luck and chance
                              778 Sacred objects and places
                              779 Theological systems

An alternative to the OCM filing system is to develop your own system that reflect topics important within the specific cultural context in which you work. Most fieldworkers, however, use what has already been developed and what has stood the test of time. This section uses the OCM category system.

If you are developing a lexical file in one field as part of your database, you may also enter cultural data by specifying the OCM reference number as another field within an entry, and the specific cultural data as a third field. This results in a database that can be used for various purposes.

A Jju entry to a database code is in (3). Each field is specified by a slash code. While this Jju entry is now dated in its format, nevertheless it includes the types of information that need to be entered into a topical database.

(3) Code for Jju database

          \j   Jju word, singular form
          \p   Jju word, plural form
          \e   English translation
          \h   Hausa translation
          \g   Grammatical category (specified as n - noun,
                      v - verb root, v, 2 - verb root of tone two: adj - adjective, etc.)
          \x   Example

\t	English translation of the example
\r	Reference number of OCM category
\a	Cultural data
\c	Compare, contrast
\s	Source (number and page of data notebook, text, book, etc.)

Sample entries using the slash codes specified in (3) appear in (4)–(6). Note that each noun has its noun class concord marker specified following the noun, a grammatical feature relevant to Jju and other Benue-Congo languages.

(4) Sample Jju database entry

\j	*gbap a*
\p	
\e	leprosy
\h	*kuturta*
\g	n
\x	*Antyok a shyyi bu gbap.*
\t	The man has leprosy.
\r	75 [OCM number for category "sickness"]
\a	Bajju refer to the first stage of leprosy in which white spots appear as *atanyrang* in the sufferer's presence. Literally, it translates as 'ringworm'. It is used euphemistically because the first stage of leprosy may be indistinguishable from ringworm. The second stage is *gbap*. This stage is manifested by the disease entering the patient's fingers.
\c	*atanyrang*, the first stage of leprosy
\s	Pastor Karik, 8/27/71, Data notebook 3, p. 5

(5)

\j	*kaWa ka*
\p	*naWa na*
\e1	abdomen
\e2	stomach
\e3	womb
\h1	*mahaifa* 'womb'
\h2	*ciki* 'stomach, abdomen'
\h3	*tumbi* 'stomach of a ruminant'
\g	n
\x	*Arembyring a shyyi bu kaWa.*
\t	The woman is pregnant.
\r	843 [OCM number for category "pregnancy"]
\a	During pregnancy a woman should refrain from eating sugar cane in order to keep her baby from gaining too much weight. Some courageous women give birth alone, though increasingly women give birth in hospitals.
\c	*diswak ti* 'pregnancy; satisfaction'
\s	Martha 9/15/83, Data notebook 3, p. 5

(6)   \j   *kwu*

       \p   *kwi*

       \e1   to die

       \e2   to be unconscious

       \e3   to faint

       \h1   *mutu* 'to die'

       \h2   *birkice* 'to become unconscious'

       \h3   *suma* 'to faint'

       \g   v, 2, 2

       \x   *A tsang a kwi.*

       \t   He is dying. / He is in a coma. / He fainted.

       \r   76 [OCM number for category "death"]

       \a   Traditionally, Bajju believed that no death was due to natural causes, other than perhaps the death of an old person. Death resulted from *nkut* or malevolent use of spiritual power. Therefore, they asked individuals within the extended family of the deceased to swear on the dirt of the grave that each was not the cause of this death. Bajju term this swearing *sswa mbyen*, literally, 'to drink the ground'.

       \c   *hywu* "sickness"

       \s   Shebayan 10/16/75, Data notebook 2, p. 11.

Later you can use this method of data entry as the basis for obtaining required data on specified topics. By using a retrieval feature of a DBMS you can specify which fields you desire. For example, specifying the fields \j (Jju), \e (English), \r (reference number for OCM), and \a (cultural data), results in a printout as shown in (7).

(7) Sample retrieval printout

> *gbap a* leprosy 75   The first stage of leprosy in which white spots appear. Bajju term *atanyrang*; the second stage is *gbap*. This stage is manifested by the disease entering the patient's fingers.

Typically, data you file under a cultural field are much more extensive than those filed under any other field within the database. Sometimes they are so extensive that they need to be divided into separate entries.

Database for dictionary construction. You can also use this type of database as the basis for dictionary construction. A dictionary can be monolingual, bilingual, or trilingual. For example, for a bilingual Jju-English dictionary select the following fields: \j, \p, \e, \g, \x, \t. The resultant dictionary example from (4) would be as in (8).

(8) Sample Jju-English dictionary printout

> *gbap a*; *gbap a*, pl.
>> leprosy. n. *Antyok a shyyi bu gbap.* 'The man has leprosy'.

You can use the computer to alphabetize entries according to which language you specify. For example, request the computer to alphabetize according to Jju, or English, or Hausa.

Coward and Grimes (1995) have produced a very helpful program and guide for making dictionaries. Features of this program are a bilingual or a trilingual format, a format for entering the national language and English, the option of single- or double-column format, the option of including or excluding sentences and working notes. It is useful particularly for your draft printouts, a reverse finderlist (e.g., Hausa-English and English-Hausa) and a sorting (alphabetizing) feature. Like the program SHOEBOX, the Multi-Dictionary Formatter provides a template for entering your data. It provides over 200 examples of possibilities for structuring your lexical data. Possibilities include glosses, definitions, homonyms, citation forms, subentries, multiple senses, example sentences, etc. It includes almost 100 field codes that you can select from and use where appropriate. A resource such as this is invaluable when you are working on a dictionary of a field language.

Database for grammatical analysis. You can also use your database for grammatical analysis. For example, you could print out all verbs with high tone, then place them in frames to check for accuracy of tonal transcription and analysis. You could also do this for nouns, adjectives, or any other part of speech.

Practical suggestions for developing a database. If you do not need a lexical field, as for example, when working either in your own language or in a trade language with an adequate dictionary available, then you would not need to include all of the above fields. For example, the \p, \x, \t, \g, \c fields could be omitted.

You need to decide the first language under which to file entries, your own or the target language. In my own research, I file according to the target language first. Frequently, there is no one-to-one translation of a local term. For example, the Jju word *kanak* translates into English rather awkwardly as a 'ritual mourning celebration'. The local term is shorter and easier to use in the field situation.

In managing your files, enter and save your data frequently, especially when working where the electricity source is erratic. After entering data, back up your entire lexical database on a diskette after every one of your significant work sessions or following entry of approximately fifty entries (Coward and Grimes 1995:5). Also, frequently send copies of your data home or to some other location outside your field research site. Events such as fires can destroy your data. Some good fieldnotes have disappeared downstream in canoes that got away. Others have disappeared in suitcases that never arrived. One fieldworker feels that some of her texts are probably at the bottom of the Atlantic Ocean—they never arrived home in the barrel she sent by ship. Two women fieldworkers watched as their thatched roof and house went up in flames, sparked by a bush fire that had been set to clear a field. They were fortunate to have moved their vehicle before it, too, went up in flames, though they lost the field data they had so carefully collected.

Coward and Grimes (1995:5) recommend that you make a hard copy of your full lexical database at least once per year. This is because field mishaps do occur. For example, lightening can fry your computer, despite your best efforts to guard against unpredictable power surges. Further, computer theft does happen. If you have a hard copy of your database, you can reenter your data and continue from there. Without a hard copy many months of valuable work may be lost.

Database reorganization

When you begin your fieldwork, you begin with one organizational structure in a specific database. As you go along, inevitably that database needs refinement and reorganization. When you find that you cannot do what you want to do with your database program, then perhaps it is time to reorganize that database.

You may find that a new more powerful database program has been developed since you did your initial fieldwork. If so, you may want to convert your data from its current program into the new database. Hopefully, the new database program will be able to read one of the formats in which the old database program can output data.

Journal or diary

In addition to keeping data notebooks and a topical database, most researchers also keep JOURNALS or field DIARIES that record the personal side of fieldwork. Here you can record your reactions to the social situation, your problems, your culture shock and stresses, the daily occurrences, and frustrations and joys. Journals focus on the ethnographic experience. They tend to be more contemplative and subjective, and they are often written when reflecting upon events without the pressure of taking things down quickly as when making entries in field data notebooks. Journals or diaries help researchers deal with loneliness, fear, and other emotions that occur in fieldwork. They chronicle what researchers feel and how they perceive the situation. They reflect our common human frailties, self-doubts, and fieldwork moods.

Glimpses into the cultural activities of the fieldwork experience emerge in journal entries. As such they are independent cultural activities that record the culture of fieldwork. Fieldwork can be an intense experience that changes cultural researchers in significant ways. You are not quite the same again. Usually, fieldwork expands your perspective, thus allowing you to see your own culture differently and more objectively.

Journals may be cathartic for you, in that writing down your problems, frustrations, personal psychological crises, etc., enables you to continue research. They allow you to "let off steam" in a benign way. For example, the intensely personal diary of Malinowski (1967), an early Polish ethnographer who studied people on the Trobriand Islands, served this purpose. In it we learn of Malinowski's human side, his egocentrism, his feelings towards the Trobriand Islanders and other expatriates. He kept it as a means of self-analysis, and it provides fascinating reading. Just as Malinowski used his journal for self-analysis, you can, too. When reading through your journal, you can see things that really bother you or things you can face directly, and then perhaps find solutions to.

Journals can be useful in several ways. For example, they may later serve as the basis of novels, short stories, personal essays, or even autobiographies about the field situation. Or if you choose to write up your results within a self-reflexive post-modern framework, journals place you within that situation and are, thus, invaluable for writing your research results. They may help you reconstruct the process by which you came to a gradual understanding of some cultural theme that eluded you at first.

Since journals are a kind of data notebook, they need some organization such as date and place for each entry. Further, include page and book numbering, and an index or table of contents.

Some anthropologists combine what they write in their data notebook with journal-like entries. Keeping a number of separate notebooks and files can become too time consuming and cumbersome for some fieldworkers. They prefer to enter one type of record that combines the functions of both data notebooks and the personal side that is usually written in a journal. I keep these two separate in my own fieldwork. One's data notebooks should be such that if another fieldworker reads them, that person will learn about the culture you are studying, not about your reactions to it.

Log

A LOG gives a running account of how you spend your time. Some keep a separate log for expenditures. You can prepare a log in advance, with a proposed time schedule on one side of a notebook page and room for recording what you actually do on the other, or with a proposed budget on one side and actual expenditures on the other.

Suggestions for collecting ethnographic data

Some suggestions for collecting ethnographic data include recording data as soon as possible after arriving at your research site. This is the time when you will find the local behavior patterns fresh, striking, and new. Furthermore, you need to take advantage of recording data on occurrences of some events which may occur infrequently. When first there, you may not know whether some event occurs rarely or not, so begin recording data right away.

If you find out that a special event will occur soon, ask your research assistant or other local person about it beforehand, then go, participate and observe, and write fieldnotes

---

Bajju chieftaincy celebrations

Bajju have two chieftaincy celebrations: one occurs at the installation of a chief soon after he has been selected, and the other occurs approximately one year after his installation. The second celebration takes place when he is firmly in power, and far surpasses the initial celebration. Since Bajju chiefs usually hold their chieftaincy positions for life, we collected data when a chieftaincy celebration occurred.

Approximately four months after we moved into our village home, the village of Kamrum, which is located approximately five miles away, announced the second celebration for their chief. We asked our language assistant what would occur. He told us that on the evening before the festivities the chief would take a goat to give to his mother to thank her for her contribution to his ascendancy. The next day people would bring gifts, eat, drink, dance, and congratulate the new chief.

When the day arrived, we took our tape recorder and camera along to record the festivities. When I first arrived, our close neighbor took me by the hand to show me her gift to the new chief. We also greeted the new chief and congratulated him on his ascendancy.

People were dancing in every compound in that village. For the first time we saw the animal horns that men blow, accompanied by drums. We tape recorded their music, took photos of dancing, ate, and interacted with people in the crowd.

Soon after arriving home, I wrote up what had occurred. The next day I went over those notes with our language assistant, who added substantially to my notes.

---

when it is appropriate. Go over your observations with your research assistant or a knowledgeable person afterwards.

In the example in the following box, if we had simply recorded what we saw happen at that celebration, we would have missed the important event of the chief thanking his mother with a goat on the evening before the celebration.

Another important data collection technique involves CROSS-CHECKING the data with more than one source. Some refer to this field method of data validation as TRIANGULATION (Fetterman 1989:89). Cross-checking should involve persons of both genders and of different age groups.

Practical considerations

Practical considerations about keeping an ethnographic record include consideration of when to write your fieldnotes. Do you write them while interviewing people or do you wait until you are away from the interviewee? The answer to this depends on a number of variables. For example, in some instances people want to be sure that you write your notes accurately. When that is the case, write your notes when interviewing. In other instances it is more appropriate to wait. You need to be sensitive to the appropriate time to write fieldnotes.

Another practical consideration is the time-consuming nature of entering detailed notes into your computer. You may come home late and be ready to eat and go to bed. Entering fieldnotes may not be an option in such instances. Consequently, you end up with fragmentary notes, or worse, notes that are unwritten, the "headnotes" that Ottenberg speaks of (Ottenberg 1990:144–46). If it is at all possible, enter your notes into the DBMS the same day you collect them. However, do not use the time you could spend with people developing good interpersonal relations to do your data entry. People are more important.

Making "scratch" notes or severely condensed notes can be problematic. They may be so abbreviated that even you cannot figure out what you were trying to describe.

The interaction between the facts of what occurred in the field and our interpretation of those facts can be problematic. Certainly, we need to be aware of the grid or framework through which we view what we observe. Our fieldnotes tend to become a record as much of our interpretation of events as records of what actually occurred. As such, they are an independent text that can be analyzed from that perspective.

Use of your fieldnotes by others

When you have worked hard at compiling an accurate record of the culture in your fieldnotes, you may find that others would like to have access to your data. Be aware that when you are collecting data, your fieldnotes are not copyrighted. The implication of this is that prior to your writing up papers, reports, and books that are copyrighted, others who have access to your fieldnotes can use the material in them for their own purposes. Unfortunately, this type of unscrupulous activity does occur within the politics of fieldwork. At times it is the power elites of the country who want access to your data for their own purposes. Most often it is other scholars who may not have done the solid fieldwork that you have and who may find that use of your data gets them ahead academically.

The stories of problems along these lines are myriad. One fieldworker shared with another scholar her findings on local medical practitioners. She reacted strongly to his betrayal of trust when she walked into a session at an anthropological meeting where he was reading a paper based on her research.

Obbo summarizes some of the potential problems as follows:

The concern over who should have access to fieldnotes is an ethical problem for all anthropologists. Once others read them, the uses made of fieldnotes are no longer controllable by the ethnographer. The problem is threefold. First, in the cutthroat, publish-or-perish climate of academia, some scholars may be ruthless in using someone else's fieldnotes to advance their own careers; others, fearing the worst, may worry unduly about protecting their work. However, considerations of self-protection in relation to fieldnotes are important, especially in the early stages of one's academic career. After all, fieldnotes are not copyrighted. Second, anthropologists increasingly work in settings where the people studied can read what is written about them. Even when pseudonyms are used in publications, communities and informants are often identifiable in fieldnotes. An indiscreet reader of others' fieldnotes may put fieldworkers or their sources in trouble by revealing the names of informants, especially in connection with unsavory activities or the confidential revelation of community "secrets." Third, where economic reprisal or political danger is an issue, anthropologists have a duty to protect their informants, particularly when working in countries with fascist or other sorts of authoritarian regimes. (Obbo 1990:290–91)

These cautions are included to make you aware of possible problems with others using your fieldnotes. You need not, however, become paranoid about this problem. For example, if you are a co-author with another scholar on a publication, then you do need to work together. This may well mean that that individual has access to your fieldnotes.

There are other instances where fieldworkers have made use of other's fieldnotes that have served useful purposes. For example, scholars, who do follow-up research in the same area years after the original research was conducted, have profitably made use of other's fieldnotes (e.g., Lutkehaus (1990) who made use of Wedgwood's notes from fifty years previously and also letters from Malinowski). Scholars need to obtain permission to use those fieldnotes from that individual or from whatever institutions or relatives have them. Such use can be helpful in studying diachronic culture change.

Uses of an ethnographic record

The data collected within data notebooks are usually nonquantifiable data, data that are useful for providing basic background information and illustrations. These data are often seen as "soft" data rather than "hard" or objective quantifiable data.

An ethical dilemma

During fieldwork, I encountered local intellectuals who strongly requested access to my fieldnotes. One person told me that if I did not let him read my fieldnotes he would be my greatest critic. Since I felt this was a form of intimidation or blackmail and it violated academic freedom, I refused. In another instance I did let a person have access to some of my fieldnotes. From the reactions I received, I regretted having done so because individual notes were misunderstood when they were not put into the context of the total project. When my final write-up was finished, I provided that person with a copy of it. Until today I find myself wondering how I could have handled those two encounters in a more positive way. Fieldnotes are a private record of our interacting with the culture. They are resources that are not intended for publication and public perusal. Yet I can well understand these two persons' concerns. This was material from their culture, and they wanted to be sure that it was not being distorted by an outsider. I needed wisdom to balance these ethical issues.

Write your research results from your ethnographic record. They provide the resource for you that includes both what is in your short-term memory as well as what is in your long-term memory. Without a written record, most of us would be lost because our long-term memories usually do not retain all that is important for write-ups of data.

Fieldnotes provide an archive of what occurred during your field research. They can provide a baseline for further research at a later date when you might want to study some area of culture change which has occurred.

Summary

This chapter focused on the mechanical side of keeping an ethnographic record, specifically through use of data notebooks, a topical DBMS, a journal or diary, and a log. Each helps make data retrievable and easily accessible. It also included a caution concerning who should have access to your fieldnotes.

A key research method for collecting data that goes into your fieldnotes is the use of informal interviews, namely talking with people. The following chapter addresses this topic.

8

Informal Interviews

After hearing me speak about early Bajju history, Tom looked incredulously at me, and asked, "How do you know all that?"

In response to this question, I responded that I had interviewed elderly Bajju. It is very difficult, if not impossible, to gain an emic perspective of another culture that has no tradition of written history without conducting informal interviews. In the above question I was dealing with the ethnohistory of this society.

Interviewing is an essential part of any fieldwork when you are collecting cultural data. Participant observation and interviewing are probably the most widely used field research methods for collecting cultural data. Interviewing involves talking with people about any topic out of a whole range of possible topics. Since the majority of culture is encoded in language, you cannot simply observe what is going on, you must also talk with people. You can also conduct follow-up interviews on an event or on a ritual you observed. You can ask for help in exegeting a text.

There are two basic types of informal interviews: nondirective and directive (Crane and Angrosino 1992:18). A NONDIRECTIVE INTERVIEW refers to asking a person for general information about some aspect of the culture. In it the speaker is allowed to respond to your open-ended questions as he or she thinks appropriate. The nondirective interviews are used early in your field research, and their use continues throughout your field project. In a DIRECTIVE INTERVIEW you narrow the questioning to some topic of specific interest to your research project and ask for more focused information.

When beginning an interview, recognize that building a relationship is more important than obtaining the information you want. Once that relationship is established, collecting data is not a problem.

When conducting informal interviews, do so at a time convenient for your interviewee. Be prepared to postpone if necessary, even when you think that you have made prior arrangements for a particular interview. Unforeseen things do come up, both for you and for the person you have arranged to interview. The place of the interview can be your house, their home, or some neutral place.

Participant observation and interviews

In cultural fieldwork, interviews are not isolated from the total fieldwork experience which includes participant observation. Interviews supplement and expand the knowledge you obtain through interaction with members of the research community. It is important to do adequate participant observation in conjunction with conducting interviews. Study the community, including its social cleavages; Cumming and Cumming found this out in their research on a mental health education program:

> Other conditions could have been made evident only by more thorough advance investigation of the community. Had such a study been made we would have been aware, for instance, that the town was divided rather sharply into a low education group, which included the Metis minority, a middle and upper educational group. We would have learned in advance that there were two segments within the educated group—"joiners," who made up the membership of most of the town's 70 organizations, and those who admired the puritan virtues and stood apart from most organizations other than the Protestant churches. (Cumming and Cumming 1955:65)

The establishment of a trust relationship is essential for interviewing. The interview process is a complex social process, and the data collected depend on how well you handle that process.

Learn to ask questions that are culturally sensitive. In order to do so, listen and observe well before asking questions. For example, in a Western context questions about the personal wealth of an individual are inappropriate; however, in a Chinese context this is one of the first questions asked. In a Latin context asking about whether or not a person is married is often inappropriate. Rather allow this type of information to emerge naturally without focusing on it. By listening to what people ask each other you can learn what questions are culturally appropriate and which are not.

Social norms in interviews

In preparing for interviews learn some of the social norms for interacting with members of the research community. In the example in the box one student found that knowledge of social space helped.

When an American goes to another person's house for a specific reason or purpose, it is business first, then social conversation. In many cultures the opposite is true. You build the relationship first, then attend to business. Hence, interviews cannot be rushed. You may have to spend perhaps an hour or even several interviews before trust has been established. Once that trust relationship has been established, you will find that your research can proceed.

Social norms are not universal, nor are they static. As an important starting point, read what others have written about social conventions in the same or a related culture area. Take an area course or courses before beginning your field assignment to provide essential guidance towards your acquiring basic knowledge of a culture that is new to you. That knowledge can help you in developing good interpersonal relations. When you are in the field, begin to operate within the cultural framework of the research community; not to do so makes you irrelevant and possibly offensive in that social context. Henige notes that,

> **Use of space**
>
> When eliciting linguistic data from an elderly Choctaw speaker, one student had trouble hearing what his language assistant said, so he moved closer. The closer he moved, the softer the speaker spoke. Realizing this, I told the student to move back; he was violating the Choctaw speaker's space. When the student did so, he found that he could hear what was being said!

> This process will not be an easy one...and it will proceed in fits and starts, even if the "alienness" of the historian [or cultural fieldworker] is at an irreducibly low level. He will commit many a blunder, experience many embarrassing moments, antagonize some informants, and end up the butt of many tall tales. Yet the adaptive process need not occur only through bitter experience. One way to limit the incidence of bad moments, cross-talking, and unnecessary misunderstandings is to ply local scholars with many questions about how best to gain the rudiments of social expertise, if only to learn what kinds of social behavior are not acceptable. (Henige 1982:42)

Violation of social norms can lead to significant problems: "Breaches of local conventions—offering cash payments instead of hospitality, not observing other forms of local protocol, failing to display acceptable dining etiquette—can easily lead to reticence, lack of interest, or silent hostility" (p. 43). Do observe the social conventions that are part of interacting with people. These include serving something such as a beverage, food, or kola nuts as part of practicing hospitality.

Interviews on sensitive topics

While the majority of questions you ask may cause your respondent no problems, there may be some sensitive topics, such as economic status, borrowing and lending money, savings, assets, profits, criminal activities, and sexual practices that may cause your respondent difficulties when discussing them in a public setting. Conduct these types of interviews in private settings. This will help them be more candid with you.

When conducting field research in India, Heyer was surprised about how much was in the public domain in areas she felt were sensitive topics. She states,

> Even topics that I expected would be private—credit, dowry gold, etc.—were quite readily discussed in the presence of others. It is important to discover what is and is not in the public domain. This itself is very culturally specific....

> Privacy, or lack of privacy, in Indian villages, is very much a matter of location and class. Among the elite, onlookers would be close kin, or neighbours who were also members of the elite. Among the poor, onlookers were rarely a difficulty: most people were simply too busy to listen in. (Heyer 1993:210)

Use of local terms to guide interviews

You often need to provide some guidance concerning what data you desire in interviews. It is helpful to use open-ended questions that are organized around specific themes. You can begin with various local terms or themes, but be sure to maintain a sensitivity to other directions of inquiry as they arise. The example in the box illustrates the direction of some of my research on local religious structure and Bajju adoption of Christianity.

In doing research on a particular topic, list the areas you want to explore. For example, Hill (1988:insert)

Mining cultural data

Using a list of terms from the local religion that I had collected previously, I conducted interviews with both men and women. I asked each about the same terms. I reasoned that when people began repeating what others had said, I would understand the meaning of each term sufficiently. To my amazement, throughout the research period people rarely repeated what others had said! I felt like there was a mine of cultural data to be explored.

suggests that Bible translators need to investigate terms such as demon, evil spirit, ghost, sin, sacrifice, offering, spirit (of a person), soul, body, shadow or silhouette or *le double*, genies, sorcerer, the power of sorcery, *guerisseur* (healer), diviner, medium or seer *(devin)*, and *amulette* or *gris gris* (amulet, charm). Also, investigate terms necessary for translation of the Christian scriptures such as Satan, devil, God, Jesus, Holy Spirit, angel, and sin.

After deciding on the content for interviews, next decide on whom to interview. In general, adults of all ages and economic levels need to be included, as well as members of various social and political groups and social classes/castes. Interviewees need to include both literate and illiterate members of the community, and both men and women. Include key individuals, specialists in various domains of knowledge.

> ### A local expert
>
> In studying the Baranzan migration narrative about the founding of Bajju villages and the entire ethnic group, each person we asked said that if we really wanted to know about Baranzan, the Bajju apical ancestor and his sons, we needed to interview Jatau. So with tape recorder in hand and our language assistant along, Norris interviewed Jatau, a Bajju elder. Jatau answered all his questions about the founding of Bajju villages, including about the founders of Sokwak who allegedly emerged from a termite mound!

Types of interviews

Local experts

In any culture there are local experts, traditionally called KEY INFORMANTS, who are specialists in certain areas of knowledge. Key informant interviewing is used to best advantage when it integrates closely with participant observation (Pelto and Pelto 1978:74). By engaging in participant observation you identify individuals to interview who have special knowledge. Seek out such individuals for interviewing. See the upper box for an example.

If you are studying a special event, interview individuals shortly before, during, or afterwards. You will likely find that they may be willing to talk and will remember relevant details more readily than if interviewed later.

Sometimes researchers interview key individuals repeatedly. When gathering data from the same individual over a period of time, ask questions on a particular topic at different times and in different ways to check on the accuracy and consistency of the data obtained. If the data differ, this may be for various reasons, including the fact that the emphasis of the oral history may change depending upon present political alignments or the desired emphasis of the teller. (See lower box for an example.)

Be aware that good cultural research usually involves information collected from interviewing more than one person. If you are engaged in salvage anthropology and if there is only one individual left from the ethnic group, then by all means interview that individual. In most research situations, however, you should base your research on interviews with more than one individual.

> ### A politically correct narrative change
>
> When we were collecting the Baranzan narrative concerning the founding of the Bajju, one man stated that there are lots of different Baranzan narratives around. For example, at one point some Bajju said that in migrating from the Jos Plateau, Baranzan stopped at an Atyap village; however, when Bajju relations with the Atyap were at a low point, oral historians conveniently changed the Baranzan narrative, leaving out the Atyap stop.

You may have the opportunity to interview key individuals only once or only very occasionally. Data that these individuals provide will likely give you direction for further research.

When interviewing local experts, if possible tape record and/or videotape the interviews, then transcribe them with your regular language or cultural assistant. In that way, not only do you have the information gained in the interviews themselves, but you also benefit from the comments of your cultural assistant. (See the following box for an example.)

Ring on her fourth toe

When in church one day, Norris noticed an elderly woman with a brass ring on the fourth toe of her right foot. He asked our regular language assistant about her. Who was she? Why did she wear that ring? Our language assistant said that she had been an *abvok*, a diviner, who had recently converted to Christianity. Further, he said that she had had twelve husbands and had been married into most of the villages around there.

Wanting to understand the work of an *abvok*, one evening we took our tape recorder, went with our language assistant to the elderly woman's compound, and asked her to tell us about her former work. Though hesitant to do so, she spent a couple of hours sharing with us.

Later, with the help of our language assistant, we transcribed and translated the recorded interview; then we asked him for explanations of some of what the *abvok* had said, including further expansions about key folk terms.

Specialized areas of information where you will need to talk to key experts include such topics as medical beliefs and practices (e.g., doctors, nurses, midwives, herbalists, pharmacists), history, craft specialists (e.g., blacksmiths, weavers, carvers, mechanics, carpenters), religion (e.g., shamans, diviners, pastors, *imams*), and law (see an example in the side box). These are suggestive only. Look for areas that require specialized knowledge and interview the relevant experts.

Men and women

Traditional medical expert

When a Canadian doctor asked about traditional medical practices to help him treat his Bajju patients, we talked with a local herbalist. This herbalist described remedies for each illness we inquired about. He typically began his description of remedies by stating, "*Dikan ən shyi!*" (There is medicine!)

Researchers have often concentrated on interviewing only men, the leaders within most societies. Their failure to interview women has skewed data. Henige addresses this issue:

> A particularly important oversight in collecting oral data has been the ignoring of women as sources. Unless researchers have been interested in a topic that happens to be relevant to the experience of women (say, the institution of the Queen Mother, women traders, or women's secret societies), they seem to have disregarded them as useful informants, presuming them to be uninterested in and unaware of larger questions relating to political or economic change or structural patterns....In some societies, of course, women are expected to dwell

in seclusion, so that male researchers have not been able to consult them even when they wished to. (1982:48)

Even when the society studied appears to be dominated by males both structurally and genea-logically, women often play more significant roles than is obvious from a surface investigation. Fur-ther, when collecting kinship data, women tend to be better sources of information than men, though this is culture specific. In some cultures it is the men who are the experts in genealogies. Check on who are the kinship experts, whether men or women.

Group interviews

Group interviews can serve useful purposes. In the context of a group interview, alternative view-points can be expressed, including those of both men and women. Sometimes a group interview brings out the pooled wisdom of a number of indi-viduals focused on the topic in question. For ex-ample, if you are investigating local terms in a particular semantic domain, the combined knowl-edge of the group may result in more clearly de-fining those terms than might be possible with a single individual.

Differing perspectives

When I was studying the men's tra-ditional ancestral organization, men said that its primary functions were (1) initiating young men and (2) keeping women and uninitiated children under control. To that end all initiates had to swear that they would not reveal the secrets of the organization to the un-initiated. Some Bajju men view this or-ganization as a men's club, similar to a fraternal society in the US.

When interviewing elderly women about this organization, they spoke of the real fear they had felt when they heard the sound of the ancestral spirits produced by men of the organization. Their fear was so great that at times they would literally shake. They spoke of being beaten for alleged transgres-sions. Their perception of this organi-zation clearly differed from that of men.

Concerning group interviews Pratt and Loizos state:

> It will be almost impossible to hold a group interview using closed questions. The aim of group interviews in part will be to encourage a collective response and to identify differences of opinion as well as areas of consensus within the group. A group interview is less likely to be successful where the members of the group are not reasonably homogeneous, as they will be inhibited and feel uncomfortable with each other if they are aware of major differences of status, class, or gender perspectives amongst them. The group interview can be a valu-able way of quickly establishing some basic common ground, information and questions for future investigation. (1992:55)

Group interviews have limitations. For example, dominant individuals tend to monopo-lize the discussion while quiet reticent persons are apt to contribute little. Social cleavages may be evident in a group interview situation that would be absent in an individual inter-view. Further, groups tend to work towards consensus in discussing an issue. The result may be that the lowest common denominator, what all agree on, comes out of a group in-terview. This homogenization of opinion may fail to allow divergent opinions to emerge. The results of group interviews provide a "public" view of what those interviewed want an outsider to know. In sum, with full recognition that there are problems inherent in using group interviews, they can be used purposefully in research in order to obtain desired information.

When you are interviewing one individual, you may find yourself in the midst of a group, as noted in the example in the side box.

Sometimes it is helpful to begin field research with a group interview followed by private sessions. Henige states, "the greatest benefit from beginning the research programme with a few group interviews and following them with private sessions is that this allows for some interesting and useful diagnosis and comparison. Knowing what certain informants say (or do not say) in company and how this differs from what they say privately can be illuminating, if sometimes disconcerting" (1982:51).

> ### Interview with an individual in the midst of a group
>
> When I was administering an interview schedule, children and other adults in the village tended to gather around to listen to the questions and answers. I remember feeling apologetic about disturbing one woman who was pounding grain to make supper; I told her that my questions would take only a short time. At the end of the interview I was glad that she could then continue pounding. When I moved on to interview at the next compound, however, she followed and enjoyed listening. I was the best show around!

Motives of interviewees

Individuals have their own perspectives, motives or agendas, and interpretations of topics under discussion in the interview situation. For these reasons, the reliability of data improves as they are cross-checked with several individuals.

When collecting data on disputes or local social cleavages, interview individuals who hold different perspectives, such as people from each faction and neutral observers. For example, Mansen (1988), who studied dispute settlements among the Guajiro in Colombia and Venezuela, collected case study data from individuals on each side of disputes, as well as from intermediaries, important individuals in any Guajiro conflict resolution. He found that intermediaries gain considerable status through effective conflict resolution.

Lying

One issue that cultural researchers encounter occasionally is lying on the part of respondents. Both Salamone (1977) and Freilich (1970) have investigated this issue. Freilich developed a typology of lies, including personal, social, and cultural lies.

Salamone points out that by cross-checking, you may be able to determine when you have received false data. If you determine that you have received false data, examine the context and process the lie. This examination expands your picture of social roles and norms. It also lets you gain information about your own standing with the cultural respondent. Salamone suggests that researchers view lies as a form of communication.

Reasons for lying include avoiding self-incrimination, shame, or losing face. People may give diplomatic answers rather than true answers. For example, in some cultures people are constrained by their culture from saying "no" or "I don't know"; to do so may be rude, or it may make them "lose face" by their not having the information requested.

Lying can be related to the type of questions you ask. In relating to others in that type of situation, you learn to phrase questions differently than you would in your mother tongue. For example, instead of asking a question such as, "Will you come to my house on Friday for dinner?" and receiving a "yes" response when the individual means "no" but is culturally constrained from so responding, you could ask, "Will you be able to come to my house on Friday for dinner or would some other time be better?" With the second question, the respondent may save face by not having to say "no" while still telling the truth. Learn to ask questions that are culturally appropriate. By asking inappropriate questions you may leave the respondent no option or leeway but to lie.

In many cultures people are anxious to please you; if that is the case, responses they give to your questions may have less to do with the truth than with maintaining good interpersonal relations and pleasing you. A hypothetical situation that one might encounter is the following: You are walking down the sidewalk, then stop to ask someone if you are going the right direction to the market by continuing to go the way you are walking. In some cultures the response would be "yes" even if the market is in the opposite direction. Pleasing the questioner is of key importance. While the respondent is not deliberately seeking to deceive, culturally he may be constrained to do so. That which is deliberate falsehood in one culture may be a culturally appropriate means of maintaining smooth interpersonal relations in another culture.

In order to arrive at a true answer in situations where politeness and protocol require a response that may not accurately reflect the truth, learn to ask several specific questions that will enable you to obtain the data you need to function. For example, suppose you are in an Asian context when working with a secretarial assistant who is entering your fieldnotes on a computer, and you request that the entering be completed by the next day. The assistant will likely reply that the notes will be ready by then. It can be frustrating to find that they are not ready when requested. Rather, when first inquiring of this assistant ask multiple questions so that gradually you can obtain the specific information desired. Questions you might ask include: "Can you have these notes ready tomorrow or would sometime within the next couple days be better? When can you be here to enter them? Can you give time to entering them today or would sometime within the next few days be better?"

Another aspect of the question of lying is what is a lie for you and what is a lie for those of the host culture. From a Westerner's perspective a lie is something said that involves false information with the intent to deceive. In some cultures the concept of shame may more accurately cover what Westerners term a lie. Giving false information becomes a source of shame only if it is discovered. This view of lying relates to other acts such as stealing. For example, in such a culture, "stealing would be the *discovered* act of taking something unlawfully" (Egner 1995:64). Egner found that some Africans she dealt with applied the term "lie" to false information; the concept of losing face or feeling shame would more accurately correspond to the Western concept of "lying" which includes both false information and the intent to deceive.

As discussed, SHAME relates to lying. Shame refers to the embarrassment and distress that an individual may experience based on the discovery by others of what the person has done. It results from strong negative external factors, and can serve as a means of social control. Some contrast shame cultures with guilt cultures, though such a contrast must be based on a preponderance of tendencies one way or the other since it is likely that they are not mutually exclusive. GUILT refers to the distress over one's actions based on moral standards that have been internalized. It relates to concepts of right and wrong. Be aware that you may encounter these two orientations within your fieldwork. When that is the case, work hard at not causing others to feel shamed.

Key questions

Investigate various cultural domains through use of key questions. These questions will initially focus on who are the participants, what is occurring, where, when, frequency of occurrence, why, and how. Gradually, the questions become more focused on specifics of the cultural domain.

Types of interviews

Types of interviews include ones that focus on an overview of what is occurring within a specific situation, detailed exploration of particular topics, requests for examples and illustrations, experience interviews in which you ask about people's direct involvement and experiences, and investigation into culturally appropriate terms, concepts, and phrases (Jorgensen 1989:86).

Research colleagues

Research colleagues are essential for conducting field research. Some are best characterized as language assistants when their primary work is helping you learn and analyze the local dialect. Others become quite skilled in helping with collecting cultural data and serve as cultural assistants. (See the following example.)

> ### Two valued research colleagues
>
> When collecting data for my dissertation on religious change, I had two primary research colleagues. Sam was a graduate student at a local seminary whose principal assigned him to work alongside me because his thesis was on a topic similar to mine. Sam, as a Bajju, knew whom we should interview. Together we rode on his battered sputtering motorcycle along bush paths to interview key individuals. Without Sam's assistance, I would not have as readily found those important individuals for interviewing as I did with him.
>
> Haruna was my second research colleague. When my family and I lived at Unguwar Rimi, Haruna lived a few miles further into the bush along the dirt road that went past our compound. We had watched Haruna grow up. By the time of this research he had received a university degree in psychology, and consequently, he readily understood the nature of my research and entered into it vigorously.

Freeman describes his relationship with and training of his local colleague as follows:

> I thought Hari had the potential to do the job I needed done. Accordingly, for several months I carefully trained him to conduct interviews among the people of his own caste, most of whom trusted him and readily confided in him in my presence. We conducted all interviews jointly. He became sensitive to the kinds of questions I asked. He learned to translate literally, to self-consciously examine ways in which he might have selectively screened or omitted information. He learned to explain to the villagers carefully and in detail what we intended to do with the information we collected, and to inform me about those households from which he could not gather information [that of his father-in-law where there was an avoidance relationship, and that of his father's cousin with whom he was feuding]. By narrating his own life history to me, Hari learned how to collect the life histories of others.
>
> Hari's most difficult adjustment had come when I told him that he would have to abandon his accustomed role as a leader because such a person often prompts people to give answers that they think will please an authority figure.

He had at first enthusiastically tried to extract information from the people of
his caste whether or not they were willing. "They are my neighbors," he said,
"they *must* tell you the truth." Later, when Muli [an untouchable] omitted details, Hari said: "We are paying him; he must tell what he knows." I insisted
that Hari never order people to divulge information, but rather that he respect
their right to offer or withhold it as they pleased. With practice he learned to
do this, as well as to ask questions unexpected of persons in authority roles,
such as his questioning of Muli's praise of Brahmans. (Freeman 1979:21–22)

While ethnographic fieldwork has often been done by solitary researchers together with
their research assistants, increasingly it is done as a team effort. Who is on the team depends upon the focus of the research. For example, it may include a linguist, an anthropological agronomist, an economist, and a medical anthropologist.

While you obtain qualitative cultural data through informal interviews, often you need to
quantify your results through use of structured interviews—the topic of the next chapter.

9

Structured Interviews:
Beyond Impressions and Anecdotes

A number of questions arise during fieldwork that are rarely considered by texts or courses on fieldwork methodology. Finding the right balance between 'numberical' (quantitative) and 'anecdotal' (qualitative) data is one such issue. (Devereux and Hoddinott 1993:35)

A primary goal of ethnographic field research is data collection with a mix of qualitative and quantitative data. By including both in your research you not only have a strong impression from observations that something is true, but you also have the quantitative data that substantiate your hypothesis. From Richards (1939) onwards, quantitative analysis has been important in ethnographic field research; she quantified her data in the areas of marriage, divorce, and labor migration. She used systematic village censuses as a primary data collection method.

Much quantitative data can be collected through observation rather than through interviews. For example, you can count children, herds, measure the sizes of fields and/or houses, or of specific parts of a house (e.g., the kitchen or outbuildings), and the number of people in a relatively small village. It is through such basic ethnographic field methods as counting and measuring that you gain significant information about the people and aspects of their culture. Some of these data can then be analyzed through statistical means. Given the importance of counting and measuring, you gain much through use of a survey instrument.

Collecting ethnographic data through structured interviews allows you to quantify them. Structured interviews help you collect a small amount of data from a potentially large population. This chapter discusses means of collecting quantitative data through use of structured formal interviews utilizing research instruments such as questionnaires and interview schedules.

Use of a survey instrument rests on certain assumptions: (1) that accurate data can be obtained through self-reporting by respondents, (2) that respondents will be honest and accurate in answering your questions, (3) that you can use a research instrument to accurately gather the data you seek, and (4) that you can analyze the data you collect. If you are unable to analyze them, it is better not to waste people's time questioning them. If you find that any of these basic assumptions raises questions, it would be well to think through and evaluate whether or not you should use this means of gathering data. Lastly, investigate and have a good idea about what statistics you plan to use before putting effort into setting up interviews. Doing so will help in formulating questions so that they do indeed test the hypotheses you are working on.

In a structured formal interview, use a research instrument such as a questionnaire or an interview schedule in order to collect data systematically and quickly. A QUESTIONNAIRE is a form with a set of questions that respondents fill out. With an INTERVIEW SCHEDULE, also a set of questions, you interview and record the responses you receive from an interviewee. Use of either an interview schedule or questionnaire involves (1) constructing the questionnaire/interview schedule, (2) testing it, (3) revising the research instrument in light of testing results, (4) selecting the sample and avoiding possible data bias, and (5) administering it. Each of these topics is discussed in this chapter. Other topics relevant to formal interviews are then discussed including a suggested minimum census database. The question, "Is a census feasible?" is also discussed. (See Marshall and Rossman 1989 for further direction in design of qualitative research.)

Participant observation, a prerequisite

Participant observation is a prerequisite to use of an interview schedule or questionnaire. This enables you to know what questions are culturally appropriate and what issues are inappropriate. It allows you to use your fieldwork in order to generate questions to include on the instrument.

An example of participant observation as a prerequisite for administering a survey comes from True and True (1977), who studied drug use in San Jose, Costa Rica.

> Confidentiality was only one of the factors figuring into the reciprocal relationships that enabled data collection. The researchers also gave of their time. They became full participants in the social life of their contacts. They visited in homes and became involved in family activities. They spent time in conversations on the street corner, in bars and cafes, and in workplaces. They participated in recreational outings, community activities, and soccer games, often being the ones providing transportation. (quoted from Marshall and Rossman 1989:70)

Interview schedule or questionnaire?

There are advantages to the use of either an interview schedule or a questionnaire. When working with a population that is illiterate, semiliterate, or a mix of literate and illiterate respondents, an interview schedule is the research instrument of choice. Further, use of an interview schedule is preferable where people feel that there is one right answer to each question. If you pass out a questionnaire in a culture where people feel that there is one right answer, a group will likely sit around discussing each question in order to arrive at an agreed upon "correct" answer. This is not appropriate when seeking to sample individual opinions.

A questionnaire is useful when working with a literate population. It has the following advantages:

1. Saves money. You do not have to pay interviewers for administering the instrument, though you do pay for postage.

2. Saves time. You may receive responses from a population quickly without having to spend time interviewing multiple individuals.
3. Convenience for interviewees. They can complete it at their convenience.
4. Anonymity of interviewee.
5. Wording of the questionnaire is standardized.
6. Avoidance of interviewer bias that might influence the interviewee.
7. Information may be readily available. The interviewee can look up information as necessary.
8. Accessibility of all interviewees. Mail goes to widely separated locations.

There are also disadvantages to mailing out questionnaires. Some of these are the following:

1. Questions are fixed. An interviewer does not have the opportunity to rephrase the question or probe further if the answer given to a question is vague or unclear.
2. Return of questionnaires may be low. You can expect that only a percentage of those who receive questionnaires will take the time to complete them. If you receive fifty percent or more completed questionnaires, you will be doing well.
3. Nonverbals are not available. You have only what the respondent writes.
4. Lack of control over the situation where the questionnaire is completed. You will not know whether the respondent has had help from another person or a group.
5. Questions are answered in the order the respondent chooses. You may have carefully designed your questionnaire in a specific order so that one question builds upon another.
6. Questions may be unanswered.
7. Spontaneous answers are not available.
8. People respond when they choose, rather than according to your schedule.
9. In the case of unreturned questionaires, there is no way of telling if the questionnaire was ignored or sent to a wrong address.
10. A simpler questionnaire may be more necessary than one that can be administered by an interviewer.
11. The sample may more likely be biased with use of a questionnaire than with use of an interview schedule. People with a conflict of interest or expert knowledge may bias your sample.

These difficulties may be more theoretical than real. For example, McDonagh and Rosenblum (1965, as quoted in Bailey 1978:159) compared the results of a mailed questionnaire with those of an interview schedule. They found no statistical difference between the results of the two research instruments which had identical questions.

Constructing a research instrument

The goals of your research lead to the specific questions you include on a research instrument. Most include basic demographic data such as age, sex, marital status, educational level attained, language background (mother tongue, other dialects, trade and national languages), residence, occupation, and, when appropriate, ethnic background.

Avoid including questions that the people will find offensive, unfair, or irrelevant. The wording of each question should be clear, so that you obtain the information that you are seeking. Sometimes it is helpful to ask your research assistant or someone else from the target group what questions he or she thinks would be appropriate to include on the re-search instrument that relate to your project. You may be surprised at areas of the culture relating to your topic that you might not have thought about which an insider may suggest asking.

In constructing a research instrument some data are discrete and have structured responses, such as marital status, with possible answers readily marked (e.g., ___single, ___married, ___divorced, ___widowed, etc.). For other information, you need to construct open ended questions.

When constructing your research instrument, you might want to add a question such as "Is there anything else important to [this topic] that I have not asked you about?" This can often lead to very useful data that add significantly to your project.

Researchers often draft research instruments in their own native language, then translate them into the language(s) of the research community, usually with the help of speakers of those languages. If you are competent in the language and know the culture, it is preferable to draft them in the local language. The questions will more likely come out sounding idiomatic in the target language if it is drafted in that language rather than in your mother tongue.

Suggested minimum census database

The Burg Wartenstein conference in 1975 focused on long-term field research. The participants proposed that those beginning anthropological research collect a minimum core database that can then be used as the basis of later research (Foster et al. 1979:333). That later research may involve study of culture change and cross-societal comparisons.

A minimum database should include samples defined in space and time and definitions of terms that are consistent and unambiguous. In addition, this core census database for each individual in the sample should include the following categories:

1. Name
2. Sex
3. Date and place of birth and of death
4. Marital and parental status (including number of all children with their dates of birth and death)
5. Unit(s) of affiliation, past and present
   a. Social
   b. Residential
6. Occupation(s) and their locations, past and present
7. Education
8. Religion
9. Resource base (minimum descriptive data)
   a. Ecological categories
   b. Economic categories
10. Sociopolitical differentiation (e.g., rank, title, caste, office, political roles, etc.) (Foster et al. 1979:333).

Sample of *all* villagers?

Prior to actual fieldwork I planned on doing a census of *all* residents of a research site. After arriving I found that the "bush village" where we settled had an estimated population of around 5,000 persons according to one census enumerator for the now discredited 1973 Nigerian census. If I had collected census data from *all* those people, I would have accomplished little else during my early research, especially given my limited knowledge of the language at that time.

A representative sample of the total village population was more appropriate than collecting census data from all residents.

Testing a trial research instrument

Before collecting data for statistical analysis, test your research instrument to evaluate the extent to which it elicits the data you desire. You need to test it for possible bias, sequencing of questions, clarity, and validity of likely responses. Based on these results you can modify the instrument until it does elicit the data you want.

Da Corta and Venkateshwarlu (1993) discuss the importance of trial interviews in their research as follows:

> Conducting as many trial interviews as possible with a cross-section of the population before implementing the survey was tremendously useful in determining the order and structure of the questionnaire so that one set of questions could flow naturally into the next. The most sensitive questions were asked at the end of the interview, or whenever the greatest level of intimacy had been established. (1993:105)

Wording of specific questions can make a difference in how people respond. Your goal is to make sure the wording of questions is respondent-friendly as well as designed to elicit the information you are seeking. Testing of your questionnaire or interview schedule should pick up on any wording and ordering problems.

All data collected in the testing stage, while your research instrument is going through various revisions, should be discarded and not used in your subsequent data analyses. While this may seem like a needless waste of good data, it allows you to carefully select your sample.

Sample selection

Carefully select your sample of individuals to interview so that the responses you receive are representative of the entire community. Decide what type of sample you desire. Do you want a random sample, a total population sample, or a convenience sample? A RANDOM SAMPLE is one in which all members of the specific population have an equal probability of being selected. A few suggestions for sample randomization include the following:

1. Assign a number to each household, then interview all adults in every second (third, or fourth, etc.) household.
2. Collect a list of all household heads, then through use of some randomization means (e.g., tossing a coin, drawing numbers out of a hat, etc.) select the households for interviewing people.
3. Assign a number to each individual, then randomly select specific individuals to interview.
4. Use a statistical computer program that has a pseudo random number generator function that can be used in sample selection. Some social sciences computer programs (e.g., Sistac) and most statistical analysis programs have this capability, including spreadsheet programs such as Microsoft Excel.
5. Use a table of random numbers such as is included in the appendices of many introductory statistics texts. Assign a number to each individual then turn to the table to see who to interview.

Be careful to avoid allowing people to choose to respond to a research instrument. A self-selected sample does not have the same validity as a random sample. Having said all this, recognize that selecting a truly random sample can be difficult, if not impossible.

A TOTAL POPULATION SAMPLE involves interviewing everyone. If data are elicited from a small ethnic group, administer the research instrument to all adults, fifteen years of age and older. In that event, there is no question as to how well the sample represents the population. Your data represent the responses of that population.

Set up criteria for the population to be sampled. For example, when planning to administer an interview schedule to a rural Bajju population, I set up the following criteria for the village:

1. The village should have a population that was not thoroughly intermixed with other ethnic groups.
2. The village needed to be readily accessible by road, though perhaps not a main road.
3. The village needed to be a long-established Bajju village, not a village whose existence in a particular geographic area was relatively recent.
4. The chief of the village approved of my administering the interview schedule to members of his village.
5. Some members of the village had converted to Christianity, as the focus of my research was Christian conversion (McKinney 1985:350–51).

A CONVENIENCE SAMPLE utilizes some randomization of the sample, but you interview only those who are at home or some specific location when you come. For example, after deciding which village to administer the interview schedule to, I interviewed adults who were fifteen years of age and older who were at home when we came to their compounds.

For an urban sample, I set up the following criteria for sample selection:

1. The population included a sufficient number of Bajju living within one geographic area to allow for randomization.
2. The population resided close enough together so that once households were selected, they would be readily accessible by walking.
3. The population lived in an urban environment.
4. Some of the population had converted to Christianity (McKinney 1985:353–54).

When these criteria were met, I then talked with an elderly long-term resident of this urban area. He provided a list of household heads of most of the Bajju households. Then by flipping a coin, the research team and I selected the compounds in which we would interview. So while my research assistant and I interviewed, Norris would flip a coin, approximately ten times, in order to decide the compounds in which we would interview next. Needless to say, his coin flipping produced questions about what on earth he was doing.

For further information on sample selection see "Populations and samples" in chapter 10.

Possible data bias

Sample selection is fraught with possibilities of bias. Simply interviewing individuals who come to public places, such as a well or river, would bias the sample to those who frequent such places. Thus, elderly individuals might be excluded from the sample, and the elders are usually the leaders in any community.

Bias may be introduced by individuals providing data that they perceive the interviewers want. For example, some researchers have asked village chiefs questions seeking information that is true for their specific villages. That may yield information that the chiefs perceive to be true, or what they would like outsiders to believe is true for their villages. Interviews with villagers would also be necessary in order to validate or invalidate the information you received from village chiefs.

Another possible source of bias in sample selection may be the researchers' ideological perspectives. For example, a Christian researcher may interview only Christians in a village where both Muslims and Christians live. Results of data from this study would apply only to the Christian population from whom the sample was drawn.

A related question concerning possible ideological bias, is whether members of the research community deliberately skew data in order to make it conform to what they believe the researcher might want their answers to be. For example, if they perceive the interviewer to be a Christian, respondents may deliberately give biased answers. This ideological bias is always a danger and is something that you need to be aware of. Ways to minimize its effect include doing good basic ethnographic research first so that you are aware of whether or not data collected through use of a formal research instrument are in line with data collected by other means. Secondly, use the local language. If you hear and understand the local language, you can often glean important information from any comments made that might indicate individuals are deliberately providing skewed or false data.

Sometimes respondents skew data in order to avoid possible problems with members of the national government, a rival ethnic group, or even members of their own group. Data about economic status frequently fall into this category. (See the side box for an example.)

Skewed data can come from interviewers providing possible responses to open-ended questions. When interviewers list possible responses, the natural tendency of interviewees is to select one of those answers, whether or not it applies. I instructed my research assistants that in administering the interview schedule they could repeat or restate questions if individuals did not understand them, but they were not to suggest possible answers. Occasionally, even when individuals understood a question, they were reticent to answer. For example, Haruna asked one elderly man how many wives he had had. The man responded evasively for a while, then asked if he had to tell. Haruna answered affirmatively. The elder finally stated that he had had eighteen wives over his lifetime, and now lived with two of them. One of his wives had been Haruna's aunt, who had stayed with him only four days before leaving!

Accurate data?

Gary Shepherd, a researcher who has spent years in Nepal among the Magar people, observed outside researchers attempt to collect data about the number of fields owned by Magar. He decided to check the accuracy by simply asking farmers the number of fields they owned. The first man he asked stated that he owned one field. Shepherd responded that he knew that the man had more than one field, so he told the man he would write down ten. The man quickly corrected him and told him to write down eight. Shepherd could only wonder at the accuracy of the data collected by the rapid rural assessment team when they arrived in a helicopter, stayed for a couple hours collecting data, then left, when even he who spoke the language and had lived with the Magar for an extended period of time had difficulty obtaining that type of data (Shepherd, personal communication, Dallas, 1989).

In an Asian context it is impolite for a younger person to answer an older person with a negative response. The result is that you will likely receive false positive answers to various questions, even though the true answers are really negative (Pratt and Loizos 1992:53). This points to the need to construct your questions so that they are asked in a culturally appropriate way. Other groups may find direct questioning offensive. To receive answers to specific questions may require patience on your part by asking questions now and then in an unobtrusive way, then writing responses down in the privacy of your own home. By asking questions in a conversational way over time you will be able to cover the content of your interview schedule without being perceived as pushy or obnoxious.

Training research assistants

If you are collecting a large sample, you will likely need to employ one or more research assistants to do some of the interviewing. Your research assistants may feel motivated in the research project if they are included in its design and development and in the testing of the research instrument. This is not always possible, especially when you are collecting data from a large sample where you must use a number of research assistants; to the extent possible, however, it helps them to be motivated.

The assistants you employ should speak the language of the population you are interviewing. This avoids potential problems with miscommunication that can occur when working with translated responses.

Administering questionnaires and interview schedules

If you choose to do a questionnaire, what is the percentage of the population that you want to complete it? Are you planning to distribute them personally, mail them out, or use some other means of distribution? Recognize that with use of a questionnaire, you can expect that you will only receive responses from a percentage of the total number of forms distributed.

An interview schedule is appropriate if you feel the need for interaction with respondents. For example, how they respond to specific questions may determine which questions to ask next. In my research on religious change I asked the following questions:

1. Are you a Christian?
2. Are you a Muslim?
3. Are you a traditional religionist?

Depending upon how an individual answered those questions, I chose one of the following questions to ask:

1. Why did you become a Christian?
2. Why did you become a Muslim?
3. Why are you not a Christian?
4. Why did you become a Christian rather than a Muslim? (This question was appropriate for this population because so few had converted to Islam even though the people who lived further north in the state were largely Muslims.)

If you decide to use an interview schedule, select the population you want to sample. Also select the means you plan to use in interviewing. For example, are you going to do so over the phone? Are you planning to go from door to door? Do you plan to accost people in shopping malls or village markets to ask them to answer your questions? Do you plan to employ research assistants?

Obtain permission from the appropriate authorities to conduct your interviews. If you plan to interview in a village context, obtain permission from the chief or other authorities who are in positions of responsibility over the population you wish to survey. If they are not in agreement, move to another group where the authorities are willing to cooperate with you. Alternatively, try to be more persuasive with them so that they see the benefit of having you do this research.

Interviews with individuals are best conducted in a quiet place, so do each interview in a private place. You can set up such an arrangement with the authorities when you request permission to conduct interviews. State that you need a quiet place where you can interview people individually. It may be under a tree, in a room, or other designated place. Be sure to follow local protocol. For example, in many situations men may not interview women, and vice versa. If you do interview someone of the opposite gender, leave the door open so that there are no questions raised about moral improprieties occurring.

Though there is a place for group interviews, when collecting data for an interview schedule, avoid group interviews because group consensus tends to introduce bias into the data. People will likely seek to arrive at a consensus answer or at an answer they feel you want to hear. They may also feel that the outcome of their answers will bring some benefit to them (e.g., a development project in their village, a language team, a well, or a factory) and, therefore, bias their answers in order to receive their desired result.

In administrating an interview schedule be sure to write down answers to all of the questions. For a questionnaire, include the instructions that the respondent should respond to all the questions. You can have a category for an answer to a specific question of "don't know" or "undecided." Be aware, however, that it can skew your analysis if answers are omitted to some of the questions.

Number of people to interview

In order for your research instrument data to have validity as being representative of a given population, the larger the number of individuals you interview the better. Larger samples are more representative of the entire population. In statistical analysis a sample of fewer than thirty individuals requires the use of small-sample tests. So as a general rule, if you plan to perform statistical tests on the data you collect, gather data from a minimum of thirty individuals.

Estimating age

One standard question on most research instruments is age of respondent. This can be problematic for individuals in many ethnic groups where age is not a commonly kept statistic. As Howell states, "…when one encounters a group of 20 or so !Kung, living in a bush camp quite isolated from events in the outside world, one necessarily doubts that the ages of these people can be determined accurately" (1979:23).

Ways of estimating ages in cultures where people tend not to keep their ages and specific dates of birth may involve asking if individuals remember a specific dated event and asking their approximate age at the time of that event. In some cultures you may use names to date individuals, especially in cultures where people receive names according to what happened around the time of their birth. Thus, names can enable you to establish approximate ages (see the side box for an example).

By constructing a local timeline of important events you can often relate the birth of individuals to specific events along that line. These events become reference points for assessing approximate ages. When constructing this event line, you need to verify the exact dates when events occurred before using them.

Another means of assessing ages is for individuals to rank themselves with respect to each other. People will often know who is older than they are and by how much. As Howell states, "People who, like the !Kung, have no notion of absolute age often have a strong cultural concept of relative age, which in the !Kung case is incorporated into regularly used terms of address" (1979:25–26). By dating one individual, as by relating his name to a specific dated event, you can estimate approximate ages to all the members of that age set.

> **Little boundary**
>
> When I wanted data on ages from elderly individuals, I used a boundary dispute that occurred twice, once in 1921, and again in 1948 between the Bajju and Agorok (Kagoro). Careful investigation by a colonial administrator established that the land belonged to the Bajju. In 1948 a Bajju representative swore an oath to the effect that the land belonged to them. Around that time that representative's wife gave birth to a son whom they named "Boundary." That son's age could be placed within the right year by knowing that this dispute took place in 1948.

The dated events may be local, regional, national, and even international. For example, an eye illness in Nigeria struck the year the US sent the Apollo manned spaceship to the moon, and that illness was called "Apollo," allegedly because people looked up into the sky to see the spaceship with their eyes, and their eyes became infected.

When dealing with the age of twins, be aware that in some cultures the baby born first is the youngest while the one born second is the oldest. We found this to be true among the Bajju. They view the oldest as the one who was first in and last out.

Kinship terms may help you estimate age. For example, where "older" or "younger," as in "older brother, younger brother," are affixed to kinship terms, these may help you estimate age.

One common problem with estimating age is AGE HEAPING, which occurs when the interviewer assigns a number of ages ending in 0 or 5, or they are heaped on socially important ages such as 18, the legal maturity age in some western cultures, or 65, the age of retirement in some cultures. A second problem is termed AGE VANITY, the tendency to report ages younger than they actually are, or older, especially in cultures where old age is respected (Howell 1979:24). A third problem may occur when the interviewer tries to estimate age from physical appearance. These types of age errors may lead to distorted conclusions. For example, when looking at a population with age distortions a researcher may conclude that one segment of the population is absent, indicating an epidemic or some other health problem.

Having discussed various means of estimating age, note that in many cultures age needs to be viewed as a "cultural truth" or a "cultural fiction." To arrive at an absolutely truthful age may be impossible. Hence, in such situations what you collect is relative age.

Gender and kinship considerations

Gender of the interviewer and of the interviewee needs to be considered when interviewing. For example, in Muslim contexts, only women may interview women. Even hearing a man's voice, other than that of a woman's husband, on a tape recorder may be taboo. Researchers have found this to be true in Pakistan.

Sometimes kinship considerations for interviewers may dictate whom they can or cannot interview. One example of this is in the side box.

Matched sample

In some surveys you need to have a matched sample with a control group and a test group. For example, if you are doing research on an experimental drug, you need one group that is composed of users of a placebo drug and another that uses the experimental drug. Such a matched sample should be as parallel as possible in terms of age, gender, health, and economic status. In order for it to be a double blind study, the persons administering the drugs should not know which individuals fall into which group, nor should the participants know. By interviewing participants and matching their responses with the drug and the placebo, researchers can assess the effectiveness and possible side effects of the drug.

> **Future father-in-law**
>
> One of my assistants, who had readily interviewed men, refused to interview one man in a village where we were working and insisted that I conduct the interview. I asked him, "Why" and found out that that man was his future father-in-law and as such it would be inappropriate for him to conduct the interview. I gladly interviewed his future father-in-law and enjoyed doing so.

In a hypothetical ethnographic example of a matched sample, you might select two closely related ethnic groups. In one group there has been conversion to Christianity while in the other people continue to adhere to their traditional religion. Further, both groups have been missionized by the same mission and have had a similar amount of missionization. Through use of an interview schedule that you administer to a matched sample you could investigate why one group converted to Christianity while the other group did not.

Other relevant questions

Is more than one questionnaire necessary?

Occasionally, researchers have decided to use phased questionnaires. This involves a first questionnaire that elicits general data, with a follow-up questionnaire that seeks more specific data on potentially sensitive topics. For example, Christensen (1993) used two questionnaires when studying issues related to economics. The second was administered after a good working relationship had been established with the respondents. Sensitive questions were interspersed with nonsensitive ones, and each was accorded the same emphasis. It may also be appropriate to use two research instruments for some projects, as use of before and follow-up questionnaires.

Synchronic versus longitudinal data

Data from a research instrument collected at one point in time, namely synchronic data, is sometimes sufficient to answer your research question(s). At other times use of multiple research instruments used over time, which yield longitudinal data, is important. Longitudinal data should come from the same cohort of respondents. Sometimes such a bounded population will be questioned at different times over a number of years. Longitudinal data collection has been very beneficial in areas such as medical studies, culture change studies, demographic studies (e.g., Howell 1979), politics, economic change, religious change, and values change.

Is a census feasible?

You should also be sensitive as to whether or not it is politically feasible to collect census data. For example, Sargent (1982:6) found that a systematic effort to collect demographic data might have aroused suspicions due to various political factors, including a mercenary invasion of the country in a coup attempt which occurred early during her research period. She decided that it would be quite inappropriate to conduct a census as part of her research. When it is politically or ethically questionable to conduct a census or administer a research instrument, the best course of action is to not do so.

After collecting data through use of a research instrument, the next step is statistical analysis of those data; this is the subject of the next chapter.

10

Statistical Analysis of Social Science Data

If we study all the cities in the United States having a population of 300,000 or more, it is quite possible that we will find a correlation between number of animals in the city zoo and crime rate. Can we conclude from this relationship that elephants and tigers are a major cause of crime? (Bailey 1978:51)

As this quote intimates you can readily draw false conclusions through statistical calculations. In fact, *How to Lie with Statistics* (Huff 1954) explores this topic. This chapter seeks to help come up with meaningful results through statistical analysis of social science data.

The goal of statistics in social science research is primarily to make statistical inferences. These inferences are based on statistical tests that are used to validate or fail to validate hypotheses to some specified degree of certainty. For example, a researcher may hypothesize that "religion correlates with occupation in three [specified] villages in northern Nigeria." This is a testable hypothesis in that data could be collected either from all people in those three villages or from a representative sample, then statistical tests run which would either validate or fail to validate this hypothesis.

This chapter looks at what you do with the results of the research instrument that was discussed in the last chapter. It should enable you to come up with quantified data through the application of some standard statistical measures and tests in order to confirm or disprove your hypotheses (see Johnson 1978, Strauss and Corbin 1990).

The information introduced in this chapter is sketchy, written more as a reminder of a few of the types of statistics you might consider. It is no substitute for a good statistics course or two, which are required in most social science curriculums.

Statistical computer programs

A number of statistical computer programs are available, and statisticians continue to develop other useful ones. Well-known statistical programs for social science research include SPSS^x (Statistical Package for Social Sciences^x 1983, 1984) and SPSS/PC+, SAS, Sistat, and Minitab. Each of these programs is available in a version for use on a personal computer. In addition, the program described in *BMDP Statistical Software Manual* (Dixon 1990) runs on most mainframe computers, minicomputers, and PCs; it does plots, simple data description, and more sophisticated techniques such as repeated measure analysis.

ANTHROPAC is a useful computer program specifically designed for anthropological research. With ANTHROPAC you can use the Guttman scaling program, analyze pilesorts and free lists, do paired comparisons, generate network questionnaires, do matrix comparisons, and run factor analyses, as well as perform other useful analytic procedures.

In the description of data analysis for statistical research presented below, examples come from analysis that made use of SPSS[x]. Other statistical programs may differ in coding and specific statistical computations available.

Normal distribution

In applying statistical tests to data, statisticians assume a NORMAL DISTRIBUTION of the data around the mean, provided that the number of samples is greater than about thirty. A graph of the normal distribution is referred to as a BELL CURVE because of its bell shape; it is also termed the NORMAL CURVE. In a normal distribution most groups of data cluster around the middle of the range. It is represented in (9).

(9) Normal or bell curve

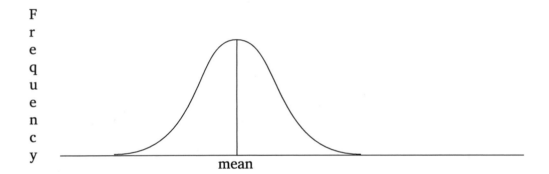

Before talking about specific statistical tests, I will define and discuss a few basic statistical concepts.

Basic statistical concepts

Populations and samples

In order to perform statistical tests on data, you must first collect data from a POPULATION. According to one way of describing a source of data in statistics, a population is a set of people or things that have some characteristic in common; for example, all the people who live in a certain village have that in common; they are a population. Other examples of a population in that village are the females, the households, the livestock (of each kind), and the tilled fields. Associated with each member of a population is any number of *variables*, each of which can have any of two or more VALUES. Examples of variables and their range of values are:

1. Sex: male or female
2. Age: 0, 1, 2, 3,…years
   (or 0, 1, 2, 3,…months, for infants)
3. Ability to speak the trade language: yes or no
   (or FSI level 0, 1, 2, 3, 4, or 5)

4. Volume (e.g., capacity of granary): capacity in liters/quarts
5. Year (e.g., of establishment of household): 1930, 1931,...

Collected data for each variable in the population are the set of measurements of that variable, either for the whole population or for a sample of the population.

Another way of describing a source of data, is that members of the population are the measurements of a variable (i.e., instances of values) themselves. Thus, the population is the set of all measurements that are of interest to you (Ott 1977:3). For example, populations in the research sample in a village might include:

1. The age of each individual;
2. The sex of each individual;
3. The number of children born to each woman;
4. The level of education of each individual;
5. The income of each individual and/or each household;
6. The occupation of each individual;
7. The area of each tilled field; and
8. The rainfall each year for the past thirty years.

Collected data are either *the* population, i.e., the set of all measurements of something, or else they are a SAMPLE, a subset of the population.

If the population is large, then the researcher usually collects a random sample of data from the total population, and infers that the results of statistical tests conducted on those data apply to the entire population. A RANDOM SAMPLE is one in which all members of the specific population have an equal probability of being selected. In order to select a random sample, use some means of randomization, such as those described in the preceding chapter.

Total population samples and random samples are treated differently, though similarly, statistically. For example, if the data are collected from each member of the entire population, the MEAN or average is represented as "mu" (μ), but if the data collected are for a sample of the population, then statisticians use "$\bar{y}$" to represent the sample mean.

Note that in data collection all questions need responses in order to have good validity for the inferences drawn from the statistical computations. It does not work very well to have 30 responses to Question 1, 29 responses to Question 2, 33 responses to Question 3, etc. If inadvertently some data on specific questions are missing, however, the way around this problem is to use statistical measures that are designed for just such a problem and to set up a dummy value for that variable entitled "no data" or "no response."

Data list, variables, and values

Included in the data file is the list of VARIABLES for a set of cases. Variables can be factors such as age, sex, village of respondent, educational level attained, literacy abilities, languages spoken, religious affiliation, test scores, income. Thus, a variable can be anything for which a VALUE can be assigned. In designing a questionnaire or an interview schedule, values can readily be assigned to responses to questions that have discrete answers. You may find it more difficult to assign values to responses to open-ended questions. Sometimes it is possible, however, to place responses to open-ended questions into discrete categories that can then be treated as discrete data.

The steps I took in analyzing the data for doctoral research on Bajju religious change will serve as an example of the general procedure for carrying out a statistical analysis on a set of data. Some of the details of the procedure you use on your data may be quite different, depending on the particular computer program that you use. For example, the old main-frame computer version of SPSS^x statistical program that I used had some limitations that would not be found on a modern PC version.

First, I labeled each variable. Variable labels depend on the research topic. For example, in my research on Bajju religious change and retention of traditional religious beliefs, I looked at variables such as age, sex, denomination, reasons for conversion to Christianity, and who is Jesus. SPSS^x limited variable labels to a maximum of eight characters. I labeled some of these variables as in (10).

(10)   Variable   Variable label

        Age of respondent   Age
        Sex of respondent   Sex
        Denomination   Denom
        Reason for conversion to Christianity   WhyXn
        Who is Jesus?   WhoisJes

Next, I assigned a NUMERICAL CODE to each value of each variable that was not already numerical. Examples for two variables are in (11) and (12).

(11)   Variable: Sex

        Value   Code

        Male   1
        Female   2

(12)   Variable: Education

        Value   Code

        No education   01
        Primary incomplete   02
        Primary completed   03
        Teachers college   04
        Advanced teachers college   05
        Secondary school   06
        University   07
        Post-graduate schooling   08
        Bible school   09
        Seminary   10
        Other   11

After entering the variables and coding each value for the variables, I instructed the computer to print out the DATA LIST so that I could check for any possible errors in data entry.

Once variable values were coded numerically and entered into the data file, I instructed the computer to calculate various statistical measures on the data for each variable and/or produce various graphical displays of the data. The statistical measures commonly include means, ranges, standard deviations, chi-squares, etc. The graphical displays of my data included scatter diagrams. Other measures you might wish to use are stem-and-leaf displays, frequency polygons or histograms, box-and-whisker charts, and cumulative percent frequency polygons. Further, you may also want to run cross-tabulations and regression correlations on various pairs of variables and/or produce scatter diagrams of the data for selected pairs of variables. The goal of statistical computations such as these is to prove or disprove specific hypotheses.

Hypotheses

At this point you are ready to begin testing specific hypotheses. The RESEARCH HYPOTHESIS, also termed the ALTERNATIVE HYPOTHESIS, is designated as H_a. A STATISTICAL TEST is based on proof by contradiction. Ott (1977:80) gives the following components:

1. A null hypothesis, H_o;
2. A research (alternative) hypothesis, H_a;
3. A test statistic, T.S.;
4. A rejection region, R.R.; and
5. A conclusion.

These components are described below:

1. Research or alternative hypothesis: A hypothesis is a researchable proposition that can presumably be put to an empirical test (in order to prove that the research hypothesis is true, you must prove that a contradictory hypothesis, termed the null hypothesis, is not true).
2. Null hypothesis: According to Shearer (1982:66) nearly all null hypotheses begin with the words "There is no difference between...," or "There is no relationship between..." Hence, you need to show a relationship between variables; if none exists, then the data represent mere coincidence.
3. A test statistic (see Statistical Test section below).
4. Rejection region: Depending upon the research hypothesis and its associated null hypothesis, set a rejection region (of the normal distribution) for the null hypothesis. The likelihood of two types of errors are determined by your choice of a rejection region:

    a. A type I error occurs if you reject the null hypothesis when, in fact, it is true. The probability of this type of error is symbolized by the Greek letter alpha (α).
    b. A type II error occurs if a null hypothesis is false yet you accept it as true. The probability of this type of error is symbolized by use of the Greek letter beta (ß).

Note that these errors are inversely related; an increase of alpha results in beta decreasing, and vice versa. These two types of errors are summarized in (13). Seek to avoid both types of errors. Researchers are much more concerned to avoid a type I error, i.e., accepting the research hypothesis H_a when it is actually false, than to avoid a type II error, rejecting the research hypothesis when it is in fact true.

(13) Rejection region: Two types of error (Ott 1977:81)

Null hypothesis

Decision	True	False
Reject H_o	α	correct
Accept H_o	correct	ß

In order to avoid accepting this type of problem, specify a tolerable probability for a type I error of the statistical test. Thus, by choosing alpha to be .01, .05, .10, etc., you specify the risk you are willing to take. For example, if you decide that one time in forty you are willing to incorrectly reject the null hypothesis, then alpha $= 1/40 = .025$. Hence, the rejection region would be .025.

As an example of a statistical test, in my research I tested the following hypotheses:

H_a The sons of Christians attained a higher level of education than the sons of non-Christians.

H_o There was no difference in the level of education attained between the sons of Christians and the sons of non-Christians.

In order to test these hypotheses, I instructed the computer to identify on the data list the entries for fathers and their religious affiliation (whether Christian or non-Christian), their sons, and their sons' educational level attainment. I then instructed it to run various statistical correlations and tests. For SPSS^x I utilized the commands "Statistics All" and "Cross-Tabs" (Cross-Tabulations). Some of the resulting statistics are in the table in (14).

Based on these statistical computations, the conclusion was that the research hypothesis was confirmed. From these data I inferred that a Bajju son's educational level correlates positively with his father's Christian commitment. From other data sources, such as informal interviews, I learned that Christians are more likely than non-Christians to send their children to school, schools that included religious knowledge as part of the regular curriculum. In the Bajju area the religious knowledge taught is Christianity, so the schools have become sources of the spread of Christianity throughout the Bajju area. While this is true for the Bajju, it would not be true for the Hausa where Islam is the subject taught in religious knowledge.

At the bottom of the table in (14) the chi-square statistical test for significance is mentioned. Chi-square is a statistical test that reflects the name of a particular distribution of a nonsymmetrical bell-shaped distribution. It is skewed to the right. It indicates that the two variables being tested are related and are not independent variables. The chi-square test is one of the statistical tests available within any number of computer statistics programs.

(14) Father's religious preference correlated with ego's highest educational attainment for Bajju urban random sample (McKinney 1985:383)

Egos' highest educational level achieved	Father a Christian? No	Yes	Row total
No education	8	9	17
Primary incomplete	2	5	7
Primary complete	0	13	13
Secondary incomplete	0	6	6
Secondary complete	0	1	1
Teachers college incomplete	0	1	1
Teachers college complete	0	3	3
Bible school incompete	1	0	1
Bible school complete	0	0	0
Technical school complete	0	0	0
Christian religious institute	0	1	1
Other	0	1	1
Column total	11	40	51

Chi-square 17.51, D. F. 9, Significance 0.0412

Clearly it is possible to come up with spurious relationships, when no relationship between variables exists. The quotation at the beginning of this chapter illustrates such a spurious correlation.

Measures of data location

Very commonly used numerical descriptive measures of a set of data are the mode, median, and mean. These measures describe the LOCATION or CENTER of a set of data.

Mode. The MODE of a set of measurements is defined as the measurement that occurs most often (i.e., it has the highest frequency). For example, 4 is the mode of the set of numbers 3334444445566.

Median. The MEDIAN of a set of measurements is defined as the middle value when the measurements are arranged in order of their magnitude. Examples of the median include the median age of persons receiving social security, the median wage increase that faculty members receive, the median scores of students on a test, etc. For example, the scores of students on an anthropology test might be as follows (note that the scores are arranged in the order of their magnitude): 62, 73, 76, 78, 84, 86, 89, 90, 92, 95. Whenever there is an even number of tokens, the median is the average of the middle two scores: Thus, the median score on the anthropology test is shown in (15).

(15)
$$\text{Median} = \frac{84 + 86}{2} \quad 85$$

Note: Determining the median can get more complicated when dealing with grouped data.

Mean. The MEAN (or AVERAGE) of a set of measurements is defined as the sum of the measurements divided by the total number of measurements. The population mean is denoted by the Greek letter *mu* (μ), and the sample mean is represented by y-bar ($\bar{y}$). From y-bar researchers make inferences about the population mean μ. The formula for deriving y-bar is given in (16).

$$(16) \qquad \bar{y} = \frac{\sum\limits_{i=1}^{n} \bar{y}_i}{n}$$

The numerator represents the sum of n measurements; hence, $\bar{y}_i$ represents the measurements in a sample of size n.

(17) $i = 1, 2, 3, ..., n$

For example, in order to get the mean of the above anthropology class test scores, add all of the scores, then divide by the total number of scores.

(18) $y = \dfrac{62 + 73 + 76 + 78 + 84 + 86 + 89 + 90 + 92 + 95}{10} = 82.5$

Numerical descriptive measures of data spread

Different sets of data or different populations have different amounts of SPREAD or DISPERSION. In some cases the data cluster relatively closely around the mean, while in other cases they are spread more widely. There are several useful measures of spread in data sets. Common descriptive measures of variability include the range, the percentiles, the variance, and the standard deviation.

Range. The range of a set of measurements is the interval between the largest and the smallest measurements of the set. The range is the simplest measure of variability of the data. For example, the range of the test scores in (18) would be $95 - 62 = 33$.

Percentile. The PERCENTILE of a set of n measurements arranged in order of magnitude is calculated by the following. The pth percentile has the value of p% of the measurements below it and $(100 - p)$% above it. For example, the score 92 in the set of anthropology test scores mentioned above is in the 80th percentile because 80% of the scores are lower than 92. Percentiles are frequently used to describe the results of achievement test scores. They rank a person's exam score in comparison to the scores of the rest of the people who took the exam.

Variance. The VARIANCE of a set of values of a variable is a measure of the amount of variation of the variable. In order to have some measure of variance around the mean for a given measurement, you can compute the sample variance as an estimate of the corresponding population variance. The variance of the values of a variable for an entire population is the population variance σ^2; and the variance of a variable for a sample from the population is the sample variance s^2. This variance is of a set of n measurements y_1, $y_2, \ldots y_n$ with mean $\bar{y}$. The sample variance is computed by use of the formula in (19).

(19)
$$s^2 = \frac{\sum\limits_{i=1}^{n} (y_i - \bar{y})^2}{n-1}$$

The population variance is computed by use of the formula in (20).

(20)
$$\sigma^2 = \frac{\sum\limits_{i=1} (y_i - \mu)^2}{n-1}$$

Standard deviation. The STANDARD DEVIATION of a set of measurements is defined to be the positive square root of the variance of the measurements. Statisticians use s to denote the SAMPLE STANDARD DEVIATION and σ to denote the POPULATION STANDARD DEVIATION. In order to derive the standard deviation, take the square root of the result of the formula above. For example, five measurements for a specific test score might result in the table in (21) from Ott (1977:34). In this example the sample mean is 3.2:

(21)

y_i	$y_i - \bar{y}$	$(y_i - \bar{y})^2$
5	1.8	3.24
4	.8	0.64
3	$-$ .2	.04
1	-2.2	4.84
3	$-$ .2	.04
Totals 16	0	8.80

In order to derive the variance, put these numbers into the formula as in (22).

(22)
$$s^2 = \frac{\sum\limits_{i=1}^{5} (y_i - \bar{y})^2}{4} = \frac{8.80}{4} = 2.2$$

Then in order to derive the sample standard deviation take the square root of 2.2 as in (23).

(23)
$$s = \sqrt{2.2} = 1.48$$

Statistical tests

Depending on the data, hypothesis, and type of results desired, select a specific statistical test or group of tests. (See Andrews et al. 1981 for guidance in selecting statistical techniques.) One commonly used means of running the data is to request the computer to run "Statistics All" or whatever the equivalent command is for the computer statistical package you are using. With that command the computer performs all of the tests available within the program. Some commonly run tests include the chi-square goodness-of-fit test, cross- tabulations, and the Student's T test.

Chi-square goodness-of-fit test

This test is used for an asymmetrical distribution of the data. Note that there are many chi-square distributions. To obtain a particular one, specify the degrees of freedom (df)[4]. The test statistic for computing chi-square (X^2) is shown in (24).

(24)
$$X^2 = \sum_{i=1}^{k} \left[\frac{(n_i - E_i)^2}{E_i} \right]$$

In this equation "n_i represents the number of trials resulting in outcome i[,] and E_i represents the number of trials that we would expect to result in outcome i when the hypothesized probabilities represent the actual probabilities assigned to each outcome" (Ott 1977:268).

The chi-square test tells you that there is an association between the variables; it does not tell the direction of that association.

Cross-tabulations

The cross-tabs procedure produces tables that are the joint distribution of two or more variables that have a limited number of distinct values. The frequency distribution of one variable is subdivided according to the values of one or more other variables.

For more information on statistical tests the reader should consult statistics books or statisticians.

The following chapter deals with a related topic, demography, the science of populations.

---

[4]Concerning degrees of freedom (df), Ott states, "Everyone seems to want to know what df really means. There is no valid explanation; df is a parameter (a numerical descriptive measure) of the t distribution. As we stated, df = n - 1 for this t distribution" (1977:102).

11

Demography

When we ask what the future size of world population will be...we are really asking how many children today's youth will have. (Carl Haub, as quoted in *Population Today*, 1998 26(5):1)

Population growth over the next 50 years will affect every facet of life, including housing, income, education, health care, and the environment—and the demand for food. (Bender and Smith 1997:7)

Whether you work with people who are experiencing rapid population growth, such as Bender and Smith speak about, where there is land shortage and unemployment, or with a tiny population that is in danger of dying out, studying demography should be part of your research in the field. DEMOGRAPHY is the science of populations. Undertaking some demographic investigation is important in cultural research to understand significant aspects of the composition and dynamics of the populations studied. This chapter gives a very brief introduction to some basic concepts of demography, an important discipline on its own.

Begin your study of demography by finding out current demographic indicators for the country and region where you are going. One resource for this is the "World Population Data Sheet" published yearly by the Population Reference Bureau (PRB). It includes population, birth rates, death rates, natural increase rates, doubling time, population estimates, infant mortality rate, total fertility rates, percentage under 15 years and over 65 years, life expectancies (total, male, female), percent urban, maternal mortality, and so on. It gives these indices by country, by region, and the world.

Uses of demographic data

Some uses of demographic data include understanding the density of the population within a given area, insight into migration patterns (whether circular, rural urban, seasonal), marriage patterns and the frequency of each type of marriage, incidence of illnesses and deaths, discernment into whether the population is growing or declining, etc. Demographic data can help in public health, in land use planning as in where to construct a hospital, school, clinic, or market, in public utility planning, family planning programs, setting immigration and emigration policies, and for many other uses.

Demographic statistics are the underpinnings of national plans for economic development and other projects (Shryock, Siegel, and Associates 1976:2). In cultural and linguistic research, collection of demographic data may contribute to decisions about initiation of a

125

language program, knowledge of which languages are spoken in what contexts, degree of bilingualism and multilingualism by age and by sex, understanding of the age-sex distribution of the population, consideration of public health projects, possible social impact studies of specific projects, understanding of migration dynamics of the population studied, and understanding of specific problems of small populations (see Headland 1986), as well as many other uses.

For example, Headland found that collecting demographic data helped him understand problems faced by the Agta, a minority Negrito group in the Philippines. He states the problem as follows:

> The anomaly of the Agta culture [sic]. In spite of the progress and westernization which has come to the Casiguran area since WWII, the Agta continue to roam nomadically through the jungles, seemingly without adequate food, clothing or shelter, refusing to send their children to the public schools, and resisting repeated government efforts to settle them on their own land and help them take up farming. This occurs in spite of the apparent poverty under which the Agta live—a way of life which appears pathetic to outside observers, and which Agta themselves are quick to tell you is *mehirap* ('hardship'). (1986:19)

The Headlands based their demographic data on censuses that they began collecting in the 1960s. These data included vital statistics such as births, marriages, deaths, migrations, places of birth, ages, female reproductive histories, and causes of death (Headland 1986:48; Headland and Headland 1982). The Headlands combined collection of demographic data with time allocation studies that enabled them to know how Agta spent their time. If the Agta were not taking up agriculture, in spite of numerous efforts to convince and coerce them to do so, how were they spending their time? They found that the Agta could earn a better living by adapting their hunter-gatherer foraging techniques and its accompanying ideology of sharing than they could by taking up horticulture, despite logging companies cutting large areas of the forest and despite large numbers of lowlanders migrating into the Casiguran area.

A second example of the usefulness of collecting demographic data comes from my Bajju research, in which I administered an interview schedule to 266 individuals, both in rural and urban environments. The first questions on the schedule were standard census questions concerning age, sex, educational level attained, religion, marital status, number of children, etc. In fact, the very first question asked for the age of the respondent. Since Bajju rarely knew their ages, that question often began the interview with laughter. On occasion it brought the response, "Whoever knows a thing like that!" (For aid in estimating relative age see the section on "Estimating Age" in chapter 9.)

Since my goal in administering the interview schedule focused on religious change, I included a number of questions on that topic, as well as questions on language usage. Standard demographic data were collected in order to correlate them with specific data on religious change (see McKinney 1985, 1986). Concerning literacy, results indicated that 74% of male respondents in the sample were able to read Hausa, the trade language, while only 41.7% of female respondents could do so. In general, literacy for females correlated with the age of respondents; this was not true for males. Women of approximately forty years of age and older tended to be more nearly monolingual with a lesser grasp of Hausa than younger women. These data point to the need for any Bajju literacy campaign to use Jju particularly for women, rather than Hausa, the trade language (see McKinney 1990).

Other uses of demography include EPIDEMIOLOGY, the science devoted to the study and control of endemic diseases. Epidemiology is a population discipline. It seeks to reduce the prevalence of disease in particular populations. When epidemics are present in multiple countries epidemiologists speak of pandemics rather than epidemics. AIDS is an example of a pandemic disease. Epidemiologists often speak of the incidence and prevalence of particular diseases. They locate centers where the disease began and the transmission routes. For example, ebola virus is so deadly that major international health initiatives work to contain it, eradicate it in specific populations, and to keep it from spreading more widely. Occasionally, this involves quarantines of particular populations.

Resources for study of demography

For aid in analysis of demographic data, the *Population Handbook* by Haupt and Kane (1985) published by the Population Reference Bureau (PRB) is extremely helpful. (See "Resources" in the appendix for the address and telephone number of the PRB.) The PRB publishes this useful booklet in an English international edition, an English Caribbean-oriented edition, and Arabic, French, and Spanish editions. It also publishes monthly *Population Today*, a short bulletin that features current demographic indicators on specific countries as well as timely topical articles.

You should also have access to some standard computer statistics program that will help you with the analysis of the data you collect. Some of these were discussed in the previous chapter on statistics.

You may analyze demographic data you collect in terms of counts, rates, ratios, proportions, constants, cohort measures, and period measures. Each of these is briefly discussed next.

Counts

The COUNT is "the absolute number of a population or any demographic event occurring in a specified population in a specified time period..." (Haupt and Kane 1985:8). This is the basis for all subsequent analysis.

Counts may be obtained from censuses, sample surveys, questionnaires, interview schedules, and files of population registers such as registered vital events (births, marriages, deaths, divorces, etc.), or by counting the population or demographic event. For example, in one study on birth weights of infants delivered in a health clinic in northern Benin, Sargent collected data from the clinic's records (Sargent, McKinney, and Wetherington 1986).

Rates

RATES refer to,

> The frequency of demographic events in a population in a specified time period (e.g., birth rate: 15.5 live births per 1,000 population in the U.S. in 1983). Rates tell how frequently an event is occurring—how common it is. Crude rates are rates computed for an entire population. Specific rates are rates computed for a specific subgroup—usually the population at risk of having the event occur (e.g., general fertility rate: births per 1,000 women aged 15–44 years). Thus rates can be age-specific, sex-specific, race-specific, occupation-specific, etc. (Haupt and Kane 1985:8).

Rates represent synchronic or transversal data. Common rates computed include birth rates, general fertility rates, age-specific fertility rates, completed fertility rates, total fertility rates, death rates, infant mortality rates, life expectancy, marriage rates, immigration and emigration rates, etc. While a few rates are dealt with here, there are numerous important rates not covered in this chapter (see Haupt and Kane 1985, Shryock, Seigel, and Associates 1976).

In computing rates first specify the population at risk, that is, "the population at risk of having the event occur" (Haupt and Kane 1985:8). The population at risk forms part of the total population or universe of people. In computations of rates the population at risk goes into the numerator, while the total population forms the denominator. Since many rates are computed per 1,000 people, the result of the fraction is multiplied by the constant k = 1,000.

Crude birth rate. When computing the CRUDE BIRTH RATE, the population at risk would be the number of births in a year, and the total population would be all women aged 15–44 years (or 15–49 years, as used by some researchers). In the formula in (25), which is used for computing the crude birth rate (CBR), B equals the number of births in a year, and P equals the total population of women in that age group.

(25)
$$CBR = \frac{B}{P} k$$

Completed fertility rate. The COMPLETED FERTILITY RATE indicates the number of children ever born to a woman who has completed her family. This rate is based on retrospective event history, so data are usually collected from women who have completed their childbearing years (45 or 49 years of age and older).

Data collection for this rate may be problematical, as for example in some societies where children are not considered to have a soul until they are seven days old. In such societies women would likely omit any children who died before this age. In general, in collecting reproductive histories women are apt to omit children who are deceased. Sometimes it is helpful to use one's hand in collecting data on children, with each finger representing a child; then you can ask for any children who were born between children, using the spaces between your fingers as a handy visual aid. In societies where abortion occurs, fetuses may not be considered children and as such may be omitted. If you want the number of children aborted, you would likely need to ask, though be aware that this is a sensitive personal topic.

Many societies have an ideal birth interval. Many groups have two years as the ideal birth interval for children to be born. Among other groups it may be longer; for example, for the !Kung in southern Africa it is four years (Howell 1979:134) and for the Dani in Irian Jaya it is five years (M. Gregerson, personal communication, 1988). If in collecting data the reported birth spacing is greater than the typical interval, you may suspect that an infant died. Therefore, ask if this occurred.

Completed fertility rates (CFR) are computed in terms of the number of births for women born in a specific year. For example, the completed fertility rate for a specified female population (FP) for the year 1925 is given by using the formula in (26) where FP_{1925} is the number of females of that population born in the year 1925, and B is the number of births to those females.

(26)
$$CFR = \frac{B}{FP_{1925}}$$

Since the completed fertility rate is based on the births for women who were born within a specific year, this is a cohort statistic. A COHORT is a group of people who share a common demographic characteristic and who are observed over time. Cohort measurements are the basis of longitudinal studies, studies which continue over a period of time, e.g., five- or ten-year increments. Typically, rates may be calculated for ages:

15–19	or	5–24
20–24		25–34
25–29		35–44
30–34		45–54
35–39		55–64
40–44		65–74
etc.		etc.

(For information on calculating cohort cumulative fertility rates, see Shryock, Seigel, and Associates 1976:289.)

Cohort measurements may also be made by years, for example,

1926–1935
1936–1945
etc.

When analyzing data for any one year, as in example (26) for 1935, the data are divided midyear (January–June, July–December).

Cohort statistics contrast with PERIOD STATISTICS, statistics that apply to a population or sample population for a specified time interval such as a year or other specified period.

Infant mortality rate. The INFANT MORTALITY RATE (IMR) is the number of deaths of infants under one year of age per 1,000 live births for a specific year, and is a transversal measurement. It is computed with the formula in (27).

(27)
$$IMR = \frac{D_{<1 \text{ year of age}}}{Births} k$$

As Haupt and Kane point out, "The infant mortality rate is considered a good indication of the health status of any given area" (1978:29). For example, Townsend (1985) found that the infant mortality rate for the Saniyo-Hiyowe, a lowland group in Papua New Guinea, was 400 per 1,000 live births. Given this high infant mortality rate, she explored causes. She found that though infanticide accounted for a minority of cases, the basic causes were preventable infectious diseases such as respiratory diseases. Yaws was also common, though gastrointestinal diseases were infrequent (Townsend, personal communication, 1998).

Migration can affect infant mortality rates. Populations move for reasons such as to escape war, desire for missionary and/or government aid, education, famine, drought, or invasion of their land by colonists or multinational corporations.

Frequently, there are striking differences in infant mortality between rural and urban areas due to differing availability and/or quality of health care. Maternal education is also a factor in infant mortality, as is social class.

Cause specific death rate. If you study or encounter a specific epidemic, such as measles, you may want to compute a CAUSE SPECIFIC DEATH RATE by use of the formula in (28).

(28)
$$\text{Cause specific death rate} = \frac{\text{number of (specified cause of) deaths}}{\text{total population}}\ k$$

You may want to know how well a specific population is doing in their new ecosystem. The infant mortality rate is a useful one to apply. For example, Dye and Dye found that after the Bahenimo moved from their mountainous environment into a lowland mosquito infested area in Papua New Guinea, no infants survived in their new ecosystem for at least the first eight years (Wayne and Sally Dye, personal communication). Clearly, that population could not survive unless they learned to deal with mosquito-borne diseases or unless they moved out of that mosquito-infested environment. In this case, the Bahenimo remained in this mosquito-invested area by a lake. They learned to use mosquito nets and also learned to treat for malaria very quickly. They eventually lobbied successfully for an "Aid Post" that was staffed by a government health worker.

You may also be able to compute death rates due to infanticide although such data may be very sensitive and require that you strongly respect confidentiality. For example, traditionally among the Bajju, infants who were mentally deficient, physically deformed, and in general who did not thrive were believed to be water spirits rather than human. Therefore, they were returned to the water, a form of infanticide through drowning (McKinney 1985:147–49).

Life expectancy

LIFE EXPECTANCY is an estimate of the average number of additional years that a person currently living might expect to live based on continuation of current mortality trends observed for any given year, namely the current mortality rates. For example, the life expectancy at birth for babies born in the United States mid-1998 was 76 years, which divided into 73 years for males and 79 years for females (PRB: "1998 World Population Data Sheet"). Life expectancy is a theoretical concept that indicates health conditions at the time of its measurement; in this it is like the infant mortality rate. Breakthroughs in treatment of specific health problems can extend life expectancy. For example, the introduction of smallpox vaccine extended significantly the life expectancy of populations that formerly were plagued by this health hazard with its high mortality rates.

Short life expectancies of infants in many developing countries are due partially to high infant mortality rates. If individuals in such places survive past one year of age, their life expectancies increase.

Life expectancy contrasts with the concept of LIFESPAN. Lifespan is a theoretical average of the upper limit to human life, a factor that is assumed to be built into the biology of humans.

Ratios

RATIOS give the relationship between two segments of the population. This section discusses three ratios: the sex ratio, the dependency ratio, and the child-woman ratio.

Sex ratio. The SEX RATIO gives the relationship of the number of males to the number of females in the population, and it is usually expressed in terms of the constant k = 100. The sex ratio is computed as in (29).

(29)
$$\text{Sex ratio} = \frac{M}{F}\ k$$

Sex ratios may give clues to practices such as sex specific infanticide within a population.

Dependency ratio. The DEPENDENCY RATIO is the ratio of the economically dependent segment of the population to the economically productive segment. Demographers arbitrarily define this as the ratio of the elderly or seniors (persons sixty-five years of age and older) and the young (those under fifteen years of age) to the population within the economically productive years (those fifteen to sixty-four years of age). In addition to the young and the old, the unproductive or marginally productive segment of people in a population includes those who are inactive at any given time due to injury, physical illness, mental illness, etc. This ratio is computed by use of the formula in (30).

(30)
$$\text{Age dependency ratio} = \frac{\text{Population under 15 + Population 65 and over}}{\text{Population aged 15–64}}\ k$$

Child-woman ratio. The CHILD-WOMAN RATIO looks at the number of children who are under five years of age, compared to the number of women in their productive years (ages fifteen to forty-four years) per 1,000 women. It may be represented as in (31).

(31)
$$\text{Child-woman ratio} = \frac{\text{Number of children under 5}}{\text{Number of women aged 15–44}}\ k$$

This ratio provides a rough indicator of the fertility of a population.

Age-sex composition of populations

Collect data on the age and sex characteristics of the population you research. These data may come from vital statistics records kept by the national government, or you can collect them either from the entire population or from a random sample subset of the total.

Based on age-sex data, demographers construct AGE-SEX PYRAMIDS which provide a picture of the population in graphic form. In an age-sex pyramid males are placed on the left, and females on the right, with age cohorts in the middle. The pyramid represents 100 percent of the population described. Across the bottom of the pyramid are either percentages or counts (absolute numbers) of the population. An example of an age-sex pyramid from the United States around 1960 is in (32). In dealing with a small population, you might want to have counts of individuals included across the bottom of the pyramid instead of the percentages such as is illustrated in (32).

(32) Percent distribution by age and sex of the population of United States around 1960 (adapted from Shryock et al. 1976:137)

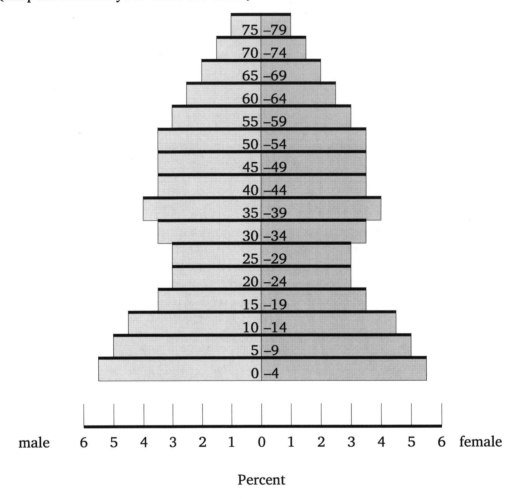

Based on the age-sex pyramids for specific populations, demographers characterize some populations as young populations and others as old populations. A YOUNG POPULATION is defined as one in which forty percent or more of the population is under 15 years of age, and an OLD POPULATION is one in which ten percent or more of the population is over 65 years old. Young populations include many in Africa, the Caribbean, and South America, while old populations are found in Scandinavian countries, France, and Germany; countries whose populations are neither young nor old include the United States, Korea, and Canada.

Besides revealing whether or not a population is young, old, or neither, an age-sex pyramid more generally displays information about the population, such as whether women outnumber men or men outnumber women, and whether one cohort is considerably smaller or larger than another, and so forth. When looking at age-sex compositions of populations, demographers distinguish between those which are expansive (populations with a larger number of individuals in the younger ages than in other cohorts), constrictive (populations that have few individuals in the younger ages), or stationary (populations with roughly equal numbers of people in all age ranges, though gradually declining in the older cohorts) (Haupt and Kane 1978:14).

Population change

POPULATION CHANGE is represented by the formula: population change = births − deaths + net migration. The first part of this formula includes NATURAL POPULATION INCREASE, that is births minus deaths. NET MIGRATION, another factor in this formula, involves computing immigration minus emigration. Further, births plus immigration indicates POPULATION GROWTH, and emigration plus deaths indicates POPULATION LOSS.

In addition to collecting the raw data and calculating rates and ratios, look at the social processes that tie them together. A few suggestive questions that you might want to look at concerning migration include, Why are people migrating? What are the economic benefits of migration? How does migration affect those who do not migrate? Is circular migration occurring (for example, do migrants spend a period of time in the wage economy before returning to their home villages, and repeat this cycle as necessary)? Are there government policies that encourage or necessitate migration? What are the stages of the migration? What are social support systems for migrants? What roles do kinship, voluntary associations, and ethnicity play for migrants? What are the beginning and end points of migration? Is the migration pattern primarily rural-urban or is some urban-rural migration also occurring, as, for example, the return to the rural area of those who retire or those who do not make it in the wage economy?

Demographic regime or demographic profile

The DEMOGRAPHIC REGIME, also termed a DEMOGRAPHIC PROFILE, involves understanding family planning, fecundity, fertility, mortality, and migration for a given population. It also studies these factors holistically. Demography not only adds births, subtracts deaths, adds immigrants, and subtracts emigrants, it also moves beyond simple arithmetic to understanding the social processes that tie together the statistical data for a population.

For example, in a population that has high fertility, there is also often high infant mortality. Cordell, Gregory, and Piche state,

> The most commonly suggested link between infant mortality and fertility stresses the replacement hypothesis, that high fertility attempts to compensate for the probable loss of a substantial fraction of offspring at very young ages. But the relationship is not unidirectional. High fertility in and of itself can contribute to higher infant and fetal mortality, through diminished maternal health and repeated risks associated with pregnancy and childbirth. Reduced birth intervals can also contribute to increased mortality at young ages. (1992:41–42)

A population may have a decline in infant mortality rates without a concomitant decline in fertility. This excess of births over deaths is part of the rapid population growth in many areas worldwide. Traditionally, demographers refer to this as DEMOGRAPHIC TRANSITION, the historic shift from high birth and death rates to lower levels for any given population. The shift to lower death rates usually precedes the shift to lower birth rates. As researchers are looking at this phenomena worldwide, however, some speak of an apparent independence of birth and death rates (p. 42).

In populations dependent upon labor-intensive subsistence patterns it makes sense to continue to have high fertility. The more children there are, the more laborers are available for horticulture, pastoral activities, household chores, craft activities, etc. If a population is also being heavily taxed or encouraged strongly to grow cash crops rather than for their subsistence needs, then some members of any given household will likely migrate to areas where they can work in the cash economy. Often such migrants send remittances home to help with the household budget.

Collecting demographic data

In order to collect demographic data, follow the procedures of developing and administering a questionnaire or interview schedule that were discussed in chapter 9. On your research instrument include basic demographic variables such as age, sex, marital status, education, occupation, etc. Next decide on aspects of the demographic regime that you want to include. Do the computations for rates and ratios that are specific to your project. Construct an age-sex pyramid which allow you to see readily a profile of the population. Next focus on the social processes that tie the demographic data together.

This chapter focused on the significant aspects of the composition and dynamics of the population, namely demography. The next chapter focuses on mapping, a topic that covers the physical setting of cultural research. It involves mapping the specific ecosystem where the population lives.

12

Maps

When driving in Jos, Nigeria, we stopped and asked directions to a certain location from a middle-aged man who was standing beside the road. He thought and thought, then finally slowly and seriously replied, "You can't get there from here!"

One important aspect of cultural research is the physical setting where people live and where you collect data. Mapping is an activity that you can do early in your field research when your command of the language is limited. You can draw sketches of the location, produce maps, and in general describe where activities take place. Maps are representations, usually on a surface that is flat, of the physical features of an area. Various types of maps are helpful to you, including initial sketches, folk maps, artistic sketches, professional-quality maps, and historical maps. Each type of map has its place within cultural research.

Physical space and social interaction can be mapped on a micro level in order to understand where specific behavior occurs. For example, in a court room, who sits or stands where is important and highly prescribed. A sketch of the court room is relevant when describing a court case. Alternately, maps may be on the macro level, as for example, to illustrate where a particular ethnic group lives within the nation. Both types of maps are helpful and have their place.

Maps should include the physical and topographic features of the area as well as the socially relevant aspects of culture as they relate to space. For example, there is the importance of the concept of territory or "turf" for urban teenage street gangs (Suttles 1968 as cited in Pelto and Pelto 1973:271). Mapping an area enables you to know settlement patterns. Who lives where? How are people related to one another, and does kinship correlate with residence patterns? What are the socioeconomic correlates of settlement patterns? As you map, note that physical space often correlates with social facts.

Mapping helps you understand residence patterns and contributes to your understanding of kinship. For example, in the process of mapmaking it may emerge that a particular section of a village belongs to one clan. You often find that extended families and closely related kin live close together. Genealogical data that you collect as a correlate of mapping may be key to your understanding the entire social system. You may map compounds and layouts of extended family houses, each of which may be indicated by hearths.

Mapping allows you the opportunity to observe the regular round of daily activities that occurs within the physical space. That understanding is particularly important when studying a foraging or hunting and gathering society, nomadic people, and pastoralists. What is their concept of the territory they utilize? What is their regular seasonal migration pattern?

135

What is the relationship between their migration trails and land usage of the settled population? Is MIGRATORY DRIFT occurring in which a migration route gradually shifts? An example of migratory drift comes from Fulani migration patterns. These pastoralists, who live in the Sahel region of Africa, probably began their migration in Senegal, and they have gradually pastured their animals eastward so that they now extend from Senegal into Sudan. Their seasonal migratory pattern includes a southward migration during the dry season and a northward one during the rainy season, together with a gradual shifting of their territory eastward over the centuries.

Be aware that mapping can be a sensitive issue in many countries or areas. It can arouse suspicion about your motives. Local fears may involve the possibility of increased taxation, of government confiscation of their land with mapping being a preliminary activity, or of mapping being a precursor to a *coup*. Aerial mapping is particularly suspect of spying activity in some countries. If that is the situation, it is better to avoid or discontinue mapping in order to complete your other research goals and avoid doing harm to the community. One way to find out in advance whether mapmaking might arouse suspicion is to talk with researchers who have already worked in that or a nearby area. Talk also with the local leaders and explain what you want to do, then enlist their cooperation with your mapmaking. You need to work with the local people from the beginning of your mapping. They know what is significant and important in their ecosystem.

Mapping is one activity that you can share with a research colleague. His or her contribution, particularly if that individual is from that area, can aid you greatly in understanding the local social situation. That person can help explain to the local people what you are doing, and thus facilitate your research.

In mapping, find out local concepts of distances. For example, one man told Norris about his uncle who was sick. He stated, "Why, he's so sick that he cannot even walk ten miles!" Sometimes distances traditionally have been measured in terms of the length of time it takes to walk them. Local concepts of space usually involve knowledge of local landmarks, distances, and directions.

Initial sketches

When you first enter a new culture, you can begin by making initial sketches of what is visible and measurable. Initial sketches may not require knowledge of the local language.

In initial sketches you may assign a number to each house or compound as a means of reference. Numbers may later be correlated with households headed by specific people. These data can serve as the basis for random selection of houses within which to administer an interview schedule or questionnaire if that is part of your research plan.

In making initial sketches you can pace off specific fields or plots of land, thereby gaining some idea of the amount of land each household has. Many people conceive of the amount of land they farm in terms of plots of land. If you want to convert the number of plots into hectares, you must calculate the conversion in terms of average size of individual plots.

Initial sketches include features such as roads, paths, railroads, schools, buildings used for religious purposes (e.g., churches, mosques, temples, synagogues, and other local religious buildings), sites of ritual activities, markets, transportation parks for public transport, cinemas, bus stops, shops, governmental offices, cemeteries, ball fields, public facilities (e.g., wells, washing areas, parks or plazas, stadiums, etc.), factories, hospitals, dispensaries, farms, hills, rivers, streams, forests, orchards, etc. Since researchers use maps and sketches to document their specific research projects, what is included depends upon your research location and purpose.

Early in your fieldwork project, map and describe items of material culture and technology. Further, note patterns of ownership. For example, it is fairly common that trees are owned separately from the land on which they grow.

As your research progresses, rework your initial sketches in order to make them more accurate. After gaining a working knowledge of the language, you or your cultural assistant may produce a folk map in order to better describe the culture.

Folk maps

FOLK MAPS depict what is significant from an insider's perspective. Depending upon the focus of maps and the research you are documenting, folk maps may indicate specific areas and objects such as sacred trees, areas where specific activities occur, areas where spirits are known to dwell, and so forth. Either an outside researcher with the aid of an insider or an insider to the culture may produce folk maps. In either case resultant maps detail information relevant to an insider's knowledge of the area and culture. You may desire several folk maps, each of which focuses upon a different aspect of the culture.

In producing a folk map, pace off distances. The length of a person's walking pace tends to be remarkably uniform, so pacing off an area can give a rough idea of actual distance. After pacing off a distance, you can then roughly compute it. Alternatively, you can use a measuring tape or other distance indicating device for more accurate measurements.

Artistic sketches

Some researchers, particularly those with some artistic talent, produce artistic sketches that go a long way toward enabling a reader to visualize the social scene they describe. While sketching helps in visualizing social scenes, photographs can also be taken. Since close observation is necessary in sketching, photographs have the advantage of helping you take into account each detail of the situation.

Depending on the type of map you want to produce, sketches can be incorporated into some maps. Sketches can be used to illustrate aspects of the culture you want to highlight.

Artistic sketches can illustrate differences in types of houses, granaries, local designs, village layout, household items, clothing, etc. See the side box for an example.

If you work with a pastoral people, such as one of the groups in the east African cattle complex, you might want to sketch the animals. Physical observable patterns of the animals are important to understand the local worldview. For example, you might want to sketch the patterns of horns of different animals, patterns that the people often deliberately develop. You might also want to sketch the hide pattern of different animals including their spots and colors. Cattle, including their color patterns, horn patterns, behavior, etc., are part of the oral traditions and songs of the people. Your sketches can serve to illustrate patterns mentioned in the oral traditions you collect.

Quiché sketches

Margaret, one of my roommates in college, had spent the previous year in Guatemala with the Quiché people. She had inadvertently left her camera at home in California. So she decided to draw significant aspects of their culture. Throughout the time we lived together, those delightful pictures graced our apartment walls. Though I had not been there, from her sketches I knew what people looked like, what clothes they wore, and what activities they engaged in.

In west Africa some sheep are two-toned, with a white back half and a dark brown front half. For the reader of your write-up who may not have seen sheep with this type of color pattern, a sketch or photograph will definitely help. Other animals that your reader may be unfamiliar with can also be sketched. Since animal patterns sometimes inform other aspects of the culture, such as names, songs, riddles, and other folklore, this information may be important for your understanding of a particular ethnic group.

Sketches are useful for understanding use of social space for social events. For example, who sits where? What is the significance of seating and standing patterns? What is the central focus of the particular social event? What buildings are used for what purposes? Spatial patterning often reflects important information that can come out clearly through sketching that social situation. Understanding of spatial patterning is one component of understanding social events. Mapping thus forms part of your write-up of data which you collect through participant observation within that social setting.

An artistic sketch may show clearly techniques that are involved in making a material object, such as a pot, basket, or textile. You can sketch each step in the process done by an artisan.

Spending time doing artistic sketches is also a delightful way to be with the people and to receive their input on what you are sketching. Sometimes it is a means of discovering local artists, too.

While the focus here is primarily on your doing artistic sketches, local artists' sketches are also important. They will include what is significant from their cultural perspective. For example, a local artist in sketching a jaguar in South America will likely include different aspects of that animal than would an outsider to the area.

Professional maps

For publication you will need a professional map of the area. When none is available for a specific area, this becomes your responsibility. As a start in producing such a map, most countries have federal geographic survey offices that produce maps, frequently made from aerial photographs; these maps can serve as the basis of the new, more detailed, map(s). Frequently aerial maps fail to identify specific villages, though they may indicate residence clusters by dots on the map. Further, such maps may be out-of-date about locations of current villages.

You may find that more than one map is necessary for the local area. For example, one map may have names of villages in the trade language, while another map may present village names in the minority language. Names for villages, towns, cities, rivers, lakes, and other geographic features may be different in the national, trade, and minority languages.

You can then use the available maps as the basis for producing professional quality maps of the local area, adding data you collect locally. Prior to publication, cultural researchers and historians frequently have cartographers or artists produce final professional quality maps. For such professional maps, identify the source maps to give some idea of the reliability and quality of the finished products. Produce the new maps in such a way that they do not violate copyright laws. For example, avoid using any special symbols, particular design, or copyrighted typeface designs that are specific to the source map. Be sure to indicate the scale of the map so that the reader can know what reduction applies.

Be careful about drawing lines around the area of a specific ethnic group. Members of a neighboring group may see this as an attempt to claim land for another group that they themselves claim. This can set off local land disputes. It is better to label the map as the land of the ethnic group and their neighbors, and to omit any lines around the area. In a technical anthropological article one anthropologist encircled on his map the area of the specific ethnic group on which he was focusing and thereby set off a major land dispute. The neighboring group accused him of claiming some of their land for the ethnic group he was writing about, and that dispute took local governmental diplomatic mediation to bring about a resolution.

If it does seem desirable to delineate an area on a map, use some disclaimer. For example, McMillan states on one of her maps, "The boundaries, denominations, and any other information shown on this map do not imply, on the part of the World Bank Group, any judgment on the legal status of any territory, or any endorsement or acceptance of such boundaries" (1995:xxiv–xxv).

Historical maps

You may desire to include in your write-up historical maps that illustrate boundary disputes, areas where significant events occurred such as wars, migrations, trade routes, locations of former villages and camps, and so forth. Sometimes such maps are available in archives, and at other times you must produce them based on information you collect locally.

Features of maps

Every map should have the following seven features:

1. Title of map or sketch.
2. The map itself.
3. An indication of direction. This is the first feature to place on your map, with north being at the top of your map. For example, you can use something like the following:

   N
   ↑
   W ←◇→ E
   ↓
   S

4. Scale of the map. This may be in kilometers or miles. If it is not to scale, you need to specify that. The scale you select limits the amount of information you can include on a map. The specific scale you select depends on the use you plan to have for the map. All maps involve a reduction of the physical features of the geography they display.
5. Landmarks. Maps usually indicate cities, villages, rivers, and roads. Some include topological features. The specific landmarks you choose to include depend upon your purposes in making the map.
6. Date of the map.
7. Key for the map. What things you indicate in your key depends upon the focus of your map. Common keys are as follows (check suggestions on other maps):

Railroad   Telephone   Airport   Bus

Health and social services   Taxi   Church   etc.

Mapping of physical features is related to the study of material culture, the topic of the next chapter.

13

Material Culture

While I was in the market bargaining for a beautifully carved calabash, a Fulani friend asked me, "Why do you want to buy a calabash when you have such beautiful tin cans?"

This Fulani woman preferred tin cans to calabashes as calabashes can break while cans do not. Further, she preferred the cans with securely fitting lids, such as powdered milk cans. Calabashes have a significant role within the social structure of some Fulani. For example, the semisedentary Fulani in the north are divided into north, south, east, and west sections. The central compound has calabashes from each section, thus symbolizing the relationship between all of the sections. Gradually, enamelware bowls and basins are replacing calabashes in northern Nigeria. Enamelware is currently preferred over calabashes because of durability and the adornment with colorful designs; however, calabashes have served both utilitarian and symbolic purposes.

Research on material culture involves study of both form of specific objects and their function within the culture. While material objects are interesting in and of themselves, the study of material culture must be placed within the larger cultural context. What do objects tell us about the culture of the people who use them? What do the decorations symbolize and what ceremonies are they a part of? Who makes and uses those objects? Their study also relates to the inventiveness and creativity of people, and to questions of how people think and how they view their world.

Studies of culture change often look at material culture to help in understanding borrowings and diffusion that have occurred. Cultures often readily accept objects that are brought in from outside. You may be able to trace relationships between different communities and ethnic groups by study of material culture.

Cultural artifacts are often what remains in the archeological record. Archeologists seek to reconstruct past cultures from artifacts.

You can study material culture early in your field research without having the benefit of knowing the local language. This is true especially when looking at the form of objects. You can possibly combine the study of material culture with mapping of the research area. While studying material culture and the technical processes involved in manufacture you begin to gain rapport with the local people.

Material culture includes clothing, body paint, piercing, scarification (e.g., tribal marks), personal adornments, buildings and houses, granaries, furniture, layout of the village or urban area, decorations, food and items used in preparation, eating, and cleanup, hunting

141

and fishing equipment (e.g., guns, bows and arrows, blowguns, nets, spears, sling shots, bait), objects associated with different occupations and craft specialties, basketry and pottery, musical instruments, sewing, spinning and weaving items, weapons, means of transportation, artistic design and expression, and so on. The list can be expanded indefinitely. The point is to select a few of the significant areas for the culture you are studying and describe in detail the objects, their manufacture, and their uses within the culture.

As is illustrated in the upper side box, the study of material culture can lead to significant findings about other areas of the culture. In this example, it led to understanding a bit about the religious beliefs of the Bahenimo.

Chewing arrow types

As Wayne Dye and a fellow anthropologist sat in the men's house researching arrow types in the Bahenimo culture in Papua New Guinea, the old man who was carving the arrow shafts with a marsupial tooth pointed to a carving hung on the wall. He said, "Do you see that carving? He's chewing on the arrow, and that's what makes it straight." This was Wayne's first clue that the carvings in the men's houses are believed to have magical powers in them (W. Dye, personal communication, May 29, 1998).

Symbolism

In studying symbolism, investigate the meanings behind objects. For example, in the lower side box, the number of pig jawbones in the men's house represents the prestige of the lineage.

The meanings associated with material culture are often immediate and pragmatic. They can also be ambiguous, however, so that you cannot readily understand their meaning apart from what people tell you. Even when talking with people, they may not be able to tell you meanings, as for example, when particular art forms have been passed down through the generations. For example, the crosses on Tuareg saddles date back to the pre-Muslim Christian era of North Africa, though present-day Tuareg have no recollection of that era of their history.

Pig jawbones

Alex Bolyanatz reports that among the Sursurunga in New Ireland, Papua New Guinea, men hang the jawbones of pigs in the men's house after having consumed the meat at a mortuary feast. He states, "The number of pig jawbones hanging in the rafters of a men's house are [sic] an index of, among other things, the prestige of deceased lineage members, and of the lineage itself" (Bolyanatz 1994:208).

Holism and material culture

Holism refers to the integration of parts of culture into the whole. It is because of this integration of culture that a change in one part of the culture may also unintentionally change other parts of the culture. Note, however, that all cultures have mechanisms for dealing with change, including the introduction of new items of material culture.

Some anthropologists deplore introduction of new material objects and ideas as changing the culture in negative ways. It is no longer "pristine." While some things introduced, such as alcoholic beverages and tobacco, do have a negative impact upon the health of people, other objects should be viewed as neutral with respect to core values of the culture. Further, it is questionable whether any culture is or ever was "pristine." Cultures in contact with each other, particularly within the same culture area, readily borrow items of material culture.

Changes in material culture

Modernization is most evidenced in the area of material culture. For example, generators, VCRs, and televisions have found their way into remote villages.

Within the same culture area you will likely find a similar inventory of material objects used. When an object of material culture diffuses from one culture to another, the form of the object may be retained or modified somewhat, and its function will likely change. Thus, a toothbrush borrowed into a culture that uses a tooth cleaning stick will likely be used for something other than to brush one's teeth. Form and function of diffused and borrowed objects of material culture should be considered separately.

As mentioned in chapter 2, it is important not to focus solely on traditional objects of material culture. To many of the local people it would appear that that focus leads to their being presented as "backward" to outsiders, a perspective that they would eschew.

Suggestions for study of material culture

A few suggestions for the study of material culture include the following:

1. Inventory the material culture present.
2. What are men's, women's, and children's items of material culture? Study the toys and other objects that are used by children.
3. What items are prestigious? What are high prestige items and what are of low prestige?
4. Who manufactures objects of material culture? What are the processes of their manufacture?
5. How do these items function within the culture?
6. What is the emic meaning of the items you are studying? For example, though the slogans in the side box are interesting, to really understand what the owner of the vehicle had in mind, it would be necessary to ask for their meanings.
7. Note the size, color, and design of the object.
8. Clothing, adornment, body paint, scarification, and circumcision:
   a. What clothes do men, women, boys, and girls wear?
   b. If people wear no clothes, or few, what are means of maintaining modesty?
   c. Who makes clothes?
   d. Is there an apprenticeship involved in making clothes?
   e. Who makes the cloth? What is the process involved?
   f. What dyes are used? How is cloth dyed?
   g. Do the people use body paint? Are there specialists in body painting? What are typical designs? When do people have their bodies painted (e.g., at rites of passage such as initiation and weddings)? What do they use as paint (e.g., henna, chalk)? Is there tattooing?

> ### Slogans on vehicles in northern Nigeria
>
> Blessed be to God
> If men were God people should have safer
> Grace to God
> A New Chance
> God's Will
> VC-10 (on an earth mover)
> No King as God
> No God as King (on a dilapidated dump truck)
> Up Jet
> Rock of Ages (on a dump truck)
> One with God is Majority
> Time is Money
> God Never Sleep Transport Service
> V.I.P. No. 1
> Jesus Only
> Love bug (on a car)
> Have Mercy! Oh Lord
> The Lord is My Shepherd
> If Men were God, People would have suffer
> Enter with Love

    h. Is male circumcision practiced? At what age are males circumcised? Who are the circumcisors? What training do they have? Must young men be circumcised before they marry? How is the circumcision carried out? What object is used to do the circumcision? (Note that circumcision for both males and females touches on a number of areas other than material culture. It involves ritual, a rite of passage, perhaps formation of an age set, etc.)

    i. Is female circumcision practiced? At what age are females circumcised? Is it practiced for religious or cultural reasons? What is the ideology behind female circumcision? Who are the circumcisors? What training do they have (e.g., an apprenticeship)? How is the circumcision carried out? What object is used? What is the status of female circumcision in the country? (Note that many countries are looking for ways to abolish this practice.)

    j. What ornaments do people wear and what are their significance? Are there necklaces, bracelets, ear decorations, nose decorations, headbands, feathers, armbands, etc.? What special ornaments are worn on specific occasions?

9. Pottery
    a. What is the source of clay for the pottery?
    b. What are the sizes and shapes of pottery commonly made?
    c. Who are the potters (e.g., men or women, people in a specific village or ethnic group)? Who are the middle people who sell the pottery?
    d. What are typical designs on the pottery, and what is their significance?
    e. How does the design tradition of one ethnic group compare with that of nearby groups?
    f. Are there specific villages which specialize in pottery and other crafts? What is the means of distribution of their products?
    g. How is pottery fired?

10. Art, artists, and artistic expression
    a. What art forms are associated with what artifacts?
    b. What are common or typical styles that can be used to define an art tradition?
    c. Who are the artists and how are they trained?
    d. What are the mediums used for art, e.g., rock art, clothing, architectural styles, decorations, paper, canvas, etc.?
    e. What are religious artistic expressions, e.g., icons, crosses, menorahs, geometric designs, idols, jujus, murals, etc.?
    f. What symbolism is associated with specific art forms?
    g. Are artifacts discarded once their use, as in a particular ceremony, is completed? For many people art is pragmatic. It is not "art for art's sake."
    h. Artisans and artists:
       i. Are artists full time or part time specialists?
      ii. What are means of remuneration for artists?
     iii. What is the status of artists within the culture?
     iv. Is the position of artisan inherited?
      v. Do artists and artisans marry endogamously?
    i. What materials are used in specific art objects? Where are dyes obtained? Where is clay obtained?

11. Tools for farming, manufacturing, blacksmithing, basketry, sewing and weaving; utensils and containers for cooking and serving; means of transportation, weapons, fishing gear, etc.

Documentation of material culture

Documentation of material culture includes photographing, producing ethnographic film, videotaping, collecting artifacts, sketching artifacts, etc. Remember that however you document the material culture that exists within a specific cultural context, that context must be respected and understood. Analysis of material objects apart from their cultural context leads to focus on form alone without regard for meaning.

Photography

Photographing documents material culture in field research and communicates information to a larger audience. It makes images available to those not there.

In using photography in field research there are certain cautions to be aware of:

1. People may perceive that you plan to exploit them by selling their pictures, with the result that you become wealthy while they remain in poverty.
2. People may feel that you are capturing their soul on film. This can strike fear and terror into people.
3. Find out the typical local attitude towards taking people's pictures. You need to obtain permission from those photographed in advance and even "tip" them.
4. Many want copies of their pictures. While a reasonable request, it may be a difficult request to meet when photo processing is either unsatisfactory or else not readily available. One way to comply with their request is to have a Polaroid camera with you, take their pictures with it and give them the pictures from it. One researcher had the type of Polaroid that puts the picture into a box; he/she sent that picture back to the person from the next village. If you give them the picture while you are there and also take a picture with another camera for your own use, sending it back from the next village can help you avoid the problem of their wanting both pictures, one from each camera.
5. Many may want you to become the resident photographer, taking up so much of your time that you are unable to continue other important aspects of your research.
6. People may want remuneration for your taking their picture. For example, when some people and I were photographing ceremonies at the Santa Clara Pueblo in New Mexico, local men came to each of us requesting a fee for photographing the ceremonies. They then gave a red tag to each of us to hang on our clothing indicating that we had paid for permission to photograph.
7. Obtain their permission prior to publication of their pictures.
8. In the study of body adornment "A camera is the ideal instrument for preserving the momentary art of body decoration and face paint" (Carpenter 1995:490).
9. If you are in a trouble spot in the world, avoid photographing anything related to the military, including soldiers, military installations, bases, etc. Also avoid taking pictures of sensitive places such as airports, radio and television stations, government buildings, border crossings, and even bridges and highways. To photograph these may lead to your arrest as a possible spy.

A few suggestions for picture taking are:

1. Prior to going, make a list of all the photo supplies that you will likely need. These include a camera or two, film, lens cleaning solution and tissues, batteries, camera bag,

plastic bags for your film and camera, and any lenses you may decide on. Then systematically collect those objects. If you are going to a rain forest area, bring desiccants with you. These draw moisture out of the air. Place them into the plastic bags with your film and with your camera.

2. Choose your film speed (ASA/ISO number) according to the type of pictures you will be taking. ISO 100 or 200 is ideal fine grained film. When photographing moving objects use a higher ISO film, such as ISO 400 or 800. Some choose to use ISO 400 as their standard film. The difference between ISO 200 and 400 films becomes significant if you plan to blow up a picture to 11" x 14" or larger where the ISO 400 film will be grainier.

3. Use color as well as black-and-white film. Color provides documentation of the appropriate colors of objects, while black-and-white film has greater longevity. If using black-and-white film you can use the traditional Kodak Tri-X Pan film, or, for ease in development, use chromogenic black-and-white film. The latter is processed in the same chemicals as color film, making it easier to get black-and-white prints. Examples of chromogenic black-and-white film are Kodak Professional T-Max T400 CN, Ilford XP-2, and Konica VX Pan 400.

4. Check the expiration date on the film you purchase. Avoid purchase of out-of-date film. Since pictures are important for documenting the material culture, choose the best quality film.

5. Store your film (especially color film) in as cool and as dry of an environment as possible. Most photographers keep their film in the original box and often in a plastic bag or container in the refrigerator. In a field situation high heat and humidity can be problematic. If you have or have access to an electric or kerosene refrigerator, use it for film storage. Refrigeration extends the life of your film. When you take the film out of the refrigerator to use, allow it to warm up first before loading it into your camera. I sometimes hold my film in my warm hands before loading it into the camera.

6. Check for correct settings on your camera and use good lighting for your pictures.

7. When photographing objects, place a ruler next to the object in order to give some indication of the size of the artifact.

8. If shaking is a problem, as with use of a telephoto lens, use a tripod. Select the type of tripod with legs that screw and pull down rather than release then pull down. Alternatively, to avoid a shaky picture, rest your camera on a stable object (rock, fence, table, etc.). Using a higher ISO film speed also helps to mitigate against the effects of shakiness. The problem with shooting while shaking is that the picture will be blurry.

9. Avoid leaving film in your camera for extended periods of time, especially after it is exposed. Leaving it exposed in your camera may cause deterioration in its picture quality. As a rule of thumb, it is a good idea to have film processed within a month or two after shooting it. If you are in a field situation where you cannot have your film processed right away, put your exposed film in the refrigerator. Heat can deteriorate film that is left in a hot place. It can also deteriorate the seals in your camera. So avoid leaving your camera in your car or other hot place.

10. Have your exposed film processed at a photofinisher that uses archive quality procedures and materials. Hazards of poor quality processing include slides that turn green over time, colors that are off (e.g., skin tones may be off), too light or too dark, etc. If the colors or lightness–darkness are off, request that they redo the picture. Most photofinishers will do so for free.

11. Have duplicate pictures made and store them in a safe place different from the place of the originals.

12. Use paper that is acid free around prints, slides, and negatives. Mount prints on acid free paper.
13. Store negatives in archival quality print files without PVC. These are sleeves that have individual slots for negative strips. They are available at most photofinishing stores.
14. Keep a record of all your photographs. Label all negatives (e.g., write the information in the space at the top of the print files), slides, and prints. Do so in such a way that they correlate with the record or log that you keep.
15. Use only a soft lead pencil when writing on the backs of prints. Many photographers avoid writing on the backs of pictures at all.
16. Check your prints, negatives, and slides regularly to ascertain that no fungi, insects, or other means of deterioration are actively destroying your pictures.
17. Be careful in handling prints. Use gloves that are available at most photofinishing stores for handling prints in order to avoid finger prints on pictures.
18. Keep your lens clean prior to shooting pictures. Take lens cleaning tissue and solution with you and use them regularly. Keeping your lens dust free assures that you do not have dust spots on negatives.
19. When changing batteries check for leakage of your old batteries. If leakage has occurred, clean the inside of the battery compartment with a pencil eraser prior to placing the new batteries into your camera.
20. Store your camera in a dust free environment to the extent possible. You can place your camera in a plastic bag that seals, then place it into your camera bag. If you find that you have dust within your camera compartment, blow it out, being careful not to touch the shutter. Dust is an enemy of good pictures. Sand and salt water are also hazardous to cameras.

There are some general considerations to be aware of when taking a camera abroad. For example, though you may take an inexpensive point-and-shoot camera, it may be an object for theft in some areas. Precautions include keeping your camera in view at all times, writing down the serial number of your camera and keeping it in a safe place so that you can prove ownership if it is recovered after being stolen, locking your camera in your luggage or in a hotel safe rather than leaving it in your room, and being aware of distractions. Thieves frequently work in pairs, with one creating a distraction while the other steals your camera or other objects you may have with you. Sometimes they deliberately bump you or spill food on you. If that happens hold on tightly to your purse, camera, and camera bag. In spite of all your precautions, if your camera is stolen, you may decide to wait until you return home to replace it as cameras are frequently more expensive abroad. Perhaps you can buy a one-time-use camera(s) until you return home.

When traveling through security at airports, request that your film be hand inspected rather than passed through the x-ray machines. Take the film cartridges out of their boxes and place them in a clear plastic bag. Alternatively, you may purchase special lead lined bags that are specifically designed to shield your film from x-rays. If you have such in your suitcase, it is likely that the security personnel will request that you show them what is causing the blank spot on their x-ray monitor. If film goes through x-ray machines repeatedly, a "fog" may build up on it.

Always carry your camera with you rather than place it in your luggage. Some luggage goes through high damaging radiation as the security searches for plastic explosives and other dangerous material. When going through security, hand your camera to the attendant for inspection, rather than passing it through the x-ray machine.

Ethnographic films and video taping

Ethnographic video taping and film producing have been a part of cultural research for decades. One early film is *Nanook of the North*, a film that continues to serve as an important documentary.

Producing ethnographic film and taping videos are a huge field. The fact that video cameras are now in the price range that most fieldworkers can own them and take them to the field means that increasingly good films can be produced of people in field sites around the world. Many of the cautions mentioned above also apply to this area of research. For more information on this important field method see Hockings' book entitled *Principles of Visual Anthropology* (1995) and other references on cinematography.

Collecting artifacts

Collecting artifacts is important if you plan to display them in a museum or use them for an exhibit. Be aware, however, that many countries do not allow antiquities out of the country. Some countries allow you to do so if you have first had them approved by the local museum. Their allowing you to take them out of the country will be selective, with the department of antiquities or the local museum making decisions on what you may or may not take. They then give you the appropriate papers to allow you to take them through customs. Objects that continue to be manufactured by local artisans tend not to present the same problems as do antiquities.

14

Kinship

Relatives cannot be washed [separated]. (Bajju proverb)

This Bajju proverb states that we do not choose our relatives as we do our friends. Whether we like them or not, relatives are still relatives. This chapter concerns relatives as they fit into kinship systems. Kinship systems differ from culture to culture, though some common patterns are found. When living cross-culturally you will likely find that events such as weddings, fights, funerals, etc. make no sense unless you know the relationships of people to each other.

In most societies understanding kinship relationships is essential to understand the people and to know how to relate appropriately and effectively to others. For example, among the indigenous Australians, mothers rarely tell their children what they should do; however, they share kinship relationships, expectations, and responsibilities with them daily. Kinship is a central focus of their culture. This focus is evident in other cultures as well, as for example among the Navaho:

> The worst that one may say of another person is, "He acts as if he didn't have any relatives." Conversely, the ideal of behavior often enunciated by headmen is, "Act as if everybody were related to you." (Kluckhohn and Leighton 1946:100)

KINSHIP SYSTEMS are culturally defined, orderly groupings of social and biological relationships based on marriage (affinal relationships) and birth (consanguineal relationships). They address kin relations, groups, responsibilities and obligations, and the system of classifying kin within a society. They are embedded within the total cultural context, including religion, politics, economics, and especially social organization. Social organization includes residence patterns, descent, inheritance, divisions of labor, roles and statuses, voluntary organizations, marriage patterns, interaction, and visitation. Analysis of kinship systems can serve various purposes such as understanding rights, duties, privileges, responsibilities, expected behaviors, and obligations correlated with different kin categories.

Kinship studies can help you know where you might fit within that system. In some cultures you need to fit into a kin category, and based on that you can then relate to others within that culture. In other cultures, while perhaps being addressed by a kin term, you fit into the category of "visitor" or "stranger." This is especially true in Africa. If you have children, however, you will likely be called the "mother/father of..." with the name of your child inserted in the blank space (e.g., Mama Susan). Heyer found that among the

Kipsigis in Kenya, "they seemed unable to treat me as an outsider. I *had* to have a role that was identifiable in their terms. They ascribed to me the role of an unmarried daughter in the household in which I was living. It was not always easy to live up to this, but by and large it worked." (1993:207, italics added)

Shaw similarly found that he needed a close relationship with the Samo people in order understand them. He writes,

> In March of 1973 they decided to initiate me in order to properly assign kinship terms to myself and my family. This helped establish the proper interaction patterns necessary for appropriate relationships within the community. My initiation greatly increased my credibility among them and established me in a close relationship with a group of male and female coinitiates that continues to the present. (Shaw 1996:7)

Being incorporated into Samo kinship brings obligations as Shaw soon found out:

> Upon returning from a field break, I was greeted as "older brother" by a young man who came out to meet us. As we went up the trail to our house others came to help and all used kin terms, designating relative age. I was delighted and reflected on this while we were unpacking. Soon a commotion at the open doorway caught my attention, and I went to see what was happening. An older man greeted me as "younger brother" and asked if, perchance, in our travels we might have brought some tinned fish back with us. Indeed we had, and I was happy to give him a can. Busying myself with settling back in, it was not long before there was more coughing at the door, and a younger woman greeted me using the term for "older brother" and wondering if I had returned with some soap. I was happy to give her a bar of soap and she went happily on her way. Soon there was another disturbance, and a young man warmly greeted me only to ask for some matches. As I looked beyond into the forest people were lining up to greet us and ask for some small item (pp. 40–41).

Shaw soon learned that anyone who leaves the village and returns is expected to share with the entire community.

Kinship terms of reference and address

Kinship analyses are based on KIN TERMS OF REFER-ENCE, terms which people use to refer to others when talking about them. KIN TERMS OF ADDRESS are those people call each other in face-to-face contact. For example, my children refer to me as "mother" but they address me as "mom." While fieldworkers regularly collect both sets of terms, their analyses of kinship systems are based on terms of reference.

When doing a kinship study, collect kinship data with reference to one individual who is specified as EGO. In the side box about the Bajju, the sex of ego determines the choice of kin terms.

Sibling terms

The Bajju have cross-sex sibling terms. A male ego refers to his sister as *anap* and a female ego refers to her brother as *asam*. A male ego would not refer to a male sibling as *asam*, as that term refers only to a cross-sex sibling, nor would a female ego refer to her female sibling as *anap*. Same sex siblings are referred to either by the generic term for sibling, *awumba*, or by specific terms that indicate birth order.

Kinship charts

Cultural researchers construct kinship charts in order to indicate graphically the relationships and genealogical ties between individuals. This section shows the anthropological conventions used for charting kinship. Begin with charting a small family before moving on to charting larger units.

Male: △

Female: ○

Sex unspecified (whether unknown or irrelevant):   □

Ego: ▲   ●

Marriage, affinal relationship:

The equal symbolizes marriage as does the upward bracket. A bracket downward symbolizes a sibling relationship:

Marriage to multiple wives:

Mating relationship that does not involve marriage: △   ≈   ○

Lineal relative, descent, consanguineal relationship:

Multiple birth:

Fictive kinship, adoption, ritual kinship:

Deceased: ⊘   or   ⊗

Divorce or annulment of marriage: Δ   ≠   ○   or   Δ ○

When charting siblings, by convention the oldest is on the left side of the chart, with subsequent siblings charted according to age from left to right. If you find that keeping siblings in their birth order interferes with keeping a husband and wife together on your kinship diagram, be sure to keep the husband and wife together so that you can readily chart their children as their descendants. Note that there may be separate terms for sibling categories, such as for oldest sibling, adjacent sibling, nonadjacent sibling, and youngest sibling. When that is case you may want to display siblings separately such as the Bajju example in (33).

(33)

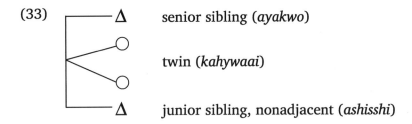

senior sibling (*ayakwo*)

twin (*kahywaai*)

junior sibling, nonadjacent (*ashisshi*)

While vertical charting is unusual, it can help show the relationship between siblings. Other Bajju sibling kin terms are (McKinney 1983:285):

(34)   Sibling (general term):   *awumba*, sg.; *bawumbeyang*, pl.
       Br (term used by a female ego): *asam*, sg.; *basam*, pl.
       Si (term used by a male ego):   *anap*, sg.; *banap*, pl.

Kinship charts can expand quickly, especially when dealing with ethnic groups with polygynous marriages, as illustrated in the side box.

Adoption, fictive kinship, and ritual kinship

Adoption, fictive kinship, and ritual kinship are charted by use of dashed lines. A kinship chart does not distinguish between these three relationships, but rather coalesces them into one.

ADOPTION is a means whereby a person or persons legally becomes the parent(s) of another person's biological child. It changes the status of the adoptee. The position of parent legally changes from that of the biological parent(s) to the sociological parent(s) and their kin group; it is similar to a congenital relationship.

FICTIVE KINSHIP is a relationship based on fiction. While not kin by blood or marriage, through an agreed upon fiction a person becomes part of the kinship system of another nonkin. This is important for you as a fieldworker to understand as it may be the only way whereby you can enter another culture. The

---

Ten wives

When I was collecting data for a kinship chart from Bulus, I found that ego's father had had ten wives and many children, so many that Bulus did not know all of them. In the process of collecting these data, I quickly filled several 8½" by 11" sheets of paper. I learned a lot about expected behaviors that correlated with specific kin categories. For example, I learned about burial practices for women suspected of being witches. One wife had been so accused and received a dishonorable burial to keep her from returning through reincarnation.

example of Shaw being assigned the status of "older brother" to a younger person or "younger brother" to an older person is a fictive kinship relationship. It provides the local people a way to interact with the fieldworker.

By contrast, RITUAL KINSHIP involves formal rites that establish a kinship tie between two individuals and also between their two kin groups. Shepherd reports that ritual kinship among the Magar in Nepal is so strong that it can never be broken. Further, it passes down from father to son (Gary Shepherd, personal communication, 1987).

Correlating kin terms with expected behavior

Kinship analysis involves collecting both kin terms of reference and the expected behavior that correlates with each kin category. Categories for some commonly found, expected behaviors include joking, familiar, and avoidance relationships.

Joking and familiar relationships

JOKING RELATIONSHIPS are "patterned behavior between relatives that calls for mild to taunting or ribald joking" (Schusky 1965:91). Joking relationships are part of the broader category of familiar relationships. Winick defines FAMILIAR RELATIONSHIPS as, "certain freedoms which can be taken with specific relatives. A typical example is the joking relationship between nephew and paternal aunt in many...cultures" (Winick 1977:201).

Joking relationships can occur on various levels of social organization, for example, between specific kin categories (e.g., mother's brother or sister with sister's son or daughter), between alternate generations (the generation above ego, termed the +1 generation, and the generation below ego, termed the –1 generation), a male ego and ego's brother's wife (this typically occurs in patrilineal societies that have the levirate and widow inheritance), between villages, and between ethnic groups.

When joking relationships occur between alternate generations, an elderly grandmother may joke with a boy in the second generation descending from her that he is her husband or that she wants to marry him. When we lived in Africa our young sons never quite appreciated this type of joking.

As already mentioned, in many societies mother's brother and/or mother's sister have a special relationship to mother's sister's son and/or daughter. That special indulgent relationship may be one of privileged familiarity, such that an individual can go to his or her mother's brother's or sister's house and take whatever he or she desires, and may also reside there in the event that problems occur at home. This pattern of familiarity between mother's brother and sister with ego exists for the Bajju and Atyap in southern Kaduna State (McKinney 1983). This relationship contrasts with that within the family where there is an authority relationship with one's parents, especially with one's father.

Since mother's brother and/or mother's sister have a special relationship to ego in societies with either patrilineal or matrilineal descent groups, be sure to inquire about these relationships when researching a group with unilineal descent.

Caricaturing villages
In one ethnic group in Africa the people in one village caricatured people in an adjacent village as having thick lips, those in another they teased that their knees protrude, and they told members of a third village that they used locust bean cakes as a perfume, cakes which smell so bad that you would not want to be down wind of them.

Joking relationships between villages is illustrated by the example in the side box on previous page. Biebuyck and Matenne reported a joking relationship between ethnic groups in the Congo: "To the entire Nyanga population, they [various Pygmy groups] stand in some sort of joking relationship in that, for example, they are allowed to freely harvest plantains in all banana groves" (1969:2).

Avoidance relationships

An AVOIDANCE RELATIONSHIP involves avoidance in speech and physical contact of another culturally specified relative. Winick defines an avoidance relationship as, "the prescribed minimization of contact between relatives in certain…societies. The regulations governing avoidance usually apply to individuals of opposite sex" (1977:53).

Avoidance relationships are a means of showing respect, respect that is symbolized by social distance. Cultures may also have prescribed avoidance behavior in certain situations to prevent potential conflict. For example, among the Apache in North America a male ego traditionally maintained a social distance from his sister from age six or seven onwards (Opler 1955:193–94).

Some cultures have mother-in-law avoidance, as for example among the Navaho where a man avoids his mother-in-law. Other societies have avoidance relationships for other kin categories. For example, the Hausa foster a couple's first child (when he or she is weaned) to a close relative such as to father's mother; similarly, the second child may be fostered to a relative such as mother's mother. This tends to result in mother-first son avoidance with its accompanying social distance.

Genealogical method

The GENEALOGICAL METHOD refers to collecting kinship data from one person, data that include all the relatives who are related to ego. For example, Rivers stated, "It is a familiar fact that many peoples preserve long pedigrees of their ancestors, going back for many generations and often shading off into the mythical" (Rivers 1910:1). The "living dead" or ancestors may also be included in genealogies.

Using the genealogical method, collect kin data for all kin of a particular individual, including terms of reference for each individual who is related to ego. As you collect the genealogy of a particular ego, you also collect other related information, such as expected behaviors of different relatives as they relate to ego, the clan of each person, the totem of each clan, the residence sites of the persons included, birth places and dates, and to the extent that people know them, reciprocal relationships, names of individuals in the genealogy, and adoptive and fictive kin.

In many societies women are the experts in keeping genealogies. In others the men are the kinship experts. Find out who are the local kinship experts, whether men or women.

In former French West Africa you can collect genealogies from a male praise singer, termed a *griot* or a female praise singer, termed a *griotte*. Some researchers refer to male praise singers as *griot*-genealogists. For example, praise singers often keep long genealogies of leaders in a culture. In their praises they may focus on genealogies, wars, history, praise or ridicule of specific leaders, etc. The domain of female praise singers tends to be weddings and naming ceremonies.

Collecting genealogies can present problems if you encounter name taboos in which a deceased ancestor can never be referred to by name. Shaw encountered this when working with the Samo in Papua New Guinea:

> I quickly discovered that collecting a genealogy with any depth was virtually impossible. The Samo did not keep genealogical records because of each individual's relationship with the ancestors. The dead were never referred to by name, individuals would not use their own name, and others with the same name were referred to by using a special reciprocal term, *lonlin*. Name taboos were also frequent between allies. Clearly the ancestors were central to understanding the importance of names. (1996:39)

Further, Shaw states that household residence is more important than specific genealogical relationships. Cooperation, interaction within the community, gender, and the initiation cycle are of prime importance for the Samo, rather than genealogical relationships (pp. 42–43).

In some instances, collecting genealogical data can be threatening to the local people. For example, Gerlach found that the Digo in Kenya, east Africa, felt threatened about providing genealogical information because it tied in closely with property rights disputes (Gerlach, as quoted in Pelto and Pelto 1970:197). It is true that you may want to understand these disputes; however, balance your quest for understanding with what people are willing to tell you. The key to success in collecting genealogical data is to be sensitive as to when it is or is not acceptable within the local context.

The Yãnomamö of Venezuela and Brazil have name taboos after individuals die. The word used as a person's name can no longer be used in the language. Hence, they tend to name their children after very specific and minute parts of things and animals. Chagnon (1977:10) reports that names like "toenail of some rodent" may be given a child. The Yãnomamö can thereby maintain both the words of "toenail" and the "rodent" but they may no longer speak of that animal's toenail. Because of this name taboo Chagnon ran into difficulties collecting genealogies in general. He states,

> They enjoyed watching me learn these names. I assumed, wrongly, that I would get the truth to each question and that I would get the best information by working in public. This set the stage for converting a serious project into a farce. Each informant tried to outdo his peers by inventing a name even more ridiculous than what I had been given earlier, or by asserting that the individual about whom I inquired was married to his mother or daughter, or the like. I would have the informant whisper the name of the individual in my ear, noting that he was the father of such and such a child. Everybody would then insist that I repeat the name aloud, roaring in hysterics as I clumsily pronounced the name. I assumed that the laughter was in response to the violation of the name taboo or to my pronunciation. This was a reasonable interpretation, since the individual whose name I said aloud invariably became angry. After I learned what some of the names meant, I began to understand what the laughter was all about....

> I was forced to do my genealogy work in private because of the horseplay and nonsense. (p. 11)

Data to collect

In gathering kinship data, note the following:

1. Source(s)
2. Culture

3. Where the data are collected
4. Date
5. Kin terms of reference
6. Expected behavior(s) correlated with each kin relationship

In general, kin called by the same kinship term have the same expected behaviors towards ego. Check whether or not kin terms for same sex siblings are different from terms of opposite sex siblings.

When eliciting kin terms collect them out to the borders of the system in order to find the patterns of that kinship system. In other words, ask about all the kinship categories of people who might possibly be related to ego. Collect the kin terms according to the genealogical method with the following kin relationships in mind.

Mo (mother)	Oldest sibling	FaBrDa	HiSoSo	SiSoSo
Fa (father)	Youngest sibling	WiMo	HuSiDa	SiSoDa
So (son)	Nonadjacent sibling	WiFa	HuBrSo	SiDaSo
Da (daughter)	Twins	WiMoMo	HuBrDa	SiDaDa
Wi (wife)	DaHu	WiMoFa	HuSiDaDa	SiSoWi
Hu (husband)	DaDa	WiFaFa	HuSiDaSo	SiDaHu
CoWi (co-wife)	DaSo	WiFaMo	HuBrDaDa	Etc.
a. First wife	SoDa	WiSi	HuBrDaSo	
b. Second	SoSo	WiSiSo	MoBr	
wife, etc.	SoDaDa	WiSiDa	MoSi	
FaFa (father's	SoDaSo	WiSiDaDa	MoBrSo	
father)	DaSoDa	WiSiDaSo	MoBrDa	
FaMo (father's	DaDaDa	WiBr	MoSiSo	
mother)	DaSoSo	WiBrSo	MoSiDa	
MoMoMo	DaDaSo	WiBrDa	MoBrSoSo	
MoMoFa	SoSoDa	WiBrDaDa	MoBrSoDa	
MoFaMo	SoSoSo	WiBrDaSo	MoSiSo	
MoFaFa	SoWi	HuMo	MoSiDa	
FaMoFa	FaSi	MoFa	MoSiSoSo	
FaMoMo	FaBr	MoMoMo	MoSiSoDa	
FaFaFa	FaSiHu	HuMoFa	MoSiDaSo	
FaFaMo	FaBrWi	MoFaMo	MoSiDaDa	
Si/Ƶ (sister)*	FaSiSo	HuFaFa	SiHu	
Br (brother)	FaSiDa	HuSi	SiSo	
Adjacent sibling	FaBrSo	HuBr	SiDa	

*Si is more common in American kinship studies, while Ƶ is more often used by British researchers. Either may be used to indicate sister.

The basic terms Wi, Hu, Br, Si, Mo, and Fa imply the gender of ego. Other kin terms may possibly be different for a male ego than for a female ego; however, this is likely limited to very close relationships, such as between siblings (e.g., the Bajju example in (33)).

It may be too difficult for a person who is giving you kin terms to think of some of the relationships in abstract terms such as MoSiDaSo. It will be much easier for that person to give you kin terms if you have him or her to be ego and give you the name and kin term for each actual relative (i.e., implement the genealogical method). Start with the closest relatives and work outward through the system until no new kin terms are forthcoming.

Family

The most basic unit of kinship is that of the mother and her child. The role of father may be filled by the biological or a sociological father; the role of mother may be filled by the biological or a nonbiological mother, as in the case of adoption or fostering.

The FAMILY is composed of at least one married couple and their children; the NUCLEAR FAMILY is the minimum unit composed of just one couple and their children. The nuclear family is also referred to as the CONJUGAL FAMILY and the ELEMENTARY FAMILY.

An EXTENDED FAMILY includes two or more married couples related through blood ties. For example, ego and his wife and their son and his wife would be a minimum extended family. In many societies extended families comprise residential units. Since extended families often have extensive expectations, rights, and responsibilities for family members, in societies where extended families are important, gather both ideal and actual behaviors associated with specific kin. Anthropologists distinguish between one's FAMILY OF ORIENTATION, the family into which one is born, and one's FAMILY OF PROCREATION, the family formed after marriage, including one's spouse and children.

Parallel and cross-cousins

People in cultures with unilineal descent (see next chapter) differentiate between PARALLEL COUSINS and CROSS-COUSINS. The sex of the linking relative determines whether a person is one's parallel or cross-cousin. For example, father's brother's children and mother's sisters children are ego's parallel cousins. The linking relatives are father's brother, who is the same sex as ego's father, and mother's sister, who is the same sex as ego's mother; hence, their children are parallel cousins. Another way to state this distinction is that parallel cousins are children of siblings of the same sex. Mother's brother's children and father's sister's children are ego's cross-cousins. Cross-cousins are children of the siblings of the opposite sex. See the diagram in (35) for the distinction between parallel and cross-cousins on a kinship chart.

This distinction between parallel and cross-cousins is significant for understanding different marriage patterns within unilineal kinship systems. In some cultures the preferred marital partner for a male ego is his cross-cousin, and in other cultures it is his parallel cousin.

Kinship systems

There are six canonical kinship systems that were first described by Lewis Henry Morgan in 1871. He named each system based on where he first found it. For example, the Hawaiian system is so named not because it occurs only in Hawaii, but rather because Morgan first received data on that kinship system from there. These models lump together or separate kin in their kin terminology.

In your fieldwork view these as models or frameworks only. Analyze all the data you collect according to its own system, then compare it with one of these systems. Specific data may differ significantly from the most similar model, but the models describe what anthropologists frequently encounter.

(35) Ego's parallel and cross-cousins

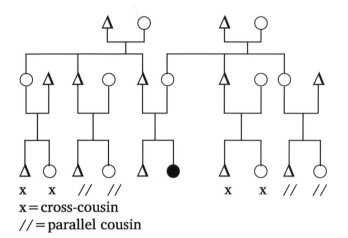

x = cross-cousin
// = parallel cousin

The six most common kinship systems are the Hawaiian, Eskimo, Iroquois, Omaha, Crow, and Sudanese. Some of these systems occur much more frequently than others. For example, in terms of the total number of kinship systems in the world, the Eskimo is rare while the Iroquois is much more widespread.

In the kinship figures below spouses are omitted, other than ego's mother and father. In these kinship figures I have used English kinship terms for specific kin categories; these indicate individuals covered by specific kin terms.

Hawaiian kinship

The HAWAIIAN KINSHIP SYSTEM has the fewest kin terms. Basically, everyone in the first ascending generation from ego is "mother" and "father," everyone in ego's generation is "sister" and "brother," and everyone in the first descending generation is ego's "son" and "daughter." For example, ego's father and father's brother are both "father." This system is termed a GENERATIONAL SYSTEM.

(36) Hawaiian kinship terms

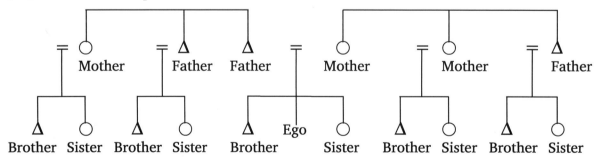

Eskimo kinship

The ESKIMO KINSHIP SYSTEM is that which most English cultures have. One's biological father and mother are termed "father" and "mother," respectively.

(37) Eskimo kinship terms

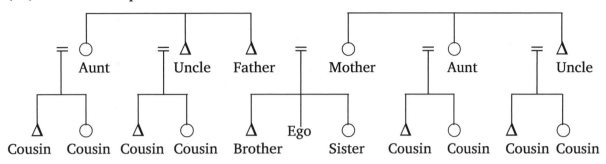

Mother's brother and father's brother are both called "uncle," and mother's sister and father's sister are termed "aunt." The descendants of mother's brother and mother's sister, as well as father's brother and father's sister, are all termed "cousin." Hence, this kinship system does not distinguish between the mother's and the father's descent line. They are collapsed, as seen in the kinship terms. Ethnographers refer to this as a BIFURCATE MERGING system. The system bifurcates or divides into two, the two descent lines for mother and father, and it merges terms from those two sides.

Iroquois kinship

In the IROQUOIS KINSHIP SYSTEM father's sister and brother are termed differently from those of mother's sister and brother. Mother's sister is called "mother", and mother's brother is termed "uncle." Father's sister is called "aunt," and father's brother is called "father." Thus, the term "mother" refers to ego's mother and ego's mother's sister. Similarly, the term "father" refers to ego's father and father's brother. To state this relationship another way, the parents of ego's cross-cousins are "aunt" and "uncle," and the parents of ego's parallel cousins are "mother," and "father." In this system, parallel cousins are distinguished from cross-cousins. Ego's parallel cousins are classified together with ego's biological brothers and sisters, and ego's cross-cousins have their own terms.

(38) Iroquois kinship terms

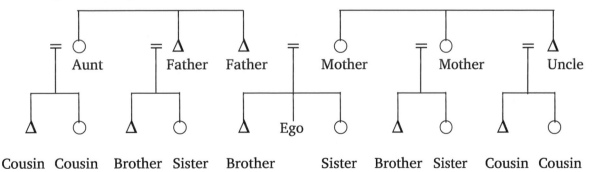

Omaha kinship

In the OMAHA KINSHIP SYSTEM ego's father and father's brother are both termed "father," and ego's father's sister is called "father's sister." Ego's mother and mother's sister are both "mother," while ego's mother's brother is "mother's brother." The terms "mother" and "mother's brother" both apply to relatives in ascending and descending generations from ego. For example, mother's brother's daughter is "mother," and mother's brother's son's daughter is "mother"; similarly, mother's brother's father is also termed "mother's brother," and mother's father's sister is "mother." In other words, a few specific kin terms are not tied to one generation, but rather transcend generations. Cross-cousins are also distinguished from parallel cousins. The Omaha kinship system typically occurs with patrilineal descent. (See the next chapter for a discussion of descent.)

(39) Omaha kinship terms

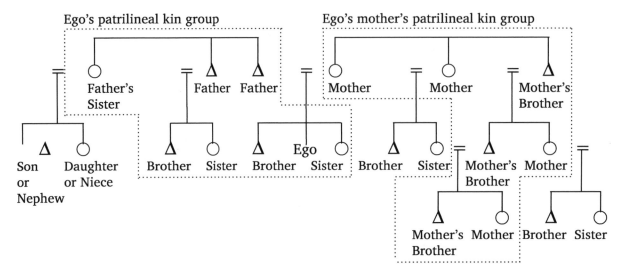

Whereas the kinship systems considered to this point are symmetrical in the way they deal with ego's father and mother's sides of the family, the Omaha and Crow systems are different.

Crow kinship

The CROW KINSHIP SYSTEM is similar to the Omaha system in that specific kin terms transcend generations. For example, ego's father's sister's daughter is "father's sister" and ego's father's sister's son is "father." Parallel cousins are classified with siblings, and cross-cousins are classified separately. The Crow kinship system occurs with matrilineal descent.

(40) Crow kinship terms

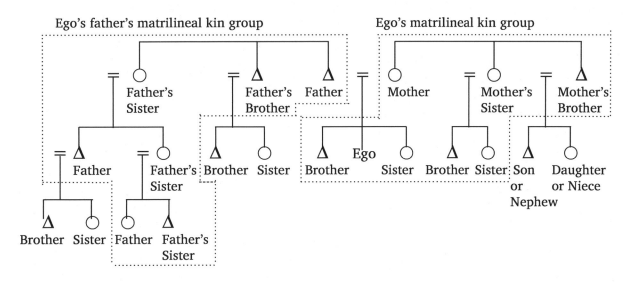

Sudanese kinship

The SUDANESE KINSHIP SYSTEM has a maximal number of kin terms, with different terms for father, father's brother, father's sister, mother, mother's sister, and mother's brother. Parallel cousins are classified separately from cross-cousins. The terms brother and sister apply only to ego's siblings.

(41) Sudanese kinship terms

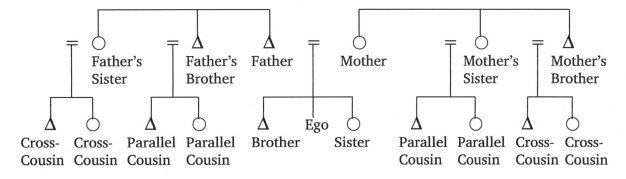

Discussion of kinship systems

These six kinship systems provide a framework or set of models that can help you understand the data you collect. You may find that the specific kinship data you collect do not fit into any of these six canonical patterns. What ethnographers typically do is describe their data with respect to one of these models. For example, you could say, "The kinship data I collected are similar to the Omaha system, with the exception of...." You then describe how your data differ from the model.

Note that people do not take their kinship system, with all its obligations and duties, as a rigid model that they must follow. Rather, people modify it according to their own wants and needs. Be aware also that kinship systems change. People modify them according to influences from neighboring groups, central governmental policies, individual innovations and motivations, and a host of other reasons for changing culture. The kinship systems described here relate to whom ego may or may not marry. Marriage, descent, and residence are the topics of the following chapter.

15

Marriage, Descent, and Residence

We don't marry wives from villages where we marry sisters. (Bajju saying)

This tradition was asserted by a Bajju elder. Who are wives versus married sisters? Are they not wives too? It took a certain amount of investigation to begin to understand about villages with marital alliances between them, namely villages where men agreed to marry each other's sisters. This contrasted with marriage to women who had already been married, namely wives, who could come from any village around. This seeming contradiction exemplifies why one must study kinship in order to understand what people tell you about kin relations. Further, many minority societies are kin-based, so in order to begin to understand their society, you have to study their kinship, marriage, and descent patterns.

Birth, marriage, and descent are the three bonds that hold all kinship systems together. In collecting data on any population, ask people their marital status; it is a variable in most social science research. Related to marital patterns are residential patterns. Residence typically reflects economic activities, though preferential residence tends to follow descent patterns.

Marriage

MARRIAGE refers to the customs, rules, rights, and obligations that establish a special relationship between a sexually cohabiting male and female, between them and any children they have, and between them, their kin group, and the wider society. Though marriage and the family rest on the biological complementarity of male and female, marriage and the family are cultural patterns that differ from society to society. Marriage is a cultural universal, and, therefore, one of the most adaptive solutions to human problems. Marriage serves a number of functions:

1. Provides for the linkage between the married couple and their family and kin groups;
2. Contributes to the survival of humankind;
3. Constitutes a socially recognized union between a man and a woman that accords legitimate birth-status rights to their children;
4. Provides for the intense care of human infants and the prolonged care of children; and
5. Provides for the exchange of products and services between men and women.

In some societies it is helpful to think of marriage as a process that encompasses marital negotiations, exchange of gifts and/or money, a wedding ceremony, and evidence of a woman's fertility as shown by the birth of a child before the marriage is socially recognized. If she proves to be barren, she has been unable to fulfill an important function of the marriage, namely, continuing the family line and, thus, may be sent back to her family. Marriage ends by death, abandonment of a spouse, divorce, or annulment.

Types of marriage

The most common types of marriage are MONOGAMY, one man married to one woman, and POLYGYNY, one man with two or more wives (SORORAL POLYGYNY refers to a man marrying sisters). Other marital patterns include SERIAL POLYGAMY or serial monogamy (marriage, divorce, then remarriage, with the potential for this pattern continuing). Rare patterns include POLYANDRY, one woman married to two or more men (FRATERNAL POLYANDRY refers to a woman marrying brothers), and rarely POLYANDROUS POLYGYNOUS MARRIAGES, a woman is married to two or more men, and her husband is married to two or more women. POLYGAMY is a general term meaning marriage to more than one spouse. It covers polygyny, polyandry, and polyandrous polygynous marriages.

Anthropologists have encountered polyandrous polygynous marriages as a traditional marital pattern only in a limited area of the world (see Levine and Sangree 1980; McKinney 1992; Muller 1980; Muller and Sangree 1973; Sangree 1969, 1974a, 1974b, 1980, 1982; Smith 1953, 1980; VerEecke 1989). Traditionally, it occurred in central Nigeria both on the Jos Plateau and in southern Kaduna State. In this pattern a man could have more than one wife, and a woman could have more than one husband, though she resided with only one at a time. Among the Bajju and related groups in southern Kaduna State a wife could return to live with each husband provided that the bridewealth had not been returned and provided that she had had a child by that husband. In effect, other than in instances of barrenness, men rarely returned the bridewealth even when their wives married other men. They lived with the hope that some day their wives would return to them. While this pattern occurred traditionally, it occurs only rarely today, and it is no longer accorded respect by the Bajju. What often happened was that when men became elderly, previous wives would come to live with them when their other spouses had died.

Polygyny. Reasons men commonly give for desiring polygynous marriages include the following:

1. Economic motivations. More wives can farm, cook, and prepare food for more members of the family. More wives and their children can help farm more land, and through their efforts generate more income for the household. Children provide ready labor where farming activities are labor intensive.
2. Continuation of household functions. To be married polygynously allows for continuing the household functions when one wife is unavailable for reasons such as illness, recent childbirth, or traveling. In those cases, another wife can continue household duties.
3. Prestige and status. In traditional societies men with many wives received prestige and status by having large families and by demonstrating that they could lead them well. In some societies for a man to receive the status of an elder he has to have demonstrated that he can handle a polygamous family well. Some parents desire to contract polygamous marriages for their daughters in order to be well provided for in

their old age. A man who can afford more than one wife is usually wealthy; therefore, parents may seek such husbands for their daughters for their own economic security. Status is also related to having a good funeral. As Ayandele states concerning the Yoruba,

> Socially parents were very keen on having a large number of children so that at death expensive and elaborate obsequies, lasting many weeks, might be observed, a custom to which much importance was attached, as it meant that parents buried in such manner would occupy a high status in the other world. (1966:335)

Chiefs, kings, and wealthy individuals traditionally had multiple wives, and some continue to do so today.

In some traditional societies if the first wife finds that she has too much work to do, she may encourage her husband to marry a second wife. In fact, she may select who that individual will be; she will usually pick someone with whom she relates well. Her status increases as does that of her husband through his being married polygynously. By her husband having a junior wife or wives, she may then be free to engage in her own economic activities. Further, as the first wife, she directs the other wives.

4. Children. In many places people without children are considered to be a shame to society. In horticultural societies, the more children and especially male children, the more land a family can farm. In Africa the goal is for each wife to have at least four children (Ishola 1991:133). Other reasons for polygamy include the desire for both male and female children. In a patrilineal family men need male children to continue the patrilineage; if one wife has only females, her husband may seek another wife in order to try to have male children.

5. Barrenness. In many cultures a primary reason for marriage is having children to continue the lineage and clan. Because of the value placed on children, a man may marry another wife if one is barren. Consequently, the life of a barren woman is difficult. A barren wife may foster the child of one of her co-wives as though that child were her own.

6. Mortality and morbidity. In many societies mortality and morbidity rates are high. In the event of the death of one wife, a man married polygamously would have one or more wives left. The man then views polygamy as a means of safeguarding himself from being alone when one spouse dies or is incapacitated through illness.

7. Sex and birth spacing. In areas where people use little or no artificial birth control and where there are cultural restrictions against intercourse during pregnancy and when a woman is nursing her baby, in order to continue sexual intercourse a man may choose to have more than one wife. The period of sexual abstinence following delivery varies from society to society. Bajju couples traditionally wait until the child is able to talk, a period of two to three years. Other groups have longer periods of abstinence, as for example, the Dani people, in Irian Jaya, who abstain from intercourse for five years following the birth of a child.

If one wife reaches menopause, a man may take another wife. Ishola relates seeing women who have reached menopause put on mourning clothes because they are no longer able to have children and they no longer have a romantic relationship with their husbands (p. 133).

8. Religion. Islam allows a man to marry up to four wives provided he treats and provides for each equally. In traditional societies where witchcraft beliefs exist, some men may take another wife if one wife is accused of witchcraft.

9. Custom. In some societies polygamous marriages have been the traditional custom. In such cultures men married at older ages than did women. Men tended to marry around 30 years of age, while women married earlier (12 to 20 years of age). Consequently, there were more women available in the population than men within the younger age-sex category (12–29 years of age) of the population than within the next adjacent age-sex category (30–39 years of age). In societies where being unmarried resulted in a stigma, even being married polygamously was preferable to remaining single. There is certainly a holdover of this way of thinking in many traditional cultures worldwide.

10. Disapproval of divorce for marriages with problems. Some societies disapprove of divorce, so when a marriage is not working out for various reasons, the husband may marry another wife. The practice of polygyny ensures that a woman is not abandoned, but is cared for by her husband even when her husband takes other wives. A divorce breaks up an extended family, and this would likely be opposed by both spouses' families. If a marriage ends in divorce, in Africa and in Islamicized areas the woman loses her respect. She may be stigmatized for having been divorced.

11. Provision for unwed mothers. In Africa if a teenager becomes a mother outside of the bond of marriage, she has brought shame upon her family. Rarely would a single man choose to marry such a woman, and his family would also bring pressure on him not to marry her. For an unwed mother to marry, in most situations she would have to marry a man who is already married.

12. Levirate. In societies that practice levirate marriage, a man's brother or other close male relative must marry a man's wife or wives upon his death. This custom keeps the family together.

Polyandry. Polyandry, marriage of a woman to two or more men, occurs only rarely. There are a few places where it continues to be practiced for a variety of reasons, for example in Sri Lanka and in northwest Nepal. It is the wealthy and the very poor who practice polyandry. For the wealthy it is a means of keeping land within the family and limiting the number of children. For the poor, it allows two men, often brothers, who cannot afford two wives, to obtain one. When their economic situation improves, often one will find another wife, and end the polyandrous marriage.

It is instructive to look at the types of marriage and nonmarriage that are practiced by a Tibetan ethnic group in northwest Nepal. Schuler (1987:48) found high incidences of nonmarriage in the village of Chumik—the following percentages of women had never married:

    32–34% of women aged 15 +
    23–26% of women aged 20 +
    20–23% of women aged 25 +
    21–24% of women aged 35 +
    26–30% of women aged 45 +

In addition, religious celibacy was practiced: 8% of women 15 years and above lived as religious celibates, and 7% of men 14 years or older lived as Buddhist religious celibates (p. 55). She also found that although polygyny is rare, it is an accepted practice, and that fraternal polyandry was common, with women having two, three, or four husbands. Given marital demographics such as this, the question that Schuler raised and sought to answer was why, What functions do nonmarriage, religious celibacy, and fraternal polyandry play within that society? She found that,

> Fraternal polyandry, along with a virtual absence of polygyny, and the fact that there are more adult women than men in the population, is one important factor skewing the incidence of marriage by concentrating eligible men in polyandrous unions....it is an intentional strategy, viewed by Chumikwa [the people who live at Chumik] and by Tibetans in general as keeping land and people concentrated within the co-residential family and by limiting the number of potential heirs (pp. 55–56).

Discussion of multiple marriage. Women view polygyny differently from men. For example, among the Temne, in Sierra Leone, women tend to focus on difficulties in interpersonal relations that result from being married polygamously, while men look more to economic advantages gained through having additional wives. There is also a difference in desire for additional wives among men in rural and urban settings (Dorjahn 1988:378).

Problems with polygynous marriages, as summarized by Evans Odei, a Ghanian, "But polygynous marriages have brought untold hardships and hatred to the families. Children of this type of marriage have always had hatred and rivalry. Also, there is rivalry and bitterness between wives because of the preferential treatment given by the husband. Instead of economic success the man most often ends up becoming poor because of many children he is not able to bring up properly" (Odei, 1996, unpublished student paper). The rivalry between co-wives often extends to their children, thus contributing to conflict in the household.

> **Bajju polygyny**
>
> As part of a larger study on religious change among the Bajju, I collected marital data. In my Bajju sample of ninety-seven men, I found that all males who were thirty-five years of age and older were or had been married polygynously!

Polygynous marriages are declining in many urban areas, where monogamy tends to be more highly valued. Since more children are surviving due to the availability of modern medical care, and since it is expensive to educate children, many couples are opting to have only one spouse and a limited number of children.

Religious factors are also contributing to the decline of polygynous marriages. Christians value monogamous marriages, and Muslims find treating each wife equally almost impossible, so many opt for monogamous marriage. In a society where the levirate is practiced, if a man becomes a Christian, he will likely still be responsible for raising the children of his deceased brother or other close relative. However, he may choose not to marry that relative's wife or wives.

Exogamy and endogamy. Rules of EXOGAMY specify which kin ego may not marry, and conversely rules of ENDOGAMY specify kin categories that ego must marry into or is strongly encouraged to marry into. Most kinship systems prohibit marriage to those defined as kin who are too closely related to ego, and they allow, even require, marriage within other categories. Marriage is encouraged within most ethnic groups, with exogamy the practice within most families, lineages, and clans; to marry within them is considered INCEST. For example, in India the caste is endogamous, and in Africa the clan is exogamous.

Since every society has rules about mating, including incest prohibitions, elicit those rules. For example, with whom is marriage permitted, and with whom is marriage prohibited? Some societies have extensive rules of exogamy.

Bride service. BRIDE SERVICE traditionally occurs in some cultures in which the prospective groom works for his fiancee's father. It usually occurs within horticultural societies, and the service rendered is help with farming. Societies stipulates the number of years a young man has to provide bride service before the wedding can occur. This practice continues within some horticultural societies. Where bride service occurs, the bridewealth tends to be less as the service comprises some of the bridewealth.

Bridewealth. BRIDEWEALTH or BRIDEPRICE refers to marital payment given by the groom's family to the bride's family. The groom's family usually gives several gifts, with the main gift (frequently monetary) being given just prior to the wedding. When the family gives a number of gifts, the recipient family may distribute them according to regular patterns. For example, several gifts may be for the bride, one or more for the bride's mother, some for other close relatives, and the largest for the bride's father. Further, the bride's family may give the bridewealth to another family for another man within the bride's patrilineage to contract his own marriage. Thus, bridewealth tends to circulate as people within the lineage and clan marry.

Bridewealth compensates the bride's family for the loss of one of its members, including her labor and fertility. In some West African groups a further way to compensate a woman's family is to send a daughter to the woman's parents to replace her. Bridewealth also gives legitimacy to the marriage in the eyes of the wider society.

The bridewealth gives stability to marriages. It insures that the family takes an active interest in that marriage. In the event of divorce, the bridewealth must be returned to the groom's family. The exception is that the bridewealth is usually not returned if a child has been born. Since the bride's family will be reluctant to return the bridewealth, they bring pressure to bear on the young couple to reconcile their differences.

Typically, higher bridewealth is associated with lower divorce rates. Since the bridewealth in some sense relates to the worth of the bride, high bridewealth may operate to strengthen the marriage.

> **A topic for gossip**
>
> I remember the day I learned how a person gossips in Jju. On our porch two elderly women discussed the scandalous actions of some young people who lived together without paying money. When these women discussed this topic, they dropped the pitch of their voices an octave, a pitch pattern that indicated that they were gossiping. Clearly, without payment of the bridewealth the wider society disapproved of the marriage.

Dowry. DOWRY refers to marital payment given by the bride's family to the groom or to the couple. Sometimes it is seen as the early bestowal of the girl's inheritance. When it is an early bestowal of her inheritance, she may retain considerable influence over these resources. Dowry is common on the Indian subcontinent, while bridewealth is the pattern in Africa.

Annulment and divorce. When studying marriage, collect data on ANNULMENT and DIVORCE; both are methods of terminating marriages. In societies that use bridewealth as a means of giving stability to marriages, return of the bridewealth terminates the marriage.

Marriages in matrilineal societies tend to be more fragile and more frequently end in divorce than those in patrilineal societies. Marriages may also be fragile in societies where women are in seclusion (*purdah*) due to Islam. (See Smith 1954 for a description of Hausa marital practices.) Divorce is a means of temporarily withdrawing from the strictures placed upon women by seclusion.

Marital data to collect. When studying marital patterns in the culture in focus, explore the function of each marital pattern. Also collect demographic data to determine age-sex ratios of the population that follows each marital pattern.

> **Grain is the blessing**
>
> Since Bajju women marry into patrilineages, they are prohibited from certain activities such as taking grain out of granaries. The grain in the granary represents the blessing of the household. If a woman who married into the patrilineage were to enter a granary and then leave the marriage, she might take the blessing of that household with her.

Marital patterns and their functions need to be set within the total pattern of gender interrelationships. In studying marriage, look for answers to the following questions:

1. How are spouses selected and by whom? Do parents or marital guardians select spouses for their children or wards? If so, what does an individual have to say about whether or not to marry the selected mate?
2. What are the rules of endogamy and exogamy?
3. What is the bridewealth or dowry? Is it paid in kind or in money? If in kind, what items or animals are included? Does the groom perform bride service for his prospective wife's family?
4. Who takes part in the marital negotiations? Who is likely to be the go-between in the negotiations, a relative or a nonrelative?
5. What ceremony and celebrations occur when the couple marries? What gifts are commonly given to the new couple? Who are the primary officiants?
6. How are marriages dissolved? Include annulment, divorce, and abandonment. Who initiates divorce? Note that in patrilineal groups women are more likely to initiate divorce than men while in matrilineal societies the men are more likely to do so.
7. Are there patterns of wife exchange?
8. What are the prescribed roles of each marital partner?
9. What is each wife's and husband's responsibilities within the marriage? For example, in a polygynous household, usually the first wife has more status than the other wives and is responsible for directing the work of the junior wife or wives. The first wife may even by called "mama" or by an equivalent word by the other wives.
10. If specific marital patterns are being abandoned (e.g., if young people object to parental selection of their spouses), what patterns are replacing them?
11. How does the husband typically relate to each wife in a polygynous marriage?
12. What are the usual behavior patterns with respect to a marital partner, e.g., how does each show the other respect?
13. What are patterns of extramarital relations? How is adultery dealt with?
14. What is the role of widows and widowers in the culture? May widows remarry or must they remain single for the rest of their lives? Might a woman be inherited after a set mourning period following the death of her husband? Is the sororal levirate, in which a man marries sisters, practiced? How does the culture provide for widows?
15. What happens to a barren woman? What is her status within the society? What roles are available to her?

16. Are there marital alliances between villages so that an individual can more readily obtain a spouse from another village within the alliance? Is it men or women that marry into villages that have marital alliances? Who are the wife givers, and who are the wife takers? Similarly, who are the husband givers, and who are the husband takers?

Many minority ethnic groups around the world are experiencing rapid culture change due to such factors as economic development, political changes, the introduction of another religious system (e.g., Buddhism, Hinduism, Christianity, Islam), imposition of a national legal system on minority groups with unique marital patterns, and the influence of television and videos. Because of the impact of rapid culture change, it is important to study the changes that are taking place in marital patterns.

Since barrenness carries a stigma in many societies, investigate them. Do barren women become prostitutes, servants, beer-brewers, or have some other local low status occupation? Are they discriminated against, and if so, how? Are they economically disadvantaged? Does the husband of a barren woman take another wife? What do leaders in local churches or other religious institutions (e.g., Muslim mosques, Hindu temples) teach about marriage to another wife in the event of barrenness? Is a barren woman returned to her father or does her husband continue to care for her?

> **Law and matrilineality clash**
>
> The Asante, who live in Ghana, are a matrilineal society (Oliver and Crowder 1981:78); however, laws tend to favor patrilineal descent. As a result of those laws, Asante women now take their husbands to court to force them to pay child support, a function previously fulfilled by mother's brother who is part of the wife's matrilineage. In these court proceedings, women are not divorcing their husbands, but rather they are seeking to compel their husbands to help support their own children.

Residence patterns

Economic factors strongly influence residence patterns, and residence patterns influence daily interactions. In most societies a married couple lives with or near their kin.

Types of residence and the percentage of societies which have each type are as follows:

1. *Patrilocal* or *virilocal residence*: A residence pattern in which the married couple lives with or near the husband's parents and kin group. Daughters marry out, while sons bring their wives to live at their home. Patrilocal residence usually occurs with patrilineal descent. Sixty-seven percent of all societies follow this pattern; as such, it is the most common residence pattern.
2. *Matrilocal* or *uxorilocal residence*: A residence pattern in which the married couple lives with or near the wife's parents and kin group. This residence pattern usually occurs with matrilineal descent. Fifteen percent of all societies follow this pattern.
3. *Bilocal residence*: A residence pattern in which the married couple lives with or near either the wife's or husband's parents or kin groups. Seven percent of all societies follow this pattern.
4. *Neolocal residence*: A residence pattern in which the married couple resides apart from the relatives of either spouse. Some researchers relate the development of this pattern to the development of a commercial or monetary economy. Five percent of all societies follow this pattern.

5. *Avunculocal or viri-avunculocal residence*: A residence pattern in which the son and his wife settle with or near his or her mother's brother and group. Four percent of all societies follow this pattern.
6. *Duolocal residence*: A residence pattern in which the married couple lives apart; each lives with his or her own kin. This was the traditional residence pattern of the Nayar in Kerala State in India, where it was associated with men being away for military purposes. (Percentages are from Ember and Ember 1973:180–81.)

Residence patterns tend to have important consequences for the status of the husband or the wife. For example, in patrilocal residence, the wife tends to be an outsider to the extended family, while in matrilocal residence the husband is the outsider.

In areas where the government has introduced individual land ownership, the traditional residence pattern listed may no longer apply. Further, in the face of rapid culture change, neolocal residence is increasing.

Descent

DESCENT is based on individuals' affiliation with one or both parents; it involves lineal relationships between kin from one generation to another. It is the basis of the formation of social groups in many societies. A DESCENT SYSTEM is based on how descent is traced through lineal relatives to a common ancestor. That common ancestor may be a real person, a mythical ancestor, or an animal who purportedly founded the group. Descent systems may be organized as follows:

1. *Unilineal*: Descent is traced through one line only. Types of unilineal descent include the following:
    a. *Patrilineal*: Descent is traced through the lineal male line.
    b. *Matrilineal*: Descent is traced through the lineal female line.
2. *Double* or *double unilineal descent*: Descent is traced both through the lineal female and the lineal male lines. This system builds on a recognition of unilineal descent.
3. *Bilateral* or *cognatic descent*: Descent is traced through the mother and father, or descent is indifferent as to which lineal line it is traced through.
4. *Indirect descent*: Descent is traced to the second generation above ego. That is, alternate generations belong to the same descent group. Ego traces his or her descent to the grandparent generation rather than that of his or her parents.

The forms of descent found and the uses of them vary from culture to culture. What is presented here represents the common patterns, but be aware that you must study what you actually find as the local system and individual motivations that sustain the system. There can be variability concerning how descent is worked out between clans and villages, all of which fall under the general category of one descent type, e.g., patrilineal descent.

In the next section, levels of complexity within social organization are discussed. When seeking to discover levels of complexity within the social organization of any particular group, look for named units within the society.

Social organization levels of complexity

Lineages. A LINEAGE is a group of people who trace their descent unilineally from a common known ancestor. If it is a lineage within a patrilineal system, it is termed a

PATRILINEAGE, and within a matrilineal system, it is a MATRILINEAGE. Lineages usually have less time depth than clans. Typically, people know their lineage for four or five generations, though people in some cultures keep track of their lineal relatives in greater depth. This is especially true for the nobility. In this case knowing one's ancestors for a number of generations is valued.

Within SEGMENTARY LINEAGE SYSTEMS different descent groups form at different levels and function in different contexts. For example, among pastoralists lineages may segment during the rainy season as young people take the animals out to camps, and again during the dry season as the various lineages come together around a central water source.

Segmentary lineage systems relate directly to residence patterns that correlate with the needs of the animals. Sometimes the elderly and young remain in permanent or semi-permanent homes while the young adults take the animals out; this pastoral pattern is termed TRANSHUMANCE PASTORALISM. Both the social structure and residence patterns contribute to mutual help and physical survival. Residential mobility may be necessary in order to relocate quickly in response to ecological failures (e.g., drought, flooding) or war.

Lineages tend to be shallow within a segmentary lineage system. During times of stress, pastoralists may figuratively "forget brothers" in order to facilitate the survival of the maximum number of animals and people. Those "forgotten" may work as laborers either for horticulturalists or in the urban market context until they can reenter the pastoral sector.

Clans (sibs, gens). A CLAN (also termed a sib or a gen) is a unilineal descent group that traces its descent from a common ancestor, though its members may not be able to trace this link genealogically. That common ancestor may be mythological. Clans are composed of one or more lineages with descent traced unilineally; they tend to be named, often occupy a specified geographic area, and are frequently totemic. A TOTEM is an object toward which members of a kinship unit have a special mystical relationship and with which the unit's name is associated. A totem may be an animal, a plant, or a mineral. See the side box for an example.

A clan within a patrilineal descent system is a PATRICLAN. A MATRICLAN is a clan within a matrilineage descent system.

The duiker as a totem

The duiker is the totem of one Bajju clan in the village of Sokwak. A member of that clan would not kill or eat a duiker. A friend's father, who was from that clan, found a duiker when he was out hunting. Because of his special relationship with that animal through his clan membership, he caught it, talked to it as though talking to a kinsman, and then released it.

Clans are frequently land-holding units. If a member of a clan wants land to farm, he or she requests that land from the clan elders. They give it out on the basis of USUFRUCT, which is defined as the right to enjoy all the advantages from use of the land, though technically the clan or community continues to own the land. Introduction of privatization of land ownership by the national government may cause major changes in a number of cultural patterns where clan elders traditionally have had responsibility for allocating land to its members on a usufruct basis. Possible problems include undermining respect for elders, disenfranchisement of land ownership from the community (e.g., if it is subsequently sold to outsiders), and monetarization of land.

Clans are exogamous; to marry within one's clan is incest. Typically, clan members refer to each other by kinship terms such as brother or sister, mother or father, etc. However, if a clan expands in size to the extent that some clan members desire to intermarry, ethnic groups frequently have a way to divide a clan into intermarrying units. This process of dividing a lineage or clan into two is referred to as SEGMENTATION or FISSION. Because of the possibility of segmentation every man is potentially a founder of a lineage. See the side box for an example.

Through fission, an ethnic group continues to divide itself, resulting in the formation of new clans. Historically, over time fission can result in the formation of closely related ethnic groups that speak related dialects, resulting in DIALECT CHAINS which are closely related historically. Just as fission of clans and lineages occurs, so too does fusion. FUSION refers to the absorption of outsiders into specific ethnic groups. For example, if a Bajju man marries a non-Bajju, their children are incorporated into the Bajju within one generation. This incorporation follows naturally from the fact that children belong to the patrilineage.

> **Clan fission**
>
> Among the Bajju if a clan expands to the extent that some of the young people begin to intermarry, Bajju clan elders may decide that it is time to split the clan. They then gather to sacrifice a goat that is all one color. The color symbolizes the oneness of the unit, and the sacrifice symbolizes that this oneness is now divided into two. Bajju elders like to have some natural boundary between the two parts being divided, such as a stream, a natural rock formation, or some trees.

In many societies the family, lineage, and clan provide the social security network for the individual. Thus, when a young person moves to an urban area for economic reasons, he or she tends to maintain ties with those in the rural area. If things do not work out well in the city, whether because of unemployment, disability, or reaching time for retirement, he or she may return home and expect to be reincorporated into the rural society, including allocation of land if it is available.

Land and its associated rights, property, titles, and specific rituals may be associated with a particular descent group. The Kadara in Nigeria are an example of specific ritual property that is associated with particular clans. Each descent group must provide part of the ritual property in order for ritual celebrations to occur.

Phratries. Some societies have a more inclusive unit above the clan termed a PHRATRY, a unit composed of two or more lineages, and often clans, joined together. Two clans usually compose a phratry, and although they recognize descent from a common ancestor, that ancestor is distant. Phratries are usually exogamous.

Moieties. Two groups compose a moiety. A MOIETY is a primary social division in an ethnic group, often for ritual or intermarrying purposes. Moieties may be viewed as a particular kind of phratry (Fox 1967:82). Each moiety has a name and has one or more clans. In an ethnic group with moieties each village divides into half, and each half has the same name from village to village. For example, if there are moieties termed the Foxes and the Coyotes, each village will have sections named Foxes and Coyotes. For groups where each moiety is exogamous, a potential marital partner for a Fox must come from the Coyotes. That potential spouse can be a Coyote from one's own village or from another village.

Ethnic groups with moieties may split various divisions into halves for different purposes. For example, one division may be for intermarriage purposes, another division for games, and a third division for hunting. The people in one moiety for one purpose may be in another moiety for another purpose.

Matrilineal and patrilineal descent. PATRILINEAL DESCENT, also termed AGNATIC DE-
SCENT and MATRILINEAL DESCENT, also termed UTERINE DESCENT, are common forms of
unilineal descent. If descent is traced through the father's line, then it is patrilineal.
Matrilineal refers to descent traced through the mother and her line.

In order to ascertain which system is present within an ethnic group, investigate what rights
people have by virtue of their membership in a matrilineal or patrilineal descent group. Look
at factors such as inheritance patterns, custody of the children in the event of divorce, leadership in the lineage and clan, and land. The table in (42) summarizes what one might expect to
find with patrilineal and matrilineal descent. While factors in (42) are typical patterns, kinship
terms themselves also correlate with descent. For example, with patrilineal descent most of
ego's wife's relatives, whether male or female, may be covered by an "in-law" term.

(42) Typical patterns of patrilineal and matrilineal descent

	Patrilineal	Matrilineal
Descent	Through father and lineal male relatives	Through mother and lineal female relatives
Leadership	Male relative in male descent line (e.g., Fa or FaFa)	Usually male relative in female descent line (e.g., MoFa, MoBr)
Children	Belong to the patrilineage	Belong to the matrilineage
Following divorce/death of spouse, children stay with	Father and/or patrilineage	Mother and/or matrilineage
Land	Usually belongs to males traced through male descent; it is usually controlled by male elders in the patrilineage	Usually belongs to men/women who trace their descent through women; it is usually controlled by persons traced through females
Inheritance	Through father	Through mother, MoBro
Residence	Usually patrilocal	Usually matrilocal, or avunculocal (living with one's MoBr, or ego's uncle)

An individual may inherit some things through his father's line and other things through
his mother's line. For example, among the Malingo in northeast Cote d'Ivoire a man inherits his land, houses, and fetishes from his patriclan and his name and other movable items
from his matriclan (Barbara Moore, June 30, 1992, lecture, Limuru, Kenya). Land, the obligation to propitiate ancestors, headship of an extended family, material objects, ritual kin,
and the responsibility to avenge a death are examples of what might be inherited.

The matrilineal and patrilineal systems are not mirror images of each other. One aspect
of their difference is who continues the lineage. The children of sisters continue the lineage
in a matrilineal system, while it is the wives of related men in a patrilineal system who
produce the children who continue the lineage. This difference is summarized by Fox as
follows, "In a patrilineal system, a man gains rights over the sexual, domestic and

reproductive services of his wife: in a matrilineal system he may gain rights over the first two, but he never gains rights over the last. Rights in the woman's reproductive services remain with her lineage" (1967:121).

Bilateral descent. BILATERAL DESCENT, also termed COGNATIC DESCENT, refers to descent traced through the mother and father, namely, descent which recognizes both descent lines. In bilateral descent either men or women may own and/or control land; in the event of divorce, courts decide whether the husband or wife gains custody of the children or whether they share them equally; and residence patterns vary (e.g., matrilocal, patrilocal, or neolocal).

Kindreds occur within bilateral descent systems. KINDREDS are egocentric networks of kin. These are groups that are related based on a relationship to a common ego. Kindreds overlap with one another. Most egos have different kindreds; the exception is that siblings share a common kindred. As siblings marry, however, they become involved with other kindreds as well, namely those of their spouses. Kindreds involve some duties towards ego and have some claims upon him/her up to a certain degree (e.g., second cousin).

A kindred is bilateral when it includes relatives from both the husband's and wife's lineage, or it may be based on one gender only. For example, the Mongols have kindreds related to ego through males only through a fixed degree of relationship (Fox 1967:170).

The kinship system of most Americans is based on kindreds. People in a person's kindred are those whom one invites to weddings and funerals, and to whom one sends Christmas cards, and with whom one occasionally gets together. They may include people from both ego's mother's and ego's father's sides of the family.

Indirect descent. In INDIRECT DESCENT, a fourth descent pattern, ego belongs to the totemic clan of the plus two generation (e.g., his or her father's father) rather than that of his or her parents. This pattern is found in Australia and Papua New Guinea.

Discussion of descent

Different descent systems have different advantages. For example, within a unilineal descent system an individual is assigned to one discrete descent group. The inheritance is limited to one line only, thereby limiting the number of possible inheritors. Children are clearly assigned to a specific parent, preventing disputes over who they will reside with following death or divorce of a parent.

Cultural clashes may occur when individuals from different descent patterns interact. An example is in the side box.

When ethnic groups with different descent systems interact, one of their descent systems may gradually be replaced by that of the other group. In that event, you may expect to find vestiges of the earlier system. For example, in some areas patrilineal descent is gradually replacing matrilineal systems. Alternatively, where people of two different systems live side-by-side, borrowing of some patterns occurs with the new system composed of elements of both, though likely one will predominate; neither system is replaced by the other.

Whose are the children?

One young mother left her husband and took her four children with her. A woman from a bilateral descent system asked me what I thought the chances were of that mother keeping her children. My response was that they were close to nil, since she came from a patrilineal society where the children belong to the patrilineage. At some point that mother needed to return her children to their father.

People have ways of manipulating social systems so that they conform to their needs. For example, Longuda (Nigeria) men like to marry Waja women. Traditionally, the Longuda are matrilineal, while the Waja are patrilineal. By marrying a Waja woman a Longuda man is able to have ownership of his children rather than having his children raised by his wife's brother (Tabitha Asake 1989, personal communication, Dallas).

Just as the Longuda men have found ways around the matrilineal system, men in other cultures sometimes find ways around strict matrilocal residence. For example, the Yao in Malawi, a matrilineal group with matrilocal residence, allow the eldest brother to be exempt from the matrilocal residence rule. He remains in the village with his sisters together with his wife in order to be the headman of the village which is composed of his sisters, their children, and other matrilineally related relatives (Fox 1967:105).

Different descent systems can be present simultaneously. For example, a unilineal descent system may occur together with a kindred system. Each serves a different purpose within the society.

Studying descent

In studying descent patterns, determine to what lineage each individual belongs. For example, in Africa in societies with patrilineal descent, the wife continues to belong to her father's patrilineage; she does not become a member of that of her husband. By contrast, in India in some patrilineal societies following marriage a woman becomes part of her husband's patrilineage and ceases to belong to that of her father.

Determine the type of descent system that is present. In order to do so ask about what happens to the children following the divorce or death of a spouse. Who owns and controls land? Who inherits land and property? What is the preferred residence pattern? Does it correlate with the descent system? Who provides leadership for the extended family and clan? How is descent traced?

Fictive kinship: Ritual kinship and adoption

Two nonbiological means of entering into fictive kinship relationships are ADOPTION and RITUAL KINSHIP. In adoption a couple legally become the parents of a minor individual who is not descended from them biologically. They assume all the rights, privileges, and responsibilities of parenthood.

In ritual kinship two individuals enter into a special fictive kinship relationship and treat each other according to the rules of kinship relationships and responsibilities. They do so through a set ritual within the community. Among the Magar in Nepal once two persons become ritual kin, that relationship cannot be broken (Shepherd, 1986, personal communication, Dallas).

This chapter addressed units of social complexity such as the family, lineage, clan, phratry, and moiety. It also looked at marriage, residence patterns, and descent.

A number of other topics not covered here are important in kinship analysis. For example, topics also relevant to kinship analysis include marriage viewed as forming MARITAL ALLIANCES (ALLIANCE THEORY) or marriage viewed as consolidating lineages (LINEAGE THEORY or DESCENT THEORY).

People need to be seen as individuals, not solely as relatives of someone else. The collection of life histories, the topic of the next chapter, enables you to do just that, as well as to see them within their cultural context.

16

Life Histories

My name is Aman. I am going to tell the whole world my story, but especially my friend Rahima, who is listening here. It is also my grandmama's and my mama's story, so I'll start with my grandmama. (Barnes and Boddy 1994:1)

The above quote draws you in and entices you to read this very personal story of Aman, a Somali woman. This is one of the functions of a life history, namely, to bring to the reader an understanding of the realities of life from the perspective of one individual. A life history brings the abstractions of an ethnographic description to the individual level. It looks at significant events including beliefs and practices about pregnancy, birth, naming, childhood, puberty, age-sets, marriage, employment, and other activities that a person has had in life. It mirrors significant social, political, and economic changes within a culture as they affected an individual.

In most oral societies people are event-orientated rather than time-orientated. Consequently, life histories tend to be event-orientated. Individuals divide their lives into events such as independence of their country, completion of school, marriage, births of children, war, a coup d'etat or an ecological disaster—an earthquake, flood, drought, volcano eruption, etc.

Life histories contribute to our knowledge of the socialization process. They allow us to relate the individual to the wider culture. They add time depth to a synchronic study of a culture.

Kluckhohn (1945:91) observed that life histories involve not only narratives of individuals' lives, but they also include the way researchers obtained the life histories, with some evaluation of the trustworthiness of the data, the way that individuals' lives integrate with other ethnographic data about the culture, and some interpretation of life histories into a coherent conceptual scheme. This synthesis, if included, is written either in the introductory or in the concluding chapter of a life history, or else in footnotes or endnotes. The text itself should include only what the individual tells you.

Researchers have collected life histories almost exclusively from adults, and most have collected them from males fifty years of age or older. Some scholars are beginning to correct this imbalance in research focus by writing life histories of women, as for example, Romero (1988), Blackman (1985, 1990), Allison, Jacobs, and Porter (1989), Mirza and Strobel (1989) who published life histories of several African women, Shostak (1981) who interviewed Nisa, a !Kung woman, and published her life history, Brettell (1983) who detailed the life histories of three Portuguese migrant women, and Barnes and Boddy (1994).

As fieldworkers increasingly include life histories of both men and women into their studies, gender ideologies emerge. These bring out beliefs about appropriate behaviors and rights within the culture. They also look at what is the essential nature of men and women, and the appropriate relations between them. Sometimes stereotypes of each emerge.

Some life histories look at key individuals within a society, as in the case of Barth (1985) who collected the life history of a king in the northern Pakistan state of Swat. Similarly, Deng (1986) wrote a book on the life history of his father, Deng Majok, who had been an important paramount chief among the Ngok Dinka in Southern Sudan from 1949–1969.

In order to protect individuals, some anthropologists have used information from life histories to write fictional anthropological novels. These novels are based on fact and provide a good picture of that culture from an insider's viewpoint.

Brief vignettes that focus on parts of a person's life history can be used to illustrate specific events in the lives of individuals. In studying Bajju Christian conversion, I collected conversion stories that included the individual's status within the Bajju society prior to conversion, including economic, political, religious, and social status, year of conversion, reason(s) for conversion, denominational affiliation, current status if still living, and any other significant information, such as cost of conversion, and persecution encountered (McKinney 1985:304). For example, one entry in the National Archives in Kaduna (NAK) states concerning Allahmagani, a Bajju elder,

> Allahmagani occupied a leadership role as an elder in the Bajju community in which he resided, as had his father before him. His grandfather, the chief in that village (between 1850 and 1870), died in exile in the north for refusing to produce the men who robbed a caravan [traveling] through this area. As an elder, Allahmagani was invited by the *gado* [ruling elder] of his village to help deliberate on issues relevant to the entire community. The colonial authorities noticed that in 1914, prior to missionaries coming to the area, the chief of his village no longer wanted anything further to do with the men's *abvoi* cult although he had been initiated into it. (NAK 2985, 1914)

Based on the above archival information and other data collected locally from Allahmagani's son, I wrote the following brief vignette on Allahmagani:

> Allahmagani married three wives and was considered wealthy according to local standards. He was known to be both a good hunter and farmer. Besides having a large number of animals, he had large quantities of grain which he shared with others if they were in need. He would also help men obtain their bride price if they needed help. In the 1931–1932 tax drive the chief of his village and Charles Smith, the District Officer, took ninety-nine goats plus some sheep from Allahmagani which they sold to obtain money to pay the taxes for the entire village. Allahmagani objected to this; he felt that if his people were educated, they would be able to find a means to resist such unfair seizure of property. He therefore looked to missionaries to come establish a school in his village. He considered inviting SIM [Sudan Interior Mission] but did not want the rules of following associated with their teaching. Two of his sons began attending the RC [Roman Catholic] church at Kafanchan. Therefore when RC priests came through his village in 1936, he invited them to establish a school. His primary motive for inviting the RC priests was to obtain education for his children and other children in the village in order to obtain freedom from the oppression Bajju and he personally had experienced. The colonial administrators

did not accept the fact that this invitation was genuinely the desire of this individual but felt that the RC priests had put him up to it, and they denied the request (NAK Zarprof 2944, 1938–1944). When these efforts were frustrated, he sent one son away for education. That son continued as a leader within the Bajju community and sought solutions to the wrongs which the Bajju experienced under colonial and emirate administration. He also became a leader within the RC church. Because Allahmagani had three wives when the RCs came, he was not baptized until just before his death in 1977 by which time only one wife remained. According to his son, though his father's goal was education, the Bajju received something far more valuable than education when they received Christianity. (McKinney 1985:305–307)

This vignette was not narrated by Allahmagani—he was deceased by the time of my research.

Collecting life histories

The following are suggestions for collecting life histories:

1. Do basic ethnographic research first before working on a life history, research that includes participant observation, informal interviews, etc. This helps you know significant areas to include; it should also help you avoid possible sensitive areas of the culture. Alternatively, you may feel the need to explore sensitive areas of the culture, but do so with care and consideration for the privacy of the people involved.
2. Select a source individual carefully and establish good rapport with him or her.
3. Visit this individual in his or her natural setting to see what types of interactions he or she has with others in order to assess his or her reliability and representativeness.
4. "Prime the pump" by telling stories about your life. Sharing something personal helps to build trust.
5. Be as nondirective as possible. Use open-ended requests, such as, "Tell me the story of your life." Start with questions such as, "When and where you were born?" and "What are some important events in your life?" or "What was it like to grow up here?" If you are collecting a life history that requires more than one session, between sessions think of questions arising out of the previous session to ask in the next session. Be aware that when eliciting a nondirective life history you allow the individual to place the emphasis on what he or she feels is important.
6. Refrain from interrupting.
7. Be aware that the subject matter you are collecting is personal. This is where a trust relationship with that individual is essential.
8. Maintain your ethical responsibility to protect that person. This may involve disguising names, places, and other individuals through use of fictitious names for people and places. You may also consider having him or her be a co-author. If he or she is a co-author, the individual then has the prerogative to edit the manuscript. Publishers may require written permission from any individual who contributes a life history before publication.
9. Tape record the data. Record date, place, interviewer, interviewee, and anything else that is significant (e.g., others present).

10. Transcribe the tape recording verbatim (see Ives 1980). In the tape-recorded data note the use of folk terms, special phrases, and local ways of describing events which add color and interest to a life history.

11. If you are collecting several life histories, collect the same basic core data from each person who gives you a life history as well as information specific to each individual. For example, Francis collected life histories from sixty individuals. She included "...age (or approximate age), father's occupation and approximate size of his landholding and herd, education level, marital, migratory and occupational history of self and spouse, current landholding and land bought or sold, stockholding, crops currently grown and sold and long-term changes in these, investments, current economic activities and sources of income, children's education and occupations, and whether the children provide economic support" (1993:95–96).

12. Begin slowly, remembering that you need to build a relationship first before proceeding to collecting a life history.

13. Go with the flow. When you find that the respondent gives you only brief answers, move on to another topic. If she or he continues to volunteer information, however, then by all means pursue the topic at hand.

14. Begin with nonthreatening topics and then move to more sensitive ones.

15. Use the usual conversational conventions present in that language that serve to keep the conversation moving, such as "yes, okay, that's the way it is, uh-huh," and so on. As an example, among the Bajju in Africa, the use of a few uvular clicks (i.e., nasally released) is a way to express sympathy for or disapproval of some tragedy that occurred in that person's life.

16. Follow up on remarks that indicate a significant area to investigate. Many important areas to investigate emerge only during the interview.

17. When appropriate, ask the respondent to be more specific.

18. Remember to show compassion, understanding, and affirm the individual as the story progresses.

19. Structure the interview around the major life events of the individual or the community. Since many people are event-orientated, specific dates may be irrelevant to them, but major events such as puberty, engagement, marriage, birth of children, employment, locations where they lived, wars, famines, floods, droughts, and so on are remembered. By structuring your interviews around major events in life, you are more apt to elicit the information you want.

20. Give a copy of the life history to the individual from whom you collected it. This demonstrates respect for that individual and helps to maintain a good relationship with him or her.

Analyzing life histories

Factors that are likely to arise in collecting and analyzing life histories include the following:

1. Translation;
2. Sequencing of events;
3. Interpretation;
4. Chronology: If there is no sense of an accurate chronology, note that in your introduction. Problems with establishing an accurate chronology may be addressed by developing a local timeline based on specific local occurrences. Sometimes you can assign dates

based on significant events that have occurred. You can also have people tell you who is older or younger than the respondent. Sometimes you will run into problems with people collapsing or telescoping the past by using a phrase such as "long ago" something occurred. (For further discussion of assessing relative age, see chapter 9.)

5. Representativeness of ages and sexes;
6. Insufficient life histories collected from an ethnic group to allow for comparison and assessment of the extent to which those individuals are representative of others in that ethnic group. This should not be a factor in your collecting a life history; it only becomes important if you want to generalize the information you glean from life histories and apply it to the culture in general.
7. The time-consuming nature of the collection and transcription of life histories;
8. Motivation of individuals may be a problem. Some individuals may feel the need "to let off steam" over some issue.
9. Exaggeration by individuals;
10. Researcher pleasing: Some may tell you what they think you want to hear rather than what actually occurred.
11. Over-prompting and putting words into people's mouths: These are temptations you need to avoid.
12. Nostalgia by respondents about the past, to the extent that they tend to idealize it;
13. Misleading information or even outright lying: Sometimes lying can be identified by inconsistencies in the information or by its being implausible. You may want to discretely check the information to tell whether or not you are dealing with this type of problem.
14. Seeking sensitive information too quickly before a trust relationship has been established;
15. Withholding information: This may occur if the information is of a personal nature or if the individual feels ashamed or embarrassed about something. Some may feel ashamed of aspects of their lives such as having little or no education, coming from a dysfunctional family, a past failure, of being expelled from school or fired from a job, an attempted suicide, or of time spent in prison.
16. Other factors that are outside of your control, such as problems in the relationships between the government of your host country and that of your country or general distrust towards outsiders.

When collecting a life history from a specific person, you may discover that the individual is atypical of the culture. At that point you must make a decision whether or not to continue. Freeman faced this situation in recording the life history of an untouchable man in India. He stated,

> I determined that as part of my two-year anthropological study of Muli's village, I would collect the first detailed life history of an ordinary Indian untouchable, perhaps Muli's if he were willing...Muli was articulate, detailed, voluble. I asked him if he would tell me the story of his life. He looked puzzled, "What does the story of my life mean?"

> "Oh, about what you did when you were a child, the games you played, how you became married, the work you do, your friends, things like that."

> "Sure, why not?" (1979:6, 7)

As the research proceeded with almost daily interviews over a six-month period, Freeman found he had selected a pimp with an attraction to transvestites.

> I now realized with dismay that not only had I selected him, but he had se-
> lected me as a way to earn easy money and possibly involve me with his
> prostitutes. Clearly by his own account, he was a deviant in his culture, a weak,
> sickly man unable to do men's work, often living entirely on his wife's earnings,
> constantly embroiled in scandals, a self-confessed liar and scoundrel whose
> schemes often brought disaster not only to himself but to everybody associated
> with him. (p. 20)

Because this was not the type of person Freeman had intended to collect a life history from,
he decided to discontinue interviewing this untouchable who so clearly fit the stereotype held
by the high castes that untouchables are lazy, ignorant, and unreliable. His research assistant
dissuaded him from doing so, however, because at that time in the agricultural cycle other
men would not be available, and because he recognized that many of the things Muli said were
true. Some of what Muli narrated seemed so atypical that Freeman and his language assistant
discretely checked with others to verify his narratives. This was especially important to do
when working with a man who was a self-admitted liar.

Freeman asked himself about the representativeness of Muli's life history,

> The details and the manner of telling the stories reflect Muli's distinctive style,
> but the environment of extreme poverty, social stigma, economic exploitation,
> and discrimination against untouchables is a reality shared by all Bauris
> [untouchables] of Muli's community and most Bauris elsewhere. Muli's own life
> style represents one of only three possible adaptations ordinarily available to
> Bauri men and women: the life of unskilled laborers; the life of shamanistic
> faith healers; and the life of transvestites, pimps, and prostitutes. These life
> styles are neither incompatible nor mutually exclusive, but like Muli most
> Bauris emphasize one of them more than the others. (p. 34)

Given this information Freeman decided to continue with Muli's life history.

Motivations of interviewee

Just as Freeman's interviewee had his own motives for telling his life story, so, too, do
most interviewees. Boddy writes concerning Aman's motives as follows,

> Her original goals, to validate her actions to people back home, talk about the
> problems faced by young girls who run away, find the Italian boy she had loved as
> a child and, certainly not least, make money, were now complicated by the need
> to locate a daughter missing in northern Somalia, and inform the west about the
> value of her now destroyed and tragically maligned country. (1997:11)

Clearly, Aman's motives and goals were complex and differed significantly from those of
the scholars who wrote down her story. For the reader of Aman's life history there are
other benefits. Boddy writes concerning reviews of this life history,

> most reviews I have seen in the popular press exhibit an understanding of the
> account: that Aman defies a society whose patriarchal institutions rarely work
> as the literature describes; that her story questions the myth of female passivity
> and dismantles received notions of African womanhood; that it demonstrates

the profound dislocations produced by colonization, the Fascist state, ensuring ethnic divisiveness and rapid urbanization—all these were remarked upon as important insights contained in the book. (p. 13)

Cultural baggage of researcher

What perspective and cultural baggage does the researcher bring to his or her field research in general, and specifically to the collection of life histories? Romero states concerning the contributing authors in the book she edited on life histories of African women,

> The same individuality [as that of the women written about] is also present in the contributors to this volume. They, like their subjects, have their own cultural baggage which they carry with them to their fields of specialization. Several different scholarly disciplines are represented here—yet even among specialists sharing the same field, methods and questions differ. Harold Scheub is a folklorist. The questions he asks of his living subject, Mrs. Zenari, differ from those historian Ivor Wilks requests from his documents. In addition, Scheub as a linguist, is concerned not only with the content of the life history, but also with *how* the story is told. (1988:1–2)

Folklorists, historians including oral historians, linguists, anthropologists, and other social scientists bring their own perspectives to the collection of life histories. They do so by various means including the questions they ask, the subjects they choose to investigate, the types of material they collect, and the types of analyses they do.

Ethnographic descriptions. Some fieldworkers use life histories, including short life histories, in ethnographic descriptions primarily as illustrative or explanatory material. They provide anecdotal material from the culture in focus. An important question in using life histories is whether they are representative of others in that culture. You would have to collect perhaps a minimum of thirty life histories in order to begin to make statements about statistical representativeness of people in the culture. Since few cultural researchers collect that number, most use them to bring the abstractions of ethnographic description and analysis to the level of reality in individuals' lives.

Linguistic research. In order to discover discourse features of languages and natural grammatical style, most linguists collect a corpus of texts for linguistic research. This is an excellent opportunity for linguists to learn about the culture. Life histories provide good cultural data that can contribute to language and culture learning.

Collecting a life history is helpful not only for the text collected, but also for language practice. The social interaction involved in collecting a life history helps a linguist learn about the culture. It gets the linguist away from the desk and out into the community.

Historical research. When you are doing historical research on an oral culture and you are using life histories as one component of your research, ask direct questions about specific events. This contrasts with the nondirectedness advocated earlier for the collection of life histories.

You need to ask leading questions. For example, you could ask, "Do you remember when they built the railroad through this area?" If the individual answers affirmatively, then you might ask questions such as, "Tell me about its construction. Did you work on it? How much were you paid per week?"

Development research. Those who are interested in development research may make use of life histories, and oral histories more generally, in order to understand land owner-ship, long-term patterns of rainfall in arid areas, land use, child labor practices, and so on. For example, if you are interested in child labor practices, you may decide to do life histo-ries from several individuals. You might use a set of questions with each person that will elicit information on when she or he began to work, what type of work did she or he do, what remuneration if any does she or he receive, and more generally that person's work history.

Francis (1993) used life histories to study the long-term processes of economic differenti-ation in her study of the Luo in Kenya. Her goal was to explore how changes in the politi-cal economy of the area affected those at the local level. To do so she collected sixty usable life histories.

Individuals presented in life histories interact with others within societies through social networks. The following chapter addresses the collection and analysis of social networks.

17

Social Networks

In Taiwan, village women form informal but powerful groups [networks] that arbitrate many aspects of women's lives, from marriage decisions to attitudes about pregnancy or children. Women use these groups to mediate a difficult situation at home or to get advice about a difficult child or mother-in-law. (Riley 1997:24)

An understanding of these social networks formed by Taiwanese women is important for fieldworkers working in Taiwan. The study of such social networks is the focus of this chapter. Social network research involves a technique for tracing the flow of goods, services, information, and social relationships between individuals or groups or both. According to Jennings, "Networks, which can be defined as the people with whom an individual maintains consistent contact, may also include some social aggregations as solidarity groups and voluntary associations" (1995:15). Network analysis is appropriate for RELATIONAL DATA which Scott defines as,

> the contacts, ties, and connections, the group attachments and meetings, which relate one agent to another and so cannot be reduced to the properties of the individual agents themselves. Relations are not the properties of agents, but of systems of agents; these relations connect pairs of agents into larger relational systems. (1991:3)

The goal of network analysis is to construct the structure of the system of social interaction and to understand the relationships of different parts of a social system. It allows a fieldworker the opportunity to look at both the formal structure and the informal interpersonal relationships.

This field method within anthropology received its impetus in the United Kingdom from British social anthropology, particularly from the work of Clyde Mitchell (1967; see also Boissevain and Mitchell 1973) and in the United States from Harrison White (1963, 1970). Network analysis has also received attention from sociologists and social psychologists in their analyses of groups and individuals' relations within groups. For example, Moreno (1934) described social configurations that formed from "the concrete patterns of interpersonal choice, attraction, repulsion, friendship and other relations in which people were involved" (Scott 1991:9). These have their bases in social aggregates, including the state and the economy. The sociogram was developed to represent the formal properties of such social configurations (Moreno 1934). A SOCIOGRAM is a diagram or map of social relations, with individuals or groups represented as points and relationships between them as lines.

Social network analysis is an integral part of an analysis of social structure. Nadel (1957:12) states that social structure is "an overall system, network or pattern of relations, which the analyst abstracts from the concretely observable actions of individuals" (as quoted in Scott 1991:30). A network is "the interlocking relationships whereby the transactions implicit in one determine those occurring in others" (Nadel 1957:16). Nadel saw social structures as networks of roles.

Many societies may be termed relation-centered. You will find that social relationships are much more important than having things occur on time or that specific goals are met. When dealing with this type of society, use of network analysis may help you understand the insiders' perspective better than other field methods. Who is important to ego, and how does ego deal with debt, find a job, retain a job, get his or her child into school, etc.? In a relation-centered society look at how ego maintains smooth interpersonal relations.

Further, in a relation-centered society the relationships may be more enduring. They will likely go beyond simply relating one individual to another; they will involve both individuals' entire families. Relationships may also be inherited.

While this chapter focuses on social network analysis as a research tool, an awareness of social networks has aided some in the research process itself. For example, Sargent (1982:5), in studying birth practices among the Bariba in northern Benin, identified other midwives to interview by following social networks of midwives whose names she obtained through the government. This might be termed a "snowball sample."

Researchers have used social network analysis for research into voluntary associations (Little 1965), the adoption of Christianity (McGavran 1955), political power as reflected in relationships with political candidates (Mayers 1966), and other similar topics.

Social network research topics

Through social network research you can explore social groups, their corporate structures, and their interrelationships. Networks can involve the transfer of goods and services and/or the flow of information. Several suggested areas where investigation of social networks might produce profitable results include the following research topics. Note that some relevant questions associated with each research topic are included.

1. Migration: When migrants first move into urban contexts, what social networks provide for their transportation, housing, food, and employment? What are the common migration routes? What are the contacts that aid migrants along their migration routes? Are there seasonal rural-urban, urban-rural migration patterns? If so, what are those seasonal migration patterns?
2. Pastoralism: What are the regular migration routes of pastoralists? What are the seasonal migratory cycles? Do pastoralists have different pastoral areas, such as wet season areas that typically are the poorest ecologically, dry season areas close to water supplies that typically provide better pastoral resources, and pastoral reserve areas that are little-used except during times of drought? What types of symbiotic relationships exist between pastoralists and nonpastoralists? How are conflicts handled when pastoralists' animals damage crops of horticulturalists? Is migratory drift going on in which migration routes are gradually shifting; and if so, why and in what direction? Do the pastoralists practice NOMADISM where everyone moves together with their animals or transhumance where some move while others (e.g., the young and old) remain in permanent or semi-permanent villages?

3. Religion: What are the usual networks along which religious ideas flow resulting in religious conversion or resistance to conversion? Do people convert through the influence of persons in a kinship network? Who in the kin group has the most influence toward others converting?

4. Markets: What are sources of commodities? How do village and regional markets feed into national and international market networks? How are peasants in villages tied to national and international economies?

5. Kinship: What is the kinship structure of a particular ethnic group? Does ego live within a unilineal descent system with lineages and clans or within a bilateral one with kindreds? How do specific individuals relate to ego? What ideas, commodities, occupations or employment opportunities are kinship-based and what are nonkinship-based?

6. Communication: What social networks provide for the transmission of information in basically face-to-face oral interactions, for example, networks that are used as the local "bush telegraph," the local gossip and information network? What roles do modern communication (e.g., newspapers, news magazines, radio, television, videos, e-mail, fax) have within the society?

7. Community structure: What is the structure of the community? What are the major groupings and cleavages? What are the residence patterns within the community? What is the ethnic composition of the community? Are there different sections of the community based on ethnic identity?

8. Political constituencies: Who are the political constituencies of a candidate? What is the resource base from which a candidate might expect financial and personnel support? Who are likely to vote for a given candidate and why?

9. Power structures: What is the hierarchical structure of a particular power structure, e.g., a corporation? What are the formal and informal means of acquiring and maintaining power? How might one influence a particular power structure? What roles do bribery and corruption have in maintaining that structure? What are elements of interdependence within particular power structures? How does any one power structure (e.g., a state) relate to other power structures? What are regions of influence of a particular power structure? What are open or public versus clandestine power structures? How can these power structures be influenced?

10. Epidemiological studies: Along which lines have specific diseases spread? Who has been infected by whom? What is the specific vector, virus, or bacterium responsible for a particular disease? Who is likely to become infected as traced through a network of social contacts?

11. Multinational corporations and industrial studies: What is the corporate structure? What are effective means of accomplishing the goals of the organization? Who relates to whom about what?

12. Social relationships: What are the social support groups of ego? What are the bases of such social support groups (e.g., is it based on kinship, friendship, religion, some other common factor)? When is ego likely to make use of his social support system?

13. Friendships: When are these formed? Are they long-lasting, as from childhood? Are they essential to conduct business? Are they called upon to provide essential support during life-crises occasions (birth, marriage, death)? Do they provide financial support? Are there bond-friendships? Are there fictive kinship or ritual kinship relationships between nonblood friends?

Network analysis is particularly useful when studying vertical and horizontal relationships. The following list is suggestive of possible areas of research.

1. Vertical relationships:
   a. Patron and client relationships, master and apprentice, teacher and student
   b. Oppressor and oppressed
   c. Minority ethnic group and majority ethnic group
   d. Chief and villagers
   e. Pastor and parishioners
2. Horizontal relationships:
   a. Cross-ethnic relationships: For example, network analysis may be useful in the study of symbiotic relationships between groups with different subsistence patterns (e.g., hunter-gatherers and horticulturalists or horticulturalists and pastoralists, peripatetic groups and horticulturalists).
   b. Relationships within unilineal descent groups or between descent groups: For example, members of two clans may belong to one church. If a church split occurs, it may occur along clan lines. Alternatively, if the ethnic group is divided into sections and if you inadvertently relate to members of only one section, you may exacerbate the rivalry between sections; hence, study of relationships between sections aids in good field research.
   c. Reciprocity and trading relationships: This includes customer–seller relationships in a market context. For example, a seller may assert to a potential customer, "You are my customer" in an attempt to establish a commercial relationship. Through this customer–seller relationship both may receive an economic advantage: the buyer by receiving a good price for commodities purchased and the seller by having regular sales.
   d. Your social network in a community: Keeping track of your social network within a community may help you be aware of your need to broaden your interactions. With whom do you interact?
      i. With marginal members of society only?
      ii. With Christians/non-Christians or with Muslims/Buddhists only?
      iii. With Christians in one or two denominations (denominations which you consider to be evangelical or liberal) only?
      iv. With the chief and his elders only?
      v. With your cultural research assistant only?
      vi. With other expatriates, missionaries, and other "strangers" only?
3. Ritual kinship relationships: What is the function of ritual kinship relationships both within and between ethnic groups? Is the ethnic group highly stratified so that a cross-cutting relationship such as ritual kinship exists to reduce tensions because of rigid social stratification (e.g., between people within different castes)? Such relationships need to be studied both vertically and horizontally.
4. Fostering relationships: Do fostering relationships exist? Who typically fosters children, and why do they do so? Again these social networks need to be looked at both vertically and horizontally.
5. Market relationships
6. Voluntary associations

Social network analyses are useful as part of extended case studies and situational analyses. For example, network analyses are helpful in studies of dispute resolutions. They are also helpful in studies of marital negotiations, particularly in cultures where there is bridewealth or dowry. They can help in the study of patterns of decision making.

Up to this point specific areas where social network analysis might be useful in your cultural research have been described. In looking at any social network, be aware that besides an internal system there is also an external one, namely, that network's relationship to its external community. Social network research looks not only at how people in the network relate to each other but also at the way they relate to wider society and adapt to their ecosystem.

In some network analyses people have looked at integration and social cohesion. In others researchers have used this research method to look at conflict and change. When looking at conflict and change, focus on power relations, negotiations, bargaining, and social coercion.

Network analysis terminology

Before describing the field methods that you might use in collecting data for the study of social networks, there are several terms and concepts to define. Plan to collect RELATIONAL DATA (Scott 1991:3). These data include the contacts, ties, and connections that relate one individual to another.

Types of networks

An EGO-CENTERED social network, also termed a PERSONAL NETWORK, is one in which each person has his or her own node. What occurs in an ego-centered network relates to links that surround particular agents or groups of agents. Social networks can also be studied from a SOCIOCENTRIC APPROACH, which looks at the patterns of the connections within the network as a whole.

In ego-centered network study gather data with reference to a specific individual who is represented graphically by a star. Interactions between ego and another individual or a group are termed LINKS or PATHS. A person with whom ego interacts is termed a NODE and is represented by a circle. Ego is linked to one or more nodes. The relationship between ego and a particular node is termed a TIE; it consists of ego, the link, and the node.

(43)

```
              tie*
   *_____ o
   ego   link/path   node
```

Since links may be unidirectional, arrows may be added to indicate the direction of the transaction, as in (44).

(44)

```
   *_____>o  or     *<_____ o  or     *<_____>o
```

If necessary add a plus (+) or a minus (–) to indicate whether or not the link consists of a positive or negative relationship or a net gain or loss.

(45)

```
   _____>*<_____
       +              –
```

A social network display is divided into ZONES. The FIRST ORDER ZONE consists of those nodes linked directly to ego (see (43) and (44)). The SECOND ORDER ZONE consists of those individuals not in the first order zone who are linked to individuals in the first order zone; in a second order zone a person relates to ego through a connecting link. The middle node represents an intermediary or go-between. In (46) the middle node is in the first order zone and the right-hand node is in the second order zone. The middle individual is the intermediary or go-between.

(46)

```
*————————>o————————>o
```

In a CLUSTER-CENTERED NETWORK each star or node represents a group of people, or an organization; thus, each group of people has its own node. These clusters have also been termed cliques or blocks, and they represent cohesive subgroups within a social network. Sometimes these subgroups are formally organized and at other times they are informal intimate nonkin groups which come together for certain purposes. Some of these formal and informal subgroupings within a community include one's family, church or other religious affiliation, co-workers, interest associations (e.g., tennis club), occupational groups, and so on. The diagrams in (47) are an example of a cluster-centered network, indicating directionality. It is based on Cohen's work on the long-distance cattle and kola nut trade in Nigeria, West Africa.

(47) Cluster-centered network of northern Nigeria (based on Cohen 1969)

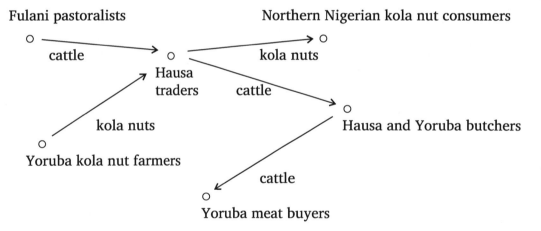

Note that this network indicates the direction of the flow of cattle and kola nuts; who is involved in this trade is shown at each node. The network begins with producers and ends in each direction with consumers. This traditional network adapted well to use of trucks and railroads. Transactions totaling hundreds of thousands of naira (the Nigerian unit of currency) occur with few written records.

A further type of social network is an UNDIRECTED SOCIAL NETWORK, in which there is no ego or group as the focal point; rather, each node is assumed to have the same type of relationship to every other node. An undirected social network does not use arrows, though plus or minus signs may be added to indicate the direction of relationship that exists between nodes. An undirected social network is shown in (48).

(48)

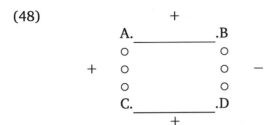

Complex social networks

Complex social networks derive from simple structures. You may have overlapping or superimposed networks. For example, within clusters there may be layers, with some individuals participating in the core of the group, others in the next layer who relate to some of the core members, and then a further layer with people bound together only infrequently. It is almost as though one were looking at concentric circles with members of the outer circles being only peripherally linked to the network; they are almost like nonmembers.

Large complicated networks are balanced. For example, Scott asserts that "...the relations *within* each of these subgroups will be positive, while those *between* the subgroups will be negative" (Scott 1991:15, based on Cartwright and Harary 1956). The two subgroups within a balanced complex social network will be in an antagonistic or conflictual relationship with each other. Where this does not occur, e.g., where all of the relations within a network are positive, then all of the nodes in the network fall into one grouping. In large complex networks, however, this usually is not the case, and some conflict and antagonism does exist.

Collecting social network data

Specific data to collect for social network analysis include the following.

1. The number of ties that ego has
2. The frequency of interaction of a tie
3. The strength of interaction of a tie
4. The density of the interaction of a tie
5. The content of the relation

As you collect your data for network analysis, you can collect it on a matrix or chart. An example of a work chart for tabulating network data is shown in (49).

(49) Ego-centered social network work chart

Name	Relationship to ego of persons observed	Frequency of interaction	Where	When (date/ hour)	Content of interaction
1.					
2.					
3.					

While the table in (49) presents one format to follow in collecting relational data, there are certainly other possibilities. What you collect depends upon the research question(s) you are studying. For example, (50) illustrates the use of names down the left-hand column and the events that particular individuals participated in across the top. You can also group individuals by sex, age, social class, ethnic group, or other relevant criteria.

(50) Person-events matrix

	Events								
People	A	B	C	D	E	F	G	H	etc.
1. John									
2. Peggy									
3. Matt									
4. Christy									
5. Eric									
6. Mark									
7. Susan									

Collection of relational data for network analysis involves many of the research methods already discussed in this field guide. For example, it involves such methods as language learning, if necessary, participant observation, direct observation, interviews, question-naires or interview schedules, spot checks of who relates to whom, and use of historical documents. All of these go into your ethnographic record.

Analysis of social networks

In analyzing the data, look at direction, frequency, and intensity of each tie. Mitchell (1969:24–29) speaks of reciprocity, intensity, and durability which are similar concepts. Mitchell also adds a measure called density, a concept borrowed from graph theory. Analysis of the strength, density, and directionality of the ties in the social network are discussed next.

Strength of the relationship

Once data are collected, the first step in network analysis is to divide the interactions according to the strength of the relationship, which may be characterized as strong, medium, and weak. In order to determine the strength of the relationship, take into account the following.

1. Frequency with which the link is activated
2. Effect
3. Kinds of exchanges
4. Kinds of things exchanged

Strong ties involve persons that an individual interacts with frequently and with whom the person is closest. They often include one's family, close friends, and coworkers. These individuals may interact with each other in multiple contexts, and they tend to possess a common body of knowledge.

Granovetter (1974:54) focused on the strength of weak ties. They, too, have their function. His study specifically deals with the means by which individuals acquire information about new employment opportunities. It is through the weak ties that involve less frequent contacts that new and different information becomes available to ego about new employment possibilities. The information most often passes to ego through a social network with one intermediary. Granovetter found that links with more than one intermediary rarely occurred. Hence, short weak ties were the most important in people obtaining information about new employment opportunities.

Density of the relationship

After determining the strength of the relationship, the next step in analysis is to calculate the density of the interaction. The density is obtained by use of the formula in (51).

(51)
$$\text{density} = \frac{n(n\text{-}1)}{2}$$

where n = the number of interactions.

You could also look at the density of the entire social network. The formula to use for computing the density of the graph is:

(52)
$$\text{density} = \frac{l}{n(n\text{-}1)/2}$$

where n = the number of interactions and l = the number of lines in the graph (Scott 1991:74)

Direction of the relationship

Next, indicate the direction of the ties, whether unidirectional or bidirectional. In (47) directionality is significant. The direction is determined by ecological factors: cattle cannot survive long in the southern rain forest due to disease transmitted by the endemic tsetse flies, and kola nuts need the moisture of the rain forest to grow, so they do not grow in the north. Kola nuts are a perishable commodity that must be kept moist in transport. The network illustrates the distributional system developed by Hausa and Yoruba.

Indicate the content of each interaction between two nodes. In (47), the content is indicated by specifying the ethnic group in each node and the commodity transmitted along each link.

Ways to display a social network

The results of network analysis may be presented in a network diagram (47), or in a matrix such as shown in (53).

(53)   A   B   C
        _____
        1
        _____

        2
        _____

        3
        _____

An example of such a matrix using data from the long-distance cattle and kola nut trade from northern Nigeria is presented in (54).

(54) Matrix of network in northern Nigeria

Ethnic group	Commodities	
	Cattle	Kola nuts
Hausa	Purchase in north, transport to south, sell in south to Hausa and Yoruba butchers, who sell to consumers	Purchase in south, transport to north, sell to kola nut salesmen, who sell to consumers
Yoruba	Purchase from Hausa	Grow, utilize some within household, sell to Hausa and Yoruba kola nut traders

In analysis of social networks look for characteristics and processes such as stability, cohesion, integration, cleavages, reciprocity (specify type), and conflicts and antagonisms in relations. For example, is there an optimal number of nodes in a specific network after which it is likely to divide?

Problems in network analysis

Problems that you may encounter in conducting network analysis include:

1. Errors in respondents' answers;
2. Limitless nature of network analysis. It is difficult to analyze more than forty units, though use of computers alleviates this problem;
3. Time consuming; and

4. Relations in dynamic flux. For example, if you are doing a network analysis of a market context, different produce is ripe at different times of the year; therefore, social networks differ depending on the commodity and the time of year.

While recognizing that there are potential problems with doing network analysis, the benefits far outweigh the costs. Some information is best gathered using this type of analysis. For example, to understand markets in terms of suppliers, sellers, and buyers you need to use some type of network analysis.

Computer programs for network analysis

There are a number of computer programs for social network analysis. These include GRADAP (Graph Definition and Analysis Package), STRUCTURE, UCINET (University of California, Irvine, Network). A computer program for network analysis needs to develop graphs and do multidimensional scaling and positional analysis.

Social network analysis is a valuable research tool for understanding interactions between different individuals and/or groups. In the next chapter, worldview and its component parts are discussed. Understanding of a worldview provides a researcher with an insider's perspective on the culture.

Practice in network analysis

The following are suggested exercises you can use to practice collecting data on social networks and analyzing them.

1. Find someone to serve as ego. Keep track of all the significant social contacts of that person. With whom does he or she interact? Collect data for five days. Present the data in terms of a chart or matrix, together with a write-up of your significant findings.
2. As a group assignment, select a small church or mosque that is willing to cooperate. Interview all individuals fifteen years of age and older (adults) to ascertain the networks through which they converted to Christianity or Islam. Present the data in a chart or matrix, together with a write-up of your significant findings.

18

A Cognitive Approach to Worldview

In African traditional medicine there are two causes for illness—an immediate cause (e.g., a bacteria or virus) and an ultimate cause (e.g., someone is using his or her spiritual power against another person). Both must be dealt with, though the ultimate cause tends to be more important than the immediate one.

Any health worker who works within an African health services context would need to know the local illness etiology. The local people operate from that perspective, and information communicated with patients by medical personnel should be understandable to them. This basic distinction concerning causes of illness falls under the category of a worldview proposition.

The study of worldview falls within a cognitive approach to culture. D'Andrade (1995:1) states that COGNITIVE ANTHROPOLOGY, is "the study of the relation between human society and human thought." One aspect of cognitive anthropology is the study of the linguistic categories that people use to describe their culture. ETHNOSEMANTICS, the study of the domains of cultural meaning, is one area within cognitive anthropology, as is ETHNOSCIENCE, the study of biology, zoology, astronomy, and similar topics from an emic perspective within a specific culture. Sometimes each of these areas is referred to with the prefix ethno- added (e.g., ethnobiology).

WORLDVIEW study concerns the basic underlying assumptions, whether on tacit or overt levels, that people hold about reality. Another way to understand this area of study is to view it as the study of the emic categorization of knowledge within a culture. As Bernard states,

> Today, anthropologists are studying many interesting domains—things people do on weekends, ways people believe they can succeed in business, traits that people think of when they think of particular ethnic groups, categories of fast foods, and more. The goal is to understand what people think, how they think it, and how they organize the material. (1994:239)

Cognitive models come from shared assumptions of members of a specific culture, though at their core they are properties of individuals within a culture (Goodenough 1965). Hence, you can expect to find some variation between people in their cognitive models within any given culture.

Data collection for a cognitive study involves investigation of the categorization of folk knowledge and folk inquiry and the content of those categories. The goal of a cognitive analysis is to understand a system of knowledge, a system of thought, a system of technology, cosmology, the classificatory system, and a theory of existence from the perspective of insiders of the culture. Folk classifications form systems within the total lexical and semantic structure of the language and culture.

Some cultural researchers have apprenticed themselves to local specialists in order to investigate folk knowledge. This is one possibility that you might consider, depending upon the subject of your research. Much local knowledge is treated as proprietary; it is passed down to apprentices over a period of time, sometimes years. For example, Stoller (Stoller and Olkes 1987) apprenticed himself to a diviner in order to learn his craft while working in Niger with the Songhay, and Sargent (1982) apprenticed herself to a Bariba midwife in Benin. Some categories of folk knowledge lend themselves to apprenticeship more than others as for example, knowledge of religious and medical practitioners. Since some of this knowledge is proprietary, it should be published only with permission. It is also true for craft specializations such as tailoring, leatherworking, glass blowing, woodworking, blacksmithing, mask carving, weaving, and other crafts. When exploring any of these specializations, expect to find lexical terms that are specific to those domains of folk knowledge.

Elicitation of specific domains of folk knowledge involves use of key terms in informal interviews. Key terms for ethnosemantic analyses include FOLK TERMS, terms which people use to construct cultural domains. For example, the terms *family, brother,* or *sister* within a Christian context may be folk terms used to refer to other Christians, and sometimes only to those within a specific group.

Methods for collecting cognitive data

Commonly used methods for collecting cognitive data include the use of informal interviews, free listings, frame elicitations, triad tests, pile sorts, rank order tests, and paired comparisons (Weller and Romney 1988).

Informal interviews

Informal interviews on key words from folk domains are the first and probably most important means of doing cognitive analysis. In exploring cognitive domains, first obtain a list of key words within that domain, then interview those who are likely to know something about them. For example, if studying the local medical system, with your key words in hand, interview a local herbalist, a diviner, or a shaman. Also interview those who may be the recipients of therapy from these specialists.

Cognitive data collection is similar to mining of cultural data, mining which follows a rich vein of ore of cultural knowledge. There is usually much information encapsulated within each term.

Data collected for cognitive study can be analyzed for recurrent patterns according to several types of analyses: domain analysis, componential analysis, and taxonomic analysis. These will be looked at later in this chapter.

Free listings

When eliciting data through free listing, choose a cultural domain to investigate. For example, if you asked an individual to name all the days of a week, that person could readily do so. You can apply this method to a multitude of cultural domains. For example, you can ask an individual to "Please list all the _____ that you know about" or "What kinds of _____ are there?" (e.g., What kinds of trees grow here?).

Use free listing when investigating any of a multitude of categories such as types of flora and fauna, types of music and musical instruments, medical domains within cosmopolitan, regional, and local medical systems and overlaps between them, diseases, tools, crops, foods, clothing, occupations, snakes, farming tools, spirits, bugs, feelings, and so on.

Sentence frame elicitations

For years linguists have elicited data within sentence frames. For example, in order to study tone within a language, a linguist sets up a frame into which the language assistant puts a list of words. As an example, a linguist may set up a frame such as, "Say _____ again" or "It is a _____."

Similarly, you can elicit cultural data through use of sentence frames. For example, you could state, "I prefer to eat ____," with your cultural assistant inserting the names of kinds of foods.

Yes/no questions

You can also set up questions that can be answered "yes" or "no," or "true" or "false."

Triad tests

When doing triad tests, show the individual three things, and then ask which one does not fit or which two best go together. You can use physical items, photographs, pictures from magazines, items you write on cards, and so on. Be sure to tell people that when putting two of the three things together, you are interested in why they do so. After they make their selection, ask them their reason for making that selection. Triad testing works best when you have only a few items within a cultural domain.

Note that when giving triad tests to various individuals, randomize the order you present the terms to them. This avoids the possible bias effect of ordering.

Pile sorts

When doing a pile or card sort of items within a specific cultural domain, write items on cards or slips of paper. Ask your respondent to put cards into piles with things that are similar in the same pile. That individual needs to define similar for you so that you know the criteria he or she uses. Further, each item can go only into one pile. That can cause problems since cultural domains can often be viewed from several perspectives, so that one item could potentially be placed in more than one pile. Alternatively, you can do multiple pile sorts with the same object.

If you ask several people to do the same pile sort, you may observe that some individuals will lump things together and some will split things into multiple piles. This is what Weller and Romney (1988:22) refer to as the lumper–splitter problem.

When your respondent is doing a pile sort, in order to give that individual time to work out his or her categories, think of something else to do for a few minutes. It is best not to hover over a person. After the individual has arranged items into piles, ask him or her the reasoning or criteria used for constructing the piles.

Use of pile sorts can help you in constructing taxonomic trees of culturally significant data (see below for a discussion of taxonomic analysis). For example, you may find that a language has no word for "plant" per se, yet the concept of plants as distinguished from animals becomes quite evident when using pile sorts of lists of lexical items. You can ask a respondent to put together those things that are most like one another. You can then ask the respondent to further subdivide them, and ask the basis of the divisions that person used.

When using pile sorts to apply to individuals within a community, you can put the names of people on each card, then ask your respondent to put together who goes with whom (e.g., who belongs to different clans). You can elicit categories such as statuses and roles within a community through this means.

Rank order tests

When doing rank order tests, ask people to rank behaviors or concepts based on some criterion. For example, you could list occupations and ask your respondent to rank them in terms of prestige. In a caste system you would want to rank castes in order to study the social hierarchy present. Sometimes languages can be ranked depending upon their social prestige. One friend who was doing field research made a list of "sins" and then asked people to rank them in terms of their seriousness. By that means he found that in that culture adultery was ranked as only a small sin as opposed to theft which was ranked higher. Note that not all behaviors and concepts lend themselves easily to ranking.

Paired comparisons

Use of pairs for comparisons is another means to rank folk terms within a cultural domain. For example, if your list of folk terms has twenty words or phrases, ask the respondent to pair together items. The questions asked when doing paired comparisons need to include some comparative word or phrase, such as smaller, greater, or more than, less than, bigger than, smaller than, brighter than, and so on. When doing paired comparisons, ask about only one comparison at a time. Further, paired comparisons typically explore only a limited number of terms at a time.

An example comes from the Bajju folk classification, where there are two major categories of diseases, those from God and those from man. Given knowledge of this underlying classification, one could do a paired comparison. The question one might ask is, Which disease is from God and which one is from man? From an emic Bajju perspective there are no medicines that can cure diseases from God. They come because of God's punishment upon one's actions. For all other diseases a western medical specialist, a herbalist, or a diviner would likely have medicine.

Semantic relationships

There are various types of semantic relationships that are important within cognitive anthropology. Some of these are hierarchical, such as those displayed in (55). Each type is discussed in turn.

Taxonomic analysis

TAXONOMIC ANALYSIS identifies folk knowledge of people within a specific culture or sub-culture. Taxonomies indicate how phenomena are structured in hierarchical systems of classification.

Taxonomic analyses move from the general to the more specific. A taxonomic analysis begins with a domain represented with a single category represented by a cover term (also known as a HYPERNYM). Within that taxonomy are a number of included categories that have a hierarchical relationship to each other. It represents a hierarchical structure of class-inclusion that expands a category to its subcategories. For example, the category of domesticated animals may include cats, dogs, horses, donkeys, some pigs, etc. A taxonomy is often illustrated by a tree diagram. A taxonomy indicates relationships between members of a set or of a subset to the whole. The table in (55) gives the types of relationships that typically occur within taxonomies.

(55) Semantic Relationships

Semantic category	Relationship	Form
Taxonomy	Class-inclusion	X is a kind of (or is a subset of) Y
Meronomy	Spatial Sequence	X is a place in Y X is a step (stage) in Y X is a part of Y
Metonomy	One part stands for a whole within/of the same domain	X stands for Y
Interpropositional	Means-end	X is a way to do Y
Relationships	Rationale Location-for-action Cause-effect	X is a reason for doing Y X is a place for doing Y X is a result of Y

Whereas you can do a taxonomy based on analytical social science categorization, from an emic perspective you need to ascertain the local categorization system. FOLK TAXONO-MIES illustrate how people categorize and comprehend their world. Kay states that folk taxonomies are "a means of organizing relations of meaning among items in natural languages and cognitive systems" (1971:872). Conklin defines a folk taxonomy technically when he states that it is a "system of monolexemically labeled folk segregates related to hierarchical inclusion" (1962:128). Folk categories do not exist a priori in the real world, but rather are culturally constructed based on people's observations, their interaction between things, what seems natural to them, how they feel things go together, all of which derive from cultural traditions. Sometimes that system of classification exists on the subconscious level.

Since specific cultures classify data differently based on their conceptual systems, the basis of their taxonomies needs to be explored when doing fieldwork. In some languages clues to folk taxonomies come from linguistic markers of categories. Lakoff notes that "Classifier languages—languages where nouns are marked as being members of certain categories—are among the richest sources of data that we have concerning the structure of conceptual categories as they are revealed through language" (1987:91). For example, in Benue-Congo languages, including the large subclassification of Bantu languages, a noun is marked for the noun class to which it belongs; and noun classes are based to some extent on semantic criteria. Denny and Creider (1986) correlate the noun class system of Proto-Bantu with semantic-based classification with respect to configurational features, i.e., the shapes of the objects within the classes. As this feature has come down into current languages, it is vestigial in many noun class systems. In some languages, however, such as Tyap in Nigeria, configurational features are a major semantic component in the use of classifiers (Follingstad 1991:71).

When doing taxonomic analyses, be aware that alternative interpretations or styles of taxonomies are possible (Goodenough 1956). Further, some words or types of words are not subject to taxonomic analysis.

Flora and fauna particularly lend themselves to taxonomic analysis. Berlin, Breedlove, and Raven (1973:214–15) give five universal ethnobiological hierarchical levels that a researcher might explore. They are as follows:

Level 0	Unique-beginner (kingdom)
Level 1	Life-form
Level 2	Generic
Level 3	Specific
Level 4	Varietal

Some folk taxonomies have an intermediate level between levels 1 and 2. For example, an intermediate level in English has the word "pine" in it, a term that covers redwoods, spruces, fir trees, etc. Trees in this intermediate level contrast with other trees by virtue of having needles as opposed to having leaves (D'Andrade 1995:97).

Each level within a folk taxonomy is termed a RANK. The top level is termed the zero rank; it is the single cover term for the entire taxonomy. For example, the zero rank might be "plant" or "animal." This rank represents the unique-beginner. Many fieldworkers who do research in ethnobiology use these universal ethnobiological hierarchical levels, and compare the data they gather with these levels. Typically, the largest percentage of data they collect falls into the generic level.

Within folk taxonomies fieldworkers have found a limited number of levels. Typically, there are five levels distinguished. In some languages there is no word for the zero rank. For example, there might be no word for "plant," rather there are specific types of plants only. This contrasts with modern biology which distinguishes at least twelve levels within the plant domain (D'Andrade 1995:93).

Criteria for placing specific terms within these categories varies depending on the culture. Within a western ethnobiological taxonomy the usual criterion is structural; however, other cultures use function, behavior, structure, or some other defining factors for specific taxonomies. For example, the Guahibo in Colombia classify animals according to where they live. One category consists of animals that live on the ground, and another category has animals that live in trees (Kondo 1991:25). They do not include structural criteria of the animals' anatomy (e.g., teeth, claws, etc.) within their defining criteria for animal classification.

Many folk taxonomies have very large fields, some with 100 to 500 terms. For example, classification of folk botanies may well contain as many as 500 terms. Tree diagrams rarely contain more than fifty terms, and usually considerably fewer. With large taxonomies, outline format better displays the data than does a tree diagram.

In order to analyze a taxonomy Spradley (1980:84) suggests use of a worksheet that includes the following:

1. Semantic relationship: (class-inclusion);
2. Form: "X is a kind of Y";
3. Example: "Participant observation is a kind of ethnographic research";
4. Cover term for the category; and
5. All included terms (the subcategories within the category).

In order to investigate and develop a taxonomic analysis, begin with a list of "either" objects. For example, begin by looking at the nouns within your database. These can serve as either the cover term or as included terms. Alternatively, you can begin by focusing on verbs that can serve as types of semantic relationships. You can base your taxonomy on folk terms (the terms the people use), analytic terms (the terms that derive from social science terminology), or a combination of both.

In working on a taxonomic analysis note that there may be interrelationships and interdependence between domains (Cheesing, as noted in Black 1973:551). Rules in one system may be defined in terms of other domains; for example, Black notes that, "sexual distance rules use the dimension of sexuality, which in turn is defined by maturation and age categories" (p. 551).

Display taxonomic analyses so that you can readily see the relationships between the cover terms and their included terms. In order to display levels of embedding between different cultural domains use taxonomic analysis.

Specific examples of taxonomic analyses are presented in (56)–(58). For each taxonomy the social situation is specified. Note that there can be several levels within a taxonomy. Both (56) and (58) represent only a single level taxonomy. The swimming pool data is from Craig and Mary Duddles and the Catholic church data is from Paul O'Rear, based on observations at a specific Catholic church in Oregon.

(56) Taxonomic analyses of strict inclusion relationships

    a. Social situation - swimming pool:

Included terms	Semantic relationship	Cover term
Windmiller Sidewinder Thresher Duck Smooth stroker	are kinds of	swimmers

    b. Social situation - Catholic church:

Included terms	Semantic relationship	Cover term
Use of rosary in prayer Volitional prayer Recited prayer Meditational prayer Use of rosary with meditation	are kinds of	prayers

Example (57) displays a taxonomy of Bajju animals which has two levels. Within the Bajju classificatory system, the people distinguish between two basic categories of animals: animals of the household (domestic animals) and animals of the bush (nondomesticated animals). This distinction is based on where animals live. A tree diagram is used in (57) to display this taxonomy. Note that there are more small and large animals than can easily be included here.

(57) Bajju taxonomy of animals

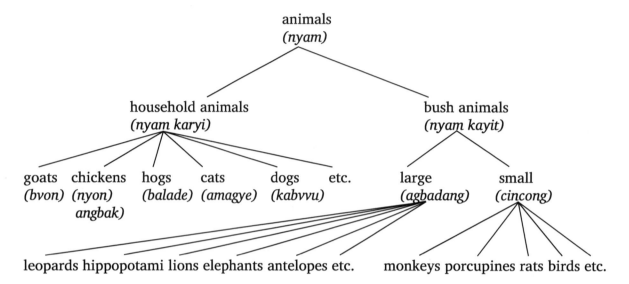

The rationale for the Bajju animal taxonomy is shown in the following list.

1. Bajju make a basic distinction between animals that they have around the house and those in the bush. This conforms to a distinction between domestic and wild animals.
2. The distinction between large animals and small ones under bush animals is because Bajju conceive of large animals having individual spirits that must be placated when a hunter kills one. If a hunter kills a large animal, he sprinkles some medicine on the animal while imploring the spirit of the animal not to harm him for having killed it. He thereby seeks to neutralize any possible harmful activities of the animal's spirit.
3. Traditionally, when a large animal was killed, the hunters would blow reed flutes as they approached their home village. People would then come out to meet them, celebrating together the hunters' good fortune.
4. Division of meat of large bush animals is much more ritualized than the division of that of small bush animals. It occurs at the hunting elder's compound, while division of meat of small animals can occur at the house of the individual hunter

Meronomy

Another type of hierarchical relationship is a whole–part relationship, termed a MERONOMY, also called a PARTONOMY. The most obvious meronomy is the human body. Another example is the automobile. Meronomies are the most common relationship that exist for human artifacts. They may also include conceptual wholes, such as events that are parts of scenarios (e.g., buying a house, enrolling in a university). The table in (58) illustrates a meronomy with data from Anita McDonald Warfol (student paper).

(58) Meronomy of spatial relationships

Social situation - child care center:

Included terms	Semantic relationship	Cover term
Cloud room Front room Art room	are parts of/ or are places in	rooms in child care center

Metonymy

METONYMY, one of the basic characteristics of human cognition, occurs when an aspect or a part of something is used to stand for the whole or some aspect of that whole. For example, Lakoff (1987:77) uses the example, "The White House isn't saying anything." In this example, White House "stands for" the president and his administration. It is this "stands for" type of relationship that characterizes metonymy.

Interpropositional relationships

Interpropositional relationships reflect different relationships between events. (59) illustrates interpropositional relationships with data from Laura Schluntz Payne and Dan Morgan.

(59) Means-ends relationships illustrating interpropositional relationships

a. Social situation - mountain climbing:

Included terms	Semantic relationship	Cover term
Walk Rappel Lowered by individual belaying a climber	are ways of	descending mountains

b. Social situation - bookstore:

Included terms	Semantic relationship	Cover term

Dim lights
Go down aisles saying,
  "We are closing in
  2 minutes."
Lock doors
	are means of	closing the store

Limitations on use of various types of semantic analyses

There are limitations on the use of various types of semantic analyses. For example, the verb "to break" can be included in one type of componential analysis and excluded in others. When used as a verb (e.g., to break a cup, scratch a fender, etc.), it can be part of a hierarchical relationship on "kinds of damage" to things. However, when used as a noun (e.g., coffee break), a distantly semantically related concept, it does not fit into the same taxonomic analysis of "kinds of damage."

Taxonomic and componential analyses do not work for a number of semantic relationships. These include situations characterized by gradations, such as: sand, gravel, pebbles, stones, rocks, and boulders differ only in size. Stages of maturation (e.g., infant, child, adolescent, adult, and elder), represent gradations based on age, and, thus, do not fit into taxonomic analyses. General, colonel, major, captain, lieutenant, sergeant, corporal, and private are rank ordered sets of military ranks that do not fit into taxonomic and componential analyses. They also do not work within color categories where colors gradually shade into other colors.

Some words do not fit readily into taxonomic analysis. These types of words are distinguished only by their collocates. Note the examples in (60).

(60) pride (of lions)   flock (of birds)
     herd (of cattle)   pack (of wolves)
     pod (of whales)   swarm (of bees)
     gaggle (of geese on the ground)   crowd (of people)
     covey (of quail)   litter (of kittens)

There are also words that are defined by their unique features. These include personal names and ISOLATES. Isolates are words with only one representative of a semantic domain.

Prototypes

One way of looking at folk classification is according to a PROTOTYPE, where one word or concept is central or an exemplar of a category. Rosch states, "By prototypes of categories we have generally meant the clearest cases of category membership defined operationally by people's judgment of goodness of membership in the category" (1978:30). Certain words or concepts are central while others are further from the ideal of what is in a particular category, yet still fall within it by means of chaining with related words and concepts. For example, in a western system, a robin is a prototype of the category of birds, yet penguins and ostriches are also birds (Arensen 1991:139). By chaining, one item is connected to another, and it to another, and so on until the original connection may not be obvious.

In the study of folk categories by use of prototypes, look for items connected to a central prototype rather than the shared features of items. In a prototypical classification system expect fuzzy boundaries with gradations and overlapping between categories. Recognize that any classification system includes things that do not fit neatly into the system.

Looking at prototypes differs significantly from the classical western classification system that is based on bounded sets with clear-cut properties or features for each category.

Schema

The development of the theoretical concepts of prototypes led to a further more complex concept of schemas. D'Andrade writes about these two concepts:

> Note that a prototype is not the same as a schema; a schema is an organized framework of objects and relations which has yet to be filled in with concrete

detail, while a prototype consists of a specified set of expectations. The filling in of the slots of a schema with an individual's standard default values creates a prototype. A prototype is a highly typical *instantiation* (i.e., an instance of a schema). (D'Andrade 1995:124)

Componential Analysis. COMPONENTIAL ANALYSES specify units of meaning within cultural categories, and in particular specify the unique clusters of attributes that are associated with those units of meaning. For the purpose of componential analysis an ATTRIBUTE or DISTINCTIVE FEATURE is any element of information that is regularly associated with a cultural category. A componential analysis includes the information noted in (61). Whereas domain analyses and taxonomic analyses focus on similarities between terms, componential analyses are based on patterns of contrast. They may be displayed in chart or paradigm format.

(61) Elements within a componential analysis paradigm worksheet (Spradley 1980:132)

Cultural Domain	Dimensions of Contrast		
	I	II	III
Cultural category	Attribute$_1$	Attribute$_2$	Attribute$_3$
Cultural category	Attribute$_1$	Attribute$_2$	Attribute$_3$
Cultural category	Attribute$_1$	Attribute$_2$	Attribute$_3$

The process whereby you can construct a componential analysis includes the following steps based on Spradley (1980:133–139).

1. Select a domain for analysis.
2. Inventory all of the contrasts previously discovered.
3. Prepare a paradigm worksheet with the cultural categories of the domain down the left-hand side and the attributes or dimensions of contrast across the top. An attribute is any element of information, component of meaning, knowledge, or particular fact that routinely occurs with that cultural category.
4. Identify the dimensions of contrast within the boxes of the paradigm. These can be either yes/no dimensions or they may state specific information, usually based on a binary contrast.
5. Combine closely related contrasts into ones that have multiple values.
6. Prepare contrast questions in order to complete the paradigm for any missing data.
7. Collect the missing data, as for example through observations, participation, and/or interviews.
8. Complete the paradigm.

The table in (62) presents an example of a componential analysis.

(62) Bajju Christian denominations—reasons for attending a specific denomination

Denominations	Approves of polygamy	Condones drinking alcoholic beverages	Allows men married polygamously to lead	Provides leadership training through the denomination
Anglican	no	yes	no	yes
Assembly of God	no	no	no	yes
Baptist	no	no	no	yes
Catholic	no	yes	no	yes
Cherubim and Seraphim	yes	yes	yes	yes
ECWA	no	no	no	yes
Methodist	no	no	no	no
United Native African	yes	yes	yes	no

Worldview

The term worldview has been used with a multitude of meanings. It is used roughly to refer to a point of view, a way of looking at something. According to McElhanon (forthcoming), the word itself comes from German *(weltanschaung)* meaning an ideology or system of thought. When used to refer to an ideology or system of thought McElhanon states that worldview deals with "the nature of God as creator and redeemer and the nature of humanity in its fallen state in need of a redeemer" (personal communication, 1997). Thus, a Christian worldview contrasts with other ideologies such as humanism, Marxism, naturalism, secularism, and other ideological systems. Within anthropology, however, the concept of a worldview is much broader than simply an ideology.

Study of worldview for any particular culture seeks the basic assumptions about reality at a high level, the macro or metatheoretical level. Worldview has been defined as "a culture's way of looking at reality consisting of basic assumptions and images that provide a more or less coherent though not necessarily accurate way of thinking about the world" (Kearney 1984:41). Haviland defines a worldview as "the conceptions, explicit and implicit, of a society or an individual of the limits and workings of its world" (1987:303). Similarly, Kraft defines the worldview of a culture as "the central governing set of concepts and presuppositions that its society lives by" (1978:4). Worldview assumptions enable a person to make sense of his or her world.

There are two differing theoretical approaches to the study of worldview (Kearney 1984:3). The first is to look at its content, which involves a description of specifics of the basic assumptions in a culture. The second is to look at its structure, the basic categories of thought. The first involves basic ethnographic description, and the second looks at what is common to all worldviews. This chapter focuses on discovering the content of a worldview, rather than the wider question of the basic structure of a worldview.

As you discover specific worldview assumptions, write these out as propositions or hypotheses. They form a cognitive model which replicates the worldview of the research community. Be aware that the research community's knowledge of their worldview may be at the tacit level or implicit level. When studying worldview, it is the task of fieldworker and his or her assistants to make these assumptions explicit.

Assertions of worldview propositions involve a much greater degree of abstraction than other topics of ethnoscience, ethnosemantics, and cognitive anthropology such as discovery of cultural domains, taxonomic analyses, and componential analyses. There is a qualitative difference because development of worldview propositions and the identification of cultural domains, taxonomies, and componential analyses. It is a form of hypothesis formulation and generalization.

Universal categories of a worldview

Compose worldview propositions in terms of the universal categories of self-other or personhood, classification, relationships, causality, space, and time:

1. Self-other: The concepts of the self and the other are defined contrastively with respect to each other. It includes one's self, and the self with respect to a we-they contrast. This self-other worldview universal can be expanded to include concepts of ethnicity, one's own ethnic group as opposed to other ethnic groups, the insider versus the outsider, the person who is in the in-group versus the stranger or foreigner, the self and all else within the universe. Concepts of the self also relate to the entire realm of pollution. For example, in a caste system if a person of high caste touches or eats with one of lower caste, the higher caste person is thereby polluted. Study of the self and the other includes investigation of the relationship between the two.

2. Classification: Under classification look at the notion of classes, and categories and the arrangement or ordering of data into those classes. In studying the classification system within a culture, you are looking at the classes that people in that culture recognize. In this chapter various analytic procedures for description of classificatory systems have been discussed. (See domain, componential, and especially taxonomic analyses; see also (55).)

   One basis of categories is groupings of things or people that have some property in common. Categories have best examples of them, termed prototypes.

   Classificatory systems tend to be arbitrary, and, as such, they differ from culture to culture. In studying classificatory systems, include what is classified as animate and inanimate (if the language has this distinction), classification of flora and fauna, objects, and so on.

3. Relationships: Under relationships look at interpersonal relationships, those between the self and the other. Study various types of exchange systems, such as balanced, reciprocal, and negative exchange. Relationships are involved in the study of market and market forces such as supply and demand. You may also study ecological relationships, the focus of ecological anthropology. How does the self fit within one's ecological niche? Is there a symbiotic relationship between the self and the other? Many ethnic groups live in symbiotic relationships with other groups within a particular environment. This is essential because of the principle of competitive exclusion that asserts that complete competitors cannot coexist within the same niche. According to this principle, if they seek to do so, one of these competitors will be eliminated.

   Study of relationships also includes investigation of the role of the self with respect to the group. For example, in Africa the self has significance in the context of the group. In other societies the self assumes greater importance through individualism and privacy.

4. Causality: The study of causality involves looking at the relationship between acts and the desired end effects. Thus, it looks at causes and effects. Durkheim stated, "The first thing which is implied in the notion of the causal relationship is the ideal of efficacy, of productive power, of active force. By cause we ordinarily mean something capable of producing a certain change. The cause is the force before it has shown the power which is in it; the effect is this same power, only actualized" (1965:406).

   In studying causality it is important to distinguish between things that are simply correlated from those which have a cause-effect relationship with one another.

5. Space: The study of space involves understanding the physical layout of the universe, including both on earth, under the earth, and in the sky. It also involves the study of proxemics. Hiebert states, "Space is theology in most tribal societies" (Hiebert, lecture, June 25, 1992, Brackenhurst, Kenya). Study of space involves understanding the significance of location and its uses. Directions can have significance (as seen on p. 212) that relate to basic worldview assumptions. Study of space can involve mathematical space, realms of supernatural beings and of ancestral spirits, and the spatial aspects of the local cosmology.

6. Time: Time for many people relates with its occupational value; it is comprised of the activities involved in the daily economic cycle. Other concepts of time include the following:

   a. Linear time: a linear view of time has a beginning and end. Time is viewed as nonrepetitive with unique events occurring along a timeline. All units of time may be of equal duration and value.

   b. Cyclical time: a repetitive view of time without beginning or end. There can be new beginnings by returning to the origins. It is commonly associated with the agricultural cycle or the cycle of reincarnation which is a rebirth of the same individual. Within cyclical time the past is that which we are all moving towards. Mbiti (1990) identifies this as the dominant temporal model in use in Africa.

   c. Pendular time: time moves and then reverses itself.

   d. Mythical time: this involves the time of the ancestors or the time of creation. Mythical time begins an origin narrative. It is the time before the gap which then deals with historic events (see p. 257).

   e. Dream time: this is time in the mythical realm. For example, Australian aborigines speak of dream time.

   f. Calendar time: time is divided into categories such as days, weeks, months, and years. This division may be based on the lunar or solar cycle. For example, Muslims base their calendar on the lunar cycle while much of the western world bases their calendar on the solar cycle. Within a western concept of time weeks have seven days; contrastively, some West African groups have four day weeks; market day is every fourth day.

When studying time, investigate which view of time predominates. For example, is the research community orientated towards the past, present, or future? What is the role of mythical time? Can time be commoditized? Are they time-orientated or event-orientated? What time distinctions are recognized locally?

   Worldview universal categories arise out of a community's need for social order and its need to adapt to its environment. These worldview assumptions serve various functions within a culture.

Functions of a worldview

Kraft (1986:50–53) lists the following functions of a worldview within a culture:

1. Explaining reality: Worldview assumptions provide explanations as to why things are as they are, the origins and nature of the universe, people, animals, plants, geographic phenomena, etc.
2. Evaluating and validating: Evaluation often occurs based on whether things are as their worldview asserts they ought to be. Thus, worldview assumptions sanction and validate basic values, morals, institutions, and goals of a society.
3. Assigning and prioritizing allegiances: Worldviews enable people to sort out the significant from the insignificant, to make specific commitments, and to form allegiances based on some prioritizing of possibilities.
4. Interpreting: Based on specific worldview assumptions people interpret and assign meaning to their perception of the world.
5. Integrating: Our worldview pushes us to integrate disparate parts of our culture. For example, in many western cultures' worldviews individualism is extremely important. These assumptions push us to evaluate, then to integrate each area of our culture that might relate to these basic parts of our worldview.
6. Adapting: Each culture's worldview assumptions enable members of a culture to adapt to changes. People's initial response to a challenge to their worldview may be to become defensive and reject that challenge. When the challenge persists, however, the culture tends to respond by adapting in a culturally appropriate way. Sometimes people hold contradictory assumptions. When the assault on a culture is too great, the influences too numerous, and the population too small, demoralization and ethnocide may occur with resultant loss of the worldview.

A worldview also serves a psychological reinforcement function during times of anxiety or crisis, and by so doing it serves to provide security and support for group behavior (Kraft 1978:5).

Cultural themes

Worldview assumptions may be stated as CULTURAL THEMES. Opler defined a cultural theme as "a postulate or position, declared or implied, and usually controlling behavior or stimulating activity, which is tacitly approved or openly promoted in a society" (1945:198). Themes are underlying ideas or central topics within a culture that explain why people do what they do. They explain underlying motivations for cultural behavior. Cultural themes have a high degree of generality. They encapsulate significant cultural meaning of what is going on within the culture. Cultural themes can be stated as hypotheses or brief assertions that need to be supported by specific data from the culture.

Fernandez (1985:754) points out that propositions, or cultural themes, are part of the metatheory about culture and are stated as highly metaphorical statements (in this position he follows Collingwood). He further speaks of the importance of images, visual or sense-modality representations in the minds of people, that must be studied as part of our understanding of any worldview. Such images and representations are often stated as metaphors.

Simply stating propositions or cultural themes based on processes of organizing principles or rational logic is inadequate. Culture themes are expressions of a people's worldview, and worldview is a matter of both logic as expressed in language and aesthetics or art. Thus, in the study of worldview, pay attention to such components of culture as art, music, performances, oral traditions, metaphors, proverbs, commonly known sayings, stylistic integration, and images. By so doing researchers can root their inquiry into worldview within the local images and metaphors (Fernandez 1985:756).

Discovering cultural themes and worldview propositions

Whereas other types of ethnosemantic analysis discussed in this chapter, such as domain, taxonomic, and componential analyses, are fairly straightforward, cultural themes are not. The discovery of cultural themes and worldview propositions is a form of hypothesis formulation that often involves a leap of logic from observed behavior to answering the question, "Why do people behave as they do?" Cultural themes often involve people's motivations for their behavior.

Prior to focusing on the worldview for a given culture, you need to have engaged in adequate participant observation and to have become well acquainted with the culture. There is not one set of questions which if applied in a formulaic manner will result in your discovering components of the worldview. Rather, there are some areas you might want to explore. For example, clues for discovering cultural themes come from folk sayings, mottoes, proverbs, recurrent expressions, songs, art, music, oral traditions, metaphors, performances, and recurrent behavior.

Spradley (1980:141, 144) asserts that cultural themes should recur in two or more cultural domains and serve as unifying relationships between differing domains. So, in addition to looking at folk sayings, mottoes, proverbs, recurrent expressions, etc., do a componential analysis of the differing cultural domains you have identified. From the results of this analysis, look for the overarching principles that tie all of the data together in two or more domains.

Another helpful way to discover one or more cultural themes is to look at the dimensions of contrast within componential analyses. Most cultural themes or hypotheses that express unifying aspects of the culture are tacit, to the point that participants do not readily express them. (See boxes for examples on the cultural themes of women and secrets, and also of rock climbers.)

Women and secrets

Both Bajju men in Nigeria and Bariba men in Benin say, "You don't share secrets with women" (Bajju quote from Asake, personal communication, Grand Prairie, TX, March 25, 1990; Bariba quote from Sargent, personal communication, Dallas, TX, March 28, 1990). A researcher studying Bajju or Bariba culture could seek specific data to substantiate this cultural theme. For example, Bajju men state that traditionally if today a man shares a secret with a woman, tomorrow she might be gone. Women marry into patrilineages and to some degree are not fully incorporated within them.

Traditionally, under most circumstances people did not accuse Bajju women of *nkut*, malevolent use of spiritual power; rather, they tended to accuse members of the patrilineage within the extended family.

Directions. Directions are another significant area to investigate when seeking cultural themes. For example, Arensen states that the east is important in Murle culture, a group that lives in southern Sudan and Ethiopia. "The sun rises in the east and is the bringer of warmth and light. It is also from the east that the rains come, bringing needed water for all the important pastures" (Arensen 1991:26).

Cultural themes of rock climbers

One student in my cultural anthropology class chose to study the subculture of rock climbing. She identified the cultural theme, "Climbers are driven by challenge," and she substantiated this cultural theme by the domains she identified as "Reasons for climbing," "The physical challenge," and "Ways of climbing."

A second cultural theme this student identified for rock climbers was "Rock climbers are purists in their outlook on climbing and life." Cultural domains used to substantiate this were "Reasons for climbing," "Kinds of equipment," "Kinds of outside interests climbers have," "Kinds of rock climbers," and "Kinds of things used for observing." She pointed out that a natural outlook on life permeates the holistic attitude climbers have towards life (Laura Schluntz Payne, student ethnography, 1987).

Lewis also states, "*Jen* is important, symbolizing the East, the source of life, where the tribe began and from where the rains come" (1972:20). The significance of the east in Murle culture is further seen in the arrangement of Murle homesteads with the senior wife receiving the honored position on the east side (Lewis 1972:4). A man sleeps facing east. In contrast, the west symbolizes death and the way of the spirits. A corpse is laid in the bush on the west side of the homestead. Other pastoralists in Sudan, such as the Atuot, have similar concepts of east and west (Burton 1981:52).

Colors. The symbolism of colors is another area to explore in looking for cultural themes. For the Bajju, black symbolizes that which is evil, bad, sinful; red symbolizes what is dangerous, bad news, sick; while white indicates purity, cleanness, and restoration of health. In India red indicates fertility while white symbolizes widowhood and death. The color blue is used to indicate god, so statutes of Krishna are blue. Traditionally in China, yellow was used to symbolize royalty, and red represented good luck. In Japan black, white, and gray are gloomy, melancholy colors. And gifts wrapped in yellow in England indicate that the gift is humorous.

Numbers. Numbers have significance beyond their numerical values in many cultures worldwide. For example, among the Pocomchi in Guatemala when individuals converted to Christianity they came to Ted Engel, a Summer Institute of Linguistics fieldworker, to ask, "Now that we are Christians how many grains of corn should we plant?" The question left the missionary puzzled until he realized that within each hole the Pocomchi planted one grain for the spirit of the mountain in addition to the corn planted for their subsistence needs (Ted Engel, personal communication, 1986).

The numbers three and four have significance for many ethnic groups in West Africa (Hansford 1995:131 and Hill 1995:131–32). Three symbolizes a male and four a female, and their significance relates to the sex organs of males and females. Seven symbolizes completeness, the result of the addition of three and four or male and female. In some groups in the southern part of West Africa markets occur every four days.

In Korea it is inappropriate to give a gift with four elements. The number four indicates bad luck, similar to what thirteen represents in some countries.

Discussion

Discovery of a culture's worldview involves doing basic ethnographic research, using tools such as participant and process observations, informal interviews, perhaps collecting some life histories, etc. This ethnographic research provides the foundation for investigation of a culture's worldview.

There is not one set of questions that, if asked, will elicit a culture's worldview. Further, for different components of a worldview, specific field methods may be useful. For example, in order to identify the classification and causality sections of a worldview, use ethnosemantic analysis such as described in this chapter. For examination of the adaptational aspects of a worldview, use methods from cultural ecology, such as time allocation studies discussed in chapter 25. For understanding the values component of worldview, study oral traditions, such as proverbs, trickster narratives, etc. Some researchers also use questionnaires to study values in which respondents indicate what they value in specific situations. For study of relationships, use social network analysis.

Be aware that competing and contrastive worldviews can co-exist within the same culture. This can result in syncretism or alternate explanations for the same phenomena. Commonly known examples of coexisting symbolism for Christmas includes both the birth of Jesus and the story of Santa Claus. Another example is the celebration of the resurrection of Jesus at Easter and the story of the Easter bunny. People have an ability to compartmentalize these potentially competing worldviews, and do so all the time. Thus, you may need to formulate more than one worldview proposition for the same aspect of a culture.

Data from worldview and cognitive analyses point to values, the subject of the next chapter.

Unity as a cultural theme

One student for a participant observation project in a cultural anthropology class chose to study a Japanese flower salesman who was selling flowers on a street corner in the United States. She spent a number of hours there with him, talking with him, observing his business, leaving the corner with him when requested to do so by a nearby restaurant merchant and setting up the business on another street corner, and in general seeking to understand his perspective of his work. Her research indicated that he had been sent to the United States from Japan by the Reunification Church established by Rev. Moon.

The cultural theme she found that recurred in a number of cultural domains could be summarized in the statement, "All activities of the flower salesman were designed to bring about unity." He felt that when his mind and body were in unity, people would purchase his flowers, thus, the cultural theme of unity brought together both his ideology and his economic activities. His work on the street corner further tied in with his ultimate goal of the unity of all religions. He felt that he must first suffer by selling flowers on a street corner to bring his own body and soul together. After doing so for three years, next he planned to speak with church pastors to encourage them towards the unity of all religions (example from Cathy Crosby Davison, Dallas, 1987).

19

Values

In order to be of help to others we must do more than learn their technical wisdom.
We must also understand their values. (Bachelor 1993:15)

VALUES are accepted or normative ideals of behavior. They involve judgment—bases of evaluation of behavior and actions. Values within various groups are part of their ethical systems that define what is perceived as right, moral, and good within society versus what is disapproved of, immoral, and viewed as wrong. Values distinguish between duty and happiness. They are the bases of many of our decisions.

Values are a cultural universal in that they point to how people should and should not behave. Every culture has a system of values. They are the core of a moral order within a culture (Powdermaker 1956:783). They provide the ideals towards which people strive; however, people often do not live up to their ideals.

Kluckholn et al. (1952:395, 403–09) describe parts of a definition of values as follows:

> Values, positive and negative, are (1) elements in the effective definition of the situation of action that designate desirable and undesirable modes, means and ends of action, i.e., normative orientations related in varying ways to cognitive and affective processes; (2) may be explicit or implicit, i.e., given directly in value judgments or inferred from verbal and non-verbal behaviors that involve approval, disapproval, blame, praise, reward, punishment, support and suppression; (3) are persistent through time and manifest directionality, i.e., there is observable consistency of response to recurrent situations; and (4) are interrelated as elements in culturally or individually distinctive patterns or systems, i.e., as differentiated but interdependent parts of a whole (as quoted in Albert 1956:221–22).

Values and worldview

Values and worldview are very closely related. For example, values can be viewed either as part of a worldview or as emerging from a worldview. Which way you choose to view them depends upon your theoretical perspective. For example, a worldview may be divided into three components: cognitive aspects that involve a person's fundamental beliefs and assumptions, affective characteristics that deal with that person's deepest feelings, and evaluative aspects that involve basic values and allegiances (Hiebert, as quoted in Bruce 1992:21). It is this latter aspect of worldview that this chapter addresses.

People often cannot explicitly state their reasons for holding specific values. Rather, you may encounter people stating things such as, "This is what is right," "It's just our custom to do it like this," "This is what we ought to do," "This is how it's supposed to be," or "That's just the way we do things." It remains your task as the field researcher to derive the basic worldview propositions that motivate specific values, and the values that grow out of those worldview propositions. Albert (1956:222) asserts that in order to derive values the researcher must use inspections, logical analysis, and successive approximations. Because values derive from the worldview of a culture, Albert notes,

> A preliminary classification indicated that the logical and functional relations between values and the general cultural conceptual system (world-view, ethnophilosophy) are so close that delineation of the world-view is an appropriate adjunct to the description of the value system (Albert p. 222).

One position some hold is that worldview refers to cosmology and cognitive assumptions only and is distinct from values or evaluative assumptions (Bruce 1992:68). Values may reflect felt needs. On the relationship between values and worldview Bruce states,

> Values might be designated as a person's treasured ideals, his commitments, and the loyalties which he chooses within the framework of his worldview. A person's worldview is his philosophy of the universe, his explanations for how it works the way it does, and the structure of the powers therein. His values form his decisions and choices in the light of that analysis and give him purpose for action and goals to attain. (Bruce 1992:21)

Worldview, values, emotions, and behavior overlap, but they apparently operate independently or interdependently in a decision-making mode (Bruce 1992:24).

Prime, focal, and specific values

Within a value system Bruce (1992:28) distinguishes three levels. PRIME VALUES tie values to the worldview of a culture. A prime value can also be termed a CORE VALUE within a culture. It deals with an individual's primary allegiance, such as to God, gods, or self. FOCAL VALUES are a second level of values that include bundles of values. From focal values emerge SPECIFIC VALUES. Behavior that is observed is an outcome of specific values. For example, in many cultures focal values deal with the desirability of maintaining smooth interpersonal relations. Out of these emerge specific values that foster good interpersonal relations.

What happens when, for a certain individual, a prime value, focal values, and specific values are inconsistent with each other? Such incongruities within a value system of an individual may result in inconsistency, compartmentalism, guilt, shame, dysfunctionality, and ineffectiveness. The lack of logical consistency is what you observe when you compare what an individual states are his or her values with that person's actual behavior.

For the purposes of this field guide, a cultural value system begins with BASIC VALUE PREMISES, PRIME VALUES, or VALUE-ORIENTATIONS. These three terms are used synonymously. They refer to the most general concepts of what is desirable and what is undesirable. Basic value premises include ultimate values, and these ultimate values are often not verbalized by members of the culture. One goal of researchers is to make explicit and to verbalize value premises. Whether verbalized or not, if you are studying values within a specific ethnic group, you need to construct prime value premises by inferences from explicit statements of individuals within the culture and from observed behavior.

From the basic value premises you derive focal and specific values. Types of focal values are impersonal, character, directive, environmental, ethical, and spiritual. Types of values, beginning with focal values, are discussed next.

Focal values as value clusters

Focal values include clusters of specific values. When you investigate a particular domain of culture, you will likely find values that apply to that domain, and then you may find specific values within it. For example, there are focal values that would apply to marriage. These include values related to the pre-wedding courtship period, the wedding ceremony and celebrations, and the expectations of the marital spouses and of the wider community. Domain, componential, and taxonomic displays may usefully be used in presenting value clusters (see chapter 18).

Impersonal values. IMPERSONAL VALUES concern events attributed to fate, God's will, one's horoscope, impersonal use of spiritual power (termed witchcraft by Evans-Pritchard 1937), and in general to phenomena over which the individual is powerless to influence or change and, therefore, is not considered to be responsible. Attributing events and actions to an impersonal category of value absolves an individual of responsibility for things that happen.

It is tempting to place an oppressive governmental system within the category of impersonal values; indeed for some individuals it does fall into this category, because they hold an unjust oppressive system responsible for their economic plight and all of their problems in general. They feel locked into a system that they cannot change and that seems unresponsive to their attempts to change it. Others would not put an oppressive system in this category but would rather attribute blame to a corrupt head of state and other corrupt governmental officials.

Character values. CHARACTER VALUES refer to virtues and vices of an individual. These are the qualities of an individual that are approved or disapproved of by members of the culture in focus. Virtues and vices reflect moral characteristics of a person.

Character values also include what a society believes about the nature of humans. They relate to questions such as, "Are people born good or evil?" "Is human nature morally neutral and completely shaped by its culture and environment?" In anthropology there is the nature-nurture question. To what extent are people born with specific qualities and to what extent does their nurturing instill these qualities in people?

> ### Parents and adult children
>
> In class, composed largely of graduate students, I divided students into groups based on their place of origin. There was a group from the western United States, another from the midwest, a third group from the south, and one from the eastern U.S. A fifth group was composed of students from Korea. Each group discussed their values. The midwesterners reported on the importance of hard work and individual effort. The westerners reported that though hard work was important, leisure was also important. The Korean group reported on the value of continuing to show respect to their parents. One young woman stated, "Our parents own our bodies, so that if we want to get a permanent or have our ears pierced we must get our parents permission."

Directive values. DIRECTIVE VALUES specify what a person should do; they are prescriptive values. Directive values also include what a person should not do, the prohibitions. Both include "laws, commandments, rules of conduct, taboos, obligations and duties, rights and privileges, and any other rules or standards which are intended to regulate conduct" (Albert 1956:226).

Environmental values. ENVIRONMENTAL VALUES deal with our relationship with the physical environment. These values involve concepts such as pollution, concern for endangered species, care for the environment, conservation, depletion of natural resources and the ozone level, sanitation, and carrying capacity of the land. Efforts to save the remaining rain forests fall into environmental values, as well as efforts to save various endangered species such as the whale and the spotted owl.

Ethical values. When looking at ETHICAL VALUES, we are looking at moral principles. These are also termed MORAL VALUES (Crapo 1993:113). They are rules which govern our interpersonal relations. Albert distinguishes between those ethical values that deal with *common decency* towards anyone, and those that deal with *duty* which refers to proper fulfillment of obligations to one's family, city, state, country, etc. (Albert 1956:234). Patriotism falls under values that relate to duty.

Spiritual values. SPIRITUAL VALUES deal with our relationship with the spiritual and supernatural realm. These values may also be termed PIETY VALUES. They concern rules or taboos that govern one's relationship with the supernatural realm. Loving God with all of one's heart falls into this category within the Judeo-Christian tradition. The Ten Commandments (see Exodus 20:2–17) are examples of spiritual and ethical values for a society.

Other types of values. In classifying values we can also look at those that apply to different realms of the society, such as political, social, economic, family, aesthetic, educational, and military values. Do so by looking at domains of a culture and investigate which particular values are present within each domain.

Specific values

Specific values include those within each of the focal value categories mentioned above.

Outline of a value system

The schema discussed above can be outlined as follows:

I. Values
  A. Prime values
  B. Focal values or value clusters
    1. Impersonal
      a. Fate
      b. God's will
      c. A horoscope
      d. Impersonal spiritual power (witchcraft)

        2. Character
            a. Virtues
            b. Vices
            c. Beliefs about human nature
        3. Directive
            a. Prescribed behavior
            b. Proscribed behavior
        4. Environmental
        5. Ethical or moral
            a. Common decency
            b. Duty
        6. Spiritual or piety
        7. Other (specify)
    C. Specific values

Values from an emic perspective

In your analysis be aware that there is the risk of error and distortion when you move from the descriptive data to cultural themes or assertions, generalizations, patterns, and inferences from which you derive values. Values that you derive from a particular behavior pattern may not be those that an insider to that culture would derive. Hence, it is important that you check any values you formulate from observed behavior or other cultural patterns with insiders of the target culture in order to obtain their emic perspective.

The results of the study of values are statements or propositions, stated in the analytical vocabulary of the social sciences, that you as the fieldworker formulate and which an insider of the culture agrees with. Sometimes what researchers formulate look nothing like what an insider of that culture would recognize. In that event you need to reformulate the values of the culture so that what you derive is in line with an emic perspective.

Values correlated with subsistence patterns

Specific values often correlate with particular subsistence patterns. For example, pastoralists consider their way of life ideal. They tend to look down on nonpastoralists, and on those pastoralists who lose their animals, perhaps due to drought and take up agriculture. Murle who no longer have cattle are referred to by the derogatory term "sugar ant" because they scurry around on the earth procuring their food as ants also do (Arensen 1991:43). While Murle pastoralists and horticulturally based Murle may call each other derogatory names, the agricultural Murle provide a haven for pastoralists when times are difficult, usually due to drought. They absorb destitute herders when there is hardship, and thus provide for them until they can reenter the pastoral segment of their society. This type of economic system has its ideal as pastoralism, but it also includes horticultural activities during hard times. This pattern occurs with other pastoralists as well within the east African cattle complex, as for example among the Maasai in Kenya.

Hunter and gatherers or foragers place a high value on sharing. The survival of the group depends upon sharing. One who does not share is viewed as being greedy or stingy. This may include a forager who also plants some crops. A forager farmer who saves grain for the next planting season is a greedy person. If you study a foraging group, the people will expect you to share all that you have. Horticulturalists, too, value sharing as part of their communal lifestyle, though not to the extent that foragers do.

People in many societies increasingly value education. It is an important means of economic advancement.

Values change

Values may change in response to factors both internal and external to a culture. When two or more cultures are in contact, such as occurs through various forms of the mass media (e.g., television, videos, motion pictures, news media, etc.), values rarely transfer intact. New values tend to be modified and incorporated into a culture based on that culture's previously held presuppositions. Further, people within a culture will incorporate new values based on their psychological needs, often in response to their anxieties as they face a new changing way of life.

Values often change based on where people are in a continuum from a traditionally oriented rural society to a modern urban society. Values may differ depending on generation, with parents in rural areas tending to hold more traditional values, and their children who have been educated tending to evaluate and in some cases adopt new values they encounter in urban areas. These second generation individuals have been socialized in the more traditional values as well as new values received through education, so some may compartmentalize their values or hold conflicting values, or both. Fallers addresses this issue when he states,

> conflicts between opposed value systems are not primarily in discrete groups of persons holding opposed systems of values and beliefs; they consist rather in the same persons, to a great extent throughout the society holding two incompatible systems of beliefs and values. (1955:302)

Williams (as quoted in Bruce 1992:125–26) describes ten types of changes in values:

1. Creation of new standards of beliefs;
2. Abrupt destruction of a value;
3. Intensification, in which a value becomes stronger;
4. Attenuation which involves a lessening of commitment to a value;
5. Extension of a value to other areas;
6. Consistency, in which a value applies throughout the value system;
7. Limitation of the area to which the value applies;
8. Elaboration, in which a value becomes more complex and embedded in a social context;
9. Specification, in which a value is redefined or applied to a particular context; and
10. Explication in which a value is enforced in philosophical terms.

Bruce (1992) examined the relationship between Christian conversion and value change, which she saw as an integral part of conversion. Many of the types of value change listed above are important in Christian conversion. For example, a new Christian may extend a value such as purity to all areas of his or her life, including sexual purity and truth in his or her interpersonal relationships.

Rapid social change in a culture (e.g., as a result of war, drought, epidemics, natural disasters, etc.) will almost always lead members of that culture to face changes in values. Often the first response of persons faced with such situations is to reassert their central generalized values. Those who do not follow those values may be labeled as hypocrites. As social change continues, however, the wider society must deal with the issue of values change.

Importance or strength of different values

Within a culture, there will likely be a cluster of values that are held by a majority of the population. Different individuals, however, assign different degrees of importance to specific values. For example, the majority of a given population may agree that God exists. Some members of that population will work to make their behavior conform to their concepts of how a holy God would want them to behave. Others will acknowledge that God exists, yet basically ignore him and any implications of that belief for their daily lives.

Resistance to value change

Bruce (1992:127–28), following Williams, cites the following examples where there will likely be resistance to change.

1. If a value is interconnected with a number of other values it will be less likely to change.
2. Values that are central and pervasive in a culture will be resistant to change.
3. Values that a society supports with powerful sanctions for transgression will be unlikely to change.
4. If there is great consensus about certain values in a culture, then they will be unlikely to change quickly.
5. If those who have prestige or who are authoritative within the society oppose change in values, then that opposition makes values less apt to change.
6. If values are congruent with other values and beliefs in that culture, then they will be less likely to change.
7. If values are symbolized in a number of ways within a culture, then they will be resistant to change.
8. Values that are central to a culture and are strongly held to are those which are most resistant to change. Further, if a resistant value does change, that change will likely affect other values that are dependent upon it.

If two important values within a culture are incongruous, or if one value is inconsistent with a central value of a culture, then various responses may occur. First, people may be persuaded to behave in a manner contrary to their values. Second, people may face the inconsistency based on new information and either change it or live with that inconsistency. Individuals can think through their values seeking inconsistencies. Counselors may assist in this cognitive process, or individuals themselves may sort them out.

While values tend to change very slowly, cyclical changes in value systems do occur within cultures. Sometimes values move from very conservative ones to more liberal, then back to more conservative positions. Cycles are of various time durations. It takes long-term longitudinal historical studies to ascertain such cyclical value changes.

Efforts to change values

Recently, there have been various educational efforts to either bring about values change or else to work on values clarification. Both have been primarily educational efforts with the goal that students see the ramifications of their actions. A third educational effort is values inculcation, in which students are encouraged to think through ethical issues and come to some conclusions as to relevant values they might adopt. Values inculcation refers to the teaching of and training in particular values.

Values may be examined and often changed through modeling, questioning of values, reasoning, confronting values, and teaching of values. Affirming and encouraging people can also lead to values change.

There are various types of educational efforts that seek to examine and clarify values. These include SUBSTANTIVE VALUES EDUCATION and VALUES CLARIFICATION THEORY.

Substantive Values Education seeks to increase student awareness of values and to help them understand their values and the values of others. This approach looks at how values can underlie and even determine behavior. It also looks at ranking of values and changes in values.

Values Clarification Theory does not work at inculcating values, but rather attempts to help students identify the values they already hold. Some have criticized this theory for failing to inculcate values, and also for teaching some values, perhaps at a latent or sub-conscious level. Those values include independence rather than interdependence, broad-mindedness that some see as too inclusive, time consciousness rather than interpersonal relationship consciousness, etc. In other words, while the goal of those who work within the Values Clarification Theory model is simply to identify and clarify values, in fact they also teach values.

There are two primary values areas within the Values Clarification Theory model that people examine. These are self value, by which an individual accepts his or her own self worth, and the value of others, by which he or she accepts the worth of others. Note that this relates to one aspect of worldview propositions, the examination of the self and of the other.

Means of transmitting values

The transmission of values occurs through various means such as advice given by elders, including parents to children, customs, taboos, gossip, songs, education, the media, and oral traditions. Outside researchers can derive values through studying what is transmitted from one generation to the next. Values often become codified into law.

Contradictory values

As noted earlier, people often hold contradictory values. People can compartmentalize values and not even realize that the values they apply in different situations are in fact contradictory. Thus, values may be applied situationally. Or an individual may face contradictory conflicting values. For example, within a traditional African family an individual derives his or her identity by virtue of being part of the group. The group is primary and the individual is secondary. Through western style education the individual may become primary and the group secondary. When the extended family makes claims upon an educated individual's salary, as for school fees for other children within the family, that individual may resist and assert that his salary is his to use as he sees fit. To do so violates the corporateness of the extended family, and any urban African would know this. Thus, he may end up with conflicting values that must be resolved in his daily behavior.

Prioritization of values

In any value system, people prioritize their values. Two individuals, e.g., a married couple, may prioritize their values differently. That difference may result in conflict between them.

One way to explore what priority people put on their values is to list their values, whether ones they have told you or ones that you have discovered and they have confirmed, then ask them to rank them in order of first importance, second importance, and so on.

If you are doing a cross-cultural comparison of values between two or more groups, you may want each group to list their values, then to prioritize them. The resultant differences in their priorities of values could help to explain areas of tension between the groups in focus.

Suggestions for studying values

Following are a few suggestions of research methods you might use to study the local value system.

Values derived through participant observation and informal interviews

When engaging in participant observation, gradually observe many of the behaviors that derive from specific values for a particular society. A few questions given below might stimulate your observations and informal interviews. You will need to develop other relevant questions within the particular target culture.

1. How do people spend their time (both work and leisure time)?
2. What do they spend their money on? For example, do they spend far in excess of their annual incomes on weddings or funerals or both?
3. What are their goals?
4. With whom do they associate?
5. What are their attitudes towards cleanliness?
6. What is their attitude towards related and unrelated ethnic groups in their area?
7. What is their attitude towards those from outside of their culture?
8. What is their attitude towards the supernatural?
9. What is their belief about ecological disasters (e.g., earthquakes, tornadoes, volcano eruptions, drought, famine, hurricanes)?
10. What advice do they give to each other? What advice do parents give to their children?
11. What issues do they discipline their children about?
12. What is their attitude towards education?
13. Do they value children highly? For example, is it a pro-natalist society or not? What is the ideal number of children a couple would desire to have?
14. Do they value the elders highly? Do they value youth? Are the elders respected? How does the value placed on age manifest itself in the culture?
15. What body shape do they value?
16. What values emerge in their music?
17. What do they value in adornment as seen in their clothes, body and facial scarification, tattoos, jewelry, make-up, etc.?

18. Which occupations have higher social status, and which have lower status?
19. What are means of motivating individuals within the culture? That which motivates individuals often points to specific values.
20. Are there different values for different social classes or social categories within the society? If so, what are they?
21. Where is it preferable to live?
22. What characterizes an ideal marital partner?
23. What skin color is valued and why? Note that this question relates primarily to those within one racial group.
24. What facial features are valued? What hair color and hair styles are valued?
25. What values do people hold towards politeness and respect? What are good manners within the culture?
26. What contributes to hospitality that is considered good or desirable within a culture?
27. What constitutes good morals within a culture?
28. What are desirable personal characteristics, and what are undesirable?
29. What are characteristics of a person of integrity within the culture? Note that their answers will differ for men and women.

Values derived from oral traditions

A second method is to collect and analyze tales or oral traditions for the values expressed. Through oral traditions people often deal with values and social tensions in a way that distances them from those situations and also in a way that entertains. In tales, values may be stated either positively or negatively. For example, Arensen collected tales that illustrated the negative value the Murle place on gluttony (1991:239–41), the importance of caring for and respecting the elderly (pp. 238–39), the importance of accepting advice and repaying kindness with kindness (pp. 241–42), the importance of showing respect to in-laws and the value they place on politeness, dignity, and respect (pp. 243–44), and bravery and courage (pp. 253–56). In addition in their oral traditions, the Murle deal with values in marriage including compatibility and the dangers of illicit love affairs (pp. 246–50).

Proverbs are one form of oral tradition that succinctly state values in metaphorical language. For example, a Bajju proverb states, "You are like water in a basket to me." The meaning of the proverb is that you are worthless or useless to me, as is water that quickly drains out of a basket. The meanings of proverbs often are not obvious but need explanation.

You may also study the value people place on speech. For example, do they value the abilities of people who can speak well? Do they value the ability to use proverbs appropriately? Do they value the art of storytelling? Are there other types of verbal art they value? Is the ability to construct and recite poetry important?

Values derived through use of ethical dilemma story completion

In order to elicit values some researchers have posed scenarios that involve ethical dilemmas and asked members of the research community either to write or to verbally complete the stories. How people deal with ethical dilemmas can often bring out their personal and societal values. For example, you could write a story about a young single woman who finds herself pregnant. You could ask respondents to complete the story, putting themselves in the place of that young woman. If they were that young woman what would they do?

Values derived through use of a research instrument

Frequently, researchers construct research instruments for collection of quantitative data about what people value. These instruments often rank responses into a range of categories such as value highly, value, value little, and no value. The questions used are about values in situations relevant to the local culture.

In administering a research instrument, ask people to rank their choices. Or give people values listed on individual cards and ask them to sort them into categories according to what they value.

Values derived from legal systems

What values are evident in the local legal system? To study this you could observe court proceedings. Or you could observe local councils as they deliberate on issues. What issues go to court? Are those issues largely interethnic rather than intraethnic?

If there is a formal and/or informal legal system, what are the basic presuppositions of each? Is the defendant presumed innocent until proven guilty or presumed guilty until proven innocent?

Douglas (1966) speaks of purity and danger as key components in the basic presuppositions of some value systems. The idea of purity relates to our concept of dirt. We can view dirt from the perspective of care for hygiene and respect for conventions in the society. Consequently, holiness and impurity form opposites on a continuum. And if there is a distinction between the sacred and the profane, then both are to be protected from defilement. One could argue that the sacred and the profane, or the sphere of religion and that of everyday life, are not separate in any given culture. This is certainly the position that Islam takes, and it is also the position of deeply committed Christians.

In looking at purity and danger— dirt versus sacredness, the holy versus the profane in a society—expect that you will be dealing with metaphors and symbolism. Your goal as a field researcher is to seek to understand the meanings inherent in these metaphors and symbols. Expect also that certain customs and conventions will govern people's relations with the spiritual and supernatural realm. Some customs will involve what, under normal circumstances, would be prohibited. Some questions you might look at include the following.

1. What constitutes pollution and danger within a society?
2. What purification rites occur and for what purposes?
3. What element(s) are associated with purification? Water? Ashes? Cow dung? Holy oil?
4. Who must undergo purification and why must individuals undergo purification?
5. Are there beliefs about the consequences of individuals' trespasses that will result in negative consequences for the entire ethnic group if people do not undergo purification? For example, if one lies when swearing an oath, what are possible consequences for that individual, his or her family, clan, and the entire ethnic group?
6. What consequences are believed to result naturally from committing adultery or fornication? How might those consequences be mitigated? If a child is born as a result of sex occurring outside of marriage, what happens to that child?
7. How do beliefs in danger relate to chiefs, kings or queens, or other heads of state? Are there supernatural aspects associated with their person? What religious beliefs help them maintain their positions? What danger is associated with them? What symbolism is associated with them that relates to purity and danger?

8. What formal rituals occur? Must there be purification before participating in those rituals? What constitutes ritual cleanliness or uncleanness?
9. What taboos are present in the society? What consequences result from breaking those taboos?

Values derived from lexical and linguistic units

In analyzing anthropological texts such as life histories, monographs, your field notes, and so on, look for indications of values. For example, what is approved of and what is disapproved of, and what attitudes and opinions are expressed? Sometimes the choice of lexical items used indicates values. It may also indicate who is included as an insider and who is excluded as an outsider.

Values derived through other research methods

A further area to investigate about values is their basic orientation. For example, do they value interpersonal relations highly or is time more important?

The material that could be used in deriving values includes life histories, field data, monographs and ethnographies, oral traditions, laws, sanctions, etc. Look for what is approved of and what is disapproved of within the culture. What are common areas of conflict?

Powdermaker (1956:800) found among girls and boys in then Northern Rhodesia, now Zambia, in the copperbelt area of Africa that many of her respondents expressed a desire to be nonhuman, including being animals, birds, flowers, trees, and rivers.

A case study

The following case study illustrates how contrastive values were derived by one researcher for two groups with different value systems. Gardner selected a group of North American missionaries and African leaders of national Bible translation organizations and used the following questionnaire to ascertain their values (Gardner 1992, unpublished paper, used with permission).

One critique of Gardner's questionnaire would be that it is aimed primarily at North American missionaries, rather than equally at the North Americans and at the African leaders. This is seen in the labels "Your values" and "African leaders' values." In order to avoid this bias the labels "North American missionaries' values" and "African leaders' values" could have been used.

The results of Gardner's study in (63) show major differences in values between these two populations. In looking at these two lists, note that there is no overlap of common values. The North American sample reflects the importance of individualism and personal satisfaction, while the African sample shows the importance of communalism, relationships, and continuation of one's name. Working cross-culturally with an African group where these are the top values would mean that the fieldworker and North American missionaries must make major values adjustments in order to understand and fit into the new community.

Values ranking

Arrange the following values in a hierarchy. Rank the items in the following list as follows:

1. Value highly
2. Value moderately
3. Value little
4. No value, unimportant to you

Your values   **African leaders' values**

1. ____ Security   ____
2. ____ Continuation of your name: your son will   ____
        carry your name on
3. ____ Your significance   ____
4. ____ Peace   ____
5. ____ Family   ____
6. ____ Power—distrust of authority and hierarchy,   ____
        but you want some voice in decisions made,
        and you want to climb up the hierarchy
7. ____ Prestige   ____
8. ____ Comfort   ____
9. ____ Happiness and pleasure   ____
10. ____ Exercising leadership   ____
11. ____ Respect for elders   ____
12. ____ Respect for strangers   ____
13. ____ Finish the work, then play   ____
14. ____ People are more important than work: ____
         relationship is more important than personal time
15. ____ Discipline of children is shared among   ____
         the community
16. ____ Discipline of children is for the parents only   ____
17. ____ Importance of and responsibility for one's   ____
         extended family; maturity is when you are
         taking responsibility for other people
18. ____ Efficiency   ____
19. ____ Accomplishing one's goals   ____

---

(63) North American missionaries' values   African leaders' values

1. Security   1. Prestige

2. Significance   2. Importance and responsibility for
                                                    extended family; maturity is when
                                                    you are taking responsibility for
                                                    other people

3. Power—distrust authority and hierarchy, but want to have a voice in decisions, and want to climb

4. Family

5. Happiness

6. Comfort

7. Job satisfaction

3. Respect to elders

4. People are more important than work; relationship is more important than personal time

5. Finish the work, then play

6. Discipline is shared among the community

7. Respect for strangers

8. Peace

9. My house will continue; my son will carry on my name

These are a few suggestions concerning collecting data on values. Another primary source of values is oral traditions, the subject of the next chapter.

20

Oral Traditions

Storytelling is a skilled art among...[the Tiv]; their standards are high, and the audiences critical—and vocal in their criticism. (Bohannan, in Spradley and McCurdy 1987:37)

For the Tiv, as for most Africans, stories, parables, and other forms of verbal art are extremely important. As Bohannan states, "Their standards are high." Jesus, as a teacher par excellence, chose to use parables in his teaching.

> Jesus spoke all these things to the crowd in parables; he did not say anything to them without using a parable. So was fulfilled what was spoken through the prophet:
> "I will open my mouth in parables,
> I will utter things hidden since the
> creation of the world." (Matthew 13:34–35)

This effective means of communication has provided the following generations with wisdom. The oral teachings of Jesus were later written down, translated, and retranslated. The parables he used drew his audience in through their simplicity and depth.

ORAL TRADITIONS are recollections of the past that are commonly known in a given culture; you can view oral traditions as verbal folk art in a culture. They include folktales, proverbs, riddles, praise songs or shouts, performances, origin narratives and founding charters, legends, poetry, music, myths, dirges, historical accounts, trickster narratives, tall tales, and other stories. Some scholars distinguish between oral history and oral tradition. Henige uses ORAL HISTORY to refer to "the study of the recent past by means of life histories or personal recollections, where informants speak about their own experiences" (1982:2; see Sitton, Mehaffy, and Davis, Jr. 1983 for aid in collecting oral histories). Vansina defines oral traditions "as verbal messages which are reported statements from the past beyond the present generation" (1985:26). They are transmitted verbally over at least one generation. Over time, oral histories may develop into oral traditions.

The term oral tradition applies both to the process and its product (Vansina 1985:3). Frequently, the process is stylized. For example, when a Bajju storyteller begins his session, he uses the formulaic saying (as translated into English), "All eyes are in front, all eyes are in back...It's a folktale."

Anthropologists, folklorists, oral historians, missiologists, linguists, and others all collect oral traditions. Investigation from several disciplinary perspectives allows researchers to bring the strengths of each discipline to their analyses.

Oral traditions exist in people's minds and are accessible only when heard over a short period of time. They are not readily accessible, except through people's memories. For centuries memories have served as faithful repositories of oral traditions, as, for example, about origins of people, explanations of why things are as they are, and how things should be done. They are selective in the material remembered and transmitted over time, and some undergo modification according to what is considered important to succeeding generations.

In predominantly oral societies traditional education consists of information transmitted visually and verbally from one generation to the next. The elders are the repositories of such knowledge. A proverb from the Ngambay in Chad illumines this when it compares an elder to a library, so that at his death people may assert, "A library has burned" (Sem Baesnel, 1990, personal communication, Dallas). Baesnel shared this proverb with Norris and me when my husband's father died and was buried on his ninety-fifth birthday. When an old person dies, that person's knowledge passes away.

Concerning the importance of traditional oral education Deng states, "For reasons of its cultural, moral, and spiritual significance, the passing of knowledge down to successive generations is more than an objective transmission of facts...transmission of the actual words implies an educational process that is both informative and normative" (1986:9).

In oral traditions the concept of the truths transmitted is fluid and dynamic. Concepts can change as the situation demands; by making changes the teller seeks to illuminate some aspect of morals, values, or other objectives. By virtue of the fact that oral traditions are oral and can be changed easily, they represent a dynamic approach to truth, one that takes into account the benefits of continued experiences. If two storytellers tell the same story, rarely do both tell it the same way except in cases where accuracy of transmission of the story is required.

Definitions of culture from the cognitive perspective relate directly to the collection of oral traditions. For example, Spradley and McCurdy define culture as "the acquired knowledge that people use to interpret experience and to generate behavior" (1975:2). According to this definition, you must study oral traditions, among other things, in order to obtain the knowledge that people have within their memories.

The collection and study of oral traditions are crucial for understanding essentially oral societies; and they serve as the bases of much of the literature of literate societies. Events in both oral and literate societies are the bases for the continued development of oral traditions.

Recording, transcribing, translating, and publishing oral literature can contribute to the dignity, sense of self-worth, and survival of a culture that has been threatened with extinction or that has been denigrated by some within the dominant culture. When in Africa, it was the oral traditions that the elders asked us to write down. They did not want to lose them.

In this chapter definitions of different types of oral traditions are discussed, then suggestions for collecting them are presented.

Types of oral traditions

The following brief definitions identify some types or genre of oral traditions. Overlap may occur between different types (e.g., as between fables, legends, and myths); in fact, the distinction between myths and folktales is fuzzy in some cultures (Arensen 1991:196). Thus, the types of oral traditions listed below are not mutually exclusive nor is the list exhaustive. Some of the categories of oral traditions listed below are western constructs. Be sensitive to the emic classification of oral traditions within the culture you are studying. As a field researcher explore what genres of oral traditions exist within the culture in focus; look for named units in the language. In the subsections to follow, several genre that you might conceivably find are listed alphabetically.

> ### Bajju oral traditions
>
> Among the Bajju there are *gan* 'proverbs', *tashikum* 'folktales', *nkhang* 'stories, news, history' (*nkhang* is a generic category), and *babvvom* 'songs'. Though this is not a complete list of oral tradition types in Jju, it gives you an idea about named types of oral traditions that you might find in a language.

Children's game stories

Associated with many children's games are stories that are well-known within various cultures. Sometimes these stories involve rhyming games, and at other times they incorporate songs, dances, and other activities. For example, in Papua New Guinea there are string games with their accompanying stories.

Dilemma tales

DILEMMA TALES are tales that place the personae in positions with a dilemma or dilemmas to be solved. The clever solutions given often point up specific values within the culture. These tales seek answers to difficult questions. In a dilemma tale there is a problem and it is presented in such a way that it will likely end in a question. The audience then is left to discuss, argue, and answer the dilemma.

Dirges

DIRGES are songs used at funerals and memorial services. They can be used either at the burial that occurs immediately after death or several months or years following burial when the official funeral or memorial service takes place. A Bajju example is in the side box.

Stone (1988:108) notes that the Akan in Ghana have funeral dirges that are without musical accompaniment. These are composed and performed during the public mourning phase of a funeral.

> ### Bajju traditional dirge
>
> At a *kanak*, a ritual mourning feast that occurred several months after death, Bajju sang one dirge that asked the deceased, "Where, where, where have you gone?"

Epics

According to Vansina (1985:25) EPICS are poetic narratives that typically contain numerous verses and usually weave a complex tale around a central person who engages in wonders and heroism. Typically, epics recount history and legend in relation to the deeds of a national hero who is on a journey which is often filled with conflicts.

Epics may contain several varieties of oral tradition, such as formal speech, proverbs, songs, and myths, often with each chained and embedded into the next story or episode. (See Biebuyck and Mateene (1969) for the epic Mwindo from the Congo; Biebuyck (1978) for a discussion of epics among the Banyanga in Zaire; and Blackburn et al. (1989) for oral epics in India.)

There are two basic components of an epic: extended length and poetic narrative. Further, epics exalt either an historical or legendary hero who relates to the supernatural.

Within an African context, scholars have identified at least twenty epics (Kesteloot 1989:203). These epics fall into two categories, "feudal" and "clan" epics (p. 204). Feudal epics recount the exploits of an historical or legendary hero. They correspond to what scholars term "Homeric" type epics within Greek epic studies. By contrast, Kesteloot states that clan epics

> are always very long narratives punctuated by musical accompaniment and enumerating the valorous exploits of a heroic figure. By and large, however, they deviate far more from the history of the peoples that produce them. They take on a distinctly fantastical character. This supernatural aspect, often reduced to ordinary magical elements in the feudal epics, here reaches exaggerated, indeed surrealist proportions…. (p. 206)

An example of an African epic is the Kpelle *woi* epic in Liberia, which combines song, narration, dance, and dramatic performance, with musical accompaniment (Stone 1988). In this epic there is a shifting of themes, with seeming discontinuity between them. In some ways performance of the Kpelle epic may be compared to polyrhythmic patterns of African music, where each part has a relatively simple rhythm, but when all are combined the result is quite complex.

In an epic, time can be viewed as multidimensional, with multiple layers that use space, motion, and telescoped time (e.g., the past enters into the present). The *woi* epic also incorporates biographical time, with each participant in the epic having an individual trajectory from birth to death, and even into ancestorship (Stone 1988:130). African epics often begin slowly, purposefully, and expansively, and end abruptly, sometimes with a single phrase or word.

The mythical founding hero often represents the aspirations of the clan. An example of an African feudal epic is the well-known Mandinka epic of Sundiata (also spelled Son-Jara or Sunjata (Niane 1965)) that tells of the founding of the Mali empire in the fourteenth and fifteenth centuries. Feudal epics provide a mine of data for historical reconstruction for particular societies. For example, in the Sundiata epic we learn the names of the early kings of the Mali empire and something of their exploits.

Epics serve as sources of wisdom and allow people to face issues of daily life. The issues faced by the hero might include problems such as lack of respect, relations with one's in-laws, interpersonal relationship problems between men and women, courtship, marital arrangements, the ideal person, cultural values, and maintenance of authority. Sometimes facing issues may help to revitalize the people through seeing how their superhero faced seemingly insurmountable odds.

Epics are performed at important occasions, for example, at the installation of a new chief where praise singers remind the new chief of his responsibilities to his people. They connect the new chief with past office holders.

In some areas a man performs a long epic in which both he and his wife contribute by singing the songs that are embedded within the narrative. Sometimes there is a praise ensemble composed of a mastersinger who narrates, a woman who sings praise poetry and songs, a female chorus, together with male musicians (Hale 1994:80).

In the oral recounting of epics, there are usually promptings from the audience or the accompanist. These promptings should also appear in your recording of epics. Some have done so by noting them at the appropriate places where they occur, then putting them in footnotes. Others incorporate them into the text itself, as within parentheses. In recording an epic include these promptings and other features of the context (e.g., audience participation, laughter) and where, when, and why the epic is recited.

Explanatory tales

EXPLANATORY TALES seek to explain the origin of a particular aspect, whether ideas or objects, of a culture. Many explanatory tales begin with an introduction that refers to an early period in history, such as "Long, long ago...," "In the beginning...," "Once upon a time," or something similar. These tales usually contain references to things within the environment and experiences of the people who tell them. (See "Legends or etiological tales" for an alternate way of describing these tales.)

Fables

FABLES are short fictional stories, frequently with morals. These stories often include animals or inanimate objects as characters. They may explain how things came to be as they are.

Folktales

FOLKTALES are stories or legends of real or imaginary events which are handed down over time; they have also been termed FAIRY TALES. Some folktales are told simply to amuse, others teach moral principles, some present tragedies, and others highlight a contrast between right and wrong with resultant rewards or penalties. Some have a number of motifs that recur, and such repetitions give the tales their rhythm and allow hearers to anticipate what is coming next.

Founding charters, charter myths, and creation or origins narratives

FOUNDING CHARTERS, CHARTER MYTHS, and CREATION or ORIGINS NARRATIVES relate the origins of particular people or ethnic groups. In most instances these terms can be used interchangeably. Do not make the mistake of thinking of founding charters as only dealing with past history. They continue to have significance for contemporary people by accounting for and justifying their distinctiveness and existence as a separate people. They serve contemporary purposes, particularly for some ethnic groups in modern nations who feel embattled or who are threatened with dispossession of their land and loss of their culture. They can recreate or sometimes even reinvent that which is significant for their group. Origins narratives point people to the customs prescribed by their ancestors or the "first people," and they provide direction for behavior, particularly ideal behavior.

Genealogies

GENEALOGIES are records of ancestors. Most genealogies contain names of individuals together with kinship terms. They show continuity with the past of particular members included within them, and they anchor the present firmly within its historical context. As an African friend stated, if a person has relatives, then he is someone, and those relatives include the dead, the living, and those yet to be born. Some African groups keep long gene-alogies while others have shallow genealogies.

Genealogies may contain either lists of individual persons or lists of clans. Sometimes these two merge, with the genealogy being a list of apical ancestors, thus, a list of the founders of specific clans within the ethnic group. When that is the case you are dealing with a founding charter. For example, the record of the genealogy of Jesus Christ the son of David, the son of Abraham:

> Abraham was the father of Isaac,
> Isaac the father of Jacob
> Jacob the father of Judah and his brothers,
> Judah the father of Perez and Zerah, whose mother was Tamar,
> Perez the father of Hezron,
> Hezron the father of Ram,... (Matthew 1:1–3)

Gossip

GOSSIP is talk or rumor about the affairs, usually private, of others. Gossip offers an emic perspective on behavior. It may be intertwined with other types of oral traditions; for ex-ample, it may be included within epics. Haviland (1977:560) found listening to gossip in-sightful because of the motives and attitudes that emerged.

While gossip is often kept from you as an outsider until people trust you, be aware that gossip can provide a gold mine of data. Sometimes you can be made aware that people are gossiping by a change in intonation and other prosodic patterns. Those patterns may in-clude lowering of the register of the voice, speaking more quietly, or speaking in whispered voice. These special speech styles serve to indicate that people are gossiping and by so do-ing they express disapproval of others' behavior.

Historical accounts

HISTORICAL ACCOUNTS or QUASI-HISTORICAL ACCOUNTS refer to narratives about actual events which historians use as one resource for reconstruction of history. For example, Johnston (1966:153–57) recorded "The Death of Captain Moloney" as narrated to him by a Hausa who witnessed the event. Oral history is a useful source of historical data from preliterate cultures.

Insults

INSULTS are speech used with the intent of showing disrespect or contempt of another person or group. They are meant to discredit the one or ones insulted. In Hausa, insults are termed *zage*. They are often done in song as a form, for example, to discredit those in the opposite political party.

Jokes

JOKES are something said or done to evoke laughter. Sometimes they focus on the absurd, the ridiculous, the incongruous, or the insignificant for humorous purposes.

In different societies there are various genre of jokes. For example, in Texas there are Ag-gie jokes, jokes built around silly things that those who attend Texas A&M University supposedly do. In Papua New Guinea there are the local equivalent that might be glossed in English as "little moron stories" (Russ Cooper, personal communication, February 27, 1992). In these stories people find themselves in incongruous situations. They may include stories about the guys who are always late, or focus on the stupid things people do.

Jokes may also be built around personal experiences. In studying a different culture from yours, be aware that there may be different genre of jokes that can be elicited and studied.

Legends or etiological tales

LEGENDS explain how and why things are as they are, and they may include moral teachings or sanctions. They may be told mainly for entertainment. Sometimes these oral traditions are termed ETIOLOGICAL TALES in that they seek to explain the origins of natural phenomena and/or local customs. They tell how specific animals obtained their unique characteristics. For example, we collected one Bajju tale about how the turtle got his "cracked" shell. The Hausa have a narrative that explains how the hyena got spots (see Johnston 1966:45–46).

Sometimes specific places or themes recur in legends. For example, in the well-known Hausa legend of Daura, the well is an important place around which the events in the legend occur; similarly, for other West Africans, wells often have a central place in their legends as a focus of village life. Paths or roads are another place commonly found in legends that people travel along as events unfold.

Legends frequently develop around real people who did things that members of the culture might want to emulate and/or value. For example, according to legend George Washington refused to lie about having cut down a cherry tree. From government records we know that Washington was an historical figure. In this legend he is used to symbolize honesty, though we do not know for a fact that he either cut down a cherry tree or admitted to having done so.

Legends are used to teach about moral sanctions on people's behavior. Their purpose is mainly to teach the values of a culture.

Myths

MYTHS are sacred stories, with no evaluation made or implied as to their truth value. As Crane and Angrosino state,

> The word "myth" should not be understood as a term of disparagement. Myths can refer to *any* stories that seek a transcendent explanation of *why* things got to be as they are, regardless of whether they can be verified or whether they are part of the structure of a living religious system. (1992:109)

Hammond similarly defines myths as "traditionally based, dramatic narratives on themes that emphasize the nature of man's relationship to nature and to the supernatural" (1971:318). Myths tend to explain why things are as they are, and they verbalize a society's major concerns. They usually deal with humans' relations to nature and to the supernatural. They are tied to the central belief structure of the religious or ideological system of the culture. Myths link together to form a mythology that verbalizes a culture's major concerns. COSMOLOGICAL MYTHS are a specific type of religious myth that deal with the origins of the heavens and its celestial bodies.

The term myth, as used colloquially, refers to that which is false. The anthropological use of this term meaning a sacred story may or may not coincide with that which is false.

Crane and Angrosino (1992:109) point out that the word myth can also apply to certain nonreligious tales because they deal with people's relationship to impersonal forces. They cite a Western myth about the rugged individualist of the American frontier who has a sense of justice, honor, dignity of labor, and who is unemotional.

One theme found in myths is a reversal of the social order at some time in the past and how the social order has changed. For example, among the Mundurucú in Brazil, women at first held the power through possessing scared musical instruments, but this social order changed with women becoming inferior to men. This myth provides the rational of present-day Mundurucú sex roles (Murphy and Murphy 1974:87ff.).

Oracles

ORACLES are divine revelations, utterances, messages (verbal and/or nonverbal), or pronouncements, and they derive their authority based on the power behind the message. For example, in the Old Testament the term oracle could be translated as "the word of the Lord" (see Malachi 1:1, Zechariah 9:1), and its authority derives from "the Lord."

Individuals may receive the content of oracles in dreams or visions. They often give directions which, if not followed, result in impending doom. Frequently, those directions involve repentance, sacrifice, and a changed lifestyle. And, if followed, oracles offer hope.

Traditionally, in Nigeria the Igbo had the Agbala Oracle (Achebe 1959:104–13), the Oracle of the Hills and Caves, that bound the people and their politically autonomous villages together. Traditionally, this ethnic group had no overarching political structure, but each village was governed by a council of elders. It was oracles that gave the people a sense of political and religious cohesion.

Parables

PARABLES are short stories that illustrate a normative lesson, a truth, or moral. Often the meaning of parables is opaque, with some explanation being necessary for a clear understanding of what the parable is intended to convey.

Performances

PERFORMANCES are oral presentations, usually in front of an audience, that encompass performers, styles of performance, settings, masks, costumes, props, and texts. Okpewho states it well as follows,

> By the term *performance* is implied that total act as well as the context or environment involved in the delivery of oral literature—issues relating not only to the role of the audience...or of music but also to the narrator's use of the movement of the face, hands, and other parts of the body in giving life to the narration. (1992:16)

While oral traditions have teaching and ritual purposes, their primary function is to entertain. Different genre of oral traditions call for different types of performances. Finnegan (1986:74) speaks of a true performance as having a text composed of the verbal contents, the style of delivery (including tempo, mood, dynamics, intonation, kinesics, and use of artifacts), and audience reaction and participation. Okpewho points out that, "The moonlit square has for countless generations been the setting for songs and stories whose primary intent is more to entertain, it would seem, than to edify" (1979:2).

In entertaining, the performer(s) and audience often interact, with the performer asking questions, chanting refrains, inserting appropriate sound effects, dancing, and acting out parts of the story, and the audience responding by singing the chorus, providing background music, inserting appropriate sounds, and cooperating with the performer(s). The art of the storyteller can be utilized in a dramatic performance. In central Africa, Vansina, describes a performance as follows:

> A performer sits, often in the evening, surrounded by listeners and spins a tale. It is never just a recitation. The voice is raised or lowered, used as a means of dramatization. Nor does the storyteller just sit there. The tale is acted out with body gestures, even when the storyteller is sitting. Sometimes he or she may stand up, move around, and mime parts of the action narrated. In most cases the public is not just watching. The public is active. It interacts with the teller, and the teller provokes this interaction by asking questions, welcoming exclamations, and turning to a song sung by all at appropriate points of the action. The teller and public are creating the tale together. (1985:34)

Traditions are transmitted to the next generation in the context of oral performances. In this transmission process, performers take the listeners' knowledge of the tradition into account. Sometimes performers leave out sections or tell them only sketchily if they know the listeners have this common knowledge. What is included depends on the storytellers' emphases.

Within some state societies there are specialists who transmit knowledge such as historical accounts, epics of the state, and genealogies of rulers. Sons listen to performances and learn the important oral traditions that they in turn pass down to their sons.

Performances of oral traditions are limited, with some used only for specific ritual occasions, such as at installations of new rulers, religious celebrations, funerals, or other ceremonies. These uses indicate that oral traditions have practical purposes. Vansina makes this point,

> Each sort of tradition has its appropriate occasions for performance, and that also determines the frequency of a performance. Among the Dogon (Mali), the Sigui ritual was performed, it is said, only once every sixty years. One wonders who after such a lapse of time would still remember the details and order of the complex rituals and, indeed, in the absence of a calendar how one knows exactly when to perform them. (1985:40)

The masks and costumes of masquerades are an essential part of the performance of the Dogon, as is true for other oral performances. Hence, collection of data on oral traditions includes gathering data on these aspects of the performance.

Performances have different functions within societies. For example, one symbolic function of fiestas, festivals, and religious ethnic rituals and services is to validate identity and ethnicity. This is especially true for migrants, who are separated from their ethnic communities. For example, Guatemalan migrants in the United States, who in their home country identify themselves by their communities of residence, assert their common Mayan roots, thus stressing their identity and ethnicity. Other migrants similarly affirm their unity even though in their own communities the stress is on their diversity (e.g., that they are from different villages or even related Mayan groups).

Poetry

ORAL POETRY consists of oral traditions which are composed and performed in verse form. For example, in traditional Mayan poetry, especially within sacred material, thoughts were expressed as couplets, and occasionally in triplets (Bricker 1989:368). Other poetry occurs in free verse form.

Some poems have a paratactic structure where Smith found that "the coherence of the poem will not be dependent on the sequential arrangement of its major thematic units" (1968:99). Sections may be omitted, added, repeated, or exchanged "without destroying the coherence of effect of the poem's thematic structure" (p. 99).

Poetry can express one's deepest thoughts and feelings. It can also be used to extol leaders, a nation, state, city, clan, family, individual, inanimate object, or some aspect of nature. It can be the vehicle by which people express grievances or praise. It can record historical events, genealogies, and fictitious events.

Praise songs or praise shouts

PRAISE SONGS or PRAISE SHOUTS performed by praise singers extol the praises, virtues and sometimes the vices, and give blessings to important personages within society. Praise singers also proclaim social criticisms. The line between praise and insult may be crossed on occasion, as when singing about social criticisms. They may also give advice to those they feel are in need of it; and they may "serve as intermediaries in delicate interpersonal negotiations, and articulate the values of society at major social events" (Hale 1994:71). Praise singers or shouters receive money from those whose virtues they laud. For example, Hanns Vischer, the first Director of Education in Northern Nigeria, received the label of *Dan Hausa* (lit., the son of Hausa or a Hausa man) and was extolled in Hausa praise songs (Smith 1957). *Emirs* (lit., chiefs or kings) may employ full-time praise singers who accompany them on official occasions to extol their virtues in song for all to hear.

In Hausa culture different kinds of praise singers/praise shouters and musicians are grouped together as professional acclaimers *(maro'a)*. People so termed have low social status among the Hausa (Ames 1973:132) and tend to marry endogamously within the category of professional acclaimers.

Another example of use of praise songs comes from the Murle, pastoralists in southern Sudan and southwestern Ethiopia. Young men are given ox names at approximately eighteen years of age when they receive their own oxen, a mark of their transition to manhood. The ox names may be shouted out in praise songs at dances (Arensen 1991:56). Further, Murle men sing praise songs to the animals that are associated with each age set (p. 106).

Field researchers have also encountered PRAISE PROVERBS. Such praise proverbs may be interspersed within a longer praise narrative, and they may be used to make an interlude between episodes or to serve as preludes to the entire narrative.

Prayers

A PRAYER involves a spiritual communication with a god or some other spirit or object of worship. Prayers are often accompanied by specific postures thought to be appropriate when approaching divinity. For example, some people kneel when praying, others bow their heads and fold their hands, and Muslims intersperse standing with kneeling and prostrating themselves including touching their foreheads to the ground. The mark of a devout

Muslim who has prayed regularly throughout his or her life is a permanent mark on his or her forehead caused by prostrations in prayer.

Prayers may be formulaic, i.e., they follow a set wording. They may also be loosely structured, with the supplicant able to insert whatever he or she thinks is appropriate. Alternatively, there may be some combination of these two extremes. For example, a priest may change the request and those who attend may reply with a set formula (e.g., "Lord hear our prayer").

Proverbs

PROVERBS, also termed ADAGES, MAXIMS, and APHORISMS, are short sayings that embody some recognized truth or thought, often having moral didactic purposes. Proverbs embody folk wisdom in terse form. The language of proverbs is often metaphorical and symbolic, a quality that adds to their charm. In proverbs, animals may be used symbolically to indicate some value or possible happening, e.g., among the Bajju and other ethnic groups in West Africa the owl is a dirty bird that symbolizes death and bad news, the bush fowl symbolizes wisdom, and the mongoose stands for craftiness.

Proverbs often arise as the products of reflection on actual historical events. As such, in many communities they continue to be developed. Over time they become codified to the point that people may no longer remember the actual events that gave rise to them. Yet they continue to be multivocal in their applicability to current situations within the community. Folk wisdom embedded in proverbs also develops in response to observations of aspects of the natural environment which are then applied metaphorically to human behavior.

For Akan in Ghana the proverb is a dynamic communicative strategy in which form, meaning, and logic are in constant flux (Yankah 1989). Proverbs may focus on the absurd or the antithesis, e.g., the English proverb "marry in haste, repent at leisure." They may reflect irony or involve understatement. Alternatively, proverbs may state paradoxes or ask rhetorical questions. Hyperbole, an intentional exaggeration that is not intended to be taken literally, is sometimes the essence of a proverb. Some folktales end in proverbs that express the central meaning or value of the story.

Proverbs for particular ethnic groups may be divided into different types. For example, some Mayan proverbs are prophetic proverbs. One example states, "The vine of an unripe squash will not support a mature squash" (Bricker 1989:381). This proverb may be used to indicate that one would not expect an immature child to support his father.

Common American proverbs include, "Two can live as cheaply as one," "A stitch in time saves nine," and "The best defense is a good offense" (see Mieder, Kingsbury, and Harder (1991) for other American proverbs 1991).

Puns and tongue-twisters

A PUN is a play on words, while a TONGUE-TWISTER is a play on sounds. A pun has a double meaning for specific words. The object of a tongue-twister is to speak the words quickly and accurately without making phonetic errors. Examples of tongue-twisters are "Peter Piper picked a peck of pickled peppers" and "She sells sea shells by the seashore."

Riddles

RIDDLES are guessing games based on generalizations about experiences. They consist of two parts: the riddle and its answer. Riddles may take the form of short statements or propositions that are thrown out as challenges. They often cause people to see connections between things that are not usually juxtaposed. Riddling contests of wit may be in the form of games. They may be used for entertainment or teaching purposes. Examples (64)–(66) illustrate riddles.

(64) Fang riddle from Gabon (Fernandez 1982:74)

> *Ele e nga be tele tara nlem?*
> A tree grows in my father's heart.

> *Mintem mi tsam mesi mese.*
> Its branches spread throughout the land.

> Answer: *Ndan!* The genealogy!

(65) Chamula riddle from Chiapas State, Mexico (Gossen 1989:406)

> *Hme? kumagre haval*
> My compadre is face up,

> *Kumpayre nahal, k'usi?un?*
> My compadre is face down. What is it?

> Answer: *Tesha.* Roof tile.

(66) Yoruba riddle from western Nigeria (Okpewho 1992:247)

> What dines with an *oba* (paramount chief) and leaves him to clear the dishes?

> Answer: A fly.

The Murle use riddles in names. When a boy reaches eight or nine years of age, his father gives him a calf. Each boy then makes up a riddling name for himself based on the color(s) of his calf. The goal is for his friends to guess the color of his calf based on the riddle. For example, one youth gave himself the name *Rigizul*, meaning "hanging tail." The tail was that of a giraffe, indicating that his calf was red and white spotted (Arensen 1991:95, 1992).

There are different types of riddles, including the following:

1. Simple riddles with challenges and responses,
2. Tone riddles,
3. Song riddles,
4. Proverb riddles,
5. Oppositional riddles,
6. Nonoppositional riddles,
7. Name riddles (see Murle example above), and
8. Ideophonic riddles.

The structure of a riddle consists of two parts, a proposition and an answer, or a precedent and a sequence. Riddles use figurative or metaphorical language, and they have a tendency towards personification of what is mentioned within them.

Saga

A SAGA is a long narrative of heroic exploits. The term saga overlaps with that of epic. The word itself seems to have originated with twelfth and thirteenth century Icelandic poetic narratives. (See "Epics" for further information on a saga.)

Secret and hidden language

SECRET or HIDDEN LANGUAGE is "a form of communication based on a system of implicit meanings" (Rodman 1991:429). The goal of using "hidden talk" in Vanuatu is shame, a part of public humiliation. Another use is for instruction in which teaching occurs through use of indirect language and parable. In Vanuatu hidden language translates as "hidden talk" while in the highlands of Papua New Guinea people speak of "veiled speech." In PNG it includes children's games, love songs, public argument and debate, and formal oratory (p. 433). A similar phenomenon occurs in Surinam among the Saramakan, where older men teach younger ones using a style marked by ellipsis, concealment, and partial disclosure (Price 1983).

Sermons

SERMONS are religious discourses delivered usually within a religious context, such as within a church, synagogue, or mosque with the purpose of teaching the listeners. You can divide sermons into different types such as expository, hortatory, explanatory, and so on.

In some contexts the audience interacts with the speaker, resulting in a sermon performance. For example, in churches with black participants in the United States the sermon style often involves an interactive performance in which the audience and the pastor together create the sermon. The audience interactions may reach a crescendo, and then the service gradually draws to a close. Sometimes this performance involves physical movements including dancing, hand waving and clapping, standing, crying, and verbal encouragements to the pastor.

Tall tales

TALL TALES, also termed LYING TALES, have as their essence ridiculous exaggeration. Sometimes such tales revolve around contests between champions. For example, in Hausa tales a common key participant is a *sarki* or 'chief'. Other participants in Hausa tales may be designated as 'husband', 'wife', 'mother-in-law' (who is often portrayed negatively), *mallam* (teacher), 'thief', or individuals indicated by occupation, e.g., 'grass-cutter', 'tailor', 'blacksmith', 'hunter'.

Trickster narratives

In a TRICKSTER NARRATIVE the leading character (or characters) or FOLK HERO is both an endearing one and a pathetic figure. He may seek to fool everyone, but often ends up fooling only himself. The trickster is usually a weak animal who fools others, particularly those stronger than himself, by his cleverness. In some tales the trickster is the hero who is cunning, resourceful, malevolent, elusive, ambiguous, contradictory, and ruthless. The goal of the trickster is ultimately to have power, something that he often fails to achieve. In his failure he becomes the joke.

Perhaps the trickster's appeal is that he represents something that is in all humans. He represents the ambiguity that each person encounters in daily life. In most trickster narratives the hero himself is an animal and mostly relates to other animals, but represents humans with human traits.

The trickster does not act out of kindness, but rather out of self-interest, for his own benefit and enjoyment, a love of mischief, and a desire to get the best of others. Trickster tales tend to progress from friendship to deception.

Sometimes animals act as animals in folktales. This is especially true in etiologic tales. In other trickster tales people are apt to be disguised as animals, as evidenced by Evans-Pritchard's quote below about *ture*. When acting as humans, tricksters operate in the framework of human society. For example, the Asante and the Chumburung in Ghana as well as the Azande in Sudan have tricksters (*Ananse* (alt. *Anansi*) for the Asante and *Ture* for the Azande) who are both a spider and a man. Evans-Pritchard states,

> Ture is a monster of depravity: liar, cheat, lecher, murderer; vain, greedy, treacherous, ungrateful, a poltroon, a braggart. This utterly selfish person is everything against which Azande warn their children most strongly. Yet he is the hero of their stories, and it is to their children that his exploits are related and he is presented, with very little moralizing—if as a rogue, as an engaging one. For there is another side to his character, which even to us is appealing: his whimsical fooling, recklessness, impetuosity, puckish irresponsibility, his childish desire to show how clever he is, his total absorption in song and dance, his feathered hat, and his flouting of every convention. In spite of his nefarious conduct he is never really malicious. Indeed he has an endearing innocence. One is sorry for him when his cocksureness gets him in trouble, when he overreaches himself and sheds frustrated tears. Then he is pathetic....He is indomitable. In spite of every failure, misfortune, and humiliation he perseveres. (1967:28–29)

Evans-Pritchard translated *ture* as a human, though the word itself translates as 'spider'. Reasons for translating *ture* as human include his having human characteristics and the use of the human personal pronoun *ko* rather than the animal pronoun *u* (p. 23). Evans-Pritchard also points out that within the same story the pronominal reference can switch from human to animal and back again depending on whether human or animal characteristics are in focus (p. 26). This dual nature of the leading character exists in other Azande narratives, e.g., one narrative begins with "There was a man called Leopard," and another with "There was a man called Vulture" (p. 26).

Frequently in African literature, the trickster is represented by a human, an animal or insect such as a spider (e.g., *anansi* among the Akan in Ghana, see Rattray 1930), a turtle, a ground squirrel, a hare, a gazelle, or a jackal. Sometimes several animals appear, each with different characteristics. For example, Johnston reports,

> The Hausas...endowed the three heroes with recognizably different qualities. All three are tricksters, of course, but in the Hausa tales the spider is unscrupulous and vindictive, the rabbit gay and mischievous, and the jackal cunning and yet sagacious. (1966:xlv)

In Hausa narrative the victims of the trickster are often represented as animals, ogres, or persons (e.g., simpletons, lepers, the blind). For example, the hyena is depicted as a greedy stupid bully, who is overbearing to those he perceives as inferior to himself and subservient to those who are his superiors (p. xlv). By comparing different trickster narratives the researcher can get a good understanding of the characteristics associated with each trickster.

In trickster narratives of the Kalapalo, a Carib speaking group of central Brazil, the trickster appears in accounts ranging from creation narratives to off-color stories (Basso 1987). As such, the trickster explores the ambiguities of human experience. As seen in the Kalapalo trickster narratives, one issue to look at is the relationship between the traditional religion and the trickster. In some instances the trickster is more closely tied to religion and to their mythology than in others. In some narratives the trickster works together with God in the beginning of culture; in others the trickster performs heroic acts, yet remains foolish, laughable, always indomitable, and sometimes obscene.

All tricksters are foolers and fools, whose foolishness takes various forms: "sometimes it is destructive, sometimes creative, sometimes scatological, sometimes satiric, sometimes playful" (Pelton 1980:15).

Okpewo cites five basic motifs within trickster narratives as follows:

1. Friendship: The tale often assumes or specifies a situation of friendship or solidarity between the characters involved.
2. Contract: Next, there is frequently an agreement reached or some kind of appointment made, which has the value or aim of testing the friendship.
3. Violation: One of the parties in the contract invariably does something that amounts to a breach of faith, e.g., by deceiving or cheating the other.
4. Discovery: The deceived or cheated party frequently discovers the trick played on it or the violation of the agreement reached. In many cases this is followed by a countertrick or counterviolation from the offended party.
5. End of friendship: The final situation in this sequence is generally the termination of the cordial relationship between the parties, sometimes with the punishment or disgrace of the original culprit. (Dundes as quoted in Okpewho 1992:176–177)

Suggestions for collecting oral traditions

You can most effectively engage in the collection of oral traditions and oral history within the context of participant observation and informal interviews. Collection of some oral traditions involves extensive interviews with specialists within the culture, while collection of many others involves attending specific performances where they are recited, danced, performed, and acted out. It is through being actively involved with members of the research community that you learn the role of oral traditions within that culture and begin to understand their meanings. Be with the people when they are performed, as for example, in the evenings around the fire when the elders share oral traditions with the younger members of society.

A common problem with the collection and analysis of oral traditions has been the attempt to study them apart from their cultural and aesthetic contexts. While researchers may draw some conclusions simply from studying the internal construction of oral traditions, much more meaningful conclusions result from understanding them within their cultural contexts.

When collecting oral traditions, use a tape recorder and/or a video camera if possible. These are aids in recording oral traditions for transcription and translation of their texts and for subsequent analyses. If analyzing oral traditions for historical content, you may find it helpful to collect oral traditions from several sources to cross-check them for accuracy and detail. Seek out expert performers, attend their performances, and interview them about the meanings incorporated into their performances.

In collecting oral traditions note who is involved in telling each type of oral tradition. Are there specific hereditary roles of tellers of oral traditions? For example, does the role of praise singer pass from father to son or from mother to daughter? (Note that in West Africa a male praise singer is termed a *griot,* and a female is a *griotte.* Some researchers term male praise singers *griot*-genealogists. Male praise singers may focus on genealogies, wars, history, and praise or ridicule of specific leaders, while the domain of female praise singers may be weddings and naming ceremonies.)

How are specific verbal skills transmitted? What types of oral traditions are the province of men, what types are the domain of women, and which are told by anyone regardless of sex? For example, among the Hausa, traditions *(labari)* are the domain of men (Skinner 1968:88). Record such data carefully.

Other questions about collecting oral traditions include the following:

1. Oral traditions-genre, symbolism, culture:
    a. What are the named genre of oral traditions in the local language?
    b. What correlation is there between specific oral traditions and the culture of the people? For example, Is social stratification reflected in their oral traditions?
    c. Are there regional or dialectal variations of the oral tradition you are collecting? Expect to find such with origins narratives as well as with other oral traditions.
    d. What symbolism is involved in the oral tradition and its performance? Is that symbolism in the text?
    e. In what ways are current cultural events being incorporated into oral traditions? Are new oral traditions serving functions of social control and commentary and/or entertainment?
    f. What does the oral tradition and its performance tell about other parts of the culture, including its values and its worldview?
    g. Is there a link between magical and/or medicinal use of oral traditions and other parts of the culture?
    h. Are shortened forms of proverbs used as names? For example, Ennis (1945:3) states that the proverb-name *Mbundu* among the Ovimbundu of southwestern Africa is a shortened form of the proverb that translates into English as "the mist of the coast is the rain of the uplands" (Ennis, as quoted in Okpewho 1992:228–29). This proverb implies that customs differ from place to place.
    i. What role do radio, television, internet, and videos play in the transmission of oral traditions today?
    j. What function(s) does the performance have?
    k. In what contexts are oral traditions recited? Courts? Weddings? Funerals? Special festivals? Homes? Feasts? Specific rituals?
2. Performers:
    a. Who are the performers? Are there specialists in different genre of oral traditions, e.g., poets, praise singers, folklorists, genealogists, etc.? What are their ages, sexes, and occupations? Do those with disabilities become performers? For example, are

people who are blind more likely to become master storytellers than those without such a disability?

b. Is the position of transmitter of oral traditions acquired by inheritance? By personal acquisition? By apprenticeship? By both inheritance and apprenticeship? If by apprenticeship, how long is that apprenticeship and what is the content of it? What does the master receive from his apprentice, and what does the apprentice do for and receive from his master? How long is the apprenticeship?

c. How is knowledge of oral traditions transmitted?

d. How are oral traditions learned?

e. What clothes (costumes) are specific to the performance?

f. What status do oral performers have, and is that status inherited, as for example, together with inheritance of occupation through one's father or mother?

g. What remuneration do performers receive? Who provides it? How is it provided (e.g., among some dancers in Africa the audience shows its appreciation by putting coins and bills on the foreheads of the performers)?

h. What makes a "good" storyteller, and what skills does he or she bring to storytelling?

i. Is performance of oral traditions considered to be a craft, such as glassblowing, weaving, or leatherworking?

j. Are performers organized, and if so, how are they organized? Do the performers have leaders or chiefs, what are their roles, and what functions do they have relative to the other performers and the audience?

k. Is performing a full-time or part-time occupation?

l. What types of oral performers are there, and what is each type's specialty?

m. Are oral performers part of a professional specialists class? Do members of this class marry endogamously? For example, would a woman or her father want her to marry a praise singer or other oral performer?

n. What roles do performers have in public life? For example, do musicians, performers, or storytellers serve roles relative to the ruling aristocracy, modern political parties, etc.?

o. Are performers itinerant? Are they associated with specific families, castes, or classes (e.g., the aristocracy, chiefs)? Do they also provide services to the settled population (e.g., some peripatetic groups in India provide services to the settled population—they are entertainers, barbers, midwives, and abortionists)? If they are itinerant, what is their attitude towards the settled populace, and what is that group's attitude towards the peripatetic group?

p. Do performers have regular practice sessions? What penalty, if any, is assessed a performer who does not attend a practice or who is consistently late for one? Who directs the practice?

q. Do performers use stalls in performance? STALLS employ language that is used repetitively by performers in order to think about what to include next within the oral performance. Rosenberg states that,

> [The stall is] language used repetitively (on either a lexical or syntactical level), whose formulation is somewhat automatic, so as to give the performer time to think of what to say next. Since it is now well-recognized that the oral performer's most pressing need is to come up with the following line even while he is reciting the line of the moment, stalls are developed as an aid in composition. The results produce the "oral style."

The various forms of stalling are perhaps the most significant stylistic feature of oral narrative. (1975:76)

3. Audience and performers:
    a. Who are the usual audiences for specific types of oral performances? Are some people prohibited from attending? For example, can women and girls attend, or do only men and boys go? Can only people who have been initiated attend?
    b. What, if any, interaction occurs between the oral performer(s) and audience? Does the audience participate and, if so, how?
    c. How do members of the audience interpret the performance and does their perspective coincide with that of the performer(s)? If the interpretation of the audience and performers differs, how does it and why?
    d. What factors contribute to a "good" performance as assessed by performers, the audience, or other members of the ethnic group?

This list is suggestive only of data to collect. In order to gather some oral traditions, such as proverbs, record them as they occur in everyday speech, as well as from those who are knowledgeable in the culture about them. In many cultures there are specialists who know the origins narrative, the folktales including trickster narratives, and so on. Tape record narratives performed by those individuals, then transcribe them with your regular cultural assistant. To transcribe performances at the time they occur would interrupt them. Further, transcription is time consuming. Transcription should include morpheme-by-morpheme glosses as well as free idiomatic translations.

Increasingly, field researchers are videotaping performances. Prior to videotaping performances, evaluate the possible impact of the videotaping upon the local people and discuss it with them. Will it have a negative impact on them? Do they understand what you are doing? If you do go ahead with videotaping, be sure to give credit to those who assisted you, and give a copy or copies of it to the local people. (Note that use of videotape cameras and VCRs is widespread throughout the world, so what you want to do in videotaping a performance may not be new to them.)

With permission from the appropriate persons, record the performers' words, songs, and performance in the local languages. By so doing, the people videotaped speak for themselves without the researchers' interpretations (except for the translation). Increasingly, videotapes of cultural events do not have a narrator who places his or her interpretations on the events shown.

Following collection of oral traditions, analyze the data collected, including carefully defined terminology, constructs, and concepts used in your analyses. Analysis of oral traditions is the topic of the following chapter.

21

Analysis of Oral Traditions

"Sometimes," concluded the old man, gathering his ragged toga about him, "You must tell us some more stories of your country. We, who are elders, will instruct you in their true meaning, so that when you return to your own land your elders will see that you have not been sitting in the bush, but among those who know things and who have taught you wisdom." (Bohannan, in Spradley and McCurdy 1987:45)

The above quotation from a Tiv elder in Nigeria reminds us that the ultimate goal of telling and learning oral traditions is to teach wisdom. This is usually done in an entertaining enjoyable way. This chapter begins with a brief overview of various perspectives on the analysis of oral traditions. It then discusses a few of these analytic perspectives in more detail.

After you have collected an oral tradition, enter it into a database, then transcribe it, if possible, using some interlinear text program to assist you in entering the translation of that text. Next, decide what type of analysis you want to use, whether focusing on its form, content, means of transmission (e.g., mnemonic devices in the text), classification or genre, or on the historical data it contains. Most analyses of oral traditions have focused on content; this is especially important if you are collecting them in order to help understand the culture.

If you are interested in the form of oral traditions, analyze the linguistic structure. The linguistic structure of oral traditions can be analyzed at the discourse, sentence, clause, phrase, or word levels. You can also look at recurrent patterns in the text that provide a distinctive form of a particular type of oral tradition (e.g., recurrent patterns within an epic).

A formal means of text analysis comes from Propp (1968), a Russian scholar who provides suggestions for the classification of oral traditions into different genre. He also suggests that you derive groupings of functions into bundles in the tradition.

You can investigate means by which oral traditions are transmitted. For example, are there mnemonic devices present in the text? If so, what are they? Are they tonal? Does the use of metaphors, similes, and symbols contribute to memorization? Your analysis would seek to understand the means by which oral traditions are easily given to the next generation through some of these specific mnemonic devices present in the text.

Oral traditions can serve functions of social control and commentary. What are situations likely to be memorialized into oral traditions? When you find that the people do use oral traditions for social control and commentary, investigate the content, the context, and the occasion when these are used.

In looking at the content of oral traditions, note that they can be divided into fiction/fantasy and nonfiction including historical accounts. You can further divide the content according to the means the narrator uses in his storytelling, whether realism, satire or irony, humorous narrative, allegory, and so on.

Oral traditions can be used as sources of information for reconstructing oral history. When oral traditions are viewed as historical record, historians assess their reliability as valid sources of history. Some oral histories contain long genealogies. In their analysis you will want to decide what functions genealogies play within the culture. For example, why do people continue to tell them? What functions do mutations of oral traditions serve in the culture in focus? Lastly, the analysis of oral traditions within a political economy framework is discussed.

Folklorists, linguists, cultural researchers, historians, and others all bring useful perspectives to the analyses of oral traditions, and their writing about oral traditions will have their perspectives. Oral traditions are rich sources of cultural data.

Overview

Oral traditions database

A preliminary stage in analysis of oral traditions is to enter them into a database so that you can access them rapidly and efficiently. For example, you might use a program such as SHOEBOX, a program already mentioned (see chapter 7). This program continues to be developed for use in cultural fieldwork. Another program that could be used is FIESTA (Alsop and Johnston 1990), an acronym for Fast Interactive Editor of Scripture and Text Analysis, for rapid viewing, searching, comparing, and editing of documents.

As linguistic text

It is important to study oral traditions in the source language. To do so will significantly increase your understanding of the texts beyond what you will be able to understand when you work only with translated texts. The translation process may leave out alliteration, humor, turns of phrases, subtleties, and meanings found in the original text. Aspects of grammar, style, discourse features, and particular linguistic structures often do not translate well.

When analyzing oral traditions as linguistic text or discourse, it is important to understand the linguistic features of the language. Text analysis traces features such as the timeline, character line, event line, referential focus, background information, plot, and setting. These aspects of the text can be analyzed in terms of specific linguistic structures such as the use of cohesion, pronominal reference, topicalization (see N. McKinney 1978; Crozier 1984), and tense and aspect. In text analysis you can use various types of charting such as span charts, Thurman charts, and/or Longacre–Levinsohn charts (see Longacre and Levinsohn 1978, Peck 1984:309–14).

For example, you might use a chart or display the text divided into columns where word order is indicated. If the word order in the language is subject, verb, object (SVO), then you would divide the display as follows:

Sentence Number	Pre-Core	Subject	Predicate	Object	Post-Core

As you chart your data, use a solid line to divide main clauses, and a broken line to indicate that two clauses are closely related.

Knowing the nuances of the language, including the formulaic openings, as in a folktale, contributes significantly and sometimes critically to understanding the meaning of the text of oral traditions. Linguists have studied text analysis extensively and provide insightful guidance for their analysis (see Chafe 1980, Fleming 1988a, 1988b [especially helpful concerning charting of data], Grimes 1975, Longacre 1983, Peck 1984, Pike and Pike 1982).

Discourse analysis has been helpful in analyzing Hausa tales. For example, Ahmad discovered that the underlying elements that recur in some folktales include (1) the initial situation, (2) motivations and causes of the characters, (3) the use of repetition, (4) the use of nonverbal elements (facial gestures, body language, etc.), (5) moral perception of the characters, and (6) variation according to audience (Ahmad 1989).

Analysis of oral traditions includes the speech styles used. For example, in some formal contexts indirectness is the preferred style, especially as an indication of respect. A number of oral traditions include songs. Some oral traditions either begin or end with a proverb.

Looking at the form of an oral tradition takes into account recurrent verbal phrases. For example, many languages in Africa and Papua New Guinea make extensive use of serial verb constructions. The verbs carry the action of the narrative along.

Genre

A GENRE refers to a class or category that has a particular form. When exploring the genre of oral traditions within a culture, look for named categories in the language.

Propp (1968) studied European fairy tales and sought to set up criteria for establishing genre for oral traditions in any society. He felt that in order to define genre of tales, an analyst would have to study at least eighty tales, with more being preferable. For statistical significance, a minimum number of folktales you would need to collect to define a genre is thirty, but the more you have in your corpus the better. His emphasis points to the importance of defining genre on the basis of sufficient data.

Propp also proposed a structural linear analysis of folktales. His method involved abstracting data through looking at patterns of the predicates of folktales. These patterns he termed "functions," and he maintained that "Functions of characters serve as stable constant elements in a tale, independent of how and by whom they are fulfilled. They constitute the fundamental components of a tale" (Propp 1968:21). He further stated that "All predicates give the composition of tales; all subjects, objects, and other parts of the sentence define the theme. In other words, the same composition may lie at the base of various themes" (p. 113). Propp's method of analyzing folktales by structural linear analysis overlaps analyzing them from a linguistic perspective.

The formal approach to analyzing oral traditions advocated by Propp is from the perspective of the analyst, not necessarily from that of the people who tell them. Both formal means such as advocated by Propp and Levi-Strauss (see "Mythemes") have their place in the analysis of oral traditions.

If studying oral traditions from an emic perspective, do so from the perspective of those who tell them. For example, look for names of types of oral traditions in the local language.

Mythemes

Levi-Strauss (1963) proposed that a researcher look for patterns in oral traditions at a deep structural level of abstraction. He termed these patterns MYTHEMES, groupings of functions into bundles. He viewed mythemes as nonlinear and timeless; they relate both diachronically and synchronically. He stated, "The true constituent units of a myth are not the isolated relations but bundles of such relations, and it is only as bundles that these relations can be put to use and combined so as to provide a meaning" (1963:211). Mythemes often form dialectics or oppositions, such as male-female, or nature-nurture. To learn more about the study of mythemes read Levi-Strauss.

Transmission

In collecting data on oral traditions, collect information on how they are transmitted from one generation to another. What are the mnemonic techniques used? Are there linguistic features within the oral texts that aid in memorization? For example, Fagborun (1990) found that in Yoruba oral Ifa texts there are wordplay devices that use counting embedded within texts to aid in memorization of the oral texts as they are transmitted from one generation to another. The process of memorization is aided by wordplay, repetition, and tonal play (Fagborun 1990:173). Use of rhyme, meter, or other patterning can also aid in the transmission process of oral traditions.

Metaphor, simile, and trope

A METAPHOR is "a figure of speech in which a term or phrase is applied to something to which it is not literally applicable in order to suggest a resemblance" (Stein 1978:563).

Examples of metaphors include "the curtain of night" and "all the world's a stage." There can also be mixed metaphors, such as "the storm of protest was nipped in the bud."

Stein and Su (1978:832) define a SIMILE as "a figure of speech in which two unlike things are explicitly compared…" often through use of words such as "like, as," etc. Examples of similes include "a heart as big as a whale" and "her tears flowed like wine."

Metaphors and similes consist of three parts: the topic, the point of similarity, and the image (Larsen 1975:83). For example, a Biblical simile from Acts 8:32 (also Isaiah 53:7) marked for each of these components is as follows:

(67) *He*   *was led like*   *a sheep*
     topic   similarity   image

In some metaphors one of these components is implied rather than explicitly stated.

TROPE refers to the use of words in other than their literal sense. For example, if one said, "You're going out on a limb for me," in this context the word "limb" does not represent a tree branch but rather that the person is taking a risk to help me.

Metaphors, similes, and tropes are usually dependent upon the contexts in which they are used. They provide a picture of what something is like. A metaphor may have multiple meanings, but when used in a specific context, usually only one of those meanings is in focus.

Metaphors exemplify some of the most significant or deepest truths in cultures. They can illuminate cultural presuppositions. They are so common in cultures worldwide as to be almost universal. Much of human perception and thought is metaphorical. Lakoff states, "Primarily on the basis of linguistic evidence we find that most of our ordinary conceptual system is metaphorical in nature" (1980:3).

Metaphor is seen in art, including verbal oral traditions. For example, Vansina states concerning metaphor,

> All art is metaphor and form. Verbal art, such as poetry, song, sayings, proverbs and tales conform[s] to this rule. They express the experience of contemporary situations or events, morals to be drawn from such occurrences or situations or express intense emotions associated with them. (1985:11)

Culture may be viewed as representations, metaphors, images, or imaginations of the mind (Fernandez 1982:3). Different cultures use images or metaphors as means of representing different social realities, whether religious, social, political, material (e.g., village structure), or other components of a culture.

In writing about the Bwiti cult of the Fang in Gabon, Fernandez describes his analysis as an anthropology of the religious imagination (p. 3). Through the Bwiti cult the Fang constructed their own meaningful microcosm that turned away from modernizing influences and built upon their traditional religious past as well as on Christianity. Some of the metaphors seem strange, yet within the Bwiti cult they make sense. For example, "The harp represents the voice of the female object of devotion in Bwiti, Nyingwan Mebege, the sister of God who is syncretized with the Virgin" (p. 4).

Religious cosmologies often are rich in metaphors. Griaule found that the religious metaphors described to him by Ogotemmeli, a blind Dogon elder in Mali, used the village layout as a metaphor in describing Dogon cosmology.

> "The village," said Ogotemmeli, "should extend from north to south like the body of a man lying on his back. Lower Ogol is almost correct. The head is the council house, built on the chief square, which is the symbol of the primal field."
>
> It appeared also, from the blind man's earlier explanations, that the village should be in the form of a square with one side facing north and the streets running from north to south and east to west....
>
> On the north side of the square is the smithy, as was that of bringer of civilization. To the east and west are houses for menstruating women; they are round like wombs and represent the hands of the village. The large family houses are its chest and belly; the communal altars at the south of the village are its feet.
>
> The stones on which the fruit of the *Lannea acida* is crushed, placed in the centre of the village, represents its female sexual parts. Beside them should be set the foundation altar, which is its male sex organ; but out of respect for the women this altar is erected outside the walls. (Griaule 1965:96–97)

In southeast Asia the widespread metaphorical use of a water buffalo occurs in marital negotiations. Among the Rengao in the highlands of Vietnam the negotiating parties may refer to the bride as a water buffalo (Marilyn Gregerson, personal communication, Dallas, 1991). A similar use of a water buffalo metaphor occurs in the Philippines (Tom Headland, personal communication, Dallas, 1991).

Closely related to analysis of oral tradition as metaphor, simile, and trope is the analysis of the symbolic content of specific oral traditions. A word, phrase, or sentence may be used to represent something else that is hidden from the surface form of the oral tradition. For example, in the novel, *The River Between*, Ngugi (1965) uses a river as symbolic of the wide gap between the people who live on two mountains, people who are torn between the traditional and the new cultural and religious patterns coming to the area. When Baesnel was in Kenya, he asked Ngugi where were the two hills referred to and Ngugi pointed to specific hills. When he was further questioned about the river, Ngugi stated that there was not a physical river, but that he had used the river as a metaphor (Sem Baesnel, personal communication, 1991).

Analytic perspectives of oral traditions

As verbal art

Oral traditions when performed are VERBAL ART, art as metaphor, image, and symbol. Just as sculptures, paintings, pottery, and other art forms cannot adequately be described in words, so it is with verbal art which often involves performance. Therefore, you may choose to capture verbal art by use of audio recordings, photographs, videos, or some combination of these onto tape or computer media.

Performers use a formal language style for some verbal art, such as epics, whereas in other types of verbal art they use everyday language. Analyses of verbal art need to be done in terms of its form, function, performance, and content.

Rhythm

When analyzing the form of oral traditions, include the study of rhythm or rhyme schemes in texts. This involves analyzing the regularly patterned repetitions of syllables, words, and phrases, the metrical structure of the text, and in general understanding the part that rhythm plays in specific oral traditions. Frequently, oral traditions have rhyme schemes that you can analyze to understand the rhythm. For example, old High German music sung by the Amish tends to have a slow drawn out rhythm. Calypso music has a range of rhythmic patterns that is readily identifiable.

Russell Schuh (lecture, Dallas, 1987) analyzed the rhythms of Hausa songs as they were influenced by the Arabic language through Islam. Hausa song rhythm had changed from using their traditional rhythm to the rhythmic patterns of Arabic songs. Schuh traced changing rhythmic patterns as the Hausa increasingly returned to using the traditional rhythmic patterns of their pre-Islamic music, even when singing Islamic songs.

The Bajuni fishing songs from a northern Somali dialect usually have sixteen syllables in a line (Donnelly and Omar 1983:115). The fieldworkers noted that,

> The metrical structure is comparable to that associated with many other Swahili songs or poems…but the Bajuni songs differ from the mainstream of Swahili poetry by their high frequency of nonmetrical devices such as parallelism, linking, lead-ons, puns, etc. (Donelly and Omar 1983:115).

As social control and commentary

Most societies utilize oral traditions as a means of entertainment, transmission of culture, and education in moral and social values. Some societies have forms of oral traditions used specifically as means of social control and commentary.

Once a year the Kera in Chad perform *insult dances* and *insult dramatizations*. Hungerford, who has worked with the Kera, states,

> The insult dance performers are always men and [they] string together as many dramatizations or songs as they can to air the gossip and insult the other villagers. They collect gossip all year in preparation for the big event. One year a man stole a goat, turned around a week later and tried to sell the stolen goat at the local market in the same village! The villagers caught and beat him so bad[ly] he died the next day. The insult dancers commenced their dramatization with carrying the "corpse" (actor) in on a bier and then acting out divining the cause of death. The diviner actor went through the whole goat story then laid out the divining straws and determined the cause of death—stupidity!... the dances are even a tighter social control because all the villages in Kera country are paired off—so the dances, songs, and dramatizations aren't about someone far away but always about your close neighbors. There are two insult dance days. The first day each [of the] paired dance troupes perform and sing at village A, the second day they repeat everything at village B so there's a home court and an away game so to speak back to back. There are about 40 villages so 20 dances* [occur] simultaneously two days in a row. It is an absolute violation of Kera norms to show anger or irritation about the insults on those 2 days, though abject obvious shame and flight away from the area (to Yaounde or Nigeria) in humiliation does regularly occur. It pokes fun at individuals, yes, but also [it] reinforces village rivalry while cementing Kera whole culture norms. It was the members of the goat-stealer village who were being insulted for raising such a stupid son.
>
> The Christians stepped into this tradition in two ways (1) on the side of the handicapped, stopped all insults about blindness or lameness or retardation and (2) except for incredible exceptions that just couldn't be passed up by insult singers, the Christian community disciplines its own and protects its own from these yearly events.
>
> * "This is a guess[; it is] not accurate." (Marian Hungerford, personal letter, February 1993; used with permission).

Individuals who find themselves portrayed in such insult dances and dramatizations, quickly learn the consequences of violating societal norms. Those who witness these dramatizations also learn social norms and values, and while doing so have a good time laughing at human follies.

Some ethnic groups in the Philippines use ritual language in singing to resolve conflicts (Tom Payne, personal letter, July 1990). Use of ritual language serves to resolve conflict, to maintain social control, and to provide commentary on events where conflict is involved.

At a funeral relatives of the deceased among the Chumburung, a group in northern Ghana, act out part of the job of the deceased. For example, if the deceased was a street trader, the people mimic his actions to make fun of him, and by so doing decrease their grief (Gillian Hansford, personal letter, December 27, 1990).

Songs of personal abuse or "lampoons" and abusive poetry are recited or sung in Nigeria. These may or may not be based firmly on fact; they do provide an outlet for the individual who may have had his feelings injured. Sometimes songs of personal abuse are sung in competitions between villages or sections of villages. For example, Okpewho speaks of *udje* poetry among the Urhobo of southwestern Nigeria, who at periodic festivals vilify each other in vicious songs. He states, "In these contests, because the leaders of the song groups—or the prominent composers of songs—are usually considered the most dangerous members of their community, their rivals choose to concentrate their attacks on them" (1992:148). Such lampoons are declining due to libel laws in modern nations.

In traditional society, insult oral traditions could be used for personal vendettas. More often they were used for social sanctions against theft, adultery, lack of respect for elders, laziness, disruptive social behavior, etc. For example, Igbo women figuratively "sit on a man" by gathering at a man's compound and singing insult songs to ridicule, satirize, and insult a man for his actions, actions of which the women disapprove.

A further area to investigate is that of gossip which expresses disapproval of what people are doing that violates social norms. For example, Bajju speakers drop the register of their voices when talking about others in disapproval. In one instance I overheard two elderly women discuss how scandalous the marriages of some younger women were, in that there had been no exchange of money for the bridewealth. In that conversation each dropped the normal fundamental frequency of her voice approximately an octave, thus signaling disapproval through gossip.

As reflections of worldview and values

Many folktales begin with formulaic words and phrases that seem to put them into an imaginary world. For example, western folktales often begin with the phrase, "Once upon a time" Murle (Arensen 1991:188) and Bajju folktales begin with phrases that translate as "Long ago." These serve to place the tales outside the realm of human memory and to indicate that things were different during that mythological period. Perhaps animals talk, turtles fly, and ladders reach to heaven. While entertaining, often through the use of metaphors, these tales serve the important functions of teaching values, morals, and worldview propositions to listeners. These functions are often made explicit in the conclusions of the stories.

Arensen states, "One great benefit of analyzing tales is that since they are told about non-real characters in a remote time, the storyteller can deal with sensitive issues" (1991:200). While some stories teach only one moral or value, others are more complex with a variety of lessons portrayed.

As historical record

Some anthropologists and folklorists speak of oral traditions as "myths," and question the extent to which these traditions reflect actual historical events. For example, Lowie stated, "I cannot attach to oral traditions any historical value under any conditions whatsoever" (Lowie 1915:598). He felt that the oral traditions he collected among the Crow and Hidatsa failed to portray facts objectively (1917:163). He noted that in some oral traditions, historical fact and nonfact or myth blend. An example of this comes from the Bajju where in some versions of the Bajju origins narrative the people of Sokwak are the descendants of Ankwak, the eldest son of the Bajju founding father Baranzan. By contrast, in another version the people of Sokwak allegedly emerged from a termite mound. Increasingly, however, fieldworkers do place importance on oral traditions as reflections of history from the point of view of those who hold them.

Collecting oral historical traditions is a means of probing into the past of a particular people, including both the recent and more distant past. Collection and subsequent analysis of them need to be supported by other types of research, especially consultation of written historical documents, including records in national archives, mission records, journals of early travelers, letters, books, and any other relevant documents. You can find data on recent historical events by studying life histories or personal recollections.

In the study and analysis of oral historical traditions, understand reasons for people's behavior as well as reasons for preservation of specific oral traditions. It helps to place yourself imaginatively in the position of those you are studying; often this is a key to cross-cultural understanding and communication.

A historical record is always incomplete, and sometimes the individuals who transmit such oral histories creatively add to them by using their imagination to fill in details likely to be consistent with the setting within which the event(s) occurred. As such, oral traditions are dynamic and reflect historical facts as they are relevant for those who tell them.

Some cultures have individuals who preserve the official version of the history of a particular people. For example, as mentioned in chapter 20, *griots* are professional praise singers in West Africa who preserve historical accounts, epics, and poetry. A *griot* combines the functions of a minstrel, jester, herald, annalist, troubadour, gleeman, and poet (Pickett, in Niane 1965:ix). The position of *griot* passes down through the clan of praise singers.

Vansina describes the position and function of a praise singer among the Yoruba as follows:

> In states, an official was often found whose duty was to perform the state's official history at public ceremonies. Thus the *baba elegun* of Ketu, a Yoruba (Rep. Benin) city, had to know the city's history. The official was hereditary in the Oyede family and the information was passed from father to son. The traditions were recited at each enthronement. If the *baba elegun* succeeded on that occasion to recite the traditions without mistake, he was offered a reward. If he failed, he was deemed to be punished by supernatural sanction. Such a man was a walking reference library, to be used when state occasion demanded it. (Vansina 1985:37)

Assessing the validity and historicity of oral historical traditions. One issue about use of oral historical traditions is that of assessing their validity or authenticity. For example, Was the material collected from an eyewitness to the events reported? or Is the material only hearsay? What motives, prejudices, and biases might those giving the material bring to them? Is there physical evidence to corroborate what individuals report on? All of these issues need to be taken into account in collecting data and analyzing ethnohistories.

In your use of oral historical material, if you are seeking to develop an ethnohistory of the people in focus, the ethnohistory you develop is an abstraction from what really occurred. Perhaps the best one can say is that this is what they believe happened. You can build a better picture of the ethnohistory of a people if you use multiple sources, such as archeological evidence, linguistic data, oral historical traditions, and archival data. Even though historical reconstruction has difficulties, it is worthwhile to reconstruct the ethnohistories for particular groups of people.

A basic issue that you face is the interpretation of oral historical traditions you collected, including their historicity. Analysis of an oral historical tradition involves studying it in the source language, translating it, dating it, understanding its metaphors, and sometimes resolving differences between its several forms.

Source language. Study of oral traditions in the source language is important in the study of the ethnohistory of a group. To do so provides more significant insights and understanding than analysis in a second language. The quality of translation directly affects the quality of your analysis of those texts. As Arensen points out, translation into good second language linguistic structure may result in a good translation, "but important things like word order, focus, and thematic fronting in the original language are lost and some of these factors may be very important in understanding the full meaning of the text" (1991:180). Aspects of grammar, style, discourse features, and other linguistic structures often do not translate well.

Translation. Translating oral traditions consists of more than translation of lexical items; it involves understanding something of the richness both of that which is denoted and that which is connoted. Sometimes translation of the whole adds up to something other than the sum of the surface lexical meanings of the parts. See the side box for an example where we understood each word, yet failed to understand the meaning.

Translation includes morpheme by morpheme glosses as well as more idiomatic translation of the text. With a careful translation, the text can be used not only for establishing the historical context, but also for discourse analysis of the text in the target language.

Participants. When publishing your analysis of one or more oral traditions and performances, be sure to include information about the participants. For example, who was the source of this oral tradition, who performed the oral narrative, who translated it, who was the audience, and what interaction occurred between the narrator and audience. In some situations the accompanist and the audience of an oral narrative interject comments into the performance in order to keep the narrator going and remind him or her what comes next. Those interjections need to be included in the published format so that the reader is able to have a more complete picture of the performance.

Since the recorder of the narrative is usually not the author of the narrative, it is problematic who should be listed as the author of the published account. Perhaps the recorder should be listed as the compiler or the one who recorded and transcribed the narrative. If there is another translator, that person's name should definitely be included in any published format as well as the performer.

Dating. Since many oral cultures are event-oriented rather than time-oriented, establishing a chronology of events in oral narratives may be problematic. One dictum some

---

Pouring water?

While Norris, our daughters, and I were attending a Cherubim and Seraphim church, people began dancing towards the back of the church, and Norris indicated that we should, too. I asked my husband what we were doing. He said that the man next to him told him that we were going "to pour water." Both of us had no clue as to what that idiom meant in this context though we knew the meaning of each lexical item. We soon found out that we were dancing to a tray located at the back of the church where we gave our offering. In this context "pouring water" meant to give our offering; it did not mean to urinate, though the phrase "to pour water" does mean that in other contexts.

historians use in writing history is that no history exists without chronology. Establishing chronology when working with oral narratives may call for creative methods. While ABSOLUTE DATING may not be possible, RELATIVE DATING may be. For example, events mentioned within the tradition can be placed within a relative time span based on events outside the narrative.

Narratives frequently have three tiers: a period of myth in the timeless past, a repetitive (cyclical) middle period, and lineal time (Vansina 1985:23). These tiers may have different functions for the society. For example, the mythical past may serve as the justification for society itself, including the existence of people, plants, and animals, and the hows and whys of things as they are (see Griaule 1965 for an example of the Dogon mythical past). The repetitive cyclical middle period may serve to explain the early period of specific societies. Lineal time is more apt to reflect history as it has occurred and may be documented from historical records.

One process that occurs in oral narratives, especially within genealogies, is TELESCOPING; this involves shortening or omitting entire portions of the society's past. The portion most commonly omitted is that between a society's recent past and the time of its origins. Different oral traditions insert the gap between the recent past and the time of origins at different places; consequently, Vansina (1985:24) refers to this as a *floating gap*. The fact that telescoping occurs does not mean that the narrative has no historical reliability.

Societies that do not keep calendars have several main sources of chronological detail: genealogies (e.g., the Fang in Gabon have genealogies that extend fifteen or more generations (Fernandez 1982:67)), calculations by relative age of respondents, recurrent social and other events (e.g., age grade initiations, markets, chieftaincy celebrations, migration of animals), datable astronomical and natural phenomena termed ecological time (e.g., comets, eclipses, earthquakes, floods, droughts and resultant famines, epidemics, locust invasions, weather cycles, planting and harvesting of crops), wars, and archaeological dating. Estimates of time depth in genealogies can be based on some approximate average number of years per generation such as 25, 30, or 35 years, though Henige states, "it is questionable whether any average really ought to be applied to a particular genealogy or list of officeholders...." (1982:97–98).

Sometimes the only date and place that can be attached to a tradition is that of its performance. Unless it was composed within the memory or knowledge of living members of the society, researchers may not be able to date its composition.

Analysis of founding charters.   Oral traditions about early ancestors, including a culture hero or heroes, and the events surrounding the ancestors, serve as founding charters for cultures. Within founding charters, traditions form around an archetypal figure, the CULTURE HERO, who tends to embody the desired values of the society. He or she is used to explain what happened at an early cultural stage. Sometimes there is little evidence other than the oral tradition that this culture hero existed historically; Crane and Angrosino state that he or she is "a character credited with conferring upon mankind special artifacts or institutions, or who has expressed the highest goals of a particular culture" (1974:107).

Culture heroes are humans rather than supernatural beings, as reported by Okpewho,

> The heroes are not superior beings except in so far as their earthly deeds make them so, least of all are they gods or descendants of gods. They do not possess supernatural powers, or do battle against other-worldly creatures such as monsters and demons. They do not go on adventures to worlds beyond that of man. Nor are they wont to provide lavish feasts in palatial mansions. In short, they

are ordinary human beings engaged in ordinary human activities. Not seldom, however, the poet, in the vividness of his imagination, uses metaphor, imagery, and symbolism which transport these ordinary activities to a level of extraordinariness, and the hero is often described as fighting against monsters, or as being himself a monster or other terrible creature destroying his opponents. But this is never meant to be more than figurative. (Kunene 1971:xvi, as quoted in Okpewho 1979:18)

In analyzing founding charters, realize that the role of the culture hero continues to be important within society today; you are not just dealing with ethnohistory or origin myths. They help define ethnic distinctives, give support to current ways of doing things, and validate ethnic identities.

In African founding charters, culture heroes serve as apical ancestors, with their sons founding villages and over time these villages becoming sections of ethnic groups as seen in the Baranzan founding charter on p. 260. (See McKinney 1985:51–59 for the Bajju founding charter; see Johnston 1966:111–12 for "The Legend of Daura" on the founding of the Hausa.)

Reconstruction of history. Life histories, personal recollections, and other oral traditions can be used to reconstruct history, an important area of cultural research since there are no people without history. In collecting oral history ask leading questions in order to find out what the interviewee knows about specific events and their occurrences. This contrasts with the methodology suggested for use in collecting life histories where you allow the interviewee the freedom to select events that are important to him or her.

Much that is written under the rubric of history concerns the activities of the elite. Collecting oral historical traditions allows you to focus on the nonelite, the underprivileged, the poor, the oppressed, the losers in history, as well as the elite. Examples of this emphasis include recent research on slavery (e.g., the acquisition of slaves, slavery itself, and the lives of ex-slaves; see Lovejoy 1983). Sources for collecting oral history on slavery exist in some countries in sub-Saharan and North Africa, particularly where governments abolished slavery within the memory of some elderly members of societies.

While study of oral traditions and oral histories is used to reconstruct past history, you can also use the diachronic study of oral traditions to analyze the change process. Through participant observation over a number of years, some scholars work with primary material in which they can document changes in oral traditions. They see specific individuals taking actions, groups forming for oral performances, and the routinization and incorporation of those oral traditions into the culture. They are able to see the dynamics of culture change by a diachronic study of oral traditions. For example, Young documented the rise and decline of the Mama Chi revitalization movement in Panama (Philip Young, lecture, Eugene, Oregon, summer 1987). Followers of Mama Chi met nightly, armed themselves, and in general formed a revitalization movement in the Panama jungle.

One issue that oral historians debate is to what extent can one strip away the nonhistorical accretions and arrive at a central historical truth. For example, by collecting and analyzing multiple versions of the same event, can a fieldworker arrive at what really happened by extracting what is the same in each version? However one answers that question, the task of reconstructing historical events and processes from oral historical traditions is difficult. Oral traditions usually do collect around some facts. It is finding those kernels of fact that is problematic; however, those kernels of fact are important from the perspective of those who keep the oral traditions and, therefore, also for the study of ethnohistory.

Analysis of genealogies. Genealogies provide clues for the analysis of oral histories. They are records or accounts of one's ancestors. Their analyses includes understanding what function(s) they have within ethnic groups. Genealogies usually fall into three general areas: (1) familial or domestic, (2) legal-political, and (3) religious.

Familial or domestic functions of genealogies. Familial or domestic genealogies serve to give an individual his or her social status. That status specifies rights, privileges, responsibilities, and obligations within the family based on his or her placement within the lineage. For example, among the Bajju the oldest son takes over the position of head of the extended family upon the death of his father, and the youngest son has the responsibility of caring for his aging parents.

Genealogies can also serve the purpose of maintaining pride in one's heritage. They indicate that the individual is part of a larger kinship grouping, and having that knowledge can give an individual prestige, pride, and social status. Sometimes an individual must be able to prove ancestry to particular ancestors to be able to join a particular group. For example, for a woman to join the Daughters of the American Revolution she must be able to prove through tracing her ancestors that she is related to those who lived in America at the time of the American Revolution.

Legal-political functions of genealogies. Legal-political functions of genealogies substantiate claims to hereditary office or help with settling competing claims. As such, genealogies show continuity with past leadership, establish royal succession, and provide legitimacy for the current leadership.

Genealogies may deal with land. Sometimes they include land claims that correlate with specific clans or lineages. When that is the case, they may be used to help settle territorial disputes. They may also explain migrations and, thus, give legitimacy to the group that resides where it does.

For some groups, one aspect of legal-political function of genealogies was for military conscription. Genealogies may also explain the military organization of the group and include praise for those who performed extraordinarily well in battle.

Genealogies may serve to show how outsiders are incorporated into the group. Or they may specifically illustrate why outsiders cannot be considered as part of the group.

Since clans may be associated with different occupations, genealogies may help to explain which persons are associated with specific trades and guilds. For example, members of clans may have as their occupational specialization being potters, brass workers, wood carvers, weavers, or other craft specialists.

A genealogy may be part of a founding charter for a particular group. When that is the case, you will find that it may provide a list of the founders of clans, e.g., descendants of the apical ancestor or cultural hero. You may want to translate the phrase "father of" as "founder of…"

Genealogies in founding charters may help explain migrations and migration routes, as well as the relationship between ethnic groups in the area. See the side box for an example.

Religious functions of genealogies. Finally, religious functions of genealogies help to establish the membership of a priesthood or of other religious offices. A prime example is the tribe of Levi mentioned in the Old Testament. Priests came only from the Levites. Genealogies may include notes about specific religious occasions with respect to particular religious functionaries.

The genealogies of Jesus are recorded in Matthew 1:1–17, which follows the genealogy of Joseph, Jesus' legal father, and Luke 3:23–38, which follows the genealogy of his mother Mary, Jesus' blood relatives. The Matthew account begins with Abraham, while the Luke account traces Jesus' genealogy back to Adam and ultimately to God. One reason for this difference in emphasis is that Matthew was likely written to a Jewish audience, while Luke addressed a non-Jewish one.

> **Bajju founding charter**
>
> In the Bajju founding charter, Baranzan, the Bajju apical ancestor, moved from the Jos Plateau into southern Zaria, where he found both good farm land and good hunting. He and his wife had several sons, each of whom founded a village; each village expanded and over time gave rise to a section of the Bajju ethnic group. His brother Atakat founded the Atakar people. Because of this close kinship relationship, traditionally the Bajju and Atakar did not intermarry.

Linear and segmented genealogies. Genealogies may be linear, segmented, or both. A LINEAR GENEALOGY is based on presentation of a single line of descent. It presents only lineal descendants, e.g., the descendants of the oldest son of the oldest son. As such it does not contain the genealogies of other sons and daughters of an oldest son. Further, a linear genealogy presents the order of the descendants based on their ages.

A SEGMENTED GENEALOGY presents all the descendants of a specific ego, including those of each son and daughter. In kinship terms, it includes descendants of ego's collateral relatives. For example, if a man has three sons, a segmented genealogy would trace the descendants of all three.

Sometimes genealogies include both linear and segmented data. One type will likely predominate, with the other brought in for specific purposes.

Time depth of genealogies. Time depth of genealogies refers to the number of generations included. For some groups genealogies may be extensive, reflecting a great depth of time, while for other groups they may be very shallow. Some genealogies go back to local concepts of the beginning of time (e.g., genealogies of Israel as recorded in the Old Testament). When that is the case, sections of the genealogy may be grouped based on some criteria. For the Old Testament genealogies that criterion is numeric; it is based on the number seven. When genealogies go back to the beginning of time, you may find God intervening and/or a mythical ancestor. There may be a floating gap between him or her and historic descendants.

Genealogies tend to have a certain fluidity. Telescoping is the most common feature of fluidity in genealogies, with names and events omitted.

Short historical notes in genealogies. Genealogies often incorporate short historical notes within them. What notes are incorporated usually depends upon the function of the genealogy. The notes may be about the unusual or the special. Sometimes notes include specific individuals from other ethnic groups whose descendants are incorporated into the ethnic group in focus, and the historical note tells why, when, and how those individuals were incorporated.

Mutations of oral traditions

You may find yourself tempted to look for *the* correct version of a particular oral tradition, with resultant frustration when each person you ask to recite that tradition gives a slightly different version. Johnston, who collected Hausa oral traditions, notes,

> It has sometimes been supposed that each folk-tale possesses an authentic version which must at all costs be reverently preserved. This is of course a myth. As the stories had no known author, and were never committed to writing until the early part of this century, they tended to have as many variants as raconteurs. (1966:xliii)

It is amazing that there is as much uniformity or agreement in oral traditions as does exist (p. xliv). When a storyteller recounts a specific oral tradition, his or her goal may not be to recite one faithful version but rather to use the oral tradition for pragmatic purposes, whether to entertain, to teach social norms, or to make a specific point. Though frequency of repetition of a tale aids storytellers in remembering details, it does not guarantee its faithful recounting. The intent of the storyteller and of the audience at a particular performance may have much to do with the details of the version told.

Further, members of different societies place greater or lesser importance on faithfully reciting a particular oral tradition. Vansina notes,

> In Polynesia ritual sanctions were brought to bear in case of failure to be word-perfect. When bystanders perceived a mistake the ceremony was abandoned. In New Zealand it was believed that a single mistake in performance was enough to strike the performer dead. Similar sanctions were found in Hawaii. This implied that when a performer was not struck dead his performance had to be correct. Such beliefs however had visible effects. Thus in Hawaii a hymn of 618 lines was recorded which was identical with a version collected on the neighboring island of Oahu. (1985:41–42)

While mutations of tales occur based on storytellers' intentions, sometimes different versions arise based on different perspectives of those who preserve the oral traditions. For example, Henige notes, "Xhosa versions of these incidents [of transcultural expansion] differ in many respects from the accounts enshrined in colonial historiography" (1982:72).

Mutations of an oral tradition may occur when it is borrowed from another ethnic group. Oral traditions, as well as other cross-cultural borrowings, undergo modifications to fit their new cultural context.

In a political economy framework

A political economic analysis seeks indicators of inequality, maintenance of that inequality, and aspects of power and domination within oral traditions. This perspective may include factors such as inequality in gender, language usage, and expressive genre. For example, minority people who are at the periphery of the economic structure may use songs (including protest songs), poems, speeches, and conversations among other oral traditions to express their perspective on that peripheral status. Sometimes the perspective expressed in oral traditions of those who are powerless differs from official views expressed by the dominant people or classes.

In order to analyze the political economic context of oral traditions you must take into account the linguistic structure, the propositional content, and the context of the performance of the oral traditions. This will enable you to uncover the way(s) in which the group formulates their opposition to their situation of inequality and oppression. While some oral traditions can be used to express opposition to political inequality, powerlessness, and oppression, not all oral traditions are so used. When they are, however, it is important to analyze these oral traditions that focus on inequality as a means to challenge openly or subvert subtly dominant values and perspectives.

When analyzing oral traditions from a political economic perspective, lexical items may be changed in such a way that they communicate with the in-group while excluding outsiders. For example, prisoners sometimes change the meaning of lexical items to communicate with each other while excluding their guards by use of slang, secretive codes, and ritual language. As an example, prisoners may term the main walkway "Main Street" and the commissary "Charlie's Place" (Don McKay, student ethnography, 1991). A second example concerns the perspective of women who stay at the Salvation Army, a place they term "Sally's Place" or simply "Sally's" (Ramona Kolic, student ethnography, 1990). Further, people can take the words of others and appropriate them for their own purposes.

The language or dialect used in specific contexts may also give information about cultural dominance. For example, which language is used in bilingual or multilingual contexts can reflect political inequality. Linguistic processes such as linguistic nationalism, pidginization, bilingualism, creolization, and language standardization often have a common focus on the economy, power, and dominance (Gal 1989:356). Study of such uses of oral traditions is undertaken in the context of good ethnographic research and careful descriptions and analyses of local social and linguistic processes.

Analysis of oral traditions requires considerable knowledge of the culture, knowledge that has been gained through other methodologies such as participant observation and informal interviews. Their analysis requires knowledge of the relevant symbolism, such as the fact that in many West African cultures the sound of an owl at night signifies that someone will die soon, or that a bush fowl represents wisdom. Colors, too, are symbolic in many cultures.

Oral traditions may be analyzed from various perspectives: as history, metaphor, text, verbal art, and performance. This chapter has dealt with each of these topics. Oral traditions are multivocal; they can be used for entertainment and amusement, for transmitting culture, for justification of specific cultures through their function as founding charters, for rationalization of beliefs and attitudes, for didactic purposes to teach values, morals, and acceptable behavior, for social pressure to sanction those who deviate from culturally acceptable behavior, for contests of wit, for explanations of cultural knowledge, for preservation of folk knowledge, and for protest of political inequality. Perhaps it is their multivocality that makes oral traditions so useful.

Another type of oral tradition is music, the topic of the next chapter.

22

Music

In 1970 the railway administration and the Ministry of Information decided to spon-
sor a band to safeguard and develop Malian music. The idea was that once in
Bamako, weary travelers could tumble off the packed carriages into the Buffet Bar,
where the Rail Band was meant to provide a taste of real Manding music, with a full
modern orchestra. All the instruments are government-owned and band-members are
obliged, as state employees, to troop up the platform occasionally and knock out a
few tunes for an arriving ministerial functionary. (Broughton et al. 1994:256)

Music provides vitality to life by contributing to our joy, moods, and sense of well-being.
For example, in Mali there is Manding music, such as music played by the Rail Band, mentioned above. Evenings in the clubs of West Africa, you are apt to find highlife music, or in
Senegal it might be Cuban dance rhythms (Broughton et al.1994:264). While music is not a
universal language, it is considered to be a universal human phenomenon.

MUSIC is the art of combining sounds of various pitches to produce compositions. Music is
part of the expressive aspect of the sociocultural system within culture. Other expressive
aspects are art, dance, religion, drama, and language. The expressive aspect of culture
deals primarily with the cognitive and emotional needs of people (Kaemmer 1993:8).

The study of music can be approached from several perspectives, two of which are music
as culture and music as an acoustic phenomenon. A combination of both approaches is necessary to understand music and its function in specific cultures.

Ethnomusicologists specialize in the study of music in its cultural setting (see Chenoweth
1972; Merriam 1964; Nettl 1967; Titon et al. 1984; the journal *Ethnomusicology*). They are
trained to write down the notes, rhythms, etc. of music as an acoustic phenomenon. They
speak of the MUSICAL EVENT as the unit of study; this relates to the broader topic of the
study of ethnographic events.

While you may lack adequate training in the technical aspects for transcribing the acous-
tics of music, this should not deter you from its study from the perspective of music as culture. Study of music as a component of culture, including both the instrumental component
and the lyrics, can open areas of understanding of the local worldview that are essential for
a complete understanding of the culture in focus. For example, Chernoff states, "The study
of African music can thus also become a focus for understanding the meaning of cultural
differences" (1979:33). One aspect of African music integrated into its cultural setting is its
community dimension. While music is played, people clap, dance, sing, and act out
dramas.

Analysis of music as culture

This chapter focuses on the study of music as a component of culture. Study of music from this perspective can be substantially enhanced by working together with an ethnomusicologist who can write down the music in musical notation. Many who conduct cultural fieldwork do not have this skill; hence, working together with an ethnomusicologist would enhance your study of music in culture.

In the study of music as a component of culture, investigate the question of whether there is a word for "music" or whether there are multiple words, each of which depicts a different type of music and its performance. In many cultures there is no generic word for music per se, but rather there are words for types of music such as singing, drumming, horn blowing, and flute-playing.

As you collect specific songs, speech surrogates (drumming, whistling), and other music, study the musical event, the total context within which the music occurs. Studying musical events entails being aware of audience interaction with the performers, food and drink served, dances and drama performed, rhythm, the occasion, the instruments used, the masquerades present, and, in general, the mood of the performance.

Analysis of the musical event comprises understanding music as an integral part of the culture it reflects and informs. Just as a fieldworker cannot adequately understand other kinds of art apart from their cultural context, so music is also integrated with its cultural context. In an African context, music and art are appreciated for their utilitarian value. Music also relates to the worldview of a culture. As Kaemmer states,

> The link between world view and music often influences the significance given to music. The people of Java have linked the brass instruments of their ensembles with the powers of the universe through the association between volcanic fires and the fires needed to smelt ore for making the musical instruments. (1993:61)

When listening to non-Western music, we tend to process it in terms of our culturally defined musical categories. Similarly, when those from cultures with non-Western musical traditions listen to Western music, they may not appreciate it. For example, when my husband and I took an African couple to a Dallas Symphony Orchestra concert, the wife's question was, "Why wasn't there dancing to accompany the music?" Music and dance go together in her indigenous culture.

Genre of music

One aspect of the analysis of music as culture is to place the music collected into the genre within which it fits. Look for named types of musical genre in cultures.

The types of musical compositions depend upon the categorization of them within specific cultures. An example is the categories of shamanistic and nonshamanistic songs of some Brazilian minority groups.

Reasons why a fieldworker might want to study genre of music (based on Hollingsworth 1998, personal communication) are that:

1. Genre are present within musical systems.
2. Knowledge of genre may give ideas of where and when music is used.

3. Knowledge of genre serves as a repertoire from which to choose when encouraging in-digenous music—when encouraging its use in literacy, church contexts, social contexts, etc. There are different contexts that are appropriate for specific genre.
4. Different genre have different linguistic and poetic forms.
5. Genre with different song types relate to different musical occasions.

In noting the genre of music, note them in the indigenous language. Alternatively, you might note the functional category of songs, e.g., initiation songs, church songs, hunting songs, etc.

Worldview, ethics, and behavioral norms

What basic worldview propositions are present in each genre of music? For example, study a number of songs in one genre and then analyze the content into a number of prop-ositions to see what these tell about the local worldview. Do this with each of several genre in order to begin to understand the culture through its music.

While the people who compose and perform music may not discuss the abstractions and systemization of morality and ethics present in music, their music often reflects an ethical system of the culture. People sing about fundamental social themes and values. As such, music can be both prescriptive and proscriptive. Music serves a socialization function within cultures.

African music deals with the norms of appropriate behavior (Chernoff 1979:154–55). Music is one means by which the individual can learn implicit social expectations and, thus, be able to respond with reasonable judgments about appropriate behavior.

Functions of music

In looking at musical events in culture, explore the functions of music. When is it played and why? Musical events are integrated in social contexts. For example, music forms part of many marriage ceremonies and receptions, social club meetings, parades, etc.

Study of the verbal content of music goes hand-in-hand with study of instruments. That verbal content may be in songs, the tones of instruments such as talking drums, or whistle talk. And the study of instruments includes all those used to produce mu-sic and accompany song such as drums, rattles, flutes, thumb pianos, horns, xylophones, stringed instru-ments, calabashes, etc.

Some major categories for the description of the acoustical phenomena of music are melody, rhythm, timbre (the characteristic quality of sound relating to the mixture and intensity of the harmonics), texture (how different instruments and voices combine), scale, and musical form (e.g., call and re-sponse, theme and variations, rondo, a cyclical pattern). Further, some music is improvised as played while other music is composed and then played as composed. You can view im-provisation and composition as being on a continuum in music.

> ### Flutes welcome successful hunters home
>
> In traditional Bajju culture when hunters returned home with a large animal they had shot, they blew flutes to tell the women and others left at home to come out to meet them and to celebrate with them.

In vocal music the musician may use different voice qualities to differentiate characters and their moods. In other compositions different instruments differentiate characters and their moods (e.g., instruments are used in Prokofiev's "Peter and the Wolf" to indicate different animals). Instruments are valued for the sounds they produce and often for their symbolic meaning. For example, in Brazilian minority ethnic groups, specific instruments are used only in particular ceremonies and are not used in other ceremonies. Avery reports that for some ethnic groups in Brazil, the shape of the instruments may be more important than the sounds they produce (T. Avery, personal communication, 1991, Dallas, Texas).

The importance of music in culture is reflected in the proverb of the Dan of Liberia, "The village where there is no musician is not a place where man can stay" (Chernoff 1979:36). In traditional Bajju culture there was a similar feeling. Bajju say that traditionally a village without hornblowers would not readily attract wives for its men. Music is part of the total cultural setting within communities.

Types of music

The following brief definitions identify some types of music. These should be viewed as suggestive only; as you study music in its cultural setting note the different types of music that are present. Look for specific terms in the language for each type of music.

Songs. SONGS are words set to music. The words of songs may or may not be organized poetically or metrically. Songs depend heavily upon their cultural context.

Songs may occur within tales, sometimes with refrains repeated several times as the story unfolds. Song refrains may be key formulae within the story.

Nuer songs reflect the complex nature of the culture where song is an integral part of that culture. Svoboda (1985:1) reports, "someone is always singing in Nuerland." Song is their primary form of artistic expression. By song the Nuer in Sudan preserve their history, transmit values and ideas, exchange contemporary points of view, and express dissent. Nuer also use songs to help their children go to sleep, to arouse warriors into battle, to encourage, to help in work, to attract lovers, and to praise or damn individuals (p. 2). The skill of a performer may increase a song's impact. Svoboda states,

> The role of song in Nuer society is so powerful that if a woman sings with great eloquence that her husband beats her, she may be granted a divorce; if a young man objects in impassioned songs that his relatives take too long to negotiate a brideprice, he may speed up a sometimes years-long process. Song has even been used as evidence in a judicial hearing and may warrant a court injunction forbidding performance. (p. 2).

When studying a culture where song occupies such a central and integral position as among the Nuer and their neighbors the Dinka (see Deng 1972), collection of songs is essential for understanding the culture, including its worldview, and its political, social, and economic structures.

The Murle in Sudan, who are pastoralists similar to the Nuer and Dinka, have songs that go with specific age-sets. Each age-set also has its name and a color code, and it selects its own leaders (Arensen 1991:99).

Songs may be divided into different types including ballads, birth songs, war songs, operas, blues, jazz, calypso, hymns, love songs, classical and traditional songs, lullabies, and so on. Modern types include high-life songs which are popular in West Africa, rock and roll, country, bluegrass, and so forth. An example of different types of songs among the Fulani comes from Sow who writes,

We can now turn to Fulani oral literature, which is divided into two principal categories. The first group includes myths, *daari* (epics), *tinndi* (stories), *cifti* (riddles), *malli* (jests), *teskuyaaji* (proverbs and maxis), *payka* (oral jousts or word games), etc. The second group consists of genres that are sung (i.e., oral poetry): *Pekaan* (fishermen's songs), *Dillere* (weavers' songs), *Gumbala* (warriors' songs), *Keroone* (hunters' songs), *Fantan* (cattle drivers' songs), *Leele* (songs of rejoicing), *Yela* (songs of women griots), *Booyngal* (merchants' songs), *Raas* (songs of entertainment among Fulani nomads), *Bojal* (shepherds' songs) lullabies, and other songs composed for particular occasions by women (*fuutankoobe*), ranging from mocking taunts (*mallol*) to eulogies (*jettugal*). (1993:61)

Certain genre of songs occur together with particular dances in different societies.

Musical classification, whether of the instruments or the songs, lends itself readily to taxonomic analysis (see chapter 18). For example, the Canilla in Brazil have both slow songs and fast songs. In constructing a taxonomy of Canilla songs, place songs at the apex of the taxonomy, and then have slow songs as one branch with specific ones under that branch, and fast songs as another branch. Both types are essential for any Canilla festival. Or in Latin America you could classify different types of sambas. Musical classifications often include cultural categories that you may not encounter elsewhere in the culture.

In gathering data on songs, ask about the different types of songs that the people recognize and that are named in the language. Then collect information on each type, though you may choose to focus on one or only a few types of songs. The following list is suggestive only of some of the genre of songs which exist.

Chants. CHANTS use monotonous tones or simple tones intoned by the voice. As intoned speech they may have no clear melody. Chants are a type of song, and the means of studying them include methods similar to the study of songs.

Chants are often associated with religious contexts (e.g., Quranic recitations, church liturgies, curing rituals, etc.). For example, the chief's chants in Kuna society, both in San Blas and in the interior Darien jungle of Panama, deal with history, politics, and religion (Sherzer 1989:263).

Dance songs. Dance, the deliberate, purposeful rhythmic movement of the body, is culturally patterned and most often occurs along with music, with or without song accompanying it. Dance, while a cultural universal, varies greatly from culture to culture.

Laments. Laments express deep sorrow or regret. They are formal songs sung at occasions such as wakes and funerals to express sorrow over the death of a member of society. They are often in verse format.

Life cycle songs. As humans proceed through the various marked cycles of life, those cycles are often marked by music. Typical life cycles marked musically include birth, childhood, puberty (including initiation songs), love and courting songs, marriage, and death.

Included within birth songs are songs that mark the conception of a woman's first child. Within traditional Bajju culture, traditionally this was celebrated, culminating in the father's going hunting to demonstrate that he can provide well for his family.

Lullabies. LULLABIES are songs composed for infants, often to help lull them to sleep. They tend to contain multiple repetitions, perhaps with minor changes for different verses.

Occupational songs. OCCUPATIONAL or WORK SONGS are associated with work activities. These songs are often rhythmic. An example is "I've been working on the railroad" for railroad workers. Occupational songs may be part of those sung during the annual cycle (preparing the soil, planting, weeding, harvesting, etc.). There is a wide variety of work songs, a few of which are listed below:

GRINDING SONGS are those sung while doing the household cooking activity of grinding grain. See side box for an example.

POUNDING SONGS are composed and sung by women as they pound grain in Africa. These songs can be used as a form of social commentary and control. You can often date the composition of such songs by the historical events that they describe. For example, Vaughan (1992) collected pounding songs from former Nyasaland, now Malawi, that described a severe famine which occurred in 1949. These songs described uneven distribution of grain, relations between men and women as affected by the famine, the breakdown of social norms, praises for those who provided food for their families, and so forth. Oral traditions and songs indicated that many women were abandoned during the period of famine (Vaughan 1992:85).

> ### Bajju grinding songs
>
> Bajju co-wives often sing *grinding* songs, in which grievances can be aired. Each day one wife cooks for their husband, and on the day she cooks she grinds the grain. As she grinds, she sings about her joys and sorrows, including her problems with her co-wife. The next day her co-wife sings her response. Children often go from compound to compound listening to the current grinding songs in order to know that is happening. Grinding songs provide a socially acceptable outlet for grievances between co-wives.

In Papua New Guinea when Saniyo women process sago, a starchy food from the pulp of sago palm trees, they sing SAGO SONGS as they sit rythmically pounding and scraping the pith of the palm with their flaked stone tool hafted like an adz. The melody remains the same, but the words are composed by the women according to what is going on at the time they are working (Pat Townsend, personal communication, July 3, 1998).

HUNTING SONGS are songs of power to increase the chances of success in the hunt. Some hunting songs include dancers acting out hunting scenes, with one or more dancers playing the roles of animals and others dancers come with bows and arrows. Together they act out hunting scenes.

Political songs. Political songs correlate with political activities, usually focused on the head of the village, area, state, or national government. They may also correlate with different political parties. These may be praise songs (see below) that praise the current office holder and his ancestors. This also includes songs such as national anthems, state songs, whether official or unofficial (e.g., *Yellow Rose of Texas, California Here I Come*).

Power and recreation songs. Some Brazilian Amazonian minority ethnic groups divide songs into SONGS OF POWER (e.g., shamanistic songs, killing songs, trading songs, and hunting songs) and RECREATIONAL SONGS, which are used in casual contexts such as for social dances. Recreational songs may include travel songs, drinking songs, children's songs, etc.

Praise songs. Praise songs are composed to celebrate an important individual or event. Frequently in an African context, these are composed by praise singers who are paid for their compositions. Among the Daasanech in northern Kenya, a man may go to a woman to request that she compose such a song to recount all of his deeds and to praise him. He pays her for this composition, which often turns out to be fairly lengthy. The woman would then teach it to other women who sing it again and again (Brian Schrag, lecture, Dallas, TX, December 6, 1990).

Religious songs. Often religious ritual is accompanied by songs and chants. For example, within a Christian context there are hymns, choruses, cantatas, chants, and so one. This category includes healing songs, spirit songs, and others songs related to religious beliefs and practices.

Magic songs are one type of religious songs. They may be sung when preparing poison, as to use on arrows or darts.

Songs of power are those which deal with potentially dangerous situations and involve the spirits who emerge from the ground to aid individuals in response to their singing. Because of the correlation of spirits who live in the earth, the danger involved, and the spiritual power present, people who sing these songs sit down in order not to disturb the spirits.

Rites of passage songs. Music can protect an individual during a rite of passage within the life cycle. This is a vulnerable, transitional period for the individual.

Shamanistic and hunting songs. SHAMANISTIC SONGS are sung to produce spiritual power, to control or to manipulate power, perhaps to heal, or to aid in life threatening or dangerous circumstances. As people sing shamanistic songs they may also present food to feed the spirits or inhale drugs to allow them to get in touch with the spirits.

Social commentary and current event songs. Songs and other musical performances are often SOCIAL COMMENTARY and CURRENT EVENT SONGS. It is frequently possible to date specific songs based on the events described. While some songs are best described as significant event or occasion songs, others serve as social protest songs or commentaries on current events. For example, during the struggle for civil rights for all races in the United States, the song *We shall overcome* was widely sung. During the Biafran civil war in Nigeria a group of teenage young women composed and performed a song about Gowon and Ojukwu, the leaders of the Federal and Biafran sides of the conflict, respectively.

An example of one means of collecting data comes from Keil (1979:100), who collected data about song composers of the Tiv in Nigeria by asking Tiv students in various secondary and technical schools to write essays on "My favorite Tiv composer and why I like him." His results identified almost 100 different composers from 122 essays. Favorite composers tended to be persons that the individual students knew, often from the same area of Tivland that the students came from.

Speech surrogates. SPEECH SURROGATES replicate rhythm and tonal patterns of oral language by playing instruments or by nonverbal communication such as whistling. These duplicate the tones of oral speech and thus take the place of that communication through the use of some speech surrogacy system. Examples of instruments used include horns, whistles, flutes, bells, xylophones, and drums. Specific examples include those Carrington (1949:33–39) described on the use of sticks or tree roots, Cowan (1948) on Mazatec whistle language, and Thieme (1969:370) on Yoruba blacksmiths' greeting passersby by beating on an anvil. Yoruba drummers also announce deaths by drumming the appellations and genealogies of the deceased.

In speech surrogate drumming, Euba reports that "false syllables" may be added by the drummer that "often express single syllables by multiple drum strokes, and also insert purely decorative notes that have no textual value" (1988:45). This occurs in Yoruba *dundun* drumming in which a vowel may be lengthened as a "terminal juncture marker" (Anyidoho 1986:35). In the Ewondo, Cameroon, speech surrogacy system a drummer customarily first calls the name of his selected audience, then plays his own drum call name (Atangana and Messi 1919:303–6, Nkili 1975/76:129, Neeley 1991:107). Following this introduction he beats out the message he wants to communicate to villagers on a slit drum.

War songs. War songs include songs that prepare people for fighting, battle songs, and victory and defeat songs. In small scale societies often women stand behind the men, shouting and on occasion singing to encourage them in fighting. Victory songs may include praise names for warriors. For example, the Bajju had different praise names for warriors who killed people which correlated with specific ethnic groups.

Marches may be played while military groups march, as around a parade ground.

Music with or without song. In many cultures there are types of music which may not have songs associated with them. For example, western classical music is often instrumental only. This is often true for jazz. Both rock and pop music in the west usually have songs associated with them though they may also be performed without the vocal accompaniment.

Musical instruments and their classification

Musical instruments vary from culture to culture. When studying musical instruments, make sketches of them or photograph them. You may want to document the various stages of their construction, too.

Within a Western musical instrument classification, the most common categories classify instruments according to what vibrates, whether the air column, the stretched sting, the stretched membrane, or the nonstretched instrument itself (e.g., idiophones such as gongs). This is known as the Sachs-Hornbostel system (Hornbostel and Sacks 1961). Hollingsworth comments on this classification,

> More helpful for research purposes is the widely-used Sachs-Hornbostel system which consists of...basic groups, a group being made up of instruments assigned according to how the sound is made, i.e., what vibrates to make the sound. Within the four basic groups, the criterion used for subdividing each group is not consistent between the groups. Idiophones are classed and arranged according to the shape. Chordophones are classified as to the relationship of the strings to the body or resonator. Aerophones are classified as to how the air is set into vibration. To these four basic groups or categories, contemporary researchers add another, electrophones, to cover electric keyboards and the like. (Hollingsworth in Schrag 1998:60)

Musical instruments are classified differently depending upon the culture, and it is that classification you need to document. In other cultures instruments are classified as to whether they are men or women's musical instruments. There may also be musical instruments that both can play.

Rhythm

Rhythm is one of the fundamental characteristics of music; it refers to uniform or patterned recurrences of a beat within music or speech. The pattern of rhythm differs from musical system to musical system. In some musical systems rhythmic pattern is more important than harmony and melody, while in others it is of less importance. A few possible rhythmic patterns are presented below.

Simple rhythm. Simple rhythm divides music into standard units of time with a recurrent main beat. When the main beat is shifted to uneven or irregular rhythm, musicians speak of syncopation. The accent is then on beats that are normally unaccented.

Multiple rhythm. Multiple rhythm, termed polymeter, polyrhythm, or multiple meter by ethnomusicologists, involves the simultaneous use of different meters. This is true for African music and contrasts with western music where harmony tends to be more important. The usual pattern within African musical systems is characterized as having multiple rhythm and cross-rhythm. Chernoff states, "African music is often characterized as polymetric because, in contrast to most Western music, African music cannot be notated without assigning different meters to the different instruments of an ensemble." (1979:45)

Polymeter is complex, yet when carefully analyzed, each instrument usually has a very simple rhythm. When all of the rhythms of the instruments are combined, it can sound incredibly complex. For example, "Each musician contributes his own part in the total polymetric fabric, and there are never two or more playing the same thing unless their specific drums are the same" (p. 47). Within African music the number of beats per measure tends to be double or triple time. For example, the time signature might be 12/8 rather than 4/4 or 3/4 time as is typical of a western musical time.

Cross-rhythms. Conflicting rhythmic patterns are termed cross-rhythms. Differing intricate and changing relationships to each other are characterized as conflicting-rhythms.

Music and dance

Music and dance are intimately related worldwide. As one African musician shared with Chernoff, "'...every drumming has got its dance'" (Chernoff 1979:101). Further, the music and dance of men and women may differ. And the music and dance of different villages may also contrast. In studying music and dance, study patterns of both for different villages and ethnic groups.

Language and linguistics in the study of music

The study of music as culture is particularly important for those who desire to learn about a culture through the collection of texts for linguistic analysis. Nketia and DjeDje state, "It is generally believed that drum language and song texts should be approached from a linguistic point of view" (1984:xvii). While linguistics is important for study of music in general, it comes to the front in the analysis of the use of talking drums that transmit messages through use of the tones of the language, and whistle talk that similarly utilizes emic tone. Both these musical forms are referred to as speech surrogates. Speech surrogates tend to occur in contexts where tone has a high functional load indicating that it is very important in conveying lexical meaning within the language, though this depends upon the culture.

Language and music often affect each other, as in the case of Handel's *Messiah* and Prokofiev's *Peter and the Wolf*. Kaemmer states, "In some societies music is subordinate to language, while in other societies the reverse is true" (1993:72). He further notes that in India the text is dominated by the music. Extra vowels or syllables may be added to make the text fit the music. In other cases, as in many folk songs in America, the text dominates the music.

In tonal languages the lexical tones restrict the melodies of the music. In some languages the tone is lexical and/or grammatical. In languages such as Chinese, Navaho, and Jju, where tone is contrastive, that contrast must be reflected in the music. Kaemmer notes,

> In areas with tonal languages the pitch possibilities of drums are used to reproduce language tones. Thus drumming, as a form of icon, can actually convey linguistic messages. This practice is the basis of the "talking drums" formerly used to communicate over long distances in Zaire. (1993:116)

Similarly, in languages where stress is contrastive, this too is reflected in the rhythm patterns of music.

Linguists, cultural researchers, and ethnomusicologists all can profitably bring the strengths of their disciplines to bear on the study of music.

Collecting data on music

In studying music, collect data on music and its performers. Some field researchers become scholar performers, as, for example, Chernoff who spent ten years in Ghana studying drumming (1979). Other fieldworkers enter into musical performances and/or express appreciation for the music performed locally. Musical appreciation serves to endear you to members of the local community. The extent to which you can participate in local performances depends on you, your musical skills, and on the acceptability of your doing so by the community. For example, some fieldworkers choose to refrain from participation in local musical religious activities while others feel they can do so with no problems.

Questions for the study of music. Some questions that might guide you in the study of music include the following.

    I. How is music differentiated from nonmusic? What are the functions of music in culture? When is music played in that culture? What is "beautiful" music within the culture? How is it defined?

    II. The musical event
        A. What are the components of the total musical event?
            1. Performers (instrumentalists, singers, dancers, etc.)
            2. Audience
            3. Audience-performer(s) interaction
            4. Context of the performance
            5. Food and drink
            6. Reason for the performance
            7. Mood of the event
            8. Cultural values and behavioral norms presented or reinforced

      9. Costumes

     10. Props

     11. Masquerades

     12. Drama

     13. Leader(s) of the musical event

     14. Instruments

     15. Text

     16. Dance

     17. Other (specify)

  B. What is the local concept of music? Do birds or animals sing? Do nonhuman spirits (e.g., witches, ancestral spirits) sing or have their own music? Is whistling classified as music? Is humming music?

  C. Do the people have any story about the origin of music?

  D. Is there a word for music in general or only for specific types of music? What is the local term for the genre of music being performed?

III. Songs

  A. Who are the primary composers of songs? Are all songs composed by people who specialize in composing songs, or are some songs composed by anyone (e.g., mothers might compose lullabies, while farmers might compose farming songs)?

    1. What kinds of songs do specific composers compose?

    2. Do composers compose the words first or the music?

    3. Do they do part of the composition (e.g., words) and have someone else do the rest (e.g., the music)?

  B. Are songs improvised, and, if so, how are they improvised, by whom, and for what purpose(s)?

  C. Are lyrics of songs fixed so that no improvisation occurs?

  D. Are new songs developed creatively, or are traditional songs used without the development of new songs?

  E. Are songs owned by specific individuals or clans? If they are owned by specific individuals, can others use them? If so, how is the owner compensated? Or is their use forbidden other than by their owners?

  F. Are there song duels? If so, what is their significance?

  G. Must music be performed word perfect? If error occurs, does it invalidate the ceremony of which the music is a part?

  H. Are there songs used mainly for recreational purposes, songs that we might term traditional recreational music? Are some of them associated with specific kinds of recreational activity?

  I. What music is associated with different occupations (e.g., music used by farmers, blacksmiths, butchers, or hunters)? In what contexts are they used? For example, are there songs to accompany clearing of the underbrush, planting, weeding, and harvesting?

  J. Are there songs associated with the center of political or social power, as for example, court songs, political party songs, national songs and anthems, etc.? Songs associated with political events are termed MUSIC OF POLITICAL IN-STITUTIONS. Within this broad category are praise songs. Are there songs of magical power? Can one hire a praise singer to greet people for you on the occasion of a specific event or holiday?

IV. Instruments
   A. What musical instruments are present within a particular society?
   B. Who makes particular musical instruments?
   C. Does the craft of making musical instruments reside within a particular clan, lineage, family, craft guild, etc.?
   D. What rituals surround the making of musical instruments?
   E. How are the instruments made? What are the sources of the materials of the instruments?
   F. How long does it take to make a particular instrument?
   G. Is the construction of musical instruments a secret activity or can anyone observe their construction?
   H. Are new instruments being incorporated into the current repertoire of instruments or replacing or substituting for older types?
   I. Do the instruments have spirits associated with them? If so, how is each spirit acknowledged or thanked in performance?
   J. If the culture has stringed instruments, do different strings have different characteristics (e.g., the lowest string for the *bokotoko* harp in Chad is known as an "elephant scream" (DeVale 1984:313))? Similarly, if a culture has a number of types of drums, how is each characterized? Are kinship categories applied to different musical instruments?
   K. When an instrument is first completed, is there a ritual that must be performed before it can be put into regular use? For example, must it be consecrated or presented to the chief of the village? If so, is there sacrifice involved? What is the ritual performed?
   L. Does one instrument always start the musical event? If so, which one is it? How is the lead instrument characterized?
   M. Are there women's songs or instruments, and similarly, are there men's songs or instruments?
   N. What are children's songs, instruments, and dances?
   O. Are there different songs, instruments, and dances for boys and for girls?

V. Musicians
   A. Are the musicians professionals (people who make music their primary source of income) or nonprofessionals (people who have other professions and perform music as a secondary source of income or do so simply for the enjoyment of it)? What other economic activities do musicians engage in? Are musicians paid or not paid? Are they paid with gifts in kind or with money? If they are not paid, how are they socially acknowledged?

      Note that some who sing do not consider themselves to be musicians. For example, Hollingsworth encountered a farmer out in a field singing. When he asked what the farmer was doing, he responded "I'm farming" (Ken Hollingsworth, personal communication, 1998).

      Be aware that in French the word "musicians" implies only instrumentalists but not singers. If working in a French-speaking context, it is well to be forewarned since the English word "musician" implies both instrumentalists and singers. If you want both included, then be specific, as in any questionnaire that you might develop.

B. Are they full-time or part-time? For example, among the Hausa more than eighty percent of 153 musicians sampled by Ames (1973:130–31) derived all of their livelihood from their work as musical performers.

C. Are musicians organized and, if so, how? Is there a leader or chief of the musicians?

D. How does a person become a musician? Does a musician acquire that role by inheritance, apprenticeship, personal acquisition, imitation, by some combination of these, or by some other means (e.g., attending school with music as one's major or a music school)? If the position of musician is inherited, who is it inherited from? If a person learns music through an apprenticeship, what is the length of time involved? Does the apprentice live with his/her master? What financial arrangements are involved?

E. Are there named ranks of musicians?

F. Are there wandering or peripatetic musicians? Is musical performance their primary means of earning an income? What occasions require their presence, and how are they compensated?

G. Are there practice sessions? Is a musician fined if he or she is late to a practice session or if he or she misses a session? What is that fine?

H. Does the behavior of musicians deviate from the typical behavior patterns of nonmusicians?

I. How do nonmusicians characterize musicians as a group? What stereotypes are applied to musicians?

J. What is the social status of musicians? Is it low or high?

K. Do musicians have spiritual guardians?

L. What prescriptions or proscriptions are there about who may perform musical acts or when, where, or how they are to be performed? What prohibitions are there about who may sing or play or otherwise perform music, or about when, where, or how it may be done?

M. At what events do musicians perform? Do some events require the services of musicians?

VI. Musical traditions
  A. What musical styles are present? In what contexts are each used?
  B. Are there regional and local musical traditions? What characterizes each?
  C. Is there a tradition of extended singing, singing that can continue day and night without sleeping?

VII. Musical performances
  A. What types of music are performed and by whom?
  B. What is each performer's part in the performance?
  C. What criteria do people use for judgments of competency of musical performances?
  D. What are the personal styles of individual performers?
  E. Do those who perform music differ from oral historians and other performers of oral traditions?
  F. What are the characteristics of the particular type of musical event?

VIII. Music and society
  A. Are instruments, songs, or dance used in healing rituals?

B. Are music and specific musical instruments incorporated into the oral history of the people? If so, what role do they have in that history and what is their relevance for people today? What can be deduced concerning historical events and reconstruction of history based on music about the past?

C. How does music contribute to harmonious social relations within that culture?

D. What music is performed with which rituals? What is the function of specific types of music within each ritual?

E. What types of music are associated with birth, initiation, betrothal, marriage, and funerals (e.g., some songs are life cycle music)? Are there songs associated with different organizations (e.g., the *poro* men's secret organization or the *sande* women's secret organization in Liberia)?

F. What do the lyrics of the music tell about the culture and its worldview?

IX. Music and Religion

A. What songs, instruments, and types of music (e.g., chants, hymns, or signature songs for specific spirits) are associated with specific religions and religious rituals? These songs are religious music; this category includes the subcategory of church music.

B. Do people receive songs from some supernatural source?

C. Do people sing songs in a foreign language in religious contexts?

X. Music and cultural change

A. Is music incorporating innovations?

B. Are changes in the musical system itself occurring? What are those changes?

XI. Music and dance

A. What relationship exists between different types of music and dance?

B. Do the rhythm of the music and the dance coincide (e.g., if the basic rhythmic musical pattern consists of ten beats, does the dance have a similar ten beat pattern)?

C. What are the dance steps associated with various types of music?

D. Who are the dance performers in what contexts?

E. What special clothes are worn by dancers

F. Are the dancers professionals?

G. What events are associated with dancing?

H. When are dances held?

(For further questions to investigate, see Boring in Schrag 1998:85–91.)

XII. Speech surrogates. Are there speech surrogates, e.g., talking drums or whistle talk?

In studying music, pick questions to investigate that are of interest to you or that are significant in that culture. Do not feel that you need to find answers to all of the above questions. They are given as suggestions only of areas that you might want to investigate.

In finding answers to some of these questions, interview musicians, and attend their performances and their practice sessions. Also interview nonmusicians about music. Include in your interviews with nonmusicians their perspective on music and musicians. When do they invite musicians to perform? How much do they pay them? What types of music do they enjoy? As you study music, you will gradually build up an understanding and appreciation of the role of music in culture.

Tape and video recordings. In tape or video recording of music for acoustic and cultural analysis, first obtain permission from the performers to do so. It is best to have that permission in writing, though you may record it verbally also. Write the following information in your data notebook, and also record it on the media.

1. Your name
2. Date: time, day, month, year, and local concept of time.
3. Location: place, section of village or neighborhood, city/village, state, and country.
4. Name(s) of performer or performers: number or approximate number of people in musical group, titles of performers, contact information of performer(s) (address, phone number, e-mail address), gender of performers, approximate ages, role of each performer
5. Language(s) used in musical event
6. Brief summary of the content of the recording
7. Number of the song
   (The above list is partially based on information from Karen Boring, Personal communication, October 16, 1991, Dallas, TX)
8. Title of music or name of music
9. Context or occasion for which the music is performed, and any history of musical performance
10. Genre of music in the indigenous language
11. Instruments used: names both in local language and in your language (give a description if there is no ready equivalent), number of instruments used and their classification
12. Audience: approximate size, interaction between musical performers and audience
13. Purpose of performance: reason for performance; is it public or private
14. Culture/ethnic group of performers and of the audience

Without such documentation audio and video tape recordings are often useless.

Indiana University has a tape archive for ethnic music around the world. You may wish to add your tape recordings or CDs to this archive. Be aware that any archive will likely require evidence of the permission of the performers for your recordings.

After tape or video recording, transcribe the words of songs, and if you are so trained, also transcribe the acoustic sounds of the music. Both for the ethnomusicologist and for the nonethnomusicologist, study of the words of the songs can be a valuable window into other aspects of the culture, including its worldview.

In tape recording use new good quality tape on cassettes that are thirty to sixty minutes long. These lengths of tape are thicker than the ninety minute cassettes and, therefore, will last longer. Also use a good quality tape recorder and microphone. Some small cassette and minicassette tape recorders have a minimum of machine noise so that they can be used for good quality recordings. Further, do the recording some place as quiet as possible, a place without extraneous background noise to the extent possible. A recording studio is excellent, though in many places in the world, field researchers do not have access to such a studio.

The single most effective technique for getting good recordings is to have the microphone as close as possible to the source of the music, most especially if the sound is weak at its source. If the source is a singer, ideally the microphone should be less than six inches from the singer's lips. It should be off center at a forty-five degree angle to avoid the "wind blast" noises of aspiration puffs hitting the microphone, unless there is a highly effective wind blast filter on the microphone.

Sometimes it is helpful in transcribing traditional songs to go over your transcription with elderly people. For example, sometimes there are obsolete words and phrases in songs that they would likely understand. Or you may find that they do not understand the archaic words; however, they may be embarrassed to tell you. There may also be nonsense syllables, often termed VOCABLES or song words, inserted to aid in the rhythm that do not have an identifiable meaning per se.

In the next chapter the focus shifts from music as a component of culture to studies that relate to collection of cultural information rapidly within specific cultures.

23

Rapid Appraisals

Are we hearing the whispers of the poor, struggling majority, or the loud cries of the wealthy and often influential minority? (Batchelor 1993:12–13)

Most of the field methods developed to study cultural data and introduced in this book assume that you are doing in-depth field research. However, sometimes decisions need to be made quickly. For example, should a language project be initiated with this group? How can we best design a project to address malnutrition that is prevalent in an area? Fieldworkers often use RAPID APPRAISAL (RA), also termed RAPID ASSESSMENT, which utilizes operational procedures for collecting data on a specific topic quickly and, hopefully, effectively and economically. The goal of an RA is to have adequate, timely, relevant, useful, and appropriate information available for decisions. RAs help to identify local problems, goals, and strategies for dealing with specific problems. Further, after you have a broad knowledge of a culture, rapid appraisal techniques may be helpful for study of certain topics.

RAs have arisen as a research technique largely to meet a need within development research where longer-term anthropological research does not readily meet the needs within the time frame necessary for a development agency or project. RAs are a form of applied anthropological research.

Some general goals of those doing rapid appraisals are to hear the voices of those who are usually voiceless, to participate with them in their cares and concerns, and to meet their needs. The perspective of all members of the society needs to be taken into account, so that the society can rise together.

In rural contexts RAs are termed RAPID RURAL APPRAISALS (RRA). They are conducted by a team of specialists responding to a problem that people in the local community have identified. Another term that you may find in the literature is PARTICIPATORY RURAL APPRAISALS (PRA). The local people themselves provide the leadership and do as much of the research work as possible rather than outside researchers (Pratt and Loizos 1992:74–77). One distinction between an RRA and a PRA is the shifting of power over to the local participants, or at least sharing of power more fully with them. A second distinction is that PRA research is an unhurried appraisal. This chapter focuses on RAs, whether in urban or rural contexts. Towards the end of this chapter PRAs are discussed further as they clearly have an important role to fill.

An example of a situation in which conducting a RA might be helpful is collection of local information before introducing ORAL REHYDRATION THERAPY (ORT). Before pursuing an ORT project you would want to know to what extent diarrhea is a problem in the area in focus, what are the local beliefs about the etiology of diarrhea, what are current means of countering dehydration, to what extent do people already know about ORT, and so forth.

It would also be helpful to conduct a RA before commencing a language program in a minority language. A language program would typically include coordination with members of the language community, language learning, linguistic analysis of the language, development of a practical orthography, production of literacy materials including primers and other reading and writing material, instruction for the people in reading those materials, and production of a literature in that language.

Before undertaking a language program you may want to know answers to several questions. What percentage of the population is bilingual or multilingual and in what language(s)? What literacy materials are available in each of those languages? Are those materials being used by the minority language population and to what extent do people understand them? How do monolingualism, bilingualism, and multilingualism correlate with age and gender of members of the population in focus? In what domains are another language or languages used? What are the attitudes of people towards use of their mother tongue? What motivations or potential motivations do people have towards literacy in their own language? And so forth.

Similarly RAs may be used for appraisal of natural resources and the environment, health and nutrition projects, farming systems, and agricultural projects, as well as other development projects. The goal of many development agencies is SUSTAINABLE DEVELOPMENT, in which projects initiated will continue after development agents leave. For sustainable development to occur the local people need to have control of the project and have a feeling of ownership. Control does not mean that they do all the work. It does mean that they are involved from the outset of the project, including its initial planning. The project becomes one of partnership between the development agency and the local community. Sustainable development likely comes through participatory development projects.

Many development projects in the past have involved the goal of modernization. The result of this too often has been DEVELOPMENT REFUGEES, people who are marginalized in the process. Perhaps their land was taken over for the project, or their resource base replaced by flooding their land for a hydroelectric dam, and the local leaders had been bypassed in the planning and implementing of the project. When these types of problems occur, people become powerless. When they resist a particular development project, often one moment of resistance may lock people into feelings of perceived or real powerlessness for the rest of their lives. The goal of sustainable development is to involve them so that powerlessness does not occur.

Many development agencies have the goal of food sufficiency for a given population. A RA could be conducted to ascertain to what extent a population has sufficient food throughout the year, what are seasonal hunger patterns, and what other problems lead to food insufficiency.

A further goal of RAs is to allow planners of development projects to avoid imposition of top down projects. Rather, planners need to work with the indigenous population by incorporating their contextualized input that takes into account their particular historical and cultural circumstances.

RAs are imprecise and entail optimal ignorance (Chambers, as reported by Cernea 1985:397). As Cernea states,

> Optimal ignorance is the measure of courage necessary to concentrate on selected sociocultural indicators with demonstrated operational significance,

rather than trying for comprehensive coverage of the ethnography of the local area; appropriate imprecision is the measure of detail which is—or is not—needed for an area. (p. 397)

RAs utilize a set of research methods that enable researchers to collect data that are both time- and cost-effective. These methods are designed to allow outsiders to learn about conditions so that the information collected gives development agents a good understanding of the local situation, and potentially this information can be used beneficially. This information is relevant particularly during the initial phases of a development project, phases that include IDENTIFICATION, PREPARATION, and APPRAISAL. It is also useful later for IMPLEMENTING, MONITORING, and EVALUATING the project.

For some research purposes rapid assessment ethnographies are necessary. For example, this is true when studying various aspects of the drug culture. In order to curtail the spread of drug use, a rapid assessment of what is happening on the street is essential for health workers in making plans for addressing this problem.

A RA differs from what might be termed development tourism which some researchers use in rural areas.

Rural development tourism

Before setting forth some research methods used in RRAs, there are certain cautions relevant to fairly quick assessments in rural settings. RURAL DEVELOPMENT TOURISM requires brief visits by an urban-based professional (Chambers 1985:400–01). This has the following potential problems:

1. Spatial (urban, tarmac, and roadside): Those who are in greater need may live away from the road in less accessible areas.
2. Project: When established projects are already in progress in a particular area, additional funds tend to be funneled into those existing projects rather than into areas where there might be greater need.
3. Elite biased: Those individuals who interact with an urban research team will tend to be the more powerful and less needy elites. They may have a vested interest in what outsiders are allowed to see, or they may present a perspective that will reflect well upon the national government.
4. Dry season: Contacts are usually made with rural areas during the dry season when travel is easier and when crops have been harvested. By so doing, you may fail to observe the extent of deprivation caused by food shortages, high prices for food, high incidence of diseases, seasonal hunger patterns, and so forth, that may occur during the rainy season.
5. Politeness and protocol: When you spend only a limited time in the area, you will tend not to meet those who are poorer. Local politeness and protocol may dictate that the group "puts its best foot forward" by shielding you from the most needy.
6. Lack of rapport with respondents: Until people learn to trust you they may give misleading or incomplete answers that may hinder research and subsequent development projects.
7. Investigators: Those who are "old hands" may not listen adequately, and consequently, they may concentrate on teaching rather than learning. Thus, they reinforce misconceptions and project their own meanings into the situation.

8. Failure to observe the invisible: Important factors such as informal organizations, patron-client relationships, wages, control of assets, and decision-making procedures are not readily observable, yet are important for development projects.

9. Limited time frame: You may see only a moment within the annual seasonal activities, that you may then project for the entire year. (Points one through nine are based on Chambers 1985:400–01.)

10. Language: You may not speak the local language and thus you are dependent upon interpreters, resulting in the possibility that data are skewed in the translation process, either deliberately or inadvertently.

11. Male biased: Individuals interviewed by the urban team will tend to be males who may give data from the male perspective only, or who will provide data they mistakenly think is the women's perspective. In fact, in some cultures, as for example, in conservative Muslim communities, male researchers may be unable to interview women. Hence, the research team needs to include female researchers.

One alternative to rural development tourism is to do a thorough lengthy ethnography project. Part of a longer ethnographic project may involve administering a lengthy questionnaire that provides lots of good useful information. Too often, however, the results of such a questionnaire or interview schedule collected by development researchers are unavailable or are not available rapidly enough to those interested in doing rural development. A rapid appraisal is a compromise in length and thoroughness between these two extremes. It provides a tradeoff between timeliness, accuracy, relevance, and usefulness of the information collected (Chambers 1985:403).

Field methods to use in rapid appraisals

According to Pratt and Loizos (1992:67) a RRA, and by inference a RA, does not involve one or more specific field methods per se, but rather it involves an outlook that will enable the researchers to produce useable data within a set length of time in order to meet a deadline. It uses common sense and imagination to come up with reliable data for decision making. Having said that, there are some specific field methods and techniques which you might use. Which specific ones you use depends upon the goal of your research.

Learn from available information

In conducting a RA, start by reviewing information available on the area and people in question. Since similar ethnic groups tend to live within a culture area where there is a cluster of culturally related peoples in a similar geographic area, you can profitably read on other peoples within the same culture area. This is particularly helpful if there has been no research on the specific ethnic group in focus. Information on that ethnic group or on related ethnic groups will provide a starting point so that you can develop a set of initial hypotheses about the group in focus that can be verified when you are in the area. Such information may include what is known about the social organization, economy, religion, political organization, geography, material culture, and technology of those who live in that culture area. Further, you can talk with people who are familiar with that area.

Rapid appraisals usually require a team of people with different specialties. The members of the team will have a list of areas to look at, and they can consult with each other. Such sharing of data enables the team to check each other's biases, come up with creative ideas, and provide the emotional and moral support that each member of the team needs.

Use data from other sources

Another means of collecting data as part of a RA is to use ad hoc data collected by local residents. Such individuals know who are the key people to interview, and who might provide what needs to be known quickly and efficiently. Further, search out results of studies done by national investigators, whose results are often to be found in libraries and in other collections in local universities and colleges.

Learn from people in the area

The second step in conducting a RA is to learn from people of the area. Such people have a wealth of knowledge, including knowledge of plants, seasons, animals, agricultural practices, cooking, childcare, medical practices (both traditional and current, which are often a combination of local, regional, and cosmopolitan medical practices), and social customs. The local people, if asked, will identify their current needs and the areas in which they need assistance.

Use key individuals

Use of key individuals (key informants) is a time-honored method of data collection and is an essential component of a RA. Key individuals include local residents, social anthropologists, extension agents, teachers, local leaders and officials, and others who reside in or have knowledge of the area being investigated. Some individuals may not realize until asked that they have information needed for a RA, but they may prove to be very helpful. Further, in a RA, cross-check data you obtain in order to evaluate their accuracy. For this reason, in doing a RA work with more than one individual.

Use informal interviews

Informal interviews, often guided by a previously prepared series of questions (e.g., questions that are open-ended and others that have more structured responses), provide the main research methodology for those engaged in RAs. Researchers can quickly establish rapport with individuals by being congenial, and yet be directive enough to collect the information desired. Informal interviewers also need to appear unhurried and relaxed, with the result that those interviewed also relax and hopefully share information with you.

Conduct group interviews

Group interviews are often beneficial (Chambers 1985:409). Sometimes data emerge in a group context that would not be as readily available when working with only one individual. If, however, the group perceives that the questioner has power to control benefits or sanctions, they may skew the data they give in such a way as to be of most benefit to themselves.

Sometimes researchers get together a local panel to discuss a particular topic. Those invited are experts on the topic and, thus, they share their knowledge. For example, if you are looking at infant feeding patterns, a group of mothers of varying ages could readily provide useful information. Participation in such panels would likely prove enjoyable and informative to the participants themselves. In the discussion by panel members there would tend to be self-correcting dynamics. For example, if someone asserts something that the others know is not accurate, the others would likely correct him or her.

Conduct direct observations

To the extent that time allows in conducting RA, use direct observations. This often reveals areas of discrepancy between ideal and actual behavior. Walking, observing, and asking questions are common components of a RA.

Identify key variables

Next, identify some key variables to investigate. Ask the people themselves about what key variables are most relevant to the research project in focus. For example, if the project concerns introducing appropriate technology[5] (see Canadian Hunger Foundation 1976 on AT) to improve the economic status of those who are most in need, ask about local variables indicative of poverty.

Some variables, such as house types, are readily visible. For example, in looking at house structures, you could count the number of metal roofs versus grass roofs. Other factors, however, such as access to the wealth of a wealthy relative, may not be so readily visible. Also, social stratification and means of identifying that stratification may not be readily visible. You may want to look at access to resources, occupations, self-sufficiency in grain for a household, multiple sources of income (e.g., some members of the household migrated to urban areas and send remittances home; members of the household may hold multiple jobs), self-help or cooperative patterns, and so forth.

Use aerial inspections where appropriate

Use aerial inspections for such things as land use, crop zoning, irrigation patterns, and residences (Chambers 1985:410). Aerial inspections should be used only where they are appropriate and locally acceptable, and when your budget can afford them. If they arouse local or national suspicion that you are a spy and that you are not doing what you claim to be doing, then they should be discontinued or avoided.

Work together in research pairs

You can collect useful information through an exploratory method in which individuals are paired. RESEARCH PAIRS include a social scientist paired with another person, such as a local farmer or an agricultural scientist. Each day the two work together as they interview, observe the social situation, and engage in participant observation where appropriate, then in the evenings discuss their findings. This debriefing time provides an opportunity to assess their data and plan what further data to collect. If several are working together as a team in conducting a RA, rotate who works together with whom in order to enable

---

[5]Appropriate technology (AT) is practical application of knowledge to the methods and materials used in industry or commerce. In many developing countries where laborers are plentiful and capital resources are limited, AT is often labor intensive. It may involve simple small-scale technologies; and it is cost effective both in terms of materials used and energy consumed.

People who desire to introduce AT need to work within the existing cultural patterns, so that the AT is tailored to the felt needs and problems of the targeted community.

members of the research team to stimulate each other to understand what is going on and what additional data they need to collect.

Engage in other field methods

Other field methods Chambers recommends in RAs as follows:

> The use of small informal samples and very short lists of questions; transects (for example, walking off at right angles from a road); specialized investigations seeking a narrow band of information, such as rural innovators' services; "piggy-backing" on research in progress by asking social anthropologists in the field or those conducting longitudinal surveys to investigate a question, adding it, as it were, to their list; or monitoring a small panel of families who are understood in social anthropological depth, revisiting them at intervals to learn about changes and how and why they have come about. (1985:410)

While there are obvious problems with conducting a RA, especially the possibility of superficiality and errors, concentrated efforts to obtain good data and utilization of cross-checking to verify specific information may allow you to conduct a RA profitably.

Collecting RA data

A few suggestive questions when conducting a RA include the following:

1. What are the physical characteristics and constraints of the community? What is the physical layout of the community (water supply, food supply, waste disposal, ceremonial areas, paths and roads, markets, religious buildings, etc.)?
2. Who talks to whom, and with what effect (Spaeth 1991b:5)? What is the social structure of the community? Who makes decisions in what areas? How are decisions made? What are the networks of information within the community?
3. What are the specific perceived needs of the community in focus? Who in the community perceives those needs? What are their strategies for meeting those needs?
4. Who keeps what kinds of promises to whom and when? What happens or what sanctions come into effect if promises are broken (Spaeth 1991b:5)?
5. What are time concepts within the community?
6. What do people get excited about? What do they identify as good and bad?
7. What motivates local businessmen? Is it profit, prestige, providing for one's personal needs at wholesale prices, power, maintaining good interpersonal relations, or some combination of these?
8. What are local worldview assumptions that must be taken into account for a particular proposed development project? What are their beliefs about fate, bad luck, supernatural beings and powers, magic, propitious times for undertaking projects, etc.?
9. What local technologies are being used or might be used to meet their perceived needs?
10. Have previous development projects been implemented in the area? What were the outcomes of such projects? If some failed, why did they fail? If some succeeded, why did they succeed?
11. What use is made of credit within the local economic structure? What secures repayment of loans?

12. Do patron-client relations predominate in this society? Does the community also have relations built on contracts?
13. Is land held communally? Is land inalienable, or has it been privatized?
14. What may be used to pay specific debts? Is it money, land, or some commodity?
15. What is the typical division of labor between men and women within the community? What are men's interests as opposed to women's interests? Who will be positively or negatively affected by the outcome of the development project?

The above list of questions is suggestive only of the types of issues to investigate when doing a RA. Specific questions will depend on the information desired for the development project envisioned.

Sometimes an interdisciplinary team is most effective collecting useful information about local practices, knowledge, perceptions including the local presuppositions or understanding of their worldview, and local forms of organization including their decision-making structure. For example, the socioeconomic component of a RA could benefit from the input of economists, sociologists, and anthropologists, while sociolinguistic surveys would benefit from contributions of linguists, sociolinguists, and anthropologists.

Participatory rural appraisals

In participatory rural appraisals the emphasis is on the participation of local people in the decision-making and implementation of the appraisal. Its methodology also differs from a RAs discussed above. For example, Pratt and Liozos found that,

> One characteristic PRA procedure involves the initiators, on entering a community, to spend some time trying their hands at standard local production tasks, such as chopping wood, ploughing, weeding, or irrigating—anything needing know-how and manual dexterity. They invite the local people to comment critically on the way they perform the tasks, and since they normally perform them clumsily, there is plenty of scope for them to be corrected. This "ice-breaker" serves several purposes. First, it allows the villagers to see the visitors less as powerful, high-status people and more as vulnerable and fallible, particularly in terms of the locality and the skills it needs….From the visitors' point of view, the lesson is a reminder that the villagers are skilled people, who have survived in their environment through the development of locally-appropriate knowledge. Thus, the equation educated expert: villager = knowledgeable person: ignorant person is erased... (1992:74)

The researchers and the local people begin to perform some basic data-gathering and data-analysis together. Hopefully, this will communicate an open-mindedness so that the research team communicates well the development project goals and elicits local support.

24

Social Impact Analysis

The essence of a good evaluation is for it to be a practical exercise in team work, involving evaluators and the staff of the programme being studied. (Batchelor 1993:148)

SOCIAL IMPACT ANALYSIS (SIA), also termed a social soundness analysis or a social impact assessment, is a method for assessing social change resulting from development projects. In the United States this method received impetus through the enactment in 1969 of the National Environmental Policy Act (NEPA) that requires assessment of the projected consequences of a specific project and an evaluation of those consequences. Similarly, in any development project a SIA is important for introducing change that is minimally disruptive of the culture yet beneficial to it. In development projects, too often there have been negative social effects.

Development projects need to be successful[6] from various perspectives including those of the development agencies, the beneficiaries in the target culture, the personnel involved in introducing change, the local, regional, and national governments, and the funding sources. Each of these categories may have their own perspective and vision of the project. As an example, McMillan states, "Four distinct levels of development visions are related here: those of the foreign donors, those of the Burkinabè government, those of the settlers, and finally, those of researchers like myself" (1995:xxviii–xxix). Each of these groups may have their own definition of what a "successful" project will look like.

From the prospect of the development agency and foreign donors, success can be assessed by evaluating whether or not projects achieve their stated goals and stay within their projected budgets. From the perspective of the local people it may be in terms of their economic advancement. From the perspective of local university scholars who study development projects conducted locally, they may adopt the development model of the development agency. Hopefully, they will think through the local implications of any development project so that it accords with the local values and goals of the people involved.

Rural assessment is usually done prior to implementation of development projects in order to feed into their planning and implementation in a culturally appropriate manner; the impact of projects on culture can be great and have far reaching consequences, even ones quite unforeseen. Hence, the need for careful consideration of possible consequences. Both

---

[6]Most people and institutions engaged in development need documentation of demonstrated successful projects. For example, the Economic Development Institute of The World Bank published a book entitled *Successful Development in Africa* (1989). A second World Bank book on a similar topic is entitled *Sub-Saharan Africa, From Crisis to Sustainable Growth* (1989).

during the implementation stage of the project and at the end, an SIA evaluates the outcomes of the project. Did it meet the goals of the proposal, and did it stay within its planned perimeters? Did the assumptions upon which it was based accurately reflect the local worldview assumptions?

Since the 1969 act, a number of models of implementation of SIAs have been proposed. Since different development projects have different goals, the specific data collected by the researcher will depend on the purpose of the study.

Typically, social impact analyses have the following components: sociocultural feasibility, potential spread effect, and social impact. The sociocultural feasibility component requires examination of local values, beliefs, social structure, and organization of the target population. The potential spread looks at potential diffusion to other groups. Finally, the social impact component seeks to identify the distribution of benefits and burdens to specific groups in the population (see Derman and Whiteford 1985:23).

Project identification document

Social impact analyses are part of the research necessary for a Project Identification Document that needs to address five areas. Greeley (1986:233–34) identifies these as follows:

1. The *sociocultural context* of the project area.
2. The *beneficiaries*, including those who benefit directly from the project as well as those who might benefit indirectly from it. Those who might be adversely affected should also be considered. People of different gender, socioeconomic strata, and ages need to be considered.
3. *Possible participation* of men and women in the project. This aspect of the study should include social, economic, and political factors as contributors to or constraints on the project objectives.
4. The *sociocultural feasibility* of the project.
5. The *impact* of the planned development project. For example, does the project help the people meet their basic human needs such as food sufficiency through equitable sustainable growth? Will it unfairly impact one group differently than another group in the area?

When a development agency introduces a specific planned project for a minority ethnic group, more often than not that group enters the world market system at the bottom rung of the social, economic, and political class structure of the wider society. Members of that ethnic group become peasants. As the group moves into a peasant status, members of that group find themselves at the margins of the system with little control over prices for their commodities or over specific decisions that the majority culture imposes upon them. They may become dependent in a way that they were not prior to the specific development project. This is an area that political economists have explored under the rubric of dependency theory.

Each of these components of a SIA within the Project Identification Document research usually requires some quantitative data.

Quantitative data collection

Choice of data to collect will depend upon the specific project; this section is of necessity rather broad, and points to what you or the research team you work with might include.

Quantitative data collected in a social impact analysis are usually extensive. Such data usually include a demographic profile of the population in focus. This demographic profile is also termed the demographic regime. Such a profile or regime includes the count of the population, and may include marriage data, fertility rates, and information about mortality and morbidity. Since these are the same types of data discussed in the chapter on demography, consult chapter 11 for aid in collecting a demographic profile of the population.

Data may also include information on socioeconomic factors of the population, such as labor force participation rates, information on employment, income structure of the population, gross national product (GNP) and the relevance of that figure to the population in focus, land ownership patterns, and kinship relations as they might impact the proposed project. Since any population has a division of labor by sex and age, collect information on sex and age specific socioeconomic variables.

Collecting data on income and other measures of economic status can be extremely difficult when working with people involved in subsistence agriculture, pastoralism, hunting and gathering, etc. In order to arrive at some measure of economic status, you might want to collect data on factors such as the amount of land farmed (usually stated locally in terms of the number of plots farmed), number of animals reared, and amount of crops harvested. Further, information about land tenure is important, including specific data on the extent to which people follow the stated land tenure ideals. Some researchers have also collected data on commodities owned such as automobiles, motorcycles, bicycles, radios, televisions, VCRs, generators, and refrigerators.

As an example, if researchers were to study market patterns among the Asante in Ghana, they would need to focus on traders of different commodities. For most commodities there are chiefs who control prices, allocate space for traders, settle disputes, maintain trading networks for acquisition of trade items, etc. If researchers want to understand the economic factors relative to tomatoes, they would need to start by interviewing the woman who is chief of the tomato saleswomen.

Other quantifiable data that you may want to collect include social networks, and community organizations and facilities. These would include voluntary organizations such as churches, temples, and mosques. If doing research in some parts of Africa, they would also include information on the age grade system and an understanding of the relevance of this traditional system within the current context.

Voluntary associations often play key roles in the integration of societies; in any development projects these should not be overlooked. You may want to look at the contribution of voluntary association to economics. For example, some voluntary savings associations collect dues from their members. Each month one member receives the amount all members of that association give for that month. That member uses the money to replenish his or her inventory for his or her business venture. This type of economic voluntary association often occurs within local markets and serves a very useful function. There are a limited number of slots for persons in such economic associations. For example, some are limited to twelve persons, with one slot allocated for each month. Knowledge of such associations may help you in consideration of a development project in the area.

Other areas on which you may wish to collect data include crime rates and types of crimes, punishment or rehabilitation of criminals, and social services available. You might also want to look at means of social control that do not necessarily involve the police or military, but rather informal factors such as gossip, ridicule, ostracism, and insult songs and plays.

Knowledge, attitudes, and practices survey

Prior to planning and implementing a development project, some agencies call for a knowledge, attitudes, and practices (KAP) survey on the topic of interest to the development project agency. For example, in a KAP survey on water and sanitation conducted by Green (1987) in Swaziland, he assessed the following:

> (1) Human resources in the traditional health sector; (2) the areas and extent of cooperation possible between the traditional and modern health sectors, with special reference to the prevention and treatment of diarrheal diseases; (3) the extent to which alternative systems of health care had developed for the consumer; (4) customary law, modern legislation, and government policies regarding traditional healing and healers; (5) prospects for the development of a national traditional healers association, and a possible role for the MOH [Swaziland Ministry of Health] in promoting, monitoring, and liaising with such an association; and (6) the potential for the paraprofessional training of certain types of traditional healers (Green, in Podolefsky and Brown 1991:202).

Since acceptance of a specific development project is frequently dependent upon the values held by the population, studying values and taking them into account in the implementation of the project may be key as to whether or not it is accepted. Various values questionnaires have been developed, though each is usually culture specific.

Project paper

Many development agencies, including USAID, incorporate social impact analysis within the larger Project Paper (PP) which includes the final project design. This includes the following analyses: technical, institutional, economic, financial, social, and environmental. Depending on various factors and personnel, one of these analyses may exert influence over the other analyses in the final implementation of the project.

Too often the social impact analysis, a key component to the success of any development project, does not have the influence it should. Only later when people begin to ask why a project failed do people examine and realize the importance of the social impact aspects of the project. Far too many development projects fail. Ingersoll, Sullivan, and Lenkerd (1981:2, as quoted in Morgan 1985:24) examined the influence of social analysis in AID projects; and they found that social analysis influenced only twenty-five percent of the projects of the forty-eight Project Papers analyzed. Part of the reason for this low impact was the variable quality of the social analyses themselves. Further, social researchers often focused on the target group without also looking at the basic goals, assumptions, and logic of the project. In other words, social scientists need to interact both with the local social situation and with the technical analysts in order to have an integrated, comprehensive perspective of proposed projects. Both potential positive and negative consequences of proposed projects should be taken into account.

Practical considerations

Development involves working with people to meet their felt wants and basic needs. Some of those basic needs for a population include (1) provision of a clean water supply, (2) safe means of cooking, (3) adequate storage for grains, (4) provision of an adequate health delivery system, (5) adequate shelter, and (6) sufficient food.

Beginning with the provision of an adequate water supply, in order to eliminate problems with inadequate or impure water supply, governments, development projects, and voluntary agencies have often focused on water issues. Populations have suffered because of schistosomiasis, guinea worm, and other parasites all because of impure sources of water. Wells and dams have been common solutions to this problem. Plans and implementation must be carefully thought through before the beginning. Concerning water problems and other related issues, Batchelor states,

> Standing on a hill in the north east of Chad Republic, I looked down on an oasis with the pool of water and trees, around which a village had grown. But, for almost as far as the eye could see, there was not a blade of grass. Sheep, goats, cattle, horses and camels had been driven in from many kilometres away, two or three times a week, to drink as much water as they could. Naturally, while there, they also ate every scrap of grass in a very large area around the pool.
>
> During the Sahelian drought, watering places were littered with carcasses. Although they had enough to drink, animals were dying of starvation.
>
> Creating dams is an excellent method of conserving water, but the way in which we do it must be appropriate to other needs in the area. It may mean, for example, that we should think in terms of many small dams rather than a few big ones. In this way there could be less concentration of animals in any one spot and, hopefully, grass for all. (1993:104–05)

Changing development plans

The issue of changing development project plans with respect to planned resettlement and riverblindness control in Burkina Faso is discussed by McMillan as follows:

> The development theories and political exigencies that guided donor funding and national planning for the Sahel have changed dramatically in the two decades since 1973. The early (1974–81) top-down AVV [Authorité des Aménagements des Vallées des Volta] planned-settlement model and agricultural program, which focused on intensive commercial cotton production, was designed under one set of planning theories and evaluated under yet another; this early model was found wanting and eventually set aside. Nonetheless, the residual effects of this older planning model—set in motion in 1974—are still evident in the 1990s. They are evident in the roads and bridges that were developed in a vast area of Burkina's relatively fertile, isolated river basins, and evident again in the design of an expensive array of new rural education and health programs. The same model left an indelible mark on the training and careers of one of the most highly trained generations of Burkina's agricultural extension service. All of these interventions continue to be important. The lives (and beliefs) of thousands of farmers, policy makers, and researchers were also changed. Such long-lasting project legacies cannot be easily dismissed.
>
> For policy planners and researchers to dispose of one set of planning theories for another seemingly more appropriate set misses the point. There are important grains of truth in almost all of the development theories that have guided foreign aid and government investment in Africa since the Second World War. (1995:xxix)

This Onchocerciasis (riverblindness) Control Program (OCP) has been very successful through its long-term strategy in the control and near elemination of riverblindness, eleminating it in the human populations in eleven saharan West African countries. It has also attacked the black fly which lives in fast moving water and carries the parasite. While the OCP is not able to restore sight to those already blind, it can prevent any more people from going blind. People are now able to move back near the rivers and farm in this fertile area.

Length of development project

While there is no set length for development projects, the changes envisioned by such projects need to be viewed over a time span. For example, "Dalton...believed that one could not expect concrete, genuine social and economic change in periods of less than fifteen years" (McMillan 1995:xviii).

Evaluations

In any development project there must be ongoing evaluation of the development project. It occurs initially, as in determining whether or not a specific project is feasible, locally acceptable, wise, financially sound, and so on. It should continue to be evaluated throughout the length of the project. Evaluation is for the purposes of adjustment of what is being done, termination of the project if that is what is indicated, and decisions about new directions of the project. As a minimum, there should be evaluations initially, mid-project, and after completion. However, the number of evaluations depends upon the length, complexity, financial resources expended, and so on of the specific project.

Why do evaluations? The most basic reason is that development projects have a very high failure rate. The area where development projects most often fail is that of failure to take cultural factors seriously.

Where there is a team of two individuals involved in a project, e.g., in a language project, evaluations are often very threatening to them. They take any criticisms of the project as personal failure. Hence, they shy away from evaluations. A different, more constructive attitude would be, What can be done to make this project a success? How can we work with the community so that the project becomes theirs? How can we help you succeed in this project?

This chapter draws heavily from social impact analyses used by large aid agencies such as USAID and World Bank. To what extent does this type of analysis relate to the work of the average cultural researcher or to smaller scale development projects? The answer depends on the goals of the research or of the project. For those interested in practical applications of their research for community development or intercultural community work, assessing the social impact of a proposed project is essential.

Schanely (1983:3–4), building on principles of Larry and Willa Yost, suggests the following principles for local level community development:

1. Start where the people are.
2. Train trainers who can train others...
3. Conduct training in the village or as close to home as possible.
4. Introduce new ideas only after relationships and confidence have been established, and show how these new ideas contribute to the solving of problems the group already has.

5. Encourage interdependent relationships.
6. Involve as many of the local people as possible in all activities from the start.
7. Identify and involve local leadership.
8. Keep the program simple and uncomplicated with only one or two major thrusts at a time.
9. Cooperate with the local, regional, and national governments.
10. Train in locally acceptable facilities and format, using locally acceptable methods.

The role of partner with local people often falls on you, whether or not this is one of your primary goals in your fieldwork. SIAs were included in this book, even if they are only marginally important to most cultural researchers, because development agents who are engaged in conducting SIAs occasionally ask you, if you are doing long-term field research, for your assistance. They term this piggy-backing on the research of others who have an in-depth knowledge of the local culture. Therefore, those who do long-term field research need to have some insight as to the nature of the potential social impact of proposed development projects in their area.

25

Other Field Methods:
Time Allocation Studies, Communicative Events, Modeling, LinguaLinks

The creativity of humans has always amazed me. This creativity is evident in the continued development of research methods for collecting cultural data. As the proverb asserts, "Variety is the spice of life," in research methods as in most other areas of our lives.

Most cultural fieldworkers use a variety of research methods with the goal of discovering patterns in culture. Typically, fieldworkers use a mix of qualitative and quantitative methods. All should engage in participant observation since this is the most basic field method. Many collect a few life histories to use as illustrative material or case studies to bring the abstractions of ethnographic theory to the lives of individuals. Most do some kinship investigation. The amount of kinship study done should ideally be related to how important kinship is for understanding a given culture. In a small clan-based society it is very important, while this is less so in an urban study. Further, many do some survey on a topic that gives quantitative results.

There are other important field methods that are not included in this book, e.g., psychological tests, suggestions for study of ritual, art, and theater. This is not because these topics are unimportant; rather, focus has been on the methods that seem more important for general cultural research.

Many anthropologists and other social scientists are looking very carefully at how cultural data are collected. For example, Sage Publications publishes a series of books on various components of the fieldwork process. *Cultural Anthropology Methods (CAM) Newsletter* is devoted to field methods (see appendix for further information on this periodical).

Universities regularly have courses on cultural research methods, qualitative research, statistics, and proposal writing. Others address how to write up the results of the data collected. Before concluding, a few other specialized field methods are discussed, including time allocation studies and the study of communicative events.

Time allocation studies

TIME ALLOCATION STUDIES investigate how people spend their time. Various useful results have come from such studies. For example, Ben Wallace (personal communication, Dallas,

295

1989) and researchers on his team influenced government policies when they found that in rural Bangladesh women spend twice as much time in farming activities as men do. Prior to their time allocation research, almost all government agricultural policies and extension work had focused on men. Their results influenced the government to begin to aim agricultural programs towards women, too, and include them within its agricultural policies.

In a time allocation study among the Negrito Agta in the Philippines, Headland (1986) addressed the question of why the Agta do not take up farming. He documents various unsuccessful attempts by non-Agta to coerce them to do so. Headland's findings demonstrated that the Agta can make a better living by their hunting and gathering subsistence pattern than by farming. It is not because they do not know how to farm—an assumption some outsiders have wrongly held.

Time allocation studies have addressed the question of the amount of time the !Kung San in southern Africa spend in hunting and gathering activities (Lee 1979). Lee and others sought to answer the question, are hunter and gatherers the original affluent societies or do they live on the edge of subsistence? His results indicated that while they are not affluent, they do have sufficient calories that provide for their basic needs and that they do not spend an inordinate amount of time in their subsistence activities.

Time allocation studies can answer questions such as how much time do men and women each spend in farming, commercial activities, fishing, domestic activities, leisure activities, etc. In preparing to collect data for a time allocation project, develop a form to be filled in with people and with a list of activities community members are likely to engage in. For example, a table for university students' use of time might be as in (68). Within each box fill in the amount of time each student engages in that activity per day, then tabulate them for overall averages.

(68) Time allocation work chart for university students

Activities   Students

	Tom	Dick	Jane	Sarah
Attend class				
Study				
Work				
Eat				
Wash and dry clothes				
Shop				
Talk on telephone				
Talk with friends about nonacademic matters				
Talk about academics				
Attend school functions				
Attend nonschool functions				
Sleep				
Other (specify)				

Time allocation observations may be conducted for various lengths of time and at various times throughout the day and night. Some researchers do SPOT OBSERVATIONS for limited time periods. Spot observations allow you time to use other field methods while also obtaining useful data on how people spend their time.

The variables considered within time allocation studies can focus on a multitude of things. For example, they can look at such factors as levels of nutrition, food production, health status, leisure, and differences in productivity by age and sex of individuals observed.

Broad categories of ways people spend their time are production time, consumption time, and free time. Production time encompasses work activities, in which goods are produced and services rendered. It usually refers to work time spent outside the home. Consumption time refers to time used for consumption of goods; this category includes time utilized in eating, watching television, playing some game such as soccer, attending an amusement park, etc. Finally, free time is spent in rest, sleep, chatting, visiting, and in idleness. Whether using these categories or ones you set up that are specific to your field project, in reporting your results be careful to specify what you used. Further, specify who is being studied including age and sex.

When doing a time allocation study on some economic patterns, e.g., data from horticulturalists, collect data for one complete year because activities vary greatly from one crop season to another. The time of weeding and harvesting differs similarly. If you are studying pastoralists, the yearly cycle is also important. Often you find a dry season pasture and migration to a wet season pasture pattern.

Da Corta and Venkateshwarlu address time allocation methodology as follows,

> The optimum methodology for collecting time allocation and income data is to monitor each individual daily, but this is time-consuming and intrusive. A more widely used method is to make an inquiry once or twice a month, asking villagers to record or recall their labour use and income for the preceding period. In studies where repeat surveys over the course of the entire year are not possible, however, the long-term recall method described below may prove to be a worthwhile option.
>
> To construct proportions of (1) time allocated to different activities and (2) income earned from different activities, we followed several steps:
>
> - *Listing* all activities and discussing comparisons among them.
> - *Ranking* activities according to their relative importance.
> - *Construction proportions.* (1993:115)

In listing activities, they had villagers list their economic activities prior to 1950, then rank them from 1950 onwards in terms importance in contribution towards the time they spent and the income they derived from them, whether of first, second, or third importance. In constructing proportions, they requested villagers to estimate in fractions what proportion of time they spent on various activities and what proportion of income they derived from each of those activities.

Results from time allocation studies can indicate societies that have a time surplus or are time affluent as well as societies that have a time famine. Clearly, there is a continuum between the two.

Communicative events

Communicative event analysis grows out of a sociolinguistic approach. Hymes (1974) proposed the analysis of the ethnography of communication, and Saville-Troike (1982) expanded his work by discussing communicative events. In an ethnography that uses the communication approach, focus on the speech community—a community that shares a common culture, common identity as seen in its local name, social life network for contact, common folklore, and history. This approach looks at who speaks to whom, when do they do so, how, and why. Thus, it involves the study of oral performances.

Three discrete units define the communicative event for analysis:

1. The communicative situation (the context within which the communication occurs). It includes the participants and the setting,
2. The communicative event, and
3. The communicative act (Saville-Troike 1982).

Study of specific communicative events builds on basic data collected on a culture, including data on the social organization, the political and economic organization, artistic information, common knowledge and beliefs, information about language usage, and the linguistic code.

The components of a communicative event include the following:

1. The genre or type of event (see chapter 20),
2. The topic,
3. The purpose or function,
4. The setting,
5. The participants,
6. The message form,
7. The message content,
8. The act sequence,
9. The rules of interaction, and
10. The norms of interpretation.

Collect data on each component of the communicative event. In the analysis phase of the research, look at relationships between various components of the communicative event. For example, you might ask, How do the genre and topic influence each other? How do the genre and setting relate to each other? What relationship exists between the genre, the topic, the setting, the participants, and the message form?

An example of an analysis of a communicative event is illustrated in a Ngambay example in (69) analyzed by Ndjerareou (1986:44–45) from Chad (note: P = participant).

(69) Ngambay marital negotiation

Function/purpose:
To obtain a formal agreement from the prospective bride's parents.

Setting:
Prospective bride's home. It takes place in the morning.

Participants:
    P1 Male; mature adult, prospective bride's father
    P2 Male; mature adult, prospective bride's father's brother
    P3 Male; mature adult, prospective groom's father's brother
    P4 Male; mature adult, prospective groom's father's other brother

Message form:
    Verbal form: spoken Ngambay, silence

Act sequence:
    P3, says "Our children are visiting each other for a while now. We think it is appropriate for us to come and listen to what you have to say."
    P2 replies, "No one ever gives birth to a child and marries him. Since no one can do that, we think we are doing what we have to do. We are aware of our son's visit to our daughter. We do not have anything to say, but we want to remind our son that we are not the young lady's only parent."

Rules of interaction:
    1. The groom's father's brother speaks first because he is presenting a demand. Only the prospective bride's uncle replies, because the father cannot speak when the negotiation concerns his own offspring.
    2. This is a very tense moment, so there is always a long pause between the interactions. Each person takes time to think over his response before uttering it. Also in this kind of situation, one could note that "our" is used by parents on both sides (prospective bride's and groom's) rather than "my" and "your."

Rules of interpretation:
    1. The suitor's father's brother is referring to the visits of his brother's son to the prospective bride. It is considered that both are involved even though the young lady has not yet gone to the young man's place.
    2. The prospective bride's father's brother is saying that for a marriage to happen, somebody has to give his daughter away. The sentence itself is an official agreement. The suitor has to visit the other members of the extended family unit.
    3. An intervention of the father would be inappropriate and interpreted to mean that he does not care for his own child (own blood), as he is so eager to give her away.

Modeling

Modeling involves developing representations of the real world including its ecosystems. Modeling is most often a part of research in cultural ecology as an aid to understanding how people adjust to their ecosystems. Models are means of simplifying reality and are aids of understanding processes that produce observable results.

In developing a model, identify the processes that are relevant, processes that are observable and that can be measured. Next, based on the model you can make predictions of how things work in the real world, then check those predictions against the real world to access their accuracy. Based on your observations, refine your model.

In cultural ecology, researchers often assume that the system they are modeling is closed or bounded. Closed systems contrast with open systems, ones with constant input from outside the system. In fact, all cultural ecological systems are open systems by virtue of people being present in them. Some models assume equilibrium, though, in fact, all cultural systems change and have mechanisms to adapt to change.

Some field researchers do modeling of known factors in an ecosystem either prior to field research or soon after arriving on the field. Once a model is set up, then a researcher can use this model to form hypotheses. On the field, data gathered can confirm, modify, or refute the model.

In the field situation at an intermediate stage of their research, researchers may do simulations. Moran states, "Simulation refers to a technique for solving and studying problems by following a model's changes over time" (1979:12). By simulation the researcher is seeking to find out how different parts function and contribute to the functioning of the whole system.

LinguaLinks

LinguaLinks is an interactive computer field manual for linguistic, sociolinguistic, literacy, and anthropological field research that is being developed by SIL. The anthropological section provides directions on specific cultural topics as well as on field methods. For some topics it provides questions and areas for investigation, as well as guidance and relevance for a language project.

Completion of fieldwork

Whereas the concentration throughout this book thus far has been on specific field methods, it is important how you complete your fieldwork while still on the field. Here are some suggestions that you might want to implement as appropriate for your field situation.

Share tentative research results

Share with some of the local people some of your tentative research results. This may involve meeting together with local leaders and others who have shared information with you. This helps especially if you have used a research instrument such as an interview schedule or questionnaire. They will likely be curious about what you have found out from all who have responded. This can be problematic especially if you have not coded your data or run statistical tests on them. See the side box for an example.

Wilson agrees on the desirability of sharing some of your preliminary findings with the local people. He states,

> Throughout your work be open in informing people about your growing understanding of the situation, and tell them what you will be writing about. In my experience, people are fascinated and engage intellectually in a highly stimulating manner. Before leaving, organise

---

Preliminary field data results

Part way through data collection, I talked with a missionary in the area who was curious about the answer to one of the questions on the interview schedule I was administering. I took out my solar-powered hand calculator and made some rough calculations. I then provided him with a rough result from the question. He found it incredible that approximately twenty percent of "Christians" did not know who Jesus claimed to be. His response was, "Are we doing that poor of a job?"

meetings with members of the community and officials (both as groups and individually) to share your main findings and elicit their reactions. In addition to enabling you to convey your thanks and learn more from them as partners in the research process, such presentations can act as catalysts to local debate. Even if your presentation is limited it can enable, for example, the views of powerless groups in the population to be articulated alongside those of the dominant, and thus contribute to the initiation of developments in the future. (1993:189)

You may want to leave a brief summary of your work and some preliminary findings with one or more respected community leaders.

Sponsor a celebration

A popular option that many fieldworkers have used is to sponsor a feast or more generally to give a party. If you choose to do so, check with insiders of that culture concerning what is culturally appropriate. This includes publicizing it, selecting food and arranging for its preparation, choosing a site for it, deciding on the entertainment, and implementing it. Be prepared to learn further about the culture when you do so. For example, Lee gave a Christmas feast for the !Kung, and the !Kung used it to teach him about the consequences of his not having shared his food with them throughout his time with them (Lee 1969). His account of this adventure provides delightful reading of how the !Kung taught him about sharing and humility.

Having mentioned this as a possibility, note that towards the end of fieldwork many find their funds dwindling and, hence, may not be in a good financial position to sponsor a party. Whether you are able to do so or not, you still need to thank those who have graciously helped you in your fieldwork. This includes thanking local officials who have allowed you to do the research.

Support a local project

One possibility is to consider sponsoring or supporting a local project. Local felt needs quickly become evident to you when you live cross-culturally. You might think about what you could do to help meet one or more of those needs. It is probably best to wait until you have done sufficient fieldwork to know the community before deciding on which one you might want to help with. This gives you time to know the cultural context, and it may help you avoid identifying with only one faction which may be agitating for one project as opposed to another community faction.

Fulfill your responsibility to the local sponsoring organization

You need to fulfill any requirements that your local sponsoring organization may call upon you to fulfill. See the side box for an example.

> **Fulfilling university obligations**
>
> The local university that supported my research associateship requested that I present a public lecture on some of my preliminary research findings prior to leaving the country. The lecture I gave became a paper that was to be published locally by the sponsoring department within the university. Further, they requested a copy of my final write-up for the university library. I took it as my responsibility to comply with their requests.

26

Completion of a Field Project: Publication of Research Results

The end of a matter is better than its beginning... (Ecclesiastes 7:8a)

After a fruitful season of field research, you are ready to complete your project. You probably have used various research methods to gather and analyze cultural data; now you need to write up your research results. The model and format you select for your write-up depends on numerous factors. For example, what are the goals of your research project? To what uses will your results be put? What is your theoretical perspective that forms the framework for the presentation of the results? The complexities and even contradictions within different societies results in some scholars questioning presentation of cultural data within only one theoretical model (Marcus 1986:10). Since cultural data is interesting, there is likely to be an outlet for publication of the data you have been collecting.

Authorship

Decide whether you are going to be the author of the write-up or whether it is to be a co-authored manuscript. Remember that co-authorship of articles with members of the ethnic group or with local scholars is important both for more accurate manuscripts and for building good interpersonal relations with others in the country of the research. This is especially important when they have contributed significantly in data collection and analysis.

Another example of co-authorship is collaboration with colleagues on a manuscript in which each brings his or her own expertise. For example, some like to farm out the analysis of statistical data to others who are competent in this field. As such, that person(s) should receive recognition as a co-author.

Professors often co-author articles with students, especially with student research assistants. This is beneficial for both the professors and their students.

Goals of write-up

Traditionally anthropologists wrote ethnographies about the cultures they studied. As the field of cultural research has developed, the incredible complexity of cultures has resulted in field researchers narrowing their focus. Today, few have the goal of writing a complete ethnography, if such is or was ever possible. A complete ethnography would take a lifetime of research and writing, and even then it would be incomplete. Yet one can usefully write a less ambitious ethnographic sketch which covers each of the main areas of culture (e.g., economics, political organization, social organization, religious organization, and material culture).

Begin with papers to be presented orally to a "friendly" audience of your colleagues. Whereas they will critique what you present, their goodwill should help you to make a good paper better. This prepares you to present your findings to a wider audience, as at a conference, whether local, regional, national, or international. The feedback you receive through oral presentations prepares you to turn your paper into a journal article, thesis, dissertation, report, or book.

Beginning to write

Begin early to write up your results. Make it a discipline to write something each day. Prior to beginning, outline your write-up. If writing is difficult for you, realize that the daily discipline of writing can be learned.

Write with your audience in mind. It is often more useful to think of one individual or of a few individuals for whom you are writing, than to think of a general audience. It may surprise you to realize that in so writing, you will end up making it interesting to a general audience. Consider writing with the people you have studied as your audience.

One possible way to get you started writing is to begin by writing the goal of your personal cultural learning. This can result in writing both for yourself and writing for your colleagues who are working in similar cultures or in a similar theoretical framework so that they can give you feedback. That feedback can teach you a great deal, and it can also encourage them in their work. For example, do two related ethnic groups have similar origins narratives? Do they have similar marital patterns and clan structure?

Modules

Write your results in modules, each of which covers a specific topic. Put your stress on the topic you have the most data on. Be aware that different cultures have complexities in different areas. For example, traditional Bajju culture and other related ethnic groups displayed great creativity in their marital patterns. Because some of these patterns are specific to their culture area, other researchers and I have written on those marital patterns (see McKinney 1992, Levine and Sangree 1980).

In writing, detach yourself from the manuscript so that you are willing to edit the text and to accept editorial suggestions from others. Extensive editing usually is required to produce well-written texts. It helps to put your manuscript away for a while, say a week or two, and then come back to reread with a fresh perspective and revise it.

Use of ethnographic present

Be careful in your writing to specify the time period to which your results apply. If you are writing in the ethnographic present, specify what time period is included in it.

Illustrative material

Include case studies as illustrative material in your write-up. Doing so makes your material more interesting, and people who read it will likely feel they can visualize the people you are writing about. Even when you are primarily presenting quantified data, include sufficient detail about the culture so that your audience does not become bored in reading. Also include direct quotations of what people actually said. Local phrases, collocations, and folk terms add color and interest to your write-up.

Use of "I"

One question that can plague you is whether to write using the first-person singular subject pronoun "I." Traditionally, scholars have used the impersonal third-person pronoun, resulting in more boring, less personal manuscripts. Use of "I" or "we" to refer to the researcher was strictly forbidden, and in some circles this continues to be the case. However, this position is changing in the writings of social scientists based on the fact that the very presence of outside researchers changes the situation. While those changes may be minimal, yet they are present. Postmodern anthropologists insist that you must include yourself in a write-up. This recognizes and includes the fact that cultures change by the very fact of your presence there. You, therefore, need to include yourself in your write-ups.

However, check with the publisher's guidelines concerning this issue. If the publisher continues to insist on use of third-person pronouns, write to fulfill the requirements of that publisher. Whatever you finally decide, above all, be consistent.

Use of words in foreign languages

When you write up your research results, include some of the most significant indigenous terms together with their translations. Doing so will give other researchers the opportunity to verify the data you report. Be sure to include a glossary in the appendix of your publication, other than in a journal article, so that readers can remind themselves of the meanings of words.

A word of caution is appropriate here. Do not overload your publication with foreign words. It can overwhelm your reader. Use them sparingly.

Publication

The importance of publishing research data cannot be overemphasized. Many cultural researchers work with little-known ethnic groups. The data they collect need to be made available to the larger community in an appropriately sensitive manner. Many do invaluable research without their results ever seeing the printed page for others to read and benefit from.

There is always the temptation to wait until you know just a little more, or until the manuscript is more polished, or until you collect more information, or some other such reason. There is, however, always more data to collect and more polishing that can be done. Sometimes it is advisable to publish what you write at an earlier stage, and indicate that this research represents "preliminary" data analysis. If you collect other relevant data or devise a more insightful analysis, another paper can add to, or lead to, revision of an earlier publication.

Theses and dissertations

Much cultural field research is done with the goal of writing theses and dissertations. These rather stilted writing works have the goal of clearly presenting a piece of scholarly research. The argumentation needs to be tight and to demonstrate that you have a grasp of the material. Further, they demonstrate that you have completed new research that adds to knowledge in general. They give evidence to the scholarly world that you are able to do independent research.

Most dissertations have rather standardized formats. There is a statement of the goals, a literature review, methods used in data collection, presentation of the data, some analysis of the data, and a conclusion.

At the completion of your degree you will often be asked to sign a contract to have your thesis or dissertation published. Most universities require or at least strongly recommend that you make your findings available through University Microfilms.

Most publishers are not interested in publishing theses and dissertations in the format in which they are completed. They are written in what might be called dissertationese. Publishers are interested in finding a market for their publications. Much of what is in your dissertation will need to be rewritten so that it is of interest to a wide market. It needs to be made more readable and more interesting. Much of the literature review can be omitted or at least rewritten in such a way that it is more interesting.

Journal articles

Many researchers publish in a variety of places, whether in scholarly journals or in non-technical publications. Ask others in your field where you might consider publishing your results. Also check the types of articles particular journals publish so you can submit your article where it can fit in.

Prior to submitting your manuscript, be sure that you know and use the format of the particular journal you have selected. Often the guidelines they follow are published in each issue of the journal. At other times you must contact the publisher for an author's guide.

Some journals use peer review for all articles that they publish. These peers are usually anonymous. If the editor accepts your article and requires edits on it, you will receive their comments to guide you in revising your article accordingly. If you are interested in an academic position, it is to your advantage to publish your article in a peer-reviewed journal. Some universities ask that you specify on your curriculum vita which articles that you have published in journals were peer-reviewed.

Books

Book publishers are in business to make a profit. They look for and even solicit manuscripts for which they believe there is a market.

In looking for a book publisher, look at what each publisher is currently publishing on a similar topic. The editor might be interested in considering your manuscript for their series on that particular topic.

As a guide to publication of book length manuscripts at university presses, see *Getting Published, The Acquisition Process at University Presses* (Parsons 1989). Alternatively, some decide to do self-publication. For useful information on this topic, see Bold (1987).

Review of manuscript

If possible, prior to publication have one or more members of the ethnic group about whom you are writing read through your manuscript. This gives them a chance to correct your misunderstandings and to assure them that you have not misrepresented them.

It is also advisable to have one or more researchers who are knowledgeable about your topic review your manuscript to make suggestions for improvements in wording, sentence construction, presentation of the material, and so on. Others can see what you may not be able to because you are too close to it to make good judgment calls on edits.

Sharing your publication

Once you have published your research results remember to send one or more copies of your publication to leaders of those about whom you have written. Also be sure to send a copy to the university library in the country where you conducted your research. This makes your results available to local researchers. Often local researchers have trouble getting access to material that should be readily available to them. You can help by making your contribution available. This will also help to build good relations for future research that you may desire to do in that country.

A scholarly responsibility

In 1975 I was at a conference in Jos, Nigeria, sitting next to an expatriate who turned to me to ask what I was doing in Africa. I told him briefly about my work. His immediate response was that I had a responsibility to the scholarly community to make my results known through publication. If I met that man again, I would not recognize him; however, his admonition has stuck with me.

Electronic publishing

In this age of technology people are increasingly publishing electronically. Many books and articles are published only on the Web.

Conclusions

For many, the most fulfilling part of the process of doing cultural research is interacting with people of other cultural backgrounds and exploring their cultures. As language is patterned, so too is culture. You have the opportunity to discover those patterns. Some aspects of cultural patterns are covert or latent; the people, themselves, are not aware of them. Further, people may give you their ideals that can then be measured against what actually happens.

Fieldwork calls for adaptability and flexibility on your part as things rarely happen as you expect. What you can expect is the unexpected. Some of Murphy's Laws apply when doing cultural research. While Hill and Arensen stated some maxims as applying to missionaries, they have a wider application to fieldwork in general:

Your glass is always the one with the fly in it.
Whenever the weather gets hot and you need a long shower, the well runs dry.
Things of great anthropological interest only happen when you are away.
People only need to be taken to the hospital in the middle of the night.
If your suitcase is slightly overweight, take five heavy books out and the weight remains the same. Add a toothbrush and it increases several kilos.
The thing you need is always in the country where you are not. (Hill and Arensen 1995:51)

Finally, look forward to cultural research with anticipation, excitement, and even a bit of realistic anxiety. Realize that it will be accompanied by culture shock and stress. Once you deal with these stresses, however, fieldwork is an activity to be enjoyed, relished, and pursued wholeheartedly. It leaves you with a quality of cross-cultural sensitivity that comes only from fieldwork, one of the rich rewards of cultural research. Other benefits of field-work include a sense of accomplishment, an expanded perspective, and an understanding of basic principles taught in cultural anthropology and other social sciences. So, happy globe-trotting!

Appendix:
Resources

Various resources that you might find helpful for fieldwork are listed below.

Appropriate technology

For water filters and other appropriate technology to take with you to the field contact,

Jade Mountain, Inc.
PO Box 4616
Boulder CO 80306
Technical: (303) 449-6601, Orders 1-800-442-1972
Fax: (303) 449-8266, e-mail: jade-mtn@indra.com
http://www.indra.com/jace-mtn/

This company advertises over 4,000 appropriate technology products. These include silver nitrate filters, solar panels, transformers, lamps, and so on.

Computer programs

For information on various computer programs mentioned contact:

1. SHOEBOX and LINGUALINKS:
    Academic Bookstore
    International Linguistics Center
    7500 W. Camp Wisdom Rd.
    Dallas TX 75236

2. ANTHROPAC:
    Dr. Stephen Borgatti
    Sociology Department
    University of South Carolina
    Columbia SC 29208

Revisions of ANTHROPAC are also available.

3.   Ethnography V5.0:
        SCOLARI, Sage Publications Software
        2455 Teller Rd.
        Thousand Oaks CA 91320

The Ethnograph V5.0 is designed to help you deal with qualitative fieldnotes. You can type in your data using whatever word processor, code them using only your mouse, selectively display and print out your code or the master list of the code, attach memos to specific lines in your data file, and search for single code words. It works with Windows personal computers.

Cultural Anthropology Methods Newsletter

To order the *Cultural Anthropology Methods Newsletter* contact:

> *Cultural Anthropology Methods (CAM) Newsletter/Field Methods:*
> *CAM Newsletter*
> Department of Anthropology
> 1350 Turlington
> University of Florida
> Gainesville FL 32611-2036

As of September 1999, CAM was superceded by a new journal *Field Methods,* and it is edited by H. Russell Bernard. The advertisement for this journal states the following:

FIELD METHODS is devoted to articles about the methods used in the social and behavioral sciences and humanities for the collection, management, and analysis of data about human thought and/or human behavior in the natural world....The motto of the journal is that "methods belong to all of us" (e-mail advertisement, 1999).

Demographic information

For current demographic information contact:

> Population Reference Bureau, Inc.
> 2213 M St. NW
> Washington DC 20037
> (202) 785-4664

The Population Reference Bureau publishes *Population Today.* It also produces a "World Population Data Sheet" each year. This data sheet provides current demographic indicators.

Self-publication of manuscripts

For a guide for self-publication of book length manuscripts contact:

> Bold Publications
> PO Box 152281
> Arlington TX 76015
> (817) 468-9924

References

Aboagye-Mensah, Robert K. 1993. Mission and democracy in Africa: The problem of ethnocentrism. International Bulletin of Missionary Research 17:130–33.

Abu-Lughod, Lila. 1993. Writing women's worlds: Bedouin stories. Berkeley: University of California Press.

Achebe, Chinua. 1959. Things fall apart. New York: Astor-Honor.

Adler, Peter S. 1987. Culture shock and the cross-cultural learning experience. In Louise F. Luce and Elise C. Smith (eds.), Toward internationalism, 24–35. Cambridge, Mass.: Newbury.

Agar, Michael. 1980. The professional stranger. New York: Academic Press.

Ahmad, Saidu B. 1989. Stability and variation in Hausa tales. African Languages and Cultures 2:113–31.

Albert, Ethel M. 1956. The classification of values: A method and illustration. American Anthropologist 58:221–48.

Allison, Charlene J., Sue-Ellen Jacobs, and Mary A. Porter. 1989. Winds of change: Women in northwest commercial fishing. Seattle: University of Washington Press.

Alsop, John R. and Clay Johnston. 1990. Fiesta, fast interactive editor of scripture and text analysis. Version 4.5, April. Dallas: Summer Institute of Linguistics.

American Anthropological Association. 1990. Professional ethics, statements and procedures of the American Anthropological Association. Washington, D.C.

Ames, David W. 1973. A sociocultural view of Hausa musical activity. In Warren L. d'Azevedo (ed.), The traditional artist in African societies, 128–61. Bloomington: Indiana University Press.

Andrews, Frank M., Laura Klem, Terrence N. Davidson, Patrick M. O'Malley, and Willard L. Rodgers. 1981. A guide for selecting statistical techniques for analyzing social science data. 2nd ed. Ann Arbor: Survey Research Center, Institute for Social Research, University of Michigan.

Anonymous. 1998. Record number of youth approaching childbearing years. Population Today 26(5):1–2.

Anyidoho, Kofi. 1986. Musical patterns and verbal structures: Aspects of prosody in an African oral art. Black Orpheus 6:27–43.

Arensen, Jonathan E. 1991. Aspects of language and society among the Murle of Sudan. Ph.D. dissertation. Wolfson College.

———. 1992. Mice are men: Language and society among the Murle of Sudan. Dallas: International Museum of Cultures.

Atangana, Karl and Paul Messi. 1919. Jaunde-texte. Hamburg: L. Friederichsen and Co.

Ayandele, Emmanuel A. 1966. The missionary impact on modern Nigeria: 1842–1914: A political and social impact. London: Longmans.

Bailey, Kenneth D. 1978. Methods of social research. 2nd ed. New York: The Free Press.

Barnes, Virginia Lee and Janice Boddy. 1994. Aman: The story of a Somali girl. New York: Vintage Books.

Barnhart, Clarence L., ed. 1947. The American College Dictionary. New York: Random House.

Barley, Nigel. 1983. Adventures in a mud hut: An innocent anthropologist abroad. New York: Vanguard Press.

———. 1986. Ceremony: An anthropologist's misadventures in the African bush. New York: An Owl Book, Henry Holt and Co.

Barth, Fredrik. 1985. The last Wali of Swat: An autobiography as told to Fredrik Barth. New York: Columbia University Press.

Basso, Ellen B. 1987. In favor of deceit: A study of tricksters in Amazonian society. Tucson: The University of Arizona Press.

Batchelor, Peter. 1993. People in rural development. Carlisle, UK: Paternoster Press.

———. 1997. People in rural development. Rev. and enlarged ed. Carlisle, UK: Paternoster Press.

Bauman, Richard and Joel Sherzer, eds.1989. Explorations in the ethnography of speaking. 2nd edition. New York: Cambridge University Press.

Bender, William and Margaret Smith. 1997. Population, food, and nutrition. Population Bulletin 51(4):1–54.

Berlin, Brent, Dennis Breedlove, and Peter H. Raven. 1973. General principles of classification and nomenclature in folk biology. American Anthropologist 75(1):214–42.

Bernard, H. Russell. 1988. Research methods in cultural anthropology. Newbury Park, Calif.: Sage.

———. 1994. Research methods in anthropology: qualitative and quantitative approaches. 2nd ed. Newbury Park, Calif.: Sage.

Biebuyck, Daniel. 1978. Hero and chief: Epic literature from the Banyanga (Zaire Republic). Berkeley: University of California Press.

——— and Kahombo C. Mateene, eds. and tran. 1969. The Mwindo epic. Berkeley: University of California Press.

Black, Mary B. 1973. Belief systems. In John J. Honigmann (ed.), Handbook of social and cultural anthropology, 509–77. Chicago: Rand McNally College Publishing Company.

Blackburn, Stuart H., Peter J. Claus, Joyce B. Flueckiger, and Susan S. Wadley. 1989. Oral epics in India. Berkeley: University of California Press.

Blackman, Margaret B. 1985. During my time: Florence Edenshaw Davidson, a Haida woman. Seattle: University of Washington Press.

———. 1990. Sadie Brower Neakok: An Inupiaq woman. Seattle: University of Washington Press.

Boddy, Janice. 1997. Writing Aman: The perils and politics of the popular book. Anthropology Today 13(3):9–14.

Boissevain, Jeremy and J. Clyde Mitchell, eds. 1973. Network analysis: Studies in human interaction. The Hague: Mouton.

Bold, Mary. 1987. The decision to publish: Writer's guide to desktop publishing. Arlington, Tex.: Bold Productions.

Bolyanatz, Alexander. 1994. Matriliny and mortuary feasting among the Sursurunga of New Ireland, Papua New Guinea. Ph.D. dissertation. University of California, San Diego.

Borgatti, Stephen P. 1990. ANTHROPAC 3.02: Provisional documentation. Columbia: University of South Carolina.

Boring, Karen H. 1998. Tool S: Socio-music questionnaire 2. In Brian Schrag (comp.), The catalyst and research library: Tools for encouraging the growth of indigenous hymnody, 85–91. 3rd ed. Dallas, Tex.: Ethnomusicology Department, Summer Institute of Linguistics.

Brettell, Caroline B. 1983. We have already cried many tears: The stories of three Portuguese migrant women. Rochester, Ver.: Schenkman Books.

Brewster, E. Thomas and Elizabeth S. Brewster. 1976. Language acquisition made practical. Colorado Springs: Lingua House.

Bricker, Victoria R. 1989. The ethnographic context of some traditional Mayan speech genres. In Richard Bauman and Joel Sherzer (eds.), Explorations in the ethnography of speaking, 368–88.

Brim, John A. and David H. Spain. 1974. Research design in anthropology: Paradigms and pragmatics in the testing of hypotheses. New York: Holt, Rinehart and Winston.

Brislin, Richard W., Walter J. Lonner, and Robert M. Thorndike. 1973. Cross-cultural research methods. New York: Wiley.

Brody, Ferm and Maureen Lambert. 1984. Alternative databases for anthropological searching. Database 7:28–32.

Broughton, Simon, Mark Ellingham, David Muddyman, and Richard Trillo, eds. 1994. World music: The rough guide. London: The Rough Guides.

Brown, H. Douglas. 1994. Principles of language learning and teaching. 3rd ed. Englewood Cliffs, N.J.: Prentice Hall Regents.

Bruce, Kathleen L. 1992. Values and value change in Christian conversion. Ph.D. dissertation. Biola University.

Burling, Robbins. 1987. Learning a field language. Ann Arbor: The University of Michigan Press.

Burton, John. 1981. Gods' ants. A study of Atuot religion. St. Augustin, West Germany: Anthropos Institute.

CAM. 1989–1990. Cultural Anthropology Methods Newsletter. vols. 1 and 2.

Canadian Hunger Foundation. 1976. A handbook on appropriate technology. Ottawa: Canadian Hunger Foundation.

Carpenter, Edmund. 1995. The tribal terror of self-awareness. In Paul Hockings (ed.), Principles of visual anthropology, 2nd ed, 481–91. Berlin: Mouton de Gruyter.

Carrington, John F. 1949. A comparative study of some central African Gong-languages. Brussels: Institute Royal Colonial Belge.

Cartwright, Darwin and Frank Harary. 1956. Structural balance: A generalisation of Heider's theory. Psychological Review, 63. Reprinted in Samuel Leinhardt (ed.), Social network: A developing paradigm. 1984. Pittsburgh, Penn.: Learning Research and Development Center, University of Pittsburgh.

Cassell, Joan, ed. 1987. Children in the field: Anthropological experiences. Philadelphia: Temple University Press.

Cassell, Joan and Sue-Ellen Jacobs, eds. 1987. Handbook on ethical issues in anthropology. Special publication of the American Anthropological Association 23. Washington, D.C.

Cernea, Michael M., ed. 1985. Putting people first: Sociological variables in rural development. New York: Oxford University Press, published for the World Bank.

Chafe, Wallace L., ed. 1980. The pear stories: Cognitive, cultural, and linguistic aspects of narrative production. Norwood, N. J.: Ablex.

Chagnon, Napoleon A. 1977. Yãnomamö: The fierce people. 2nd ed. New York: Holt, Rinehart and Winston.

Chambers, Robert. 1985. Shortcut methods of gathering social information for rural development projects. In Michael M. Cernea, (ed.), Putting people first: Sociological variables in rural development, 399–414. New York: Oxford University Press, published for the World Bank.

Chenoweth, Vida S. 1972. Melodic perception and analysis: A manual on ethnic melody. Papua New Guinea: Summer Institute of Linguistics.

Chernoff, John Miller. 1979. African rhythm and African sensibility. Chicago: The University of Chicago Press.

Christensen, Garry. 1993. Sensitive information: Collecting data on livestock and informal credit. In Stephen Devereux and John Hoddinott (eds.), Fieldwork in developing countries, 124–37. Boulder, Colo.: Lynne Rienner.

Cohen, Abner. 1969. Custom and politics in urban Africa: A study of migrants in Yoruba towns. Berkeley: University of California Press.

Comrie, Bernard. 1981. Language universals and linguistic typology: Syntax and morphology. Chicago: University of Chicago Press.

Conklin, Harold C. 1962. Lexicographical treatment of folk taxonomies. International Journal of Applied Linguistics 28(2)IV:119–41.

————. 1980. Folk classification: A topically arranged bibliography of contemporary and background references through 1971. New Haven, Conn.: Yale University Press.

Cooper, Harris M. 1989. Integrating research: A guide for literature reviews. Applied Social Research Methods 2. Newbury Park, Calif.: Sage.

Cordell, Dennis D., Joel W. Gregory, and Victor Piche. 1992. The demographic reproduction of health and disease: Colonial Central African Republic and contemporary Burkina Faso. In Steven Feierman and John M. Janzen (eds.), The social basis of health and healing in Africa, 39–70. Berkeley: University of California Press.

Cowan, George M. 1948. Mazateco whistle speech. Language 24:280–86.

Coward, David F. and Charles E. Grimes. 1995. Making dictionaries: A guide to lexicography and the multi-dictionary formatter. Version 1.0. Waxhaw, N.C.: Summer Institute of Linguistics.

Crane, Julia G. and Michael V. Angrosino. 1978. Field projects in anthropology: A student handbook. Morristown, N.J.: General Learning Press.

————. 1992. Field projects in anthropology: A student handbook. 3rd ed. Prospect Heights, Ill.: Waveland Press.

Crapo, Richley H. 1993. Cultural anthropology: Understanding ourselves and others. 3rd ed. Guilford, Conn.: Dushkin.

Crozier, David. 1984. A study in the discourse grammar of Cishingini. Ph.D. thesis. University of Ibadan, Nigeria.

Cumming, John and Elaine Cumming. 1955. Mental health education in a Canadian community. In Benjamin D. Paul (ed.), Health, culture, and community, 43–69. New York: Russell Sage Foundation.

da Corta, Ludia and Davuluri Venkateshwarlu. 1993. Field methods for economic mobility. In Stephen Devereux and John Hoddinott (eds.), Fieldwork in developing countries, 102–23. Boulder, Colo.: Lynne Rienner.

D'Andrade, Roy. 1995. The development of cognitive anthropology. New York: Cambridge University Press.

d'Azevedo, Warren L., ed. 1973. The traditional artist in African societies. Bloomington: Indiana University Press.

Deng, Francis Mading. 1972. The Dinka of the Sudan. New York: Holt, Rinehart and Winston.

———. 1986. The man called Deng Majok: A biography of power, polygyny, and change. New Haven: Yale University Press.

Denny, J. Peter and Chet A. Creider. 1986. The semantics of noun classes in Proto Bantu. In Collette Craig (ed.), Noun classes and categorization, 217–39. Amsterdam: John Benjamins.

Derman, William and Scott Whiteford, eds. 1985. Social impact analysis and development planning in the third world. Boulder, Colo.: Westview.

De Vale, Sue Carole. 1984. Prolegomena to a study of harp and voice sounds in Uganda: A graphic system for the notation of texture. In J. H. Kwabena Nketia and Jacqueline Cogdell DjeDje (eds.), Selected reports in ethnomusicology, 285–315. Los Angeles: Program in Ethnomusicology, Department of Music, University of California, Los Angeles.

Devereux, Stephen and John Hoddinott, eds. 1993. Fieldwork in developing countries. Boulder, Colo.: Lynne Rienner.

De Waal, Alexander. 1989. Famine that kills: Darfur, Sudan, 1984–1985. Oxford: Clarendon.

Dickson, Murray. 1983. Where there is no dentist. Palo Alto, Calif.: Hesperian Foundation.

Dixon, Wilfred J., ed. 1990. BMDP statistical software manual. vols. 1 and 2. Berkeley: University of California Press.

Donnelly, Kevin and Yahya Omar. 1983. Structure and association in Bajuni fishing songs. In Veronika Gorog-Karody (ed.), Genres, forms, meanings: Essays in African oral literature, 109–22. Paris: Maison des sciences de l'Homme.

Dorjahn, Vernon R. 1988. Changes in Temne polygyny. Ethnology 27:367–90.

Douglas, Mary. 1966. Purity and danger: An analysis of concepts of pollution and taboo. London: Routledge and Kegan Paul.

Durkheim, Emile. 1965. [originally published 1912] The elementary forms of religious life. New York: Free Press.

Dye, T. Wayne. 1974. Stress-producing factors in cultural adjustment. Missiology 2:61–77.

Economic Development Institute of The World Bank. 1989. Successful development in Africa: Case studies of projects, programs, and policies. EDI Development Policy Case Series, Analytical Case Studies 1. Washington, D.C.: World Bank.

Egner, Inge. 1995. What's a lie anyway? In Harriet Hill and Jon Arensen (eds.), The best of ethno-info, 64–65. Nairobi, Kenya: Summer Institute of Linguistics, Africa Area Anthropology Department.

Elsass, Peter. 1987. Organisational patterns for ethnic minorities. In Roberto Lizarralde, Stephen Beckermann, and Peter Elsass (eds.), Indigenous survival among the Bari and Arhuaco: Strategies and perspectives, 60:58–77. Copenhagen: International Work Group for Indigenous Affairs (IWGIA).

Ember, Carol R. and Melvin Ember. 1973. Cultural anthropology. 4th ed. Englewood Cliffs, N.J.: Prentice-Hall.

Ennis, E. L. 1945. Women's names among the Ovimbundu of Angola. African Studies 4:3–15.

Euba, Akin. 1988. Essays on music in Africa 1. Bayreuth, Germany: Iwalowa-Haus.

Evans-Pritchard, Edward E., ed. 1967. The Zande trickster. Oxford: Clarendon Press.

———. 1976. [originally published 1937] Witchcraft, oracles and magic among the Azande. Oxford: Clarendon Press.

Fagborun, J. Gbenga. 1990. Yoruba counting verses: A linguistic approach to oral tradition. African Languages and Cultures 3:167–80.

Fallers, Lloyd. 1955. The predicament of the modern African chief: An instance from Uganda. American Anthropologist 57(1):290–305.

Fernandez, James W. 1982. Bwiti: An ethnography of the religious imagination in Africa. Princeton, N.J.: Princeton University Press.

———. 1985. Review of world view. American Ethnologist 12:749–57.

Fetterman, David M. 1989. Ethnography, step by step. Applied Social Research Methods Series 17. Newbury Park, Calif.: Sage.

Finnegan, Ruth. 1986. The relation between composition and performance: Three alternate modes. In Yosihiko Tokumaru and Osamu Yamaguti (eds.), The oral and the literate in music, 73–87. Tokyo: Academia Music, Ltd.

Fleming, Ilah. 1988a. Communication analysis: A stratificational approach. Dallas: Summer Institute of Linguistics.

———. 1988b. A field guide for communication situation: Semantic and morphemic analysis 2. Dallas: Summer Institute of Linguistics.

Follingstad, Carl. 1991. Multiple action verb roots in Tyap. ms.

Foster, George M., Thayer Scudder, Elizabeth Colson, and Robert V. Kemper, eds. 1979. Long-term field research in social anthropology. New York: Academic Press.

Fox, Robin. 1967. Kinship and marriage. Middlesex, England: Pelican.

Francis, Elizabeth. 1993. Qualitative research: Collecting life histories. In Stephen Devereux and John Hoddinott (eds.), Fieldwork in developing countries, 86–101. Boulder, Colo.: Lynne Rienner.

Freeman, James M. 1979. The untouchable: An Indian life history. Stanford: Stanford University Press.

Freilich, Morris, ed. 1970. Marginal natives at work: Anthropologists in the field. New York: John Wiley and Sons.

Furnham, Adrian and Stephen Bochner. 1986. Culture shock: Psychological reactions to unfamiliar environments. London: Routledge.

Gal, Susan. 1989. Language and political economy. Annual Review of Anthropology 18:345–67.

Gardner, Robert and Wallace Lambert. 1972. Attitudes and motivation in second language learning. Rowley, Mass.: Newbury House.

Goodenough, Ward. 1956. Componential analysis and the study of meaning. Language 32:195–216.

———. 1965. Rethinking "status" and "role": Toward a general model of the cultural organization of social relationships. In Michael Banton (ed.), The relevance of models for social anthropology, 1–24. Association of Social Anthropology Monographs 1. London: Tavistock.

Gossen, Gary H. 1989. To speak with a heated heart: Chamula canons of style and good performance. In Richard Bauman and Joel Sherzer (ed), Explorations in the ethnography of speaking, 389–413. 2nd ed. Cambridge: Cambridge University Press.

Granovetter, Mark. 1974. Getting a job. Cambridge, Mass.: Harvard University Press.

Greeley, Edward H. 1986. Social analysis in AID: Lessons from Africa. In Edward C. Green (ed.), Practicing development anthropology, 223–34. Boulder, Colo: Westview.

Green, Edward C., ed. 1986. Practicing development anthropology. Boulder, Colo.: Westview.

———. 1991 [originally published 1987] The integration of modern and traditional health sectors in Swaziland. In Aaron Podolefsky and Peter J. Brown (eds.), Applying cultural anthropology: An introductory reader, 237–42. 2nd ed. Mountain View, Calif.: Mayfield.

Griaule, Marcel. 1965. Conversations with Ogotemmeli: An introduction to Dogon religious ideas. London: Oxford University Press.

Grimes, Joseph E. 1975. The thread of discourse. The Hague: Mouton.

Guralnik, David B. 1974. Webster's new world dictionary. Cleveland, Oh.: Collins + World.

———— 1980. Webster's new world dictionary of the American language. 2nd College ed. Cleveland, Oh.: William Collins.

Hale, Thomas A. 1994. Griottes: Female voices from West Africa. Research in African Literatures, Special Issue: Women as Oral Artists 25(3):71–91.

Hammond, Peter B. 1971. An introduction to cultural and social anthropology. New York: Macmillan.

Hansford, Gillian F. 1995. Three for a boy, four for a girl. In Harriet Hill and Jon Arensen (eds.), The best of ethno-info, 131. Africa Area Anthropology Department, Nairobi, Kenya: Summer Institute of Linguistics.

Harriss, Barbara. 1993. Talking to traders about trade. In Stephen Devereux and John Hoddinott (eds.), Fieldwork in developing countries, 138–51. Boulder, Colo.: Lynne Rienner.

Haupt, Arthur and Thomas T. Kane. 1978. The population reference bureau's population handbook. Washington, D.C.: Population Reference Bureau.

————. 1985 The population reference bureau's population handbook. 2nd ed. Washington, D.C.: Population Reference Bureau.

Haviland, John B. 1977. Gossip, reputation, and knowledge in Zinacantan. Chicago: University of Chicago Press.

Haviland, William A. 1987. Cultural anthropology. 5th ed. New York: Holt, Rinehart and Winston.

Headland, Thomas N. 1986. Why foragers do not become farmers: A historical study of a changing ecosystem and its effect on a Negrito hunter-gatherer group in the Philippines. Ph.D. dissertation. University of Hawaii.

———— and Janet D. Headland. 1982. A census by families of the Casiguran Agta in June 1977. ms.

————, Kenneth L. Pike, and Marvin Harris, eds. 1990. Emics and etics: The insider/outsider debate. Newbury Park, Calif.: Sage.

Healey, Alan, ed. 1975. Language learner's field guide. Ukarumpa, Papua New Guinea: Summer Institute of Linguistics.

Henige, David. 1982. Oral historiography. London: Longman.

Herndon, Marcia, Roger Burnyate, and Norma McLead. 1980. Music as culture. Darby, Penn.: Norwood Editions.

Heyer, Judith. 1993. Contrasts in village-level fieldwork: Kenya and India. In Stephen Devereux and John Hoddinott (eds.), Fieldwork in developing countries, 200–16. Boulder, Colo.: Lynne Reiner.

Hiebert, Paul G. 1985. Anthropological insights for missionaries. Grand Rapids, Mich.: Baker Book House.

Hill, Harriet. 1988. Interface: Anthro and translation - key words survey. Ethno-info 9:insert.

————. 1995 More on three and four. In Harriet Hill and Jon Arensen (eds.), The best of ethno-info, 131–32. Africa Area Anthropology Department, Nairobi, Kenya: Summer Institute of Linguistics.

———— and Jon Arensen, eds. 1995. The best of Ethno-info. African Area Anthropology Department, Nairobi, Kenya: Summer Institute of Linguistics.

Hirschkind, Lynn. 1991. Redefining the "field" in fieldwork. Ethnology 30(3):237–49.

Hitchcock, Patricia. 1987. Our Ulleri child. In Joan Cassell (ed.), Children in the field: Anthropological experiences, 173–83. Philadephia: Temple University Press.

Hockings, Paul, ed. 1995. Principles of visual anthropology. 2nd ed. Berlin: Mouton de Gruyter.

Hollingsworth, Kenneth R. 1998. Tool E: Commentary, classification of instruments: Organology. In Brian Schrag (ed.), The catalyst and research library: Tools for encouraging the growth of indigenous hymnology, 60–65. 3rd ed. Dallas, Tex.: Ethnomusicology Department, Summer Institute of Linguistics.

Honigmann, John J., ed. 1973. Handbook of social and cultural anthropology. Chicago: Rand McNally College Publishing.

Hornbostel, Erich M. von, and Curt Sachs. 1961. (originally published 1914) Classification of musical instruments. Translated by Anthony Baines and Klaus P. Wachsmann. Galpin Society Journal 14:4–29. [Orig. Systematik der Musikinstrumente. In Zeitschrift fur Ethnologie 46:553–90, 1914.]

Howell, Nancy. 1979. Demography of the Dobe !Kung. New York: Academic Press.

————. 1990 Surviving fieldwork: A report of the advisory panel on health and safety in fieldwork. American Anthropological Association Publication 26. Washington, D.C.

Huff, Darrell. 1954. How to lie with statistics. New York: Norton.

Hymes, Dell. 1974. Foundations in sociolinguistics: An ethnographic approach. Philadelphia: University of Pennsylvania Press.

Illich, Ivan. 1970. Celebration of awareness. New York: Doubleday.

Ingersoll, Jasper, M. Sullivan, and Barbara Lenkerd. 1981. Social analysis of AID projects: A review of the experience. ms.

Ishola, Solomon. 1991. Polygamy in Africa. In Ebbie C. Smith (ed.), That all the world may hear: An introduction to missionary anthropology, 130–42. Fort Worth, Tex.: Southwestern Baptist Theological Seminary.

Ives, Edward D. 1980. The tape-recorded interview: A manual for field workers in folklore and oral history. Knoxville: The University of Tennessee Press.

Jennings, Anne M. 1995. The Nubians of West Aswan: Village women in the midst of change. Boulder, Colo.: Lynne Rienner.

Johnson, Allen W. 1978. Quantification in cultural anthropology: An introduction to research design. Stanford, Calif.: Stanford University Press.

Johnston, Hugh A. S. 1966. A selection of Hausa stories. Oxford: Clarendon Press.

Jorgensen, Danny L. 1989. Participant observation: A methodology for human studies: Applied Social Research Methods Series 15. Newbury Park, Calif.: Sage.

Kaemmer, John E. 1993. Music in human life: Anthropological perspectives on music. Austin: University of Texas Press.

Kay, Paul. 1971. Taxonomy and semantic contrast. Language 47:866–87.

Kearney, Michael. 1984. World view. Novato, Calif.: Chandler and Sharp.

Keil, Charles. 1979. Tiv song. Chicago: The University of Chicago Press.

Kennedy, John G. 1987. The flower of paradise: The institutionalized use of the drug qat in North Yemen. Dordrecht: D. Reidel.

Kesteloot, Lilyan. 1989. The African epic. African Languages and Cultures 2(2):203–14.

Kirton, Jean F. 1989. Yanyuwa—A dying language. Notes on Scriptures in Use and Language Programs 19:30–48.

Klass, Morton and Sheila Solomon Klass. 1987. Birthing in the bush: Participant observation in Trinidad. In Joan Cassell (ed.), Children in the field: Anthropological experiences, 121–47. Philadelphia: Temple University Press.

Kluckhohn, Clyde. 1945. The personal document in anthropological science. In The use of personal documents in history, anthropology, and sociology 53:79–173. New York: Social Science Research Council.

———— and others. 1952. Values and value-orientation in the theory of action: An exploration in definition and classification. In Talcott Parsons and Edward Shils (eds.), Toward a general theory of action, 388–433. Cambridge: Harvard University Press.

———— and Dorothea Leighton. 1946. The Navaho. Rev. ed. Cambridge, Mass.: Harvard University Press.

Kluckhohn, Florence. 1940. The participant-observer technique in small communities. American Journal of Sociology 46:331–43.

Koenig, Mary M. and John M. Weeks. 1989. Introduction to library research in anthropology. Boulder, Colo.: Westview.

Kondo, Riena. 1991. Taking into consideration cultural learning styles. Notes on Literacy 17(2):23–34.

Kraft, Charles H. 1986. Worldview and Bible translation. In Karl J. Franklin (ed.), Anthropological and missiological issues. Notes on Anthropology and Intercultural Community Work, 6/7:46–57.

Kraft, Marguerita G. 1978. Worldview and the communication of the gospel: A Nigerian case study. South Pasadena: William Carey Library.

Kunene, Daniel P. 1971. Heroic poetry of the Basotho. Oxford: Clarendon.

Kurin, Richard. 1980. Acceptance in the field: Doctor, lawyer, indian chief. Natural History 89(11). In James P. Spradley and David W. McCurdy (eds.), Conformity and conflict. Readings in cultural anthropology, 46–56. Boston: Little, Brown, and Company.

Lakoff, George. 1980. Metaphors we live by. Chicago: University of Chicago Press.

————. 1987. Women, fire, and dangerous things. Chicago: University of Chicago Press.

Larsen, Mildred. 1975. A manual for problem solving in Bible translation. Grand Rapids, Mich.: Zondervan.

Lee, Richard Borshay. 1969. Eating Christmas in the Kalahari. Natural History. 60(3):14–22.

————. 1979. The !Kung San: Men, women, and work in a foraging society. Cambridge: Cambridge University Press.

Levi-Strauss, Claude. 1963. Structural anthropology. New York: Basic Books.

Levine, Nancy E. and Walter H. Sangree, eds. 1980. Women with many husbands: Polyandrous alliance and marital flexibility in Africa and Asia. Journal of Comparative Family Studies. Special Issue 11(3).

Lewis, Bazett A. 1972. The Murle: Red chiefs and black commoners. Oxford: Clarendon Press.

Little, Kenneth. 1965. West African urbanization: A study of voluntary associations in social change. Cambridge: Cambridge University Press.

Longacre, Robert E. 1983. The grammar of discourse: Notional and surface structures. New York: Plenum.

———— and Stephen Levinsohn. 1978. Field analysis of discourse. In Wolfgang U. Dressler (ed.), Current trends in text linguistics, 103–22. Berlin: Walter de Gruyter.

Lovejoy, Paul E. 1983. Transformations in slavery: A history of slavery in Africa. Cambridge: Cambridge University Press.

Lowie, Robert H. 1915. Discussion and correspondence. American Anthropologist 17:597–99.

————. 1917. Oral tradition and history. The Journal of American Folk-Lore 30:161–67.

Lutkehaus, Nancy. 1990. Refractions of reality: On the use of other ethnographers' fieldnotes. In Roger Sanjek (ed.), Fieldnotes: The makings of anthropology, 303–23. Ithaca, N.Y.: Cornell University Press.

Malinowski, Bronislaw. 1967. A diary in the strict sense of the term. London: Routledge and Kegan Paul.

Mann, Brenda J. 1976. The ethics of fieldwork in an urban bar. In Michael A. Rynkiewich and James P. Spradley (eds.), Ethics and anthropology: Dilemmas in fieldwork, 95–109. Malabar, Fla.: Robert E. Krieger.

Mansen, Richard Arnold. 1988. Dispute negotiation among the Guajiro of Colombia and Venezuela: Dynamics of compensation and status. Ph.D. dissertation. University of Illinois at Urbana-Champaign.

Marcus, George E. and Michael M. J. Fischer. 1986. Anthropology as cultural critique. Chicago: University of Chicago Press.

Marshall, Catherine and Gretchen B. Rossman. 1989. Designing qualitative research. Newbury Park, Calif.: Sage.

Marshall, Terry. 1989. The whole world guide to language learning. Yarmouth, Maine: Intercultural Press.

Mayers, Marvin K., ed. 1966. Languages of Guatemala. The Hague: Mouton.

——— 1974. Christianity confronts culture: A strategy for cross-cultural evangelism. Grand Rapids: Zondervan.

Mbiti, John S. 1970. African religions and philosophies. Garden City, N.Y.: Anchor Books.

———. 1990. African religions and philosophies. 2nd ed. London: Heinemann.

McCall, George J. and Jerry L. Simmons, eds. 1969. Issues in participant-observation: A text and reader. Reading, Mass.: Addison-Wesley.

McElhanon, Ken. Forthcoming. In Evangelical dictionary of world missions, edited by Scott Moreau. Grand Rapids, Mich.: Baker.

McGavran, Donald Anderson. 1955. Bridges of God: A study in the strategy of missions. New York: Friendship.

McKinney, Carol V. 1983. A linguistic shift in Kaje, Kagoro, and Katab kinship terminology. Ethnology 22(4):281–93.

———. 1985. The Bajju of central Nigeria: A case study of religious and social change. Ph.D. dissertation. Southern Methodist University.

———. 1986. Retention of traditional religious beliefs by Bajju Christians. Notes on Anthropology and Intercultural Community Work 6/7:58–66.

———. 1990. Which language: Trade or minority? Missiology 18(3):279–90.

———. 1992. Wives and sisters: Bajju marital patterns. Ethnology 31(1):75–87.

McKinney, Norris P. 1978. Participant identification in Kaje narrative. In Joseph E. Grimes (ed.), Papers on discourse, 179–89. Dallas: Summer Institute of Linguistics.

McLead, Ruth A. 1975. Learning Xavante monolingually. In Alan Healey (ed.), Language learner's field guide, 281–96. Ukarumpa, Papua New Guinea: Summer Institute of Linguistics.

McMillan, Della E. 1995. Sahel visions: Planned settlement and river blindness control in Burkina Faso. Tucson: University of Arizona.

Merriam, Alan P. 1964. The anthropology of music. Evanston, Ill.: Northwestern University Press.

Mieder, Wolfgang, Stewart A. Kingsbury, and Kelsie B. Harder, eds. 1991. A dictionary of American proverbs. New York: Oxford University Press.

Mirza, Sarah and Margaret Strobel, eds. and trans. 1989. Three Swahili women: Life histories from Mombasa, Kenya. Bloomington: Indiana University Press.

Mitchell, J. Clyde. 1967. On quantification in social anthropology. In Arnold L. Epstein (ed.), The craft of social anthropology, 17–46. London: Tavistock.

———. 1969. Social networks in urban situations. Manchester: Manchester University Press.

Moran, Emilio F. 1979. Human adaptability: An introduction to ecological anthropology. Boulder, Colo.: Westview.

Moreno, Jacob. 1934. Who shall survive? New York: Beacon.

Morgan, E. Philip. 1985. Social analysis and the dynamics of advocacy in development assistance. In William Derman and Scott Whiteford (eds.), Social impact and analysis and development planning in the third world, 21–31. Boulder, Colo.: Westview.

Muller, Jean-Claude. 1980. On the relevance of having two husbands: Contribution to the study of polygynous/polyandrous marital forms of the Jos Plateau. Journal of Comparative Family Studies 11:359–69.

——— and Walter H. Sangree. 1973. Irigwe and Rukuba marriage: A comparison. Canadian Journal of African Studies 7:27–57.

Murdock, George P. and D. R. White. 1969. Standard cross-cultural sample. Ethnology 8:329–69.

———, Clellan S. Ford, Alford E. Hudson, Raymond Kennedy, Leo W. Simmons, and John W. M. Whiting. 1987. Outline of cultural materials. 5th rev. ed. (HRAF Manuals Ser.) New Haven, Conn.: Human Relations Area Files.

Murphy, Yolanda and Robert F. Murphy. 1974. Women of the forest. New York: Columbia University Press.

Nadel, Siegfried F. 1957. The theory of social structure. London: Cohen and West.

Nanda, Serena. 1980. Cultural anthropology. 2nd ed. Belmont, Calif.: Wadsworth.

Naroll, Raoul. 1962. Data quality control: A new research technique. Glencoe, Ill.: Free Press.

Neeley, Paul L. 1991. People of the drum of God, come!: Calling the Christians in Cameroon. M.A. thesis. University of Texas at Arlington.

Nettl, Bruno. 1967. Theory and method in ethnomusicology. New York: The Free Press.

Ngugi Wa Thiong'o. 1965. The river between. Oxford: Heinemann.

Niane, Djibril Tamsir and George D. Pickett (trans.). 1965. SUNDIATA: An epic of old Mali. London: Longman Group.

Nketia, J. H. Kwabena and Jacqueline Cogdell DjeDje, eds. 1984. Selected reports in ethnomusicology. Studies in African Music 5. Los Angeles: Program in Ethnomusicology, Department of Music, University of California, Los Angeles.

Nkili, Agnes-Marie. 1975/76. Le nkul des Mvele: Essai d'analyse semiotique. Yaoundé: Université de Yaoundé.

Nutini, Hugo G. and Betty Bell. 1980. Ritual kinship: The structure and historical development of the compadrazgo system in rural Tlaxcala. Princeton: Princeton University Press.

Obbo, Christine. 1990. Adventures with fieldnotes. In Roger Sanjek (ed.), Fieldnotes: The makings of anthropology, 290–302. Ithaca: Cornell University Press.

Oberg, Kalervo. 1960. Culture shock: Adjustment to new cultural environments. Practical Anthropology 7(4):177–82.

Okpewho, Isidore. 1979. The epic in Africa: Toward a poetics of the oral performance. New York: Columbia University Press.

———. 1992. African oral literature, backgrounds, character, and continuity. Bloomington: Indiana University Press.

Oliver, Roland and Michael Crowder. 1981. The Cambridge encyclopedia of Africa. Cambridge: Cambridge University Press.

Opler, Morris E. 1937. (Reprinted in 1955) An outline of Chiricahua Apache social organization. In Fred Eggan (ed.), Social anthropology of North American tribes, 171–239. Chicago: University of Chicago Press.

———. 1945. Themes as dynamic forces in culture. American Journal of Sociology 53:198–206.

Orefice, Paolo. 1988. Participatory research in Southern Europe. Convergence Convergencia 21(2 /3):39–48.

Ott, Lyman. 1977. An introduction to statistical methods and data analysis. North Scituate, Mass.: Duxbury.

Otterbein, Keith F. 1990. Two styles of cross-cultural research. Cultural Anthropology Methods Newsletter 2(3):6–7.

Ottenberg, Simon. 1990. Thirty years of fieldnotes: Changing relationships to the text. In Roger Sanjek (ed.), Fieldnotes: The makings of anthropology, 139–60. Ithaca, N.Y.: Cornell University Press.

Owusu, Maxwell. 1978. Ethnography of Africa: The usefulness of the useless. American Anthropologist 80(2):310–34.

Oxford, Rebecca L. 1990. Language learning strategies: What every teacher should know. New York: Newburg House.

Parsons, Paul. 1989. Getting published: The acquisition process at university presses. Knoxville: University of Tennessee Press.

Peck, Charles. 1984. A survey of grammatical structures. 2nd ed. Dallas: Summer Institute of Linguistics.

Pelto, Pertti J. and Gretel H. Pelto. 1970. Anthropological research: The structure of inquiry. 2nd ed. Cambridge: Cambridge University Press.

———. 1973. Ethnography: The fieldwork enterprise. In John J. Honigmann (ed.), Handbook of social and cultural anthropology, 241–88. Chicago: Rand McNally College Publishing.

Pelton, Robert D. 1980. The trickster in West Africa: A study of mythic irony and sacred delight. Berkeley: University of California Press.

Pike, Evelyn G. 1983. Instant language learning kit. Notes on Linguistics 25:6–13.

Pike, Kenneth Lee and Evelyn G. Pike. 1982. Grammatical analysis. 2nd ed. Dallas: Summer Institute of Linguistics and the University of Texas at Arlington.

Podolefsky, Aaron and Peter J. Brown. 1991. Applying cultural anthropology: An introductory reader. Mountain View, Calif.: Mayfield.

Powdermaker, Hortense. 1956. Social change through imagery and values of teen-age Africans in northern Rhodesia. American Anthropologist 58(5):783–813.

Pratt, Brian and Peter Loizos. 1992. Choosing research methods: Data collection for development workers. Development Guidelines 7. Oxford: Oxfam.

Price, Richard. 1983. First-time: The historical vision of an Afro-American people. Baltimore: Johns Hopkins University Press.

Propp, Vladimir and Laurence Scott (trans.). 1968. Morphology of the folktale. 2nd ed. Austin: University of Texas Press.

Radin, Paul. 1956. The trickster: A study in American Indian mythology. New York: Philosophical Library.

———, ed. 1952. African folktales. New York: Schocken Books.

Rattray, Robert S. 1930. Akan-Ashanti folk-tales. Oxford: Clarendon Press.

Richard, Audrey. 1939. Land, labour and diet in northern Rhodesia. London: Oxford University Press.

Riley, Nancy E. 1997. Gender, power, and population change. In Population Bulletin 52(1):1–48.

Rivers, William H. R. 1906. Reports of the Cambridge expedition to Torres Straits, 5 and 6. Cambridge: University Press.

———. The Todas. New York: Macmillan.

———. 1910. The genealogical method of anthropological inquiry. Sociological Review 1(11):1–11.

Robarchek, Clayton and Carole Robarchek. 1998. Waorani: The contexts of violence and war. Fort Worth, Tex.: Harcourt Brace.

Rodman, William L. 1991. When questions are answers: The message of anthropology according to the people of Ambae. American Anthropologist 93(2):421–34.

Romero, Patricia W., ed. 1988. Life histories of African women. London: Ashfield.

Rosch, Eleanor. 1978. Principles of categorization. In Eleanor Rosch and Barbara Lloyd (eds.), Cognition and categorization, 27–48. New York: L. Erlbaum Associates.

Rosenberg, Bruce A. 1975. Oral sermons and oral narrative. In Dan Ben-Amos and Kenneth S. Goldstein (eds.). Folklore: Preformance and communication, 75–101. The Hague: Mouton.

Rynkiewich, Michael A. 1976. The underdevelopment of anthropological ethics. In Michael A. Rynkiewich and James P. Spradley (eds.), Ethics and anthropology: Dilemmas in fieldwork, 47–60. Malabar, Fla.: Robert E. Krieger.

——— and James P. Spradley, eds. 1976. Ethics and anthropology: Dilemmas in fieldwork. Malabar, Fla.: Robert E. Krieger.

Salamone, Frank A. 1975. Becoming Hausa: Ethnic identity change and its implication for the study of ethnic pluralism and stratification. Africa 45:410–24.

———. 1977. The methodological significance of the lying informant. Anthropological Quarterly 50(3):117–24.

Sangree, Walter H. 1969. Going home to mother: Traditional marriage among the Irigwe of Benue-Plateau State, Nigeria. American Anthropologist 71:1046–57.

———. 1974a. The Dodo cult, witchcraft, and secondary marriage in Irigwe, Nigeria. Ethnology 13:261–78.

———. 1974b. Prescriptive polygamy and complementary filiation among the Irigwe of Nigeria. Man 9:44–52.

———. 1980. The persistence of polyandry in Irigwe, Nigeria. Journal of Comparative Family Studies 11:335–43.

———. 1982. Spirit possession cults in Irigwe, Nigeria: An indigenous response to severe separation depression. In Olayiwala A. Erinosho and Norman W. Bell (eds.), Mental health in Africa, 60–75. Ibadan: Ibadan University Press.

Sanjek, Roger, ed. 1990. Fieldnotes: The makings of anthropology. Ithaca, N.Y.: Cornell University Press.

Sargent, Carolyn Fishel. 1982. The cultural context of therapeutic choice: Obstetrical care decisions among the Bariba of Benin. Dordrecht, Holland: D. Reidel.

———, Carol McKinney, and Ronald Wetherington. 1986. Socioeconomic status and the incidence of low birth weight among the Bariba of Benin. East African Medical Journal 63(2):91–98.

Saville-Troike, Muriel. 1982. The ethnography of communication. Oxford: Basil Balckwell.

———. 1989 The ethnography of communication, 2nd ed. New York: Basil Blackwell.

Schanely, Leon E. 1983. Developing community potential. Dallas: Summer Institute of Linguistics.

Schrag, Brian, comp. 1998. The catalyst and research library: Tools for encouraging the growth of indigenous hymnody. 3rd ed. Dallas: Ethnomusicology Department, Summer Institute of Linguistics.

Schuler, Sidney Ruth. 1987. The other side of polyandry, property, stratification, and nonmarriage in the Nepal Himalayas. Boulder, Colo.: Westview.

Schusky, Ernest L. 1965. Manual for kinship analysis. 2nd ed. New York: Holt, Rinehart and Winston.

Scott, John. 1991. Social network analysis: A handbook. London: Sage.

Scotton, Carol Myers. 1975. Multilingualism in Lagos—What it means to the social scientist. In Robert K. Herbert, (ed.), Patterns of language, culture, and society: Sub-Saharan Africa, 78–90. Columbus: Ohio State University.

Shaw, R. Daniel. 1996. From longhouse to village: Samo social change. Fort Worth, Tex.: Harcourt, Brace.

Shearer, William M. 1982. Research procedures in speech, language, and hearing. Baltimore: Williams and Wilkins.

Shepherd, Gary. 1982. Life among the Magars. Tripureshwar, Kathmandu: Sahayogi.

Shezer, Joel. 1989. Namakke, Sunmakke, Kormakke: Three types of Cuna speech event. In Richard Bauman and Joel Scherzer (eds.), Explorations in the ethnology of speaking, 263–82. 2nd ed. Cambridge: Cambridge University Press.

Shostak, Marjorie. 1981. Nisa: The life and words of a !Kung woman. New York: Random House.

Shryock, Henry S., Jacob S. Siegel, and Associates. 1976. The methods and materials of demography. New York: Academic Press.

Sitton, Thad, George L. Mehaffy, and Ozro L. Davis, Jr. 1983. Oral history: A guide for teachers (and others). Austin: University of Texas Press.

Skinner, Neil. 1968. Hausa readings: Selections from Edgar's *tatsuyiyoyi*. Madison: Department of African Languages and Literature, University of Wisconsin Press.

Smith, Barbara. 1968. Poetic closure: A study of how poems end. Chicago: Chicago University Press.

Smith, Mary F. 1954. Baba of Karo: A woman of the Muslim Hausa. New Haven: Yale University Press.

Smith, Michael G. 1953. Secondary marriage in northern Nigeria. Africa 23:298–323.

———. 1957. The social functions and meaning of Hausa praise-singing. Africa 27:26–45.

———. 1980. After secondary marriage, what? Ethnology 19:265–77.

Southwell, Neville. 1989. Assessment and reassessment: A Pacific perspective. Notes on Scriptures in Use and Language Programs 19:3–12.

Sow, Abdoul Aziz. 1993. Fulani poetic genres. Research in African Literatures 24(2):61–77.

Spaeth, David H. 1991a. Development program planning: A process approach. Dallas: Summer Institute of Linguistics.

———. 1991b. A model for rapid rural assessments. ms.

Spradley, James P. 1980. Participant observation. New York: Holt, Rinehart and Winston.

———, and David W. McCurdy. 1975. Anthropology: The cultural perspective. 2nd ed. New York: John Wiley and Sons.

———. 1987 Conformity and conflict: Readings in cultural anthropology. 6th ed. Boston: Little, Brown, and Co.

SPSSx. 1983. User's guide SPSSx. New York: McGraw-Hill.

Stein, Jess and P. Y. Su, eds. 1978. The Random House dictionary. New York: Ballantine Books.

Stoller, Paul and Cheryl Olkes. 1987. In sorcery's shadow. Chicago: University of Chicago Press.

Stone, Ruth M. 1988. Dried millet breaking: Time, words, and song in the Woi epic of the Kpelle. Bloomington: Indiana University Press.

Strauss, Anselm and Juliet Corbin. 1990. Basics of qualitative research: Grounded theory procedures and techniques. Newbury Park, Calif.: Sage.

Suttles, Gerald D. 1968. The social order of the slum. Chicago: Chicago University Press.

Svoboda, Terese, trans. 1985. Cleaned the crocodile's teeth: Nuer song. Greenfield Center, N.Y.: Greenfield Review.

Thieme, Darius. 1969. A descriptive catalog of Yoruba musical instruments. Ph.D. dissertation. Catholic University of America.

Titon, Jeff Todd, James T. Koetting, David P. McAllester, David B. Reck, and Mark Slobin. 1984. An introduction to the music of the world's peoples. New York: Schirmer Books.

Tonkin, Elizabeth. 1984. Language learning. In R. F. Ellen (ed.), Ethnographic research: A guide to general conduct, 178–87. London: Academic Press.

———. 1984. Producing data. In R. F. Ellen (ed.), Ethnographic research: A guide to general conduct, 216–23. London: Academic Press.

Townsend, Patricia K. 1985. Infant mortality in the Saniyo-Hiyowe population, Ambunti district, East Sepik Province. Papua New Guinea Medical Journal. 28:177–82.

Tracy, Hubert Parker. 1988. Land: The key to Bintukwa ethnic survival, Colombia. M.A. thesis. University of Texas at Arlington.

True, William R. and Joan R. True. 1977. Network analysis as a methodological approach to the study of drug use in a Latin city. In Robert S. Weppner (ed.), Street ethnography, 125–41. Beverly Hills, Calif.: Sage.

United Nations Development Forum. 1989. Tribal groups in danger of extinction. World Christian, April, 31–32.

Vanderkooi, Mary. 1986. Village medical manual: A layman's guide to health care in developing countries. 4th ed., vol. 1: Principles and procedures, vol. 2: Diagnosis and treatment. Pasadena, Calif.: William Carey Library.

Van der Valk van Ginnen, P. H. M. 1981. Land use in northern Nigeria: The Kaje of Abet and land use problems in Abet. Internal Communication 41. Kaduna: International Livestock Centre for Africa Subhumid Programme.

Van Maanen, John. 1988. Tales of the field: On writing ethnography. Chicago: University of Chicago Press.

Vansina, Jan. 1985. Oral tradition as history. Madison: University of Wisconsin Press.

Vaughan, Megan. 1992. Famine analysis and family relations: Nyasaland in 1949. In Steven Feierman and John M. Janzen (eds.), The social basis of health and healing in Africa, 71–89. Berkeley: University of California Press.

VerEecke, Catherine. 1989. From pasture to Purdah: The transformation of women's roles and identity among the Adamawa Fulbe. Ethnology 28:53–73.

Vidich, Arthur J. 1955. Participant-observation and the collection and interpretation of data. American Journal of Sociology 60:354–60.

Weeks, John M. 1987. Tozzer library: A 'national' library for anthropology. Current Anthropology 28:133–37.

———. 1991. Introduction to library research in anthropology. Boulder, Colo.: Westview.

Weller, Susan D. and A. Kimball Romney. 1988. Systematic data collection. Newbury Park, Calif.: Sage.

Werner, David B., Carol Thuman, and Jane Maxwell. 1980. Donde no hay doctor, una guia para los campesinos que viven lejos de los centros medicos. 4th ed. Palo Alto, Calif.: La Fundacion Hesperian.

———. 1992. Where there is no doctor: A village health care handbook. Rev. ed. Palo Alto, Calif.: Hesperian Foundation.

White, Harrison C. 1963. An anatomy of kinship. Englewood Cliffs, N.J.: Prentice-Hall.

———. 1970. Chains of opportunity. Cambridge: Harvard University Press.

Wilson, Ken. 1993. Thinking about the ethics of fieldwork. In Stephen Devereux and John Hoddinott (eds.), Fieldwork in developing countries, 179–99. Boulder, Colo.: Lynne Rienner.

Wimbish, John S. 1990. Shoebox: A data management program for the field linguist. Version 1.2. Ambon, Indonesia: Summer Institute of Linguistics and Pattimura University.

Winick, Charles. 1977. Dictionary of anthropology. Totowa, N.J.: Littlefield, Adams, and Co.

Wissler, Clark. 1917. The American Indian: An introduction to anthropology in the new world. N.Y.: D. C. McMurtrie.

World Bank. 1989. Sub-Saharan Africa: From crisis to sustainable growth. Washington, D.C.: World Bank.

Yankah, Kwesi. 1989. The proverb in the context of Akan rhetoric: A theory of proverb proxis. Sprichworterforschung 12. New York: Peter Lang.

Index